STUDY GUIDE
TO ACCOMPANY

CONTEMPORARY MARKETING

10TH EDITION

LOUIS E. BOONE
ERNEST G. CLEVERDON CHAIR OF BUSINESS AND MANAGEMENT
UNIVERSITY OF SOUTH ALABAMA

DAVID L. KURTZ
THE R. A. AND VIVIAN YOUNG CHAIR OF BUSINESS ADMINISTRATION
UNIVERSITY OF ARKANSAS

PREPARED BY
THOMAS S. O'CONNOR
UNIVERSITY OF NEW ORLEANS

HARCOURT COLLEGE PUBLISHERS

FORT WORTH   PHILADELPHIA   SAN DIEGO   NEW YORK   ORLANDO   AUSTIN   SAN ANTONIO
TORONTO   MONTREAL   LONDON   SYDNEY   TOKYO

Cover Image: Courtesy of Pierre-Yves Goavec.

ISBN: 0-03-031404-6

Copyright © 2001, 1998, 1995, 1992, 1989, 1986, 1983, 1980, 1977, 1974 by Harcourt, Inc.

All rights reserved. No part of this publication may be reproduced or transmitted in any form or by any means, electronic or mechanical, including photocopy, recording, or any information storage and retrieval system, without permission in writing from the publisher.

Although for mechanical reasons all pages of this publication are perforated, only those pages imprinted with Harcourt, Inc. are intended for removal.

Requests for permission to make copies of any part of the work should be mailed to the following address: Permissions Department, Harcourt, Inc., 6277 Sea Harbor Drive, Orlando, Florida 32887-6777.

Address for Domestic Orders
Harcourt College Publishers, 6277 Sea Harbor Drive, Orlando, FL 32887-6777
800-782-4479

Address for International Orders
International Customer Service
Harcourt, Inc., 6277 Sea Harbor Drive, Orlando, FL 32887-6777
407-345-3800
(fax) 407-345-4060
(e-mail) hbintl@harcourt.com

Address for Editorial Correspondence
Harcourt College Publishers, 301 Commerce Street, Suite 3700, Fort Worth, TX 76102

Web Site Address
http://www.harcourtcollege.com

Printed in the United States of America

1 2 3 4 5 6 7 8 9   202   9 8 7 6 5 4 3 2

Harcourt College Publishers

Introduction

There have been a number of changes made in the *Study Guide for Contemporary Marketing — Wired*, Ninth Edition. As always, I made them only when I felt they would improve the essential purpose of this work — to help you, the student, obtain greater understanding of the marketing profession as it is practiced and studied today. The *Study Guide* is closely coordinated with the textbook and each of its parts is structured as a learning unit exploring a particular area of the marketing field.

Coverage of each chapter of the *Study Guide* begins with an outline of the material in the chapter. The **Outline,** when used in concert with the textbook, is designed to serve as a memory refresher to assist in recalling significant points in the text as you work through the exercises in the guide.

Other features include a section on each chapter's **Key Concepts,** a matching of important topics in the chapter to their definition; a **Self-Quiz** for each chapter's material – at least fifty questions exploring the material in the text in detail; **Applying Marketing Concepts,** a series of illustrations of how the techniques and principles described in the text are put to use; and **Surfing the Net,** the addresses of and commentaries on some Internet Web sites of particular interest to the marketing student.

In **Creating a Marketing Plan,** an episode of which appears in each of the parts of the guide, you are given information you can develop by following the adventures of three young entrepreneurs.

Each of the parts of this guide also contains a brief synopsis of the part as well as several **Cases** that call for problem solving in a marketing context.

As always, I solicit and welcome your comments and those of your teachers. Though I have made every effort to make sure that the answers match the questions and it all makes sense, I'm sure there are errors scattered here and there throughout the *Study Guide*. For these I apologize and request that if you find them, please tell me about them. I'm **toconnor@uno.edu.**

Otherwise, my best wishes to you for success in your studies and in the use of these materials.

Thomas S. O'Connor
The University of New Orleans

A Few Words of Thanks

As always, it has been a pleasure working with the people at Dryden Press. Tracy Morse has been unstintingly pleasant as we have worked our way through this revision. My thanks also go to all those folks whom I don't know who've read and commented on this work as it was in process. And my secretary, Marilyn Schiro, has ably assisted in keeping other things at bay while I pursued this project.

My family has, as usual, tolerated me well while this revision was in progress. By now they're used to it. To them I express my deepest appreciation for that tolerance. Thanks again Val, Brian, and Terrence.

Contents

Part 1 The Contemporary Marketing Environment — 1
Chapter 1 Customer-Driven Marketing — 3
Chapter 2 The Marketing Environment, Ethics, and Social Responsibility — 19
Chapter 3 Global Dimensions of Marketing — 35
Cases for Part 1 — 50
Creating a Marketing Plan: A Continuing Exercise (Introduction) — 53

Part 2 Managing Technology to Achieve Marketing Success — 55
Chapter 4 E-Commerce: Electronic Marketing and the Internet — 57
Chapter 5 Succeeding Using Relationship and Database Marketing — 73
Cases for Part 2 — 88
Creating a Marketing Plan: Getting Started (Episode Two) — 93

Part 3 Marketing Planning, Information, and Segmentation — 95
Chapter 6 Marketing Planning and Forecasting — 97
Chapter 7 Marketing Research and Decision-Support Systems — 113
Chapter 8 Market Segmentation, Targeting, and Positioning — 129
Cases for Part 3 — 143
Creating a Marketing Plan: Who's Out There? (Episode Three) — 149

Part 4 Customer Behavior — 151
Chapter 9 Consumer Behavior — 153
Chapter 10 B2B: Business-to-Business Marketing — 169
Cases for Part 4 — 183
Creating a Marketing Plan: Where Do We Go From Here? (Episode Four) — 187

Part 5 Product Strategy — 189
Chapter 11 Product Strategies — 191
Chapter 12 Brand Management and New Product Planning — 207
Cases for Part 5 — 224

Part 6 Distribution Strategy — 231
Chapter 13 Marketing Channels and Logistics Management — 233
Chapter 14 Retailing, Wholesaling, and Direct Marketing — 251
Cases for Part 6 — 270
Creating a Marketing Plan: Let's Find a Place to Hang Our Hats (Episode Five) — 277

Part 7 Promotional Strategy — 279
Chapter 15 Integrated Marketing Communications — 281
Chapter 16 Advertising, Sales Promotion, and Public Relations — 297
Chapter 17 Personal Selling and Sales Force Management — 313

Cases for Part 7	330
Creating a Marketing Plan: Now Let's Get the Message Out – We're Here! (Episode Six)	333

Part 8 Pricing Strategy — **335**

Chapter 18 Price Determination	337
Chapter 19 Managing the Pricing Function	353
Cases for Part 8	369
Creating a Marketing Plan: How Much Is Too Much? (And How Little Is Not Enough?) (Episode Seven)	373
Creating a Marketing Plan: So When Do We Start to Get Rich? (Episode Eight)	376
Chapter Solutions	379
Case Solutions & Solutions for Creating a Marketing Plan	398

Part 1

The Contemporary Marketing Environment

The marketing process creates time, place, and ownership utilities for consumers. Marketing itself is defined as the process of planning and executing the conception, pricing, promotion, and distribution of ideas, goods, services, organizations, and events to create and maintain relationships that satisfy organizational and individual objectives. Today's marketplace is global in scope. Firms can no longer limit their activities to a single or even several nations. Products and services have both been affected.

Marketing arises out of the exchange process. The emphasis on marketing activities increases as firms progress through the four eras of: (1) production orientation, (2) sales orientation, (3) marketing orientation, and (4) relationship orientation. Long-run success does not happen unless firms adopt a company-wide consumer orientation. This realization has been called the marketing concept. In recent years, the marketing concept has been broadened to include the activities of not-for-profit organizations. In the area of nontraditional marketing, we find people, places, causes, events, and organizations now being treated as though they were goods or services.

Marketers plan and coordinate the four strategic areas of product, distribution, promotion, and pricing in a marketing mix designed to satisfy the wants and needs of a specific target market, a group of people to whom the firm directs its marketing effort. There has been a revolution in the technology of marketing that has resulted in interactive marketing in which the customer controls the information received from a marketer. The development of the Internet and World Wide Web have opened new vistas on market access to both marketers and consumers.

The desirability of the development of positive long-term relationships between vendors and customers of all sorts must be recognized. Given the high cost of marketing, effective relationships confer significant competitive advantages. For marketing to take place, it is usually necessary that a firm or some combination of firms perform the eight universal functions of: (1) buying, (2) selling, (3) transporting, (4) storing, (5) standardization and grading, (6) financing, (7) risk-taking, and (8) securing marketing information.

The marketer must be aware of the five interacting environments that affect marketing activities: the competitive, the political-legal, the economic, the technological, and the social-cultural. Each of these has its own complexities and rules, written or unwritten, that affect what, how, when and where certain activities may be acceptable, necessary, or prohibited. Globalization of business has expanded the necessity to be aware of the differences between environmental components from one place to another.

The competitive environment includes all those organizations competing for the purchasing power of customers. A firm chooses its competitive environment when it chooses its markets and may face direct competition, competition from substitutes, and competition from all other organizations that seek to sell to consumers.

Marketing strategies must be adjusted in response to changes in the political-legal environment. Early antitrust legislation was aimed at maintaining a competitive environment. Later legislation arising out of the Depression conditions of the 1930s was designed to protect small competitors from discriminatory practices. Since the 1950s, a number of laws have been designed to protect consumers from harmful marketing practices and unsafe products or services. Beginning in the 1970s, it became common to "deregulate" industries that were formerly under substantial government control, yet there still exists many regulatory agencies charged with implementing existing laws. In addition, public and private consumer interest groups have an effect on this environment.

The rate of inflation, stage of the business cycle, level of unemployment, national income, and availability of critical resources all influence the likelihood of individuals parting with discretionary income. If resources are in short supply it becomes difficult to satisfy consumer demand.

Technology is changing with incredible speed. There are competitors in this environment, too, and technological breakthroughs by others may take market share away from those who don't keep up the pace.

The social-cultural environment is a significant factor to marketers. This area includes all relationships marketers have with society. Rising educational levels and better communications have lead to greater public involvement in this area. Moreover, changing dietary habits and greater consciousness of cultural diversity have presented opportunities and challenges in the marketplace. Finally, the question of ethical conduct is a very serious issue in this context – many would say that marketing's role in society now hinges on the moral/ethical issue.

Ethical considerations are an intrinsic part of operating within an environmental structure. Ethics has to do with moral values and standards of conduct. Social responsibility places increased weight on the well being of society in its relationship to a firm's desire for profits and the consumer's wish to be satisfied.

Entering the global market involves understanding the differences in the marketing environment as one moves from culture to culture. Failure to do this can mean disaster. The global market is a huge and diverse one, including over six billion people who are expected to number eight billion by 2025.

A nation's size, its per-capita income, and its stage of economic development determine its prospects as a host for business expansion. Its infrastructure, monetary stability, cultural and technological capacities, as well as the working of its legal system and view on the desirability of being a trading partner or market for foreign goods all have an effect. One of the more significant influences on a firm's activities in the global sphere is the trend toward multinational economic integration. Entry into the world market may be by importing or exporting, contractual agreement, or international direct investment. Entry strategies for marketing may be global, multi-domestic, or multinational. Product and promotional strategies include straight extension, promotion adaptation, product adaptation, dual adaptation, and product invention. Distribution and pricing may have to be modified for different target markets around the globe. American firms must also recognize that the United States is an attractive market for international entrepreneurs.

Chapter 1

Customer-Driven Marketing

Chapter Outline

Use the following as a guide in taking notes.

I. Chapter Overview – The technology revolution is changing the rules of marketing largely because of global networks made possible by communications and computer technology

II. What is Marketing?

    A. Production and marketing of goods and services – the essence of economic life in any society

    B. Organizations create form, time, place, and ownership utility – the want-satisfying power of a good or service

    C. A Definition of Marketing

    D. Today's Global Marketplace

III. Four Eras in the History of Marketing

    A. The Production Era – a quality product will sell itself

    B. The Sales Era – output increases, manufacturers seek customers for their goods, and personal selling and advertising are viewed as means to overcome sales resistance

    C. The Marketing Era – a major shift occurs as the seller's market becomes a buyer's market and organizations develop a company-wide consumer orientation

    D. The Relationship Era – firms focus on establishing and maintaining long-term value added relationships with customers and suppliers

    E. Converting Needs to Wants – achieved by focusing on the benefits resulting from the acquisition of goods and services

IV. Avoiding Marketing Myopia – Recognizing the Scope of One's Business

V. Extending the Traditional Boundaries of Marketing

    A. Marketing in Not-for-Profit organizations – NFP, organization operate in both public and private sectors

    B. Characteristics of Not-for-Profit Marketing

    C. Nontraditional Marketing

Harcourt, Inc.

1. Person Marketing
2. Places Marketing
3. Cause Marketing
4. Event Marketing

VI. Organizational Marketing – involves attempts to influence others to accept the goals of, receive the services of, or contribute in some way to an organization.

VII. Elements of a Marketing Strategy

    A. The Target Market

    B. Marketing Mix Variables

    C. The Marketing Environment

    D. Critical Thinking and Creativity

VIII. The Technology Revolution in Marketing

    A. Interactive Marketing

    B. The Internet

    C. How Marketers Use the Web

IX. From Transaction-Based Marketing to Relationship Marketing

    A. Developing Partnerships and Strategic Alliances

X. Costs and Functions of Marketing – It costs money to produce utility

    A. The exchange functions

    B. The physical distribution functions

    C. The facilitating functions

XI. Ethics and Social Responsibility: Doing Well By Doing Good

XII. Strategic Implications of Marketing in the 21st Century

a. an active advocate of the marketing concept.
   b. operating in a buyer's market.
   c. a firm with a sales orientation.
   d. unique in its analysis of marketing opportunities and target markets.
   e. a production-oriented company.

43. The fact that the steel recycled each year by Ford Motor Company alone would build 200 Eiffel Towers is a good example of
   a. an unethical activity tending to divert needed steel from other, more productive, purposes.
   b. the shortage of Eiffel Towers. Imagine how beautiful 200 more of them would be!
   c. a successful combination of sound business practice and helping to save the planet.
   d. a corporate commitment to local education and mentoring programs.
   e. a sound business practice but one that causes substantial environmental damage.

44. Not-for-profit organizations
   a. are prohibited by law from earning a profit on their operations.
   b. are very numerous in the public sector, but are seldom found in the private sector.
   c. are served by over 110 million volunteers, each of whom works an average of eight hours a week.
   d. seldom partner with for-profit companies to promote their messages.
   e. provide full or part-time employment for about one in ten Americans.

45. The City of New Orleans calls itself "The Big Easy" and New York is known as "The Big Apple." These nicknames were coined by the cities' Tourist Bureaus to create an image for them and make them desirable tourist destinations. This is an example of the nontraditional form of marketing known as:
   a. cause marketing.
   b. concept marketing.
   c. celebrity marketing.
   d. place marketing.
   e. personal promotion.

46. Standardization and grading together comprise one of the
   a. exchange functions.
   b. discriminating functions.
   c. delivery functions.
   d. physical distribution functions.
   e. facilitating functions.

47. On the way home from work, John stops at a grocery store to buy a gallon of milk. He buys the store's own brand of milk even though he's unfamiliar with it because the label says "USDA Grade A – 4 Percent Butterfat" and he's satisfied that's the kind of milk his family prefers. He pays for his purchase with his VISA card. Which of the following marketing functions have most obviously facilitated John's purchase?
   a. risk taking and securing market information
   b. risk taking and financing
   c. standardization/grading and financing
   d. transportation and buying
   e. storing and financing

48. The marketing functions of transportation and storage are most closely related to the utilities of
    a. time and place.
    b. form and time.
    c. ownership and place.
    d. ownership and form.
    e. time and ownership.

49. As an example of how important operations outside the U. S. market can be, it is important to recognize that sales outside the U.S. now account for
    a. almost 70 percent of Boeing's aircraft business.
    b. half of Gillette's sales volume.
    c. about 60 percent of Coca-Cola's sales.
    d. 20 percent of McDonald's business.
    e. 70 percent of Colgate-Palmolive's revenues.

50. The idea that customers will resist purchasing products and services not deemed essential and that the task of personal selling and advertising is to convince them to buy is typical of the
    a. production-oriented company.
    b. sales-oriented company.
    c. marketing-oriented company.
    d. relationship-oriented company.
    e. none of the above.

Name_____ Instructor_____

Section_____ Date_____

Applying Marketing Concepts

Yuri Koublitskaya, a former racing mechanic, has opened an automobile accessory and repair shop near the campus of Western Range State College. The shop does major and minor auto and light truck repair and carries an extensive line of auto audio equipment, appearance accessories, and do-it-yourself parts and supplies. The brands carried include Rockford-Fosgate, Champion, Monroe, AC-Delco, Blaupunkt, and FelPro, among others.

In a recent interview, Koublitskaya explained his business strategy: "I am convinced there is a real need for auto repair services and related supplies among the students, faculty, and staff of Western Range. I want to help satisfy this need. I do a fair amount of repair business but there is also strong demand for do-it-yourself repair products. Generally, I stock the products and brands customers ask for as long as I can get them and make a profit on the sale. Some manufacturers, like Frauenkirchen, make this a problem. Their shock absorbers are very popular among the four-wheel drive crowd, but I have had to stop dealing with them because they acted very independently, sometimes not filling orders for up to six months."

"Some of the products I stock are purchased from wholesalers because we order in small quantities. Most of our orders are shipped to us using United Parcel Service (UPS) because this insures we get the product less than a week after placing the order without incurring an exorbitant freight bill. I do most of my advertising in the school newspaper, *The Rangerider*, where I usually offer students a discount or some free product like a spark plug gapper if they buy more than a certain dollar minimum. My parts sales force is myself and two Western Range students. In general, we charge everyone the same price; our prices are comparable to those of our competitors. It's necessary to be competitive because there are several shops in the area that offer comparable products."

"Overall, I am making enough to pay the bills and make a 10 percent return on my investment. My major concern is that my marketing costs seem to be too high; they are almost 35 percent of the selling price of my goods."

Write "T" for True or "F" for False for each of the following statements.

_____ 1. Yuri Koublitskaya appears to have adopted the marketing concept.

_____ 2. The Frauenkirchen Company may be production oriented.

_____ 3. Koublitskaya's shop faces a seller's market for its do-it-yourself lines.

_____ 4. Yuri's marketing costs are higher than the national average.

_____ 5. Mr. Koublitskaya's decision to locate his store near its market created ownership utility for his customers.

Harcourt, Inc.

Circle the letter of the word or phrase that best completes the sentence or best answers the question.

6. Repairing automobiles creates
   a. form utility.
   b. place utility.
   c. ownership utility.
   d. time utility.
   e. none of the above.

7. Newspaper advertising and the three-person sales force are part of Koublitskaya's
   a. promotional strategy.
   b. pricing strategy.
   c. product strategy.
   d. distribution strategy.
   e. target market strategy.

8. Yuri's distribution strategy includes
   a. FedEx and truck distributors.
   b. pick up and delivery service on vehicles to be repaired.
   c. student discounts.
   d. free parts delivery to customers.
   e. UPS and wholesalers.

9. Mr. Koublitskaya's pricing strategy includes
   a. charging all customers the same price.
   b. prices comparable to competitors' prices.
   c. student discounts.
   d. free products in conjunction with minimum dollar purchases.
   e. all of the above.

10. The shop's product strategy is best described as
    a. stock the lowest cost products available.
    b. sell the highest quality products.
    c. offer customers the products they want.
    d. sell only nationally known brands.
    e. none of the above

Alton Altophase, who recently graduated from college with a degree in ceramic engineering (but with a minor in business), has returned home to help his father run the family business, Altophase Vitreous Products Company. Begun in 1903, the Altophase Company has long since had a reputation for making the very finest in porcelain decor items. These enameled porcelain figures, usually used as decorative details in gardens and other outdoor locations, typically represent mythical creatures like trolls and gnomes and small animals such as rabbits, squirrels, and puppies.

The first thing Alton did upon reporting for work was to apply his business training to an analysis of the firm's financial records. He was surprised to learn that during the last ten years, there had been a dramatic decline in sales of the company's garden line. When he asked his father about this, the elder Altophase replied, "Gee, son, I don't really know why that's happening. Our figures are the very best that can be bought. We're still making them exactly the same way we have for the last ninety years, using the same molds and with the same materials. I can't really understand why sales are off so badly. But I have taken steps to do something about it. Just last month, I hired a young man to go out and try and find us some new customers. We really do have to do something to try and increase sales volume."

Alton was now disturbed. He knew that his father and he had done what he thought was the right thing, but Alton thought that more needed to be done. His thinking was that the company needed to look more carefully at the marketplace. He felt that Altophase Vitreous had lost touch with its customers and with garden design fashions. Though he hesitated to do it, he felt that he had to suggest to his father that they invest in some research to find out what was happening in outdoor design and to adapt their products to what was currently popular. He though it might even be possible that the firm would find it desirable to expand or even change the nature of their product line.

11. Alton's father, judging from his distress at the decline in his company's fortunes and the fact that he can't understand why the company's figures aren't selling, is probably a victim of
    a. his inability to produce a product of the required quality.
    b. the "better mousetrap" fallacy.
    c. a general decline in the economy about which nothing can be done.
    d. too much of a commitment to a marketing orientation.

12. Altophase the elder's retention of a salesman may well be evidence that he has been converted to
    a. a philosophy of company-wide consumer orientation.
    b. a mere figurehead in his son's presence.
    c. an attitude typical of the sales era of marketing history.
    d. a belief that he's in a seller's market.

13. Alton's idea of investigating the nature of the market reveals that
    a. he is at least aware of the marketing concept.
    b. he shares his father's attitude toward the changes in the company's sales performance.
    c. his college education has been largely wasted; he should be able to analyze the problem from internal company records.
    d. he, too, is a victim of "marketing myopia."

14. "Marketing myopia" refers to
    a. defining the scope of your business too broadly.
    b. failing to define the scope of your business.
    c. defining the scope of your business too narrowly.
    d. making comparisons between your business and businesses not much like the one you're in.

Contemporary Marketing

Name_____   Instructor_____

Section_____   Date_____

Surfing the Net

Keeping in mind that addresses change and what's on the Internet as this is being written may have changed by the time you read this, let's take a look at some of the places on the Net that reflect aspects of marketing. We are not endorsing or recommending any of these sources, merely making note of the information and services that people have elected to offer through the Internet.

In this initial episode, let's mention the fact that there are many Web browsers out there, and what you see when you access the Net depends to some extent on the way your browser works. We suggest you use the most recent version of Netscape Navigator or Microsoft's Internet Explorer that is available to you. Older browsers may produce odd-looking displays when used to access sites written with newer versions in mind. On the more recent browsers, you can "shortcut" the address, leaving off the http:// in many cases. Nonetheless, we've given the entire address for each site.

So! Let's get started!

Feeling Consumed? It's supposed to be the other way around. You're the consumer! For consumer information on all sorts of products and services, order the *Consumer Information Catalog* from Uncle Sam. Just fill out the order form at **http://pueblo.gsa.gov/** It's a free service of the General Services Administration of the Federal Government.

Thinking about changing schools? There are several Web sites that offer information of one sort or another about college rankings, costs, and even how good certain programs at certain schools are supposed to be. The most comprehensive of these appears to be one at the University of Illinois Champaign-Urbana that can be accessed at **http://www.library.uiuc.edu/edx/rankings.htm.** Alternative sites include **http:nces.ed.gov**, another of those federal government sites that provide so much information about so many things. Finally, we suggest **http://www.collegeboard.com** as a general-purpose site oriented more to the high school senior than the individual already in college, but still worth a look.

Thirsty? Unless you drink only water, take a look at all the topics available on the beverage network. Devoted to information on commercially available nonalcoholic beverages, there's something there for everyone. We'd be willing to bet you haven't heard of almost all of the beverages on this site. It's at **http://www.thebevnet.com**

Into sports? Professional sports is all over the net! Just for starters, the *Sports Illustrated* site at **http:CNNSI.com** has an incredible array of current scores, standings, and articles on what's happening NOW in the world of sports. Alternatively, for something a little less slick but definitely for the fan, try **http://www.sportznutz.com** if what you want is to get your sports info from the fan's point of view.

Sites verified December 10, 1999.

Harcourt, Inc.

Chapter 2

The Marketing Environment, Ethics, and Social Responsibility

Chapter Outline

Use the following as a guide in taking notes.

I. Chapter Overview – Firms and the Impact of External Forces

II. Environmental Scanning and Environmental Management

III. The Competitive Environment

    A. Types of competition

    B. Developing a competitive strategy

        1. Time-based competition

IV. The Political-Legal Environment

    A. Government regulation

    B. Government regulatory agencies

    C. Other regulatory forces

    D. Controlling the political-legal environment

V. The Economic Environment

    A. Business cycles

    B. Inflation

    C. Unemployment

    D. Income

    E. Resource availability

    F. The International Economic Environment

VI. The Technological Environment

    A. Applying technology

Contemporary Marketing

VII. The Social-Cultural Environment

    A. Importance in international marketing decisions

    B. Consumerism

VIII. Marketing's Role in Society

    A. Evaluating the quality of life

    B. Criticisms of the competitive marketing system

IX. Ethical Issues in Marketing

    A. Ethical problems in marketing research

    B. Ethical problems in product strategy

    C. Ethical problems in distribution strategy

    D. Ethical problems in promotional strategy

    E. Ethical problems in pricing

X. Social Responsibility in Marketing

    A. Marketing's responsibilities

    B. Marketing and ecology

XI. Controlling the Marketing System

XII. Strategic Implications of the Marketing Environment, Ethics, and Social Responsibility

Name_____ Instructor_____

Section_____ Date_____

Key Concepts

From the list of lettered terms, select the one that best fits each of the numbered statements below. Write the letter of that choice in the space provided.

Key Terms

a. environmental scanning
b. environmental management
c. competitive environment
d. time-based competition
e. political-legal environment
f. economic environment
g. demarketing
h. technological environment
i. social-cultural environment
j. consumerism
k. consumer rights
l. marketing ethics
m. social responsibility
n. green marketing

____ 1. Laws and their interpretations that require firms to operate under competitive conditions and serve to protect consumer rights.

____ 2. Standards of conduct and moral values under which marketers operate.

____ 3. Producing, marketing, and reclaiming environmentally sensitive products.

____ 4. Reducing consumer demand for a product or service to a level that the firm can supply.

____ 5. Attainment of organizational objectives by predicting and influencing the competitive, political-legal, economic, technological, and social-cultural environments.

____ 6. Social force that aids and protects the consumer by exerting legal, moral, and economic pressures on business and government.

____ 7. Strategy of developing and distributing goods and services more quickly than competitors.

____ 8. The relationship between the marketer and society and its culture.

____ 9. Interactive process that occurs in the marketplace among marketers of directly competitive products, marketers of substitutable products, and other marketers competing for consumer purchasing power.

____ 10. Includes the stage of the business cycle, inflation, unemployment, resource availability, and income.

Contemporary Marketing

_____ 11. Marketing philosophies, policies, procedures, and actions intended primarily to enhance society's welfare.

_____ 12. Applications to marketing of knowledge based on discoveries in science, inventions, and innovations.

_____ 13. Collecting information about the external marketing environment in order to identify and interpret potential trends.

_____ 14. The right to choose freely, to be informed, to be heard, and to be safe.

Part 1 The Contemporary Marketing Environment

Name_____ Instructor_____

Section_____ Date_____

Self-Quiz

You should use these questions to test your understanding of the chapter material. Check your answers against those provided at the end of the chapter.

While these questions cover most of the chapter topics, they are not intended to be the same as the test questions your instructor may use in an examination. A good understanding of all aspects of the course material is essential to good performance on any examination.

True/False

Write "T" for True and "F" for False for each of the following statements.

____ 1. Environmental scanning involves detailed examination of the firm's internal structure to affect and control use of resources.

____ 2. One aspect of environmental management is activities designed to influence the marketing environment to the firm's advantage, such as strategic alliances.

____ 3. The first decision a company must make with respect to competition is whether it will compete or not.

____ 4. Compact discs by *Asleep at the Wheel* and movies starring Burt Reynolds compete with purchases of cowboy boots and Stetson hats for the discretionary purchasing power of individuals.

____ 5. The most striking aspect of the existing legal framework for marketing in the U.S. is the clear statement of the terms of the law and its consistent enforcement.

____ 6. Government regulation of business in the United States has passed through four phases: keep the environment competitive, protect competitors, protect consumers, deregulate industry.

____ 7. The antimonopoly period of government regulation saw passage of laws such as the National Environmental Policy Act and the Food, Drug, and Cosmetic Act.

____ 8. Deflation, devaluation of the money through persistent price increases, can occur at any stage in the business cycle.

____ 9. The Federal Trade Commission and state regulators cannot do anything to stop firms from using fraudulent and deceptive advertising, especially in cyberspace.

Harcourt, Inc.

Contemporary Marketing

_____ 10. Deregulation of the utility industry is expected to improve efficiency and increase consolidation due to mergers between utility companies.

_____ 11. Discretionary income is the amount of money people have left to spend after they've paid for food, clothing, housing, and other necessities.

_____ 12. Historically, periods of major innovation have been accompanied by dramatic declines in living standards and rising inflation.

_____ 13. The technological innovations embodied in the electronic calculator wiped out the market for slide rules.

_____ 14. Demographic shifts such as population growth and age distribution changes have historically had little effect on consumers' reactions to different products and marketing practices.

_____ 15. Ben and Jerry's, the somewhat unconventional ice cream producers, was able to enter the British market with little change in its marketing strategy despite competitive and cultural differences between Britain and the U.S.

_____ 16. The United States is a mixed society composed of various submarkets, each of which displays unique values, cultural characteristics, and consumer preferences.

_____ 17. Consumerism is a radical, reactionary movement that resists and contradicts the societal demand that organizations adopt the marketing concept.

_____ 18. President Kennedy's statement of consumer rights includes "the right to be safe." This means that products and services must be designed in such a way that they will be absolutely safe for anyone to use in all circumstances.

_____ 19. No marketer today can initiate a strategic decision without taking into account the society's norms, values, culture, and demographics.

_____ 20. Charges of neglect in the area of quality of life go unanswered because business people have not developed reliable indicators with which to measure contribution to life quality.

_____ 21. The only ethical standards that should influence an individual are his or her individual ethics and the organizational ethics of the person's employer.

_____ 22. The marketing system may be influenced or controlled in four ways: (1) by helping the competitive market system to operate in a self-correcting manner; (2) by educating the consumer; (3) by increasing regulation; and (4) by encouraging political action.

_____ 23. The practice of "green marketing" involves letting people know that products are made from all-new materials, thus encouraging the growth of new trees for making paper and other products and the development of new sources of metals, plastics, and similar materials.

_____ 24. It is expected that the first decade of the twenty-first century will see a reduction in the number of rules and regulations designed to control the marketing environment.

_____ 25. Business cannot successfully meet all consumer demands and still generate the profits necessary to remain viable.

Harcourt, Inc.

Multiple Choice

Circle the letter of the word or phrase that best completes the sentence or best answers the question.

26. Microsoft's recent difficulties with the U.S. Justice Department grew out of the operation of which of the environments of marketing?
    a. the social-cultural environment
    b. the economic environment
    c. the political-legal environment
    d. the technological environment
    e. none of the above

27. Which of the following orientations toward the marketing environment should the marketer take?
    a. Ignore it and maybe it will go away.
    b. Recognize that the environment has an effect on marketing activities and that the firm may, in turn, influence the environment.
    c. Realize that an individual firm cannot have any effect on the marketing environment.
    d. Do not change marketing strategies until substantial losses result from environmental forces.
    e. Make sure marketing strategies satisfy legal requirements but ignore other aspects of the marketing environment because there are no legal penalties for such behavior.

28. The effort by U.S. beer marketers to stem the rising tide of imported beer by touting the relative freshness of their domestic products is an example of
    a. sour grapes marketing.
    b. price-based promotional action.
    c. space-based competition.
    d. time-based competition.
    e. a deceptive advertising practice.

29. Major reasons why a firm may choose not to compete in a particular market include
    a. inadequate resources available to the firm.
    b. a lack of fit between the market and the firm's objectives.
    c. low profit expectations.
    d. a, b, and c above.
    e. only a and b above.

30. A correct match of a specific law and its primary objective is
    a. Robinson-Patman Act – protect competitors
    b. Sherman Act – protect competitors
    c. Wheeler-Lea Act – protect the consumer
    d. Staggers Rail Act – maintain a competitive environment
    e. Consumer Product Safety Act – deregulate industry

31. All of the following are parts of the economic environment except
    a. resource availability.
    b. inflation.
    c. Income.
    d. the stage of the business cycle.
    e. falling birth rate.

32. Firms that once held a monopoly position in the market like public utilities enjoyed, at the cost of considerable regulation, protection from the forces of the
    a. economic environment.
    b. competitive environment.
    c. technological environment.
    d. political-legal environment.
    e. social-cultural environment.

33. This recent phase in the regulation of American business has seen government working to increase competition in such industries as telecommunications, utilities, transportation, and financial services.
    a. the antimonopoly period
    b. the era of protecting competitors
    c. the deregulation of industry
    d. consumer protection times
    e. environmental development phase

34. Which of the following methods is used by the Federal Trade Commission to protect consumers?
    a. The FTC takes hostages from firms believed to be guilty of violating the law.
    b. The officers of guilty firms are arrested and imprisoned until a ransom is paid.
    c. Public service announcements identifying all firms that have used deceptive selling practices are broadcast.
    d. A cease and desist order is issued, demanding that a firm stop an illegal practice.
    e. A closure order to shut down a guilty firm's operations is issued.

35. An example of an ethical problem related to pricing strategy would be
    a. whether an automobile dealership should be required to purchase parts from the manufacturer of the cars it sells.
    b. the exaggeration of product merits or outright deceit in product descriptions.
    c. whether marketers have an obligation to warn consumers of impending discount or returns policy changes.
    d. whether packages should be kept to some standard size, rather than made extra-large or odd-shaped.
    e. whether there is an obligation to serve areas where there are few users of the firm's product.

36. The socially responsible manager has traditionally been concerned with
    a. providing quality products at reasonable prices.
    b. providing workers with adequate wages.
    c. making acceptable profits for stockholders.
    d. creating decent working conditions for employees.
    e. All of the above.

37. A correct statement about the economic environment is that
    a. during periods of recession, consumers spend more at hardware stores and do-it-yourself centers and less on convenience foods.
    b. consumer spending rises to its highest level during periods of economic recovery.
    c. the last economic depression in the United States occurred in the 1950s.
    d. the rate of inflation since 1996 has been well over 8 percent per year.
    e. unemployment does not affect marketing because consumer behavior remains the same.

38. Which force in the marketing environment is noted for improving existing products, offering better customer service, and even creating entirely new industries?
    a. the economic environment
    b. the competitive environment
    c. the political-legal environment
    d. the social-cultural environment
    e. the technological environment

39. Which of the following is an example of a demarketing strategy?
    a. Offering a second gallon of milk for half price if a first gallon is purchased at full price.
    b. Providing consumers with tips on how to make a product last longer or use less energy.
    c. Advertising the convenience of owning more than one car.
    d. Telling consumers that they should stock up on a product in abundant supply.
    e. Making substantial reductions in a firm's advertising budget.

40. Which of the following is an accurate statement about the social-cultural environment?
    a. The United States as a nation is becoming younger and less affluent.
    b. Marketing strategies that have proven themselves in the United States will work anywhere.
    c. Most marketers do not need to take the social environment into consideration.
    d. Consumer activism has been declining for a number of years.
    e. Changing social values have led to the social force called the consumerism movement.

41. A person's standards of ethical behavior based on their own personal system of values would be called
    a. organizational ethics.
    b. corporate ethics.
    c. individual ethics.
    d. professional ethics.
    e. coded ethics.

42. Which of the following would most likely not be an appropriate means for a small retailer to survive when faced with competition from a Wal-Mart Supercenter or similar megadiscount store?
    a. Offer a more complete selection of a line of products like hardware or building materials than does Wal-Mart.
    b. Stock more upscale merchandise than the discounter competitor.
    c. Extend operating hours and liberalize returns policies.
    d. Offer the same products as the discounter at the same prices.
    e. Deliver purchases for free and have an on-site repair department.

43. Which of the following situations best reflects the competitive condition of substitution?
    a. Tide, Cheer, Surf, Oxydol, and Fab in the detergent section of the supermarket
    b. gypsum board, wood paneling, Masonite sheet, and plaster as wall finishing materials
    c. rock concerts, video rentals, dining out, and wind surfing for an evening's entertainment
    d. Delta, Continental, and Southwest Airlines all offering cut-rate fares between their major destinations
    e. None of the above are examples of substitution; all represent direct competition

Contemporary Marketing

44. The most common ethical criticism levied against marketing researchers has to do with
    a. alleged invasions of personal privacy.
    b. planned obsolescence.
    c. product testing issues.
    d. the danger inherent in automotive air bags.
    e. the degree of corporate distributional control.

45. The Federal Food and Drug Act and the Nutrition Labeling and Education Act are examples of laws that
    a. are designed to help maintain a competitive environment.
    b. regulate the conditions of competition in some way.
    c. have as their objective the protection of consumers.
    d. deregulate particular industries.
    e. serve to create a new class of criminal where none existed before.

46. George, Howard, and Louis are the only three real estate brokers in the town of Pierre Part. They have the informal habit of getting together for lunch once a month to "talk things over." At their most recent meeting, George proposed that they divide the town up into sections, with each realtor taking one part as his exclusive territory. If they carry out their plan, they can be accused of violating
    a. the Consumer Goods Pricing Act.
    b. the Sherman Act.
    c. the Robinson-Patman Act.
    d. the Celler-Kefauver Act.
    e. the Federal Commission Improvement Act.

47. The Federal regulatory agency that regulates telephone companies, radio and television stations, and cable service providers is the
    a. Air Transport Commission.
    b. Transportation Regulatory Commission.
    c. Federal Power Commission.
    d. Federal Trade Commission.
    e. Federal Communications Commission.

48. The initial ecological problem to face marketing was the issue of
    a. planned obsolescence.
    b. pollution of the environment.
    c. recycling of used materials.
    d. environmental redevelopment.
    e. effluent discharge.

49. That phase of the business cycle during which marketers tend to lower prices, improve customer service, and increase promotional outlays, as well as launch value-priced offerings, is
    a. prosperity.
    b. depression.
    c. recovery.
    d. recession.
    e. exclusion.

50. During economic recovery,
    a. consumers' ability to buy increases, but their willingness to buy often lags behind.
    b. consumer buying power declines and marketers should consider increasing promotional outlays.
    c. consumer spending is brisk, and demand for premium versions of well-known brands is strong.
    d. consumer spending readies its lowest level.
    e. marketers may increase prices or extend their product lines to take advantage of brisk consumer spending.

Contemporary Marketing

Name_____ Instructor_____

Section_____ Date_____

Applying Marketing Concepts

Val Cartouche was thinking about her problems with her interior decorating business. They all began when she first decided to go into business for herself. Having found the "perfect" location for her store, she was dismayed when the city wouldn't give her a business license on the grounds that the local zoning ordinances didn't allow a store of that type in the chosen location.

After much effort, Val found a new location and was successful in getting a license to operate. She experienced trouble getting some minor renovations to the building done because of a "building boom" the city was experiencing. She also had trouble hiring salespeople and other workers because unemployment was at an all-time low and good people were at a premium.

At long last the renovations were complete, a staff had been hired, and the store was ready to open. But almost the minute the dust sheets were taken off the window displays, Val received a visit from a neighborhood committee objecting to one of her window displays. It seems the display featured a semi-nude mannequin in a rather suggestive pose on a sofa that was the window's central feature. In an effort to be accommodating, Val changed the display.

Soon Val was faced with two new problems. The building she had rented was equipped with an incinerator, which she intended to use to dispose of refuse and excess packing materials from the business. The first time it was lighted, however, the police appeared and presented her with a citation for a violation of a section of the city sanitation code. On top of that, Val discovered that the cost of the goods she was selling was going up so fast that she could barely cover the cost of replacing what she'd sold from what she was able to get for it.

The straw that broke the camel's back, however, was Val's discovery, only sixty days after she'd opened for business, that Interior Industries, a national chain of interior decorating emporiums, was about to open an outlet only two blocks away. Val knew that they could, because of their enormous buying power, undersell her by thirty percent on practically every item in her store.

Realizing that the handwriting was on the wall, Val held a sale to clear out her remaining inventory and closed her store.

Write "T" for True and "F" for False for each of the following statements.

_____ 1. Val's difficulty in getting a business license was due to the social/cultural environment.

_____ 2. Val seemed able to adapt her marketing strategy to the constraints of the environment.

_____ 3. Val's problems getting a business license could have been avoided if she had checked the appropriate environmental constraints before she decided on her first location.

Harcourt, Inc.

Part 1 The Contemporary Marketing Environment

____ 4. The actions of a company like Interior Industries – buying in bulk and selling at low retail prices – are likely a violation of the Robinson-Patman Act.

____ 5. Val may have been shortsighted in going out of business. It's possible that she may have been able to develop an appeal to a different target market than people who would choose to shop at Interior Industries.

Circle the letter of the word or phrase that best completes the sentence or best answers the question.

6. Val had problems with the
   a. economic environment.
   b. political-legal environment.
   c. competitive environment.
   d. social-cultural environment.
   e. environments in a-d above.

7. Val's citation was probably issued by the police because she
   a. was in violation of an air pollution regulation.
   b. was destroying valuable recyclable materials.
   c. used an excessive amount of natural gas firing her incinerator.
   d. had failed to get a city inspection of her store before opening.
   e. was a particular target of a "get-tough" administration.

8. Val's problems in getting her store renovated were probably due to the fact that
   a. her city was experiencing a period of recession and lots of workers had left town.
   b. the city was experiencing a prosperous period of the business cycle.
   c. she was in competition with other employment opportunities for the services of the available labor.
   d. all of the statements above are true.
   e. the statements in b and c above are true.

9. Val's inability to purchase new merchandise for what she'd paid for the old was due to
   a. her inability to manage her money so as to make sure that she'd have enough to rebuy goods.
   b. low sales volume and a high proportion of fixed costs in her store's operation.
   c. inflation which made today's dollar less valuable than yesterday's and drove up merchandise costs.
   d. unemployment at the national level which increased the cost of government services to merchants like Val.

10. From Val's point of view, Interior Industries is part of
    a. the social-cultural environment.
    b. the competitive environment.
    c. the political-legal environment.
    d. the economic environment.
    e. the ethnic environment.

Contemporary Marketing

Delbert Lewis was tired, lonely, and a little confused. When he left his home in Frankfurt to move to Candelle, he was sure it was the right thing. After all, the job he'd been offered had been a real opportunity and his prospective employer had a fine reputation. But he couldn't seem to get used to Candelle. It was so different from Frankfurt. For one thing, just getting around town involved dealing with traffic that was unbelievably frustrating. Left turns at divided intersections were against the law, and the speed limit was 25 miles an hour – even in industrial neighborhoods. This didn't seem to bother the local population, nor did the fact that their lives revolved around whether or not Precision Measurements, Candelle's single major employer, or a Japanese firm which was also bidding for it got the order for those 3,000 optical comparators from Extremely High Tech, Incorporated.

Delbert couldn't believe how hard it was to make friends in Candelle. It seemed as if everyone he met had been there all their lives and wasn't interested in anything or anyone not a Candelle native. All in all, though, it wasn't so bad for Del. His employer was great to work for and his job let him use the latest equipment in his field of eutectic TIG welding. He did all the magnetometric and X-ray testing. He felt he was on the very leading edge of scientific thought in his job at Large Metal Fabrications, and that made up a lot for having to live in Candelle. Now if he could only find some friends who thought a six-pack of beer and a bug zapper were quality entertainment, he'd be just fine.

11. Del's perception of the traffic in Candelle being frustrating was very largely due to
    a. his own rather bad driving habits.
    b. differences in the political-legal environment between Candelle and Frankfurt.
    c. his general dissatisfaction with Candelle itself.
    d. his dislike of his job.

12. Del's job appears to have been deeply involved with the
    a. economic environment.
    b. social-cultural environment.
    c. competitive environment.
    d. technological environment.
    e. development of military hardware.

13. Del's comments about Candelle people being unconcerned with anyone or anything not from Candelle is really a statement relating to the
    a. social-cultural environment.
    b. ethnic environment.
    c. competitive environment.
    d. political environment.

14. The relationship between Candelle's major industry and the Japanese company that is also bidding on the comparator contract is
    a. part of the legal environment.
    b. a condition of direct competition.
    c. a sort of indirect competition
    d. nonexistent; there is no relationship, direct or indirect, between the two firms.

Part 1 The Contemporary Marketing Environment

Name_____   Instructor_____

Section_____   Date_____

Surfing the Net

Keeping in mind that addresses change and what's on the Web now may have changed by the time you read this, let's take a look at some of the places on the Net that reflect aspects of ethical, social, or environmental influence. We are not endorsing or recommending any of these sources, merely making note of the information and services that people have elected to offer through the Internet.

If it sounds too good to be true... You may have run afoul of a fraud. To check it out, try the U. S. Postal Service's site at **http://www.usps.gov/websites/depart/inspect/consmenu.htm**, a long but informative web label belonging to the Department of Postal Inspection, for information on the legal aspects of fraud at the consumer level.

The economic environment is accessible. Why not check out the idea of credit and how to use it? There are four Web sites you might find interesting. The first is very personal, with an extensive array of frequently asked questions (FAQs) dealing with what's on a credit report, how to establish and maintain good credit, and what a credit rating is all about. It's at **http://www.acb-credit.com** and is operated by the Associated Credit Bureaus, Inc., the people who evaluate the worth of individual credit. The other sites are devoted to more specific issues concerning credit. The first is at **http://www.nacm.org** – it's the site of the National Association of Credit Managers and discusses issues related to their work. A third site can be found at **https://www.123creditreports.com/credit** and deals with how to get a copy of your own credit report and how to repair credit which may have been damaged by a credit report that is in error. Finally, a site is available that talks about the responsibilities of users of credit reports under the new Fair Credit Reporting Act – their obligation to proceed in good faith and with reasonable regard for the debtor. It is at **http://www.detection.net/infouser.htm**. If you find yourself with a sudden serious need to read the text of that very law – the FCRA – go to **http://www.ftc.gov/os/statutes/fcra.htm** That's the Federal Trade Commission's site and the file "fcra.htm(l)" is the text version of the law.

Technology up close and personal. It's the NASA homepage. A lot of this is about the space program, but NASA has a lot more than that on the burner (so to speak), and some of it is on their Web site. Try **http://www.nasa.gov**.

The social-cultural environment's worth a look. What movies are worth seeing? Try **http://www.imdb.com** for the largest database of movie reviews, analysis, and commentary around. How about a good book? Nothing great on the shelf? Check with Project Gutenberg at **http://sailor.gutenberg.org**. Their thing is bringing great writings to the Internet.

Prefer your economic environment in larger doses? You can always go straight to the Securities and Exchange Commission at **http://edgar.space.invisible.net/help/edgar.help.html** or, for more general economic information, try Washington University at St. Louis' Economics Homepage at **http://econwpa.wustl.edu**

Sites verified January 12, 2000.

… Part 1 The Contemporary Marketing Environment

Chapter 3

Global Dimensions of Marketing

Chapter Outline

Use the following as a guide in taking notes.

I. Chapter Overview – The international market may be a source of considerable revenue and other opportunities

II. The Importance of Global Marketing

    A. Service and retail exports

    B. Benefits of going global

III. The International Marketplace – Large and diverse

    A. Market size

    B. Buyer behavior

IV. The International Marketing Environment

    A. International economic environment

    B. International social-cultural environment

    C. International technological environment

    D. International political-legal environment

        1. Trade barriers

            a. Tariffs

            b. Administrative barriers

        2. Dumping

V. Multinational Economic Integration

    A. GATT and the World Trade Organization

    B. The NAFTA Accord

    C. The European Union

VI. Going Global

    A. First steps in deciding to market globally

    B. Strategies for entering international markets

    C. Contractual agreements

        1. Franchising

        2. Foreign licensing

        3. Subcontracting

    D. International direct investment

    E. From multinational corporation to global marketer

VII. Developing an International Marketing Strategy

    A. International product and promotion strategies

    B. International distribution strategy

    C. Pricing strategy

        1. Countertrade

VIII. The United States as a Target for International Marketers

IX. Strategic Implications of International Marketing

Part 1 The Contemporary Marketing Environment

Name_____ Instructor_____

Section_____ Date_____

Key Concepts

The purpose of this section is to allow you to determine if you can match key concepts with the definitions of the concepts. It is essential that you know the definitions of the concepts prior to applying the concepts in later exercises in this chapter.

From the list of lettered terms, select the one that best fits each of the numbered statements below. Write the letter of that choice in the space provided.

Key Terms

a. exporting
b. importing
c. infrastructure
d. exchange rate
e. friendship, commerce, and navigation (FCN) treaties
f. tariff
g. import quota
h. embargo
i. exchange control
j. dumping
k. General Agreement on Tariffs and Trade (GATT)
l. World Trade Organization (WTO)
m. North American Free Trade Agreement (NAFTA)
n. franchise
o. foreign licensing
p. joint venture
q. multinational corporation
r. global marketing strategy
s. multi-domestic marketing strategy
t. straight extension
u. product adaptation
v. promotion adaptation
w. dual adaptation
x. product invention
y. countertrade

____ 1. Trade restriction that limits the number of units of certain goods that can enter a country for resale.

____ 2. The same product marketed in the home market is introduced in the foreign market using the same promotional strategy.

____ 3. International trade agreement that has helped reduce world tariffs.

____ 4. A nation's basic system of communications systems, transportation networks, and energy facilities.

____ 5. A complete ban on the import of a specified product.

____ 6. Organization that succeeds GATT in overseeing trade agreements, mediating disputes, and reducing trade barriers; hands down binding decisions.

Contemporary Marketing

____ 7. Standardized marketing mix with minimal modifications that a firm uses in all of its foreign and domestic markets.

____ 8. Domestic purchases of foreign-produced goods, services, and raw materials.

____ 9. Agreement in which a firm shares the risks, costs, and management of a foreign operation with one or more partners who are usually citizens of the host country.

____ 10. Strategy in which modifications of both product and promotional strategies are used in the foreign market.

____ 11. Strategy in which a product is introduced physically unchanged to a foreign market with a unique promotional strategy for the new market.

____ 12. Marketing domestically produced goods and services in foreign countries.

____ 13. Tax levied on imported products.

____ 14. Program of market segmentation that identifies specific foreign markets and tailors the marketing mix to match specific traits in each nation.

____ 15. Controversial practice of selling a product in a foreign market at a price lower than what it receives in the producer's domestic market.

____ 16. Administrative trade restriction that controls access to foreign currencies.

____ 17. Agreement by which a firm permits a foreign company to produce or distribute goods in a foreign country or gives it the right to use the firm's trademark, patent, or processes in a specified geographical area.

____ 18. The development of a new product combined with a new promotional strategy to take advantage of unique foreign opportunities.

____ 19. International strategy wherein product modifications are made for the foreign market, but the same promotional strategy is used.

____ 20. Contractual arrangement in which a wholesaler or retailer agrees to make some payment and to meet the operating requirements of a manufacturer or other business in return for the right to market the manufacturer's or other business's goods or services under its brand name.

____ 21. Price of one nation's currency in terms of another nation's currency.

____ 22. Firm with significant operations and marketing activities outside its home country.

____ 23. Accord that removes trade barriers among the United States, Canada, and Mexico

____ 24. International agreements that deal with many aspects of commercial relations among nations.

____ 25. Form of exporting whereby goods and services are bartered rather than sold for cash.

Harcourt, Inc.

Part 1 The Contemporary Marketing Environment

Name_____ Instructor_____

Section_____ Date_____

Self-Quiz

You should use these questions to test your understanding of the chapter material. Check your answers against those provided at the end of the chapter.

While these questions cover most of the chapter topics, they are not intended to be the same as the test questions your instructor may use in an examination. A good understanding of all aspects of the course material is essential to good performance on any examination.

True/False

Write "T" for True and "F" for False for each of the following statements.

____ 1. About 5 percent of the total U.S. workforce produces goods or services for export, a 15 percent decline in the last decade.

____ 2. The United States' leading export to the rest of the world is agricultural products.

____ 3. The major trading partners of the United States include Mainland China, Canada, and Japan.

____ 4. Though many U. S. manufacturers are heavily involved in the international market, service firms have not found the international market attractive enough to induce their entry.

____ 5. One good reason to become a global marketer is that a firm may be able to gain advance notice of new products and acquire new insights into consumer behavior.

____ 6. In newly industrialized countries like Korea and Brazil where most people still engage in agriculture and per capita income is low, few opportunities for international trade exist.

____ 7. One-fifth of the world's population lives in China compared with less than one in twenty in the United States.

____ 8. Average birth rates continue to grow around the world, but death rates are declining due to better geriatric medicine.

____ 9. Indian consumers prefer to buy large quantities at one time because they know it is more economical to do so.

____ 10. International marketers must make sure they not only address potential customers in their own language, but that the message is correctly translated and conveys the intended meaning.

____ 11. Before the adoption of the Euro, prices for the same goods and services varied between 30 percent and 100 percent among European nations, dropping to only 28 percent in the first year after the introduction.

Harcourt, Inc.

_____ 12. The U.S. *Foreign Corrupt Practices Act of 1977* exempts companies from antitrust regulations so they can form export groups to serve foreign buyers.

_____ 13. Revenue tariffs, when applied by the U.S. government, are generally higher than protective tariffs.

_____ 14. Under the terms of the *Omnibus Trade and Competitiveness Act of 1988*, the United States can now single out countries that impede trade among their own domestic companies and penalize them by placing tariffs or quotas on their goods imported into the U.S.

_____ 15. The World Trade Organization has made only slow progress toward its major policy initiatives of liberalizing world financial services, telecommunications, and maritime markets.

_____ 16. The standardized operations offered the marketer by a franchise typically reduce costs, increase operating efficiencies, and provide greater international recognizability.

_____ 17. The North American Free Trade Agreement strengthens trade restrictions among Canada, the United States, and Mexico, and is the Western Hemisphere's only functioning trade bloc.

_____ 18. Companies using a global marketing strategy change their approach to the market in each foreign market in which they become involved.

_____ 19. A firm typically follows a one-product, one-message straight extension strategy as part of a global marketing strategy like Pepsi Cola's.

_____ 20. The marketing of different blends of coffee combined with different promotional programs in the various markets where those products are sold would be an example of a dual adaptation strategy.

_____ 21. Foreign markets usually offer excellent transportation systems and warehousing facilities by comparison to those available in the U.S.

_____ 22. The tried and true pricing strategies which have stood the test of time here in the United States require little adaptation for foreign markets and are seldom changed as conditions change.

_____ 23. The Organization of Petroleum Exporting Countries is an example of a commodity marketing organization that tries to control prices through collective action.

_____ 24. Countertrading is a form of exporting where goods are sold "counter to the interests" of one or both of the nations involved in the transaction; in other words, countertrading involves dealing in contraband.

_____ 25. British Itsy Bitsy Entertainment Company's newest export to the United States, the Teletubbies – Tinky Winky, Dipsy, Lala, and Po – have been quite successful in the early childhood education of U.S. youngsters.

Multiple Choice

Circle the letter of the phrase or sentence that best completes the sentence or answers the question.

26. When Howard Furniture Company, a manufacturer of wood furniture, purchases kiln-dried spruce or ash lumber from a Canadian supplier, it is
    a. acquiring goods to complement its main product line.
    b. taking advantage of foreign innovation to improve quality of its own products.
    c. forestalling foreign competition by getting involved in a market abroad.
    d. buying necessary raw materials abroad to use in its domestic manufacturing operations.
    e. speculating on the increasing scarcity of spruce and ash by laying in a supply to beat market fluctuations in the price.

27. Many eastern European currencies are "soft." This means that
    a. they cannot readily be converted into hard currencies such as the dollar, the yen, or the euro.
    b. they trade in the open money market and their value fluctuates widely from day to day.
    c. their value depends on the nature of the transaction; they may be more or less valuable depending on what's being bought or sold.
    d. they have unusual names that frequently change, along with their exchange value, with changes in the government of the country issuing them.
    e. currency dealers are reluctant to trade in them until more is known about the political stability of the countries issuing them.

28. Reflecting its "newly industrialized" status, imports to Brazil tend to be
    a. comprised mainly of pizzas bought from Domino's.
    b. few and far between; the economy can't yet support them.
    c. primarily agricultural products needed to feed the population.
    d. largely dominated by services bought from the United States.
    e. industrial goods, particularly high-tech equipment, and consumer goods.

29. McDonald's decision to offer beets as a condiment in some of its Australian outlets illustrates that
    a. new middle-class consumers often seek strange products to express their success.
    b. marketing strategies must be matched to local customs, tastes, and living conditions.
    c. the shortage of onions had to be met some way.
    d. color is an important component of product appeal. Purple goes well with beef.
    e. people can sometimes be convinced to buy almost anything.

30. The introduction of the Euro as a unit of currency
    a. destabilized the economies of western Europe and the Euro had to be withdrawn.
    b. has had little effect on domestic prices for products among European nations.
    c. reduced variations in prices charged for the same goods and services among European countries.
    d. is not expected to have any long-term consequences for European prices or national growth.
    e. serves only as an accounting convenience: domestic currencies remaining unchanged.

31. The U.S. Helms-Burton Act of 1996
    a. exempts from antitrust regulations companies forming export groups to offer products to foreign buyers.
    b. prohibits U.S. businesspeople from bribing foreign officials in soliciting new or repeat sales abroad.

c. seeks to impose trade sanctions against Cuba by allowing U.S. interests to sue foreign firms for using expropriated U.S. assets to do business with Cuba.
d. places high tariffs on goods coming from countries known to be "tainted" by internal corruption.
e. denies U. S. visas to corporate executives of firms accused of violating the act.

32. A nation's population size, its per capita income, and its stage of economic development are characteristics of its
    a. social environment.
    b. cultural environment.
    c. political environment.
    d. legal environment.
    e. economic environment.

33. When one examines the state of a nation's highway and railroad system, the availability and coverage of its radio, TV, and newspaper network, and how much energy is available from its generators, gas pipelines, and other utilities, one is scrutinizing
    a. the social environment of the country from an industrial point of view.
    b. the government's ability to deliver social services to its people.
    c. the likelihood of the country to experience a revolutionary takeover.
    d. the adequacy of the infrastructure provided by that nation's economy.
    e. the possibility of getting caught should the necessity for a fast getaway arise.

34. Administrative barriers to trade may include
    a. revenue tariffs.
    b. import quotas.
    c. protective tariffs.
    d. dumping.
    e. weak or soft currency.

35. The degree of a nation's multinational economic integration is reflected in its
    a. size, per capita income, and stage of economic development.
    b. laws, trade regulations, and political stability.
    c. membership in a customs union, common market, or free-trade area.
    d. participation in such activities as dumping, protective tariffs, and exchange control.
    e. language, educational system, religious attitudes, and social values.

36. ISO 9000 certification
    a. ensures that a company's products and services meet established quality levels.
    b. was developed in the United States to assure internationally common goods.
    c. is unavailable to small businesses – only firms above a certain size may apply.
    d. does not usually lead to increased prestige or access to more markets.
    e. is of no significance to most U. S. firms.

37. The body of international law emerges from the
    a. United States Statutes and Code of Federal Regulations for citizens of the United States.
    b. statutes, laws, and regulations of the appropriate country of jurisdiction.
    c. treaties, conventions, and agreements that exist among nations.
    d. Codes and Resolutions of the United Nations.
    e. Laws and Regulations of the Admiralty.

Part 1 The Contemporary Marketing Environment

38. The function of the *Export Trading Company Act of 1982* is to
    a. exempt companies from the antitrust laws so they can form export groups that offer a variety of products to foreign buyers.
    b. control the shipment of U.S. goods to foreign countries in ships of other than U.S. registry.
    c. empower the United States Coast Guard to search and seize vessels found to have contraband aboard regardless of whether they are inbound or outbound.
    d. encourage export of U.S. products by subsidizing American firms which actively participate in foreign trade.
    e. establish a U.S. foreign trade commission which negotiates with nations abroad for special privileges for U.S. firms.

39. Taxes levied against imported products for the purpose of raising funds for the importing government are called
    a. exchange taxes.
    b. import quotas.
    c. protective tariffs.
    d. antidumping penalties.
    e. revenue tariffs.

40. A tax levied against imported goods whose purpose is to protect domestic industry is a
    a. protective tariff.
    b. revenue quota.
    c. exchange control.
    d. general agreement tariff.
    e. revenue tariff.

41. Dumping is the practice of
    a. selling defective or contaminated goods in the international market rather than in the home market.
    b. escaping undesirable foreign contracts simply by dumping on the foreign party to the contract and abandoning the agreement.
    c. taking materials which have been seized by the government under the Contraband Products Act out to sea and throwing them overboard.
    d. selling a product in a foreign market for a price lower than that which it brings in the home market.
    e. selling merchandise overseas before it has been introduced in the home market in order to prevent foreign competitors from entering the home market once the goods do become available there.

42. The Common Market, or European Union (EU) as its members now prefer to have it called, is perhaps the world's best example of
    a. a mutual defense organization like NATO or the Warsaw Pact countries.
    b. an internally self-competitive organization of national powers.
    c. how fragile any treaty-based organization must be, as its recent collapse will attest.
    d. an economic union since 1948, when a single uniform set of regulations regarding foreign trade was implemented.
    e. a fifteen-nation customs union moving in the direction of full economic union.

43. The least risky way of entering the international market is by
    a. franchising or subcontracting.

b. exporting.
c. joint ventures.
d. dealing in contraband.
e. acquisition of a foreign firm.

44. When a domestic firm enters into an arrangement under which it agrees to share the risks, costs, and management of a foreign operation with a foreign company, it has
    a. issued a license to the foreign firm.
    b. formed a joint venture with the foreign company.
    c. engaged in foreign marketing of its products and services.
    d. laid the groundwork for foreign production and marketing by its own people.
    e. forever lost its rights to those assets which it has allowed the foreign company to use.

45. A firm that chooses to use a "global marketing strategy" will
    a. use a standardized marketing mix in every market in which it becomes involved, making minimal modifications as required.
    b. alter its products but not its promotional mix as necessary to appeal to the tastes and preferences of its various markets.
    c. alter its promotional mix but not its products as it enters various foreign markets.
    d. modify both its products and its promotional mix for each of the different markets it enters.
    e. be prepared to take whatever actions are necessary to assure itself of success in each of its different markets

46. A firm which approaches the international market with a product unlike anything it has ever sold in the domestic market is probably applying a
    a. straight extension strategy for entering the international market.
    b. promotion adaptation strategy for entering that market.
    c. dual adaptation strategy for market entry into a foreign market.
    d. product invention strategy, recognizing unique opportunities in the foreign market.
    e. product adaptation strategy for entry into foreign markets.

47. The first decision that must be made concerning distribution strategy for a foreign market is
    a. how the product will be distributed within the foreign market.
    b. the method that will be used to enter the foreign market.
    c. who is going to exercise control over distribution in the foreign market.
    d. what devices will be used to maintain product quality during the distribution process.
    e. whether the product will be packaged differently in the foreign market than at home.

48. Which of the following would be the best example of a countertrade?
    a. Cincinnati-Milacron sells computer controlled milling machines to a West German Company and the West Germans pay in U.S. dollars.
    b. General Motors sells jet engines to a British firm. The British pay in Pounds Sterling.
    c. Turnbull Cone Baking Company sells ice cream cones to a firm in Bolivia. The Bolivians pay by shipping tin ingots to the Turnbull people.
    d. Peerless Valve Company sells water valves to the city of Milan, Italy. The city pays in a combination of U.S. dollars, Italian Lire, and West German bearer bonds.
    e. Rolls-Royce ships nine Silver Cloud convertibles to the Pasha of Ranjipur. The Pasha pays in gold.

49. Pricing decisions in the foreign market

a. can always be approached the same way they are in the United States; this aspect of marketing never varies.
b. are seldom subject to political constraints; politicians recognize that without profits, products aren't produced or sold.
c. are relatively free of competitive implications; most foreign economies are much more highly controlled than is that of the U.S., and competition much less active.
d. may require modifications to recognize competitive, economic, political, and legal differences between the foreign market and the U.S. market.
e. are little affected by the actions of groups like the Organization of Petroleum Exporting Countries.

50. The dominant theme of foreign investment in America continues to be
    a. franchising outlets in the United States.
    b. foreign licensing to U.S. businesses.
    c. joint ventures between foreign and American firms.
    d. subcontracting for American manufacturers.
    e. acquisition of domestic firms by foreign interests.

Contemporary Marketing

Name_____   Instructor_____

Section_____   Date_____

Applying Marketing Concepts

CSRG, S.A, (which stands for Chattelerault, Sibley, Ribeyrolle, and Gladiator, Inc. – and now you know why it's called CSRG) is a well-established manufacturer of specialty commercial vehicles located in Chatellerault, France. Founded in 1958, the firm made its name in France by producing and marketing a line of unitized service units specially designed to serve the needs of electrical utilities. These "Gladiators" are heavy-duty vehicles that can carry a vast array of repair parts and even include a self-contained shop for use in the event reworking of a component in the field is required. Recently, CSRG was approached by Bradford, Ltd., a British truck manufacturer, who asked to enter into an arrangement to incorporate some of CSRG's patented technical features in vehicles of their manufacture, selling the resulting trucks as Bradford Gladiators. Bradford would provide the manufacturing facilities and CSRG the patents, quality control, some components, and marketing expertise. Profits would be shared between the two firms.

CSRG has told Bradford it will consider the arrangement, but in the meantime it is exploring other possibilities. It recognizes that, should it decide to enter the British market on its own, its vehicles would at least have to be modified to right-hand drive (the driver would be seated on the right of the cab, rather than the left) because of the British custom of driving on the left-hand side of the road. There is considerable concern, as well, over whether the British market can be approached the same way as the French market. Data indicate that the present British market for vehicles such as CSRG's lies with television cable companies who carry different components and work in a fashion somewhat different than that of providers of electricity. One officer of CSRG has even suggested that the company develop a truck of a totally different design to satisfy this unique demand.

Circle the letter of the phrase or sentence that best completes the sentence or answers the question.

1. If CSRG enters into the arrangement suggested by Bradford, it will have created a(n)
    a. export contract.
    b. licensing agreement.
    c. joint venture.
    d. shared-rights consortium.
    e. export trade law standard relationship.

2. If CSRG makes the modifications required by British driving custom and exports units to that country, promoting them the same way it promotes them in France, its strategy will be
    a. straight extension.
    b. dual adaptation.
    c. triple adaptation.
    d. product adaptation.
    e. promotion adaptation.

Part 1 The Contemporary Marketing Environment

3. If CSRG accepts the theory that British cable TV companies are the target market for its products in that country, modifying its promotional program as well as some features of its truck's design to better suit that market, it will be adopting a
   a. dual adaptation strategy.
   b. marginal entry strategy.
   c. promotion adaptation strategy.
   d. product invention strategy.
   e. product adaptation strategy.

4. Heeding the advice of the executive who proposes the development of an entirely different vehicles for the different requirements of the British market would result in the adoption of a
   a. dual adaptation strategy.
   b. straight extension strategy.
   c. product invention strategy.
   d. product adaptation strategy.
   e. market development strategy.

Aunt Melba's Natchitoches Pie Corporation, of Natchitoches, Louisiana, has been making and selling for over 50 years its variety of the unique fried meat pies for which that section of the state is famous. The company operates more than 30 pie stands and drive-through restaurants in northwest Louisiana, east Texas, and southern Arkansas.

Aunt Melba's recently received an inquiry from an Australian engineer working in nearby Shreveport. The engineer, Walter Christie, has apparently become quite fond of the Natchitoches (pronounced Nack-it-tosh) fried pie and believes that it would be quite a success back home in the land down under, where the inhabitants often eat a quick lunch consisting of the Australian meat pie. The Australian pie is a small potpie eaten from the hands somewhat like a sandwich. Christie has asked Aunt Melba's for the exclusive rights to produce and distribute its fried pies in his homeland.

The company, realizing that Australia's population of some 14 million people is roughly the same size as the one it now serves, countered by offering to bring Walter into the firm. After a brief training period, he would be sent to Australia to introduce the product to the market. He did not reject the offer outright, but did mention that he wanted a proprietary interest in any such venture.

Further investigation of the Australian market by Aunt Melba's officials proved very interesting. While some Australians, particularly in heavily populated New South Wales, do like to eat and run, early efforts by U. S. fast food chains specializing in sandwiches met with considerable resistance. Australians simply did not approve of the skimpy portions of meat and poor quality of bread used in the American sandwiches. One U.S. fast food executive was heard to say, "Australians are very fussy about bread. They will put almost anything in a sandwich – beans, spaghetti, even corn – but if the bread isn't up to snuff, that's the end of it." An executive of another firm commented, "They have a sandwich down there they call 'the lot.' It has everything – the lot – on it: pineapple, meat, egg, potato, whatever. We just couldn't compete with that, so we changed our product."

Armed with those observations, Aunt Melba's executives rethought their position. Why should they take a financial risk? Since Christie seemed to have financial backing, they decided to let him have rights to their fried pie in the Australian market for a number of years, provided he paid them a sizable royalty on sales.

Circle the letter of the phrase or sentence that best completes the sentence or answers the question.

5. The level of involvement of the Aunt Melba firm under Walter's proposal would be
   a. exporting.
   b. foreign licensing.
   c. overseas marketing.
   d. direct investment in foreign production and marketing.
   e. direct exporting.

6. The level of involvement of the firm under their original counterproposal to Walter would be
   a. exporting.
   b. foreign licensing.
   c. overseas marketing.
   d. direct investment in foreign production and marketing.
   e. direct exporting.

7. The major barrier to the introduction of American fast food into Australia, as shown in the testimony of the interviewed executives, was
   a. cultural.
   b. economic.
   c. trade restrictions.
   d. political.
   e. exchange rate controls.

8. Which component of the marketing mix seems to present the greatest challenge for firms entering the Australian fast food market?
   a. distribution
   b. price
   c. product
   d. promotion
   e. none of them do

Write "T" for True and "F" for False for each of the following statements.

_____ 9. It is very likely that Aunt Melba's fried pies will have to be modified to be compatible with Australian tastes.

_____ 10. It is likely that Mr. Christie and Aunt Melba's will be faced with Australian tariffs and import restrictions.

_____ 11. Wealthier countries such as Australia may prove to be prime markets for U. S. products, particularly consumer goods.

_____ 12. If Aunt Melba's and Mr. Christie come to terms, there is a real danger that Aunt Melba's will be guilty of dumping.

_____ 13. Aunt Melba's is following a global marketing strategy.

_____ 14. Mr. Christie's original proposal was in the nature of a request for a joint venture arrangement.

Part 1 The Contemporary Marketing Environment

Name _____   Instructor_____

Section _____   Date_____

Surfing the Net

Keeping in mind that addresses change and what's on the Web now may have changed by the time you read this, let's take a look at some of the places on the Net that reflect aspects of global marketing. We are not endorsing or recommending any of these sources, merely making note of the information and services that people have elected to offer through the Internet.

I don't know what they are, but you can get arabidopsis seed in an utterly astonishing array of genetic pedigrees from the Arabidopsis Stock Centre at the University of Nottingham, U.K. Their address is **http://nasc.life.nott.ac.uk/description.html**. The seed will actually come from their North American branch, the Arabidopsis Biological Resource Centre at Ohio State University if you're in Canada or the United States. These folks have their own Website at **http://aims.cps.msu.edu/aims**

Demographics and other data for Britain and much of the rest of Europe are available at the University of Bristol (U.K.) at their site **http://sosig.esrc.bris.ac.uk/.** This is the Social Science Information Gateway and has links to all sorts of sources of European Social Science Sites. It's pretty neat.

On the other hand, you can visit Australia's Charles Sturt University (no, it's not misspelled) at **http://www.csu.edu.au/** and read all about Australian education and tourism. Brazil (if you speak Portugese) can be found at **http://www.brazil.gov.br** or if you prefer your information about Brazil in English, try **http://brazilbiz.com/english**, a business-oriented site. Ireland may be visited at **http://www.commerce.ie** or **http://www.enterprise-ireland.com/english.isp** France has an interesting site at **http://www.urec.cnrs.fr/annuaire**, run by the Centre National de Recherche Scientifique or the Louvre Museum of Paris may be found at **http://www.louve.fr/louvrea.html** in English. There are, of course, many other foreign travel and business destinations. As you browse, you'll surely discover them.

Sites verified January 29, 2000.

Harcourt, Inc.

Contemporary Marketing

Name_____ Instructor_____

Section_____ Date_____

Cases for Part 1

1. Laser VideoDiscs: a Technology in Search of a Home

Introduced in 1981, RCA's SelectaVision videodiscs were the result of fifteen years and $300 million of scientific research. The result all this work and expense was a simple player which could be attached to any television set. The user inserted the 12" diameter prerecorded laser-scannable disc, flipped a switch, and watched the movie or other performance recorded on the disc.

The video cassette recorder was introduced in 1976. Its performance in reproducing recorded material was inferior to that of the SelectaVision unit, but it could record, which SelectaVision could not. On the other hand, a SelectaVision unit was initially less expensive than a VCR. Moreover, the VCR market was dominated by units produced in Japan, and SelectaVision was an American product.

By 1984, VCR prices had fallen from an average of $1,000 for a home-quality unit to about $250. A SelectaVision unit sold for $200. SelectaVision discs, at around $20, were much cheaper than prerecorded videotapes, but a tape of a movie could be rented at any of 15,000 tape shops for as little as a dollar a day.

RCA embarked on a program of rebates and freebies – at one point, the purchase of a SelectaVision player got you a $50 rebate AND a free popcorn popper – but sales remained stagnant. VCRs were outselling laserdisc units by a ratio of fifteen to one. Despite continued promotion and the introduction of newer, cheaper players, retailers ultimately refused to handle SelectaVisions, and RCA abandoned the market in 1984 after losing $200 million.

The laserdisc was not dead, however, and reappeared on the home entertainment scene in 1987 as the compact disc. Vastly superior to the alternatives – the LP phonograph record and tape recording – in sound quality, capacity, and convenience, this product rapidly established itself as the definitive sound source for music recordings played in the home. Moreover, a close relative and physical twin, the CD-ROM, became the new medium for presenting very large programs to the home computer. By 1993, the CD had completely supplanted the LP phonograph record, CD-ROMs became standard equipment on most home computers – and RCA, now a division of French electronics giant Thomson-CSF, reintroduced SelectaVision.

The new SelectaVision achieved some success, but not as a home-entertainment product. Instead, it found a niche as an audio-visual resource in the educational arena. The niche was small, however, and the product once again began to stagnate, and by the late 1990s, had for all practical purposes once again disappeared.

Harcourt, Inc.

Then, in 1997, there appeared on the scene the DVD disc. Exactly the same size as the now-common music CDs and CD-ROMs used to store large computer programs, and capable of storing and playing an entire movie with extras – the "making of" documentary, theatrical trailers, and interviews, not to mention the music video of movie's theme – the DVD product soon became a relatively popular viewing medium, though not, by millenium's end, sufficiently popular to replace the video cassette as the most common vehicle for home-entertainment viewing of motion pictures.

Questions

a. Did RCA employ the marketing concept when it introduced SelectaVision? (A simple "Yes" or "No" is not sufficient. Get into it.)

b. What environmental factors affected the original SelectaVision product's failure?

c. What changes in the environment do you think argued for the reintroduction of SelectaVision after its ten-year absence?

d. Why do you suppose that the DVD product was more successful than either of its predecessors?

Part 1 The Contemporary Marketing Environment

Creating a Marketing Plan: A Continuing Exercise

Introduction

At this location in each subsequent section of this Study Guide, you will be presented with new facts in a continuing narrative designed to give you experience in gathering information, relating abilities to opportunities, and matching the needs of the marketplace to the desire for success of three young entrepreneurs. You will create for this threesome a marketing plan that will pave their way, if carefully followed, to the realization of their dreams.

The narrative will outline the abilities, aspirations, and strengths of our dynamic trio as well as their shortcomings. You will be given some information about conditions in the real world, but it is expected that you will have sufficient motivation to go beyond what is given, especially when it is presented as an opinion of one of the participants. At the end of each of the narrative parts, questions will be posed to help you stay on the right track. Before beginning this exercise and as you are presented with new facts at the end of each section of this book, you should review the appendix to Chapter 6, "Developing a Marketing Plan," which can be found in *Contemporary Marketing*. The information that you will be given in any one section of this exercise will not necessarily follow the same order as the outline of the marketing plan in your textbook, but will be designed to help you complete a particular section of the plan. By the time you have completed all of the parts of "Creating a Marketing Plan" you will have a document that should serve the needs of the three young people for whom you have prepared it and will contain all of the essential information required for the entry into the marketplace of their marketing mix.

To assist you, we present here an outline of components that a Marketing Plan should contain.

I. Situation Analysis: Appraisal of Current Status (Where Are We Now?)
    A. History of the Firm
    B. Customer Analysis – Who are the firm's markets?
    C. Competitor Analysis – Who are the firm's competitors?

II. Marketing Objectives: Where Do We Wish to Go?
    A. Sales Objectives – Volume of sales desired in one year? Five years?
    B. Profit Objectives – Level of profits desired
    C. Customer Objectives – Our image and our services defined

III. Strategy – How Do We Get There From Here?
    A. Product Strategy – What is our product? Defining the offering.
    B. Pricing Strategy – What are our base prices and price alterations?
    C. Distribution Strategy – Channels and Physical Distribution Options
    D. Promotional Strategy – Define the mix of personal and nonpersonal selling
    E. Financial Strategy – How will we budget to achieve these objectives?

Meeting the Cast

Brian McPatrick and Terrence Michaels are cousins, and with their friend Laura Claire, were considering their future. The three had known each other since childhood, but had not thought that their careers might bring them together until recently. The two young men, after graduating together from Georgia Tech, where Terry had majored in electrical engineering and Brian in Industrial Management (specializing in computer applications), had decided to attend Internet Service Corporation's Computing Institute in

Harcourt, Inc.

Contemporary Marketing

Owasho, South Dakota, to become more familiar with the ins and outs of the World Wide Web and its potential for business and in the home. They felt that their undergraduate education had given them an excellent preparation for dealing with the nuts and bolts of computer technology, but wanted to know more about how people interacted with each other through the "intelligent machines" of the early twenty-first century. Their plan was to use this extra information to get jobs at some Internet service provider where Terry could design new utilities that would enhance the usefulness of computing machinery and Brian could work with software to make Web Surfing more "user friendly."

Imagine their surprise when, on reporting to the new class to the Institute, they met their lifelong friend, Laura. She had recently graduated with a degree in Enterprise Administration from the University of Louisiana in Lafayette and was attending the Institute because her family used a large number of computers in their wholesale food distribution business and all of the family members had attended the Institute to learn the details of computer applications for use by the firm, which was now using the Internet to maintain contact with its customers and suppliers. Laura had not yet made a commitment to enter the family firm, and was not being pressured to do so, but her mother had pointed out to her that the information she would receive at the Institute certainly wouldn't hurt her job prospects anywhere, and if she should ever decide to join the family firm she would have to attend the Institute anyway. Looking at the experience as an extension of her college training, Laura enthusiastically decided to go.

The three old friends quickly renewed their acquaintance, and soon recognized that among them they possessed a unique combination of talents and interests that might well be put to good use. Brian and Terry had a real desire to improve computing equipment itself, Brian through improvements in software systems and Terry through improvements in relationships among the hardware. Laura, as it turned out, really had little interest in distributing fruits and vegetables and wanted to do something on her own – something interesting, different, and challenging.

All three of the friends did well at the Institute, mastering the details of current thinking on circuit design and interfacing, software development, and system applications with reasonable facility. Needless to say, each was a bit stronger than the others in his or her own specialty. Terry whizzed through the circuit design and interfacing part of the course, helping the others when they found themselves in difficulty. Brian found the software logic, even the newest and most esoteric systems, a breeze, and Laura thrived on systems applications, particularly on applications where economy of configuration was important. Soon the course was over, and all of them received the diploma that certified them to be graduates of the ISC Computing Institute.

Now they were sitting around a table in a small neighborhood restaurant they had all come to know and enjoy, relaxing over a friendly repast and discussing their plans for the future. None of them really wanted to break up the set, as they had come to think of themselves, and soon the conversation turned to the possibility of the three starting their own company in a computer related field. Each felt that he or she could raise enough money to support the developmental cost of one-third of a firm in some aspect of the computing industry.

Questions and Instructions:

There are no questions for this part. Read the information that appears above two or three times and try and absorb the nature of the strengths and weaknesses of each of the three partners in this venture, whatever its nature turns out to be. After you have completed the material in Part 2 of your text, the development of the marketing plan for Telabri Enterprises will begin in earnest. (Telabri, of course, is the first two letters of Laura and Terry and the first three of Brian strung together.)

Part 2

Managing Technology to Achieve Marketing Success

Electronic commerce (e-commerce) describes marketing activities occurring on the Internet, by fax, or through telephones, computer modems, or CD-ROMs. Electronic marketing (e-marketing) is the narrower concept of presenting a marketing mix through the facilities of e-commerce. Online marketing is the pursuit of e-marketing through interactive computer systems. The Internet is the primary vehicle for online marketing through its World Wide Web of interlinked computers functioning within the Internet. The Web provides entertainment, information, and e-commerce opportunities to its users.

E-commerce impacts the economy through its business-to-business and business-to-consumer marketing resources, offering lower prices, convenience, and personalization of service often lacking elsewhere. The global nature of the Internet broadens the base of e-commerce from both the vendor's and the customer's point of view. The Internet's effect on marketing has been significant, with over 25,000 new commercial sites being added every month. But marketing has also impacted the Internet, creating new promotional techniques and channels of distribution for goods and services. Online buyers tend to be affluent, urban consumers while online vendors sell everything from auto parts to fresh vegetables delivered to your door.

Creating an effective Web presence for the marketer means more than just being there. The objective of marketing on the Web is to create a sustainable Web presence generating profit, new customers, and related benefits to the firm. The Web site must help build relationships between the firm and its customers. Managing the Web site and measuring its effectiveness become crucial activities in this context. Strategically, interactive marketing is expected to increase in importance and complexity during the next several years.

Relationship marketing is the development, growth, and maintenance of long-term, cost-effective relationships with individual customers, suppliers, distributors, and employees. It typically involves creating class ties between buyer and seller through the use of database technology to identify current and potential customers, modification of the marketing mix to target the individual customer, and monitoring of the relationship to measure the success of the resulting program. Relationship marketing replaces transaction-based marketing, and is ultimately the function of promises made, promises enabled, and promises kept. The emotional link between vendor and customer is forged through bonding, empathy, reciprocity, and trust, moving through three levels of intensity from the customer's point of view beginning with the level of economic incentive, progressing to the level of social benefit, and finally reaching the partnership level. Customers who reach the third level can often be retained for very long periods.

Affinity and frequent buyer/user programs are common tools for developing a relationship with customers. These are facilitated by the use of databases to target appropriate types of customers. Relationship marketing applies to business-to-business situations as it does to business-to-consumer interactions. The partnership level of relationship for businesses offers significant advantages to both partners. Businesses may form four types of partnership with other businesses: buyer partnerships, seller partnerships, internal partnerships, and lateral partnerships. Lateral partnerships often result in co-marketing and co-branding.

Harcourt, Inc.

A crucial measure of the value of relationship marketing is the "lifetime value of a customer," which is the revenue and intangible benefits each customer brings to the seller over a lifetime less the cost of acquiring, marketing to, and servicing that customer. The realization that has grown out of calculation of this datum is that it is far more profitable to keep an existing customer than it is to find a new one.

Chapter 4

E-Commerce: Electronic Marketing and the Internet

Chapter Outline

Use the following as a guide in taking notes.

I. Chapter Overview – Technology: The Source of Dramatic Change

II. What Is Electronic Commerce?

    A. Interactivity and e-commerce

    B. The Internet

        1. Growth of the Internet

        2. Intranets and extranets

    C. The world wide web and its three functions

    D. Accessing the Internet

III. E-Commerce and the Economy

    A. Business-to-business online marketing and its benefits

    B. Online Consumer Marketing

        1. Lower prices

        2. Convenience

        3. Personalization

    C. Benefits of Online Consumer Marketing

        1. Relationship Building

        2. Cost Reductions

        3. Increased Efficiency

    D. Online marketing is international marketing

    E. Security and privacy issues of e-commerce

IV. Reciprocal Effects of Marketing and the Internet

Harcourt, Inc.

A. The Internet's impact on marketing

B. Marketing's impact on the Internet

V. Who Are the Online Buyers and Sellers?

A. Online buyers

B. Online sellers

VI. Interactive Online Marketing Channels

A. Company Web sites

1. Electronic storefronts and cybermalls

2. Advertisements on other Web sites

3. Online communities

4. Other interactive marketing links

VII. Creating an Effective Web Presence

A. Building an effective Web site

B. Managing a Web site

C. Measuring effectiveness of online marketing

VIII. Strategic Implications of E-Commerce

Part 2 Managing Technology to Achieve Marketing Success

Name_____ Instructor_____

Section_____ Date_____

Key Concepts

The purpose of this section is to allow you to determine if you can match key concepts with the definitions of the concepts. It is essential that you know the definitions of the concepts prior to applying the concepts in later exercises in this chapter.

From the list of lettered terms, select the one that best fits each of the numbered statements below. Write the letter of that choice in the space provided.

Key Terms

a. electronic commerce (e-commerce)
b. electronic marketing (e-marketing)
c. digital tools
d. online marketing
e. interactive marketing
f. internet (Net)
g. electronic mail (e-mail)
h. intranet
i. extranet
j. internet service provider (ISP)
k. portal
l. bot

m. corporate Web site
n. marketing Web site
o. electronic store front
p. cybermalls
q. online forum
r. newsgroup
s. electronic bulletin board
t. Web kiosk
u. smart card
v. electronic currency
w. hits
x. page views

_____ 1. Number of times a page is actually accessed by a visitor to a Web site.

_____ 2. Internet application for sending written messages between computers.

_____ 3. Web site that seeks to build customer good will and supplement other sales channels rather than to sell goods and services.

_____ 4. Basic pathway that provides individuals and organizations with access to the Internet either directly or through a specially designed online site.

_____ 5. All-purpose global communications network composed of some 50,000 different networks around the globe that, within limits, lets anyone with access to a personal computer send and receive images and data anywhere.

_____ 6. Internal corporate network that allows employees with an organization to communicate with each other and gain access to corporate information.

_____ 7. Electronic technologies used in e-commerce including fax machines, computer modems, telephones, and CD-ROMs.

Harcourt, Inc.

Contemporary Marketing

_____ 8. Specialized online service that provides information on a specific topic or area of interest.

_____ 9. Small, freestanding structure with one or more sides that provides consumers with Internet connections to a firm and its goods and services.

_____ 10. Multipurpose card embedded with computer chips that store personal and financial information such as credit-card data, health records, and drivers license number.

_____ 11. Process of creating, distributing, promoting, and pricing goods and services to a target market over the Internet or through digital tools.

_____ 12. Noncommercial Internet version of online forum that is limited to people posting and reading messages on a specific topic.

_____ 13. Search program that checks hundreds of sites, gathers and assembles information, and brings it back to the sender.

_____ 14. Discussion groups located on commercial Internet services.

_____ 15. Buyer-seller communications in which the customer controls the amount and type of information received from a marketer through such channels as the Internet, CD-ROMs, interactive toll-free telephone numbers, and virtual reality kiosks.

_____ 16. Term referring to the number of times a visitor goes to a home page.

_____ 17. Marketing activities that connect buyers and sellers electronically through interactive computer systems.

_____ 18. Gateway for Internet access (originally called a search engine) through a Web site that contains various services or communities of common interests.

_____ 19. Online store where customers can view and order merchandise much like window shopping at traditional retail establishments.

_____ 20. Group of virtual stores planned, coordinated, and operated as a unit for online shoppers.

_____ 21. System of exchange that allows consumers to set up accounts at Web sites and place credits in those accounts based on a monetary amount.

_____ 22. Corporate network that allows communication between an organization and selected customers, suppliers, and business partners outside the firm.

_____ 23. Web site designed to engage consumers in an interaction that increases their desire to make a purchase.

_____ 24. Among other things, conducting customer transactions and maintaining online relationships with customers by means of telecommunications networks.

Part 2 Managing Technology to Achieve Marketing Success

Name_____ Instructor_____

Section_____ Date_____

Self-Quiz

You should use these questions to test your understanding of the chapter material. Check your answers against those provided at the end of the chapter.

While these questions cover most of the chapter topics, they are not intended to be the same as the test questions your instructor may use in an examination. A good understanding of all aspects of the course material is essential to good performance on any examination.

True/False

Write "T" for True and "F" for False for each of the following statements.

____ 1. Ordering a computer motherboard from the Treasure Chest Computers Web site with overnight delivery by Federal Express is an example of electronic marketing.

____ 2. The Internet improves the geographic protections of local businesses by demonstrating that they can usually meet or beat the terms of sale offered by distant vendors.

____ 3. Creating products to meet customer specifications – even to the extent of starting production after an order has been placed – is called interactive marketing.

____ 4. E-commerce shifts the balance of power in the market to the buyer because he or she knows an alternative supplier is just a mouse-click away.

____ 5. What we now know as the World Wide Web was originally developed as an internal document-management system at the European Center for Nuclear Research in Geneva, Switzerland.

____ 6. A recent survey of online users disclosed that the most common use of the Web by online users was searching for information.

____ 7. It is expected that almost 250 million people will be World Wide Web users by the year 2002.

____ 8. At present, most of the revenue derived by portals comes from membership fees.

____ 9. To be successful, a Web site must provide a platform for communication between organizations and their customers and suppliers.

____ 10. Business-to-business online marketing has come to have even more glitz and glamour than the business-to-consumer segment.

Harcourt, Inc.

Contemporary Marketing

_____ 11. By the year 2003, it is expected that business-to-business e-commerce will amount to $1.3 trillion, or almost 10 percent of total U.S. business sales.

_____ 12. A business-to-business site on the Web needs to be listed with the major search engines and with Internet yellow pages such as Big Book to position itself so corporate buyers notice it.

_____ 13. The cost of launching a business-to-business Web site is relatively inexpensive, seldom exceeding a thousand dollars.

_____ 14. Price is seldom a major benefit one receives from shopping on the Web because prices there tend to be higher than store prices to offset the convenience of using the Web.

_____ 15. The emphasis of consumer-oriented e-commerce has turned from mass merchandising to one-to-one marketing as marketers recognize the key role of customer satisfaction in creating loyal customers who make repeat purchases.

_____ 16. Brand loyalty is one of the offline relationships that does not transfer well to online sites.

_____ 17. One of the shortcomings of e-commerce is that less than 5 percent of retail Web sites offer immediate customer service assistance.

_____ 18. Sales made entirely through a Web site have a much greater profit margin than sales from traditional channels such as catalogs, retail stores, or phone centers.

_____ 19. The countries of Asia account for 62 percent of Internet users worldwide, the United States and Canada only 12 percent.

_____ 20. Issues of infrastructure, economy, and politics all come into play when marketers try to enter international markets using the Internet.

_____ 21. Surprisingly, as the number of Internet users has risen, the incidence of online fraud has actually declined by a substantial percentage.

_____ 22. The Internet may ultimately mean the death of traditional sales activities and "bricks-and-mortar" retailing because it is a revolutionary, rather then evolutionary, development.

_____ 23. Americans of Asian and Pacific Island origin are the most likely racial groups to use the Internet, while African Americans and Hispanics are only half as likely to do so.

_____ 24. The Internet has tended to reduce the amount of mass customization and personalization of products and services available to American shoppers.

_____ 25. Marketing Web sites seldom attempt to sell the company's products directly, but attempt to build customer good will and assist channel members in their marketing efforts.

Part 2 Managing Technology to Achieve Marketing Success

Multiple Choice

Circle the letter of the phrase or sentence that best completes the sentence or answers the question.

26. The strategic process of creating, distributing, promoting, and pricing goods and services to a target market over the Internet or by using digital tools is called
    a. electronic marketing.
    b. electronic commerce.
    c. digital marketing.
    d. virtual commerce.
    e. an out-of-body experience.

27. The fact that customers on the Internet may negotiate prices online in much the same way as customers do at a local flea market or car dealership is an example of
    a. integrated marketing over the net.
    b. what is called "right-time marketing."
    c. interactive marketing.
    d. personalization.
    e. global reach.

28. The Internet is best defined as
    a. an organization of computer users who use telephone lines to communicate with each other.
    b. a government-run database interfacing the nation's personal computers by satellite link.
    c. a conspiracy of hackers and computer geeks to obtain information from other computer users.
    d. an entirely commercial endeavor designed to change the shape of the marketplace.
    e. a global collection of computer networks linked together for the purpose of exchanging data and information.

29. The proportion of U.S. households possessing a computer now exceeds
    a. 25 percent.
    b. 35 percent.
    c. 40 percent.
    d. 50 percent.
    e. 60 percent.

30. Internal corporate networks that allow employees within a firm to communicate with each other and gain access to corporate information are called
    a. extranets.
    b. internets.
    c. intranets.
    d. outernets.
    e. undernets.

31. The individual seeking information on the Web can often identify information-oriented Web sites by looking for the domain suffixes
    a. .com and .biz
    b. .org and .gov
    c. .bmp and .frg
    d. .wpd and .dbf
    e. .aba and .kba

Harcourt, Inc.

Contemporary Marketing

32. The basic path for going online is
   a. through a Web gate accessed by cursor link.
   b. by linking with a government agency such as NASA or the CIA.
   c. through satellite feed direct to an off-planet source.
   d. by using an Internet service provider like AT&T or America Online.
   e. on your own through a domain established for the purpose.

33. The leading category of business-to-business vendors on the Internet is
   a. wholesalers of business products.
   b. professionals such as attorneys and accountants offering their services on the Net.
   c. durable goods manufacturers.
   d. computer software companies.
   e. firms offering personal and business security.

34. Many business writers have begun to label e-commerce
   a. edgy commerce because it makes competitors nervous when they see what each of them is doing to assure themselves a place on the Net.
   b. environmental commerce because it has to be examined from an environmental point of view.
   c. elementary commerce because of its resemblance to chemical processes.
   d. extensive commerce because of its rapid rate of growth and the involvement of so many buyers and sellers by comparison with other markets.
   e. easy commerce because it allows the direct interchange of information in seamless fashion without the intervention of intermediaries.

35. In a recent survey cited in your textbook, the most common motivation cited by consumers for shopping on the Web was
   a. to save money.
   b. because it is fun.
   c. better selection of merchandise.
   d. for reasons of convenience.
   e. to avoid crowds and pesky salespeople.

36. The fact that cybershoppers can order goods and services from around the world any hour of the day or night is illustrative of its
   a. privacy and security in use.
   b. ease of navigation.
   c. demonstrative capacity.
   d. warmth and friendliness.
   e. convenience.

37. An example of effective personalization on the Web would be
   a. discovering you were welcomed back to a vendor's site by name and offered a choice of several new CDs by your favorite artists.
   b. finding an impressive array of size and color choices from a number of name brand manufacturers of fashion merchandise on a site selling casual clothing.
   c. having to use a password to charge a purchase to your credit card at a Web vendor's site.
   d. having to search through several categories of merchandise on a Web vendor's site to reach the kinds of items you sought.
   e. being dumped from a Web vendor's site because it was too busy to handle your queries.

38. For large and small businesses alike, using the Web as a marketplace can
    a. build strong relationships with customers.
    b. reduce both start up and operating costs.
    c. increase operational efficiency.
    d. help them to achieve a global presence.
    e. do all of the above.

39. Cultural differences can prove to be a barrier that hampers online marketing abroad, especially
    a. in Asia, where language problems and less familiarity with catalog and telephone buying cause reluctance on the part of consumers to buy online.
    b. in Australia, where on the entire continent only 12 percent of all homes are Internet users.
    c. in nearby Canada, where an abundance of local stores cater to every need and the Internet is seldom used.
    d. here in the United States, where distrust of foreigners makes us reluctant to order from non-U. S. Internet vendors.
    e. if the local government legislates against use of the Internet.

40. A recent study by the U. S. Department of Commerce found that
    a. 65 percent of the population were either very concerned or somewhat concerned about the confidentiality of the Internet.
    b. 40 percent of the population expressed any concern at any level about the confidentiality of the Internet.
    c. over 90 percent of the population were concerned about the security of the Internet.
    d. three-quarters of the U. S. population showed some concern about privacy on the Internet.
    e. surprisingly, only about a quarter of the population were concerned about Internet privacy.

41. Among the steps being taken to address security and privacy concerns on the Internet,
    a. eBay now requires purchasers to pay vendors in full in cash before the goods are shipped.
    b. the Federal Trade Commission requires that all information obtained by commercial Web sites from their customers be published on the Internet.
    c. online shopping malls are requiring that their customers read explicit policies that make them responsible for the quality of the products they buy.
    d. all Web sites are now required to obtain permission from parents by e-mail or fax before collecting personal data from children under the age of 13.
    e. Amazon.com has stopped accepting credit cards. All payments to them must be made in cash or by a cash-equivalent method.

42. At the present time, the number of e-commerce Internet sites is growing at the rate of
    a. 10,000 new sites per year.
    b. 100,000 new sites per year.
    c. 25,000 new sites per month.
    d. 150,000 new sites per month.
    e. 200,000 new sites per year.

43. Which of the following is not something an effective Web site ordinarily does?
    a. builds customer loyalty
    b. saves organizations and customers money
    c. quickens the sales process
    d. lowers costs
    e. reduces profits

Contemporary Marketing

44. To stimulate initial demand for Internet access,
    a. marketers had to invent totally new ways of reaching the market segment of possible Internet users.
    b. very little use was made of direct-mail promotions.
    c. use of television as an advertising medium for the new concept was severely limited because both stations and networks refused to air the messages.
    d. marketers used many of the traditional channels to do their advertising.
    e. magazine advertising proved useless at bringing the Internet concept into American homes and businesses.

45. Leading the increase in consumer spending on the Internet in the most recent year were
    a. people under the age of 25.
    b. people who had never bought online before and people over the age of 50.
    c. people who had a long record of Internet purchasing.
    d. owners of new computers and people over 60 years of age.
    e. small children (under age 8) who, with their parents' permission, spent over $400 each on the Net.

46. Online marketing in the United States is more likely to reach people
    a. who ordinarily do not watch television or read magazines.
    b. of low income, regardless of where they live.
    c. who live in rural areas and lack telephone service.
    d. of Hispanic ethnicity about twice as often as those who are of Asian heritage.
    e. who are currently unemployed and did not graduate from college.

47. The most popular class of consumer goods sold on the Internet is
    a. computer hardware.
    b. books and other publications.
    c. computer software.
    d. concert and event tickets.
    e. toys.

48. A small, strip message placed in a highly visible area of a frequently visited Web site is a
    a. headline.
    b. footnote.
    c. banner ad.
    d. capstone.
    e. sidebar.

49. A freestanding computer located in a retail showroom or shopping center that delivers information on demand would typically be
    a. a video show.
    b. an online forum.
    c. an electronic storefront.
    d. a Web kiosk.
    e. a chat room.

50. A smart card is a
    a. credit card that refuses to be charged for a foolish or extravagant purchase.
    b. plastic card similar to a credit card containing a microchip storing personal and financial information.

c. common sight in Europe but a fairly rare item in the U.S. as yet.
d. credit card which will mail itself home if lost or stolen.
e. credit card that can only be scanned when it is in the possession of its authorized owner.

Contemporary Marketing

Name_____ Instructor_____

Section_____ Date_____

Applying Marketing Concepts

Treasure Hunt Antiques of Natchez, Mississippi, is a hundred and fifty-year-old establishment that specializes in antebellum household furnishings. But just because they're old doesn't mean they're slow. The Tarleton family, owners of Treasure Hunt, know well the tastes of antique buyers and have developed a Web operation they think is as good as anything out there.

Every employee of the firm is computer literate as well as "antique literate." They are all interconnected through their computers and can send and receive messages among themselves and use the company's inventory database to match what they have on hand to the desires of potential customers. Beyond that, employees can send and respond to queries from the other members of the antiquenet, a computer-based linkage of a number of firms specializing in the same general categories of antiques as Treasure Hunt.

Treasure Hunt accesses the Internet through DeepSouth.net, a firm that provides this service to several hundred thousand subscribers in southern Mississippi, southwest Alabama, and part of Louisiana. They are also listed as antique dealers with Google, Yahoo!, and HotBot.

Just recently the company began to solicit people who access the Treasure Hunt Web site for information about their interests and preferences, even their tastes in antebellum antiques. This information is entered into a database and if that person ever accesses the Treasure Hunt Web site again, they are greeted with a reference to an antique presently in stock that will probably appeal to them.

The Tarletons have been amazed at the number and diversity of the people who have visited the Treasure Hunt Web site. "Yes, indeed," says Buffy Tarleton, daughter of the present owner and shipping manager of the firm, "We have people from all over the world signing in all the time – and buying stuff to be shipped to the most outlandish locations."

Circle the letter of the phrase or sentence that best completes the sentence or answers the question.

1. The interconnection of Treasure Hunt employees through their computers and their access to the inventory database is provided by an
    a. Internet.
    b. Infranet.
    c. Intranet.
    d. Extranet.
    e. Overbite.

2. The "antiquenet" is an example of an
    a. Overnet.
    b. Undernet.
    c. Net ball.
    d. Extranet.
    e. Venturenet.

Harcourt, Inc.

3. DeepSouth.net is Treasure Hunt's
   a. Internet service provider (ISP).
   b. Search base.
   c. Security service.
   d. Engine driver.
   e. Credit department.

4. Being listed with Google, Yahoo!, and HotBot is important to Treasure Hunt because
   a. it vastly increases the prestige of the firm to be listed with these rating services.
   b. Being listed on these search engines means that Treasure Hunt's name will automatically be forwarded to the computer of anyone who types in that they are searching for an "antique dealer."
   c. It's the thing to do on the Internet these days.
   d. It is the only way that Treasure Hunt can gain access to the lists of potential customers these services have compiled in the several years that they have been in business.
   e. It's the only way Treasure Hunt will get invited to the Google, Yahoo!, and HotBot antique dealers' Christmas parties every year.

5. Treasure Hunt's solicitation of its potential customers for information about their tastes in antiques is most likely part of an attempt to
   a. lower prices industry-wide by getting as many people as possible interested in different kinds of antiques.
   b. Compile a mailing list of likely prospects to be sold to other antique dealers.
   c. Reduce costs by limiting people's access to only those kinds of antiques they really like.
   d. Personalize Treasure Hunt's relationship with potential and existing customers by catering to them as individuals.
   e. Find and develop a new pool of vendors to sell antebellum antiques to Treasure Hunt.

6. Buffy's comments about the customers who have bought from Treasure Hunt's web site are
   a. evidence of the global reach of electronic commerce.
   b. Very unusual; most internet business is done within a very few miles of the Web site's home.
   c. Well-stated, but obviously quite confused; you can't ship antiques out of the country.
   d. Strongly worded indications of the interactive nature of the e-commerce experience.
   e. Fairly irrelevant; they're typical of most businesses today.

7. Bonus question for web surfers: The domain suffix Treasure Hunt's Web site is most likely to bear is
   a. .gov
   b. .edu
   c. .com
   d. .org
   e. .web

Tyler Burmaster is an Internet freak, a true Webhead. Everything he buys, he buys on the Net. He even has custom software to search for the lowest price on the best products in their classes on the Internet. Tyler is such a well-known figure to many of the sites he visits that they welcome him by name and tantalize him with offers of his favorite products. Despite this, Tyler spends only twenty to thirty minutes a day shopping on the Net.

Tyler spends almost four hours a day taking distance learning classes from a university almost a thousand miles away, and another hour and a half surfing the Web looking for needed data and preparing homework assignments to be e-mailed to his professors. Tyler will receive his bachelor's degree in electrical engineering in December from a university he's never seen.

On an average day, Tyler will spend between an hour and two hours at MusicCity.com, listening to concerts by his favorite new wave groups. He will occasionally log on to a game site and play for a while. Sometimes he even takes a plunge and pays for the privilege of playing on the Web.

But Tyler's day is not over. At least twice a day he reads his e-mail, much of which comes to him through his own Web site from firms who wish to buy one of his unique software packages or even to have him design a software array just for them. He always responds promptly, perhaps confirming the order and stating payment terms or providing an initial estimate of the cost of any special requests for programming a form may have. Tyler, it appears, is well known in the business world as Skylark Software. He can be found listed as a "serious software developer and publisher" on every search engine and in the Internet Yellow Pages and his Web site features a broad array of testimonials and references from satisfied clients.

8. The custom software Tyler uses to get the best deal on the things he wants to buy is a
   a. dot. It seems that everything on the Internet has a dot in it.
   b. Bot. This is one of the newest e-commerce tools.
   c. Portal. It opens the doors to e-buying.
   d. Gnome. That's what these little exploratory programs are called.
   e. Lot. This stands for what the program can do.

9. The fact that Tyler only spends twenty to thirty minutes a day doing his shopping is evidence of the Net's
   a. convenience. When he's done, he's done.
   b. Entertainment value. Tyler has to seek other stimulation.
   c. Price structure. He obviously can't afford to buy much.
   d. Complexity. Tyler probably becomes confused and quits.
   e. Dedication to businesses rather than consumers. He can't find anything to buy.

10. Tyler's time spent "in class" and researching demonstrate this function of the Internet. The function is
    a. entertainment.
    b. Providing information.
    c. E-commerce.
    d. Government business.
    e. Travel planning.

11. Tyler's time spent at MusicCity.com is time spent using the Internet for
    a. entertainment.
    b. Providing information.
    c. E-commerce.
    d. Government business.
    e. Travel planning.

12. Tyler's Web site is devoted to
    a. consumer-to-consumer commerce.
    b. Business-to-consumer commerce.
    c. Consumer-to-business commerce.
    d. Business-to-business commerce.
    e. Idle gossip and flighty conversation.

13. That Tyler's software is so well known testifies not only to its quality but to
    a. Tyler's luck in getting so many people to use it.
    b. The inaccessibility of good software so that people will seek him out.
    c. Tyler's success in distinguishing his firm and its products from competitors and theirs.
    d. The power of word of mouth in getting the word out about such products.
    e. Tyler's scintillating personality and firm cocktail party handshake.

Contemporary Marketing

Name_____   Instructor_____

Section_____   Date_____

Surfing the Net

Keeping in mind that addresses change and what's on the Web now may have changed by the time you read this, let's take a look at some of the places on the Net that reflect aspects of ethical, social, or environmental influence. We are not endorsing or recommending any of these sources, merely making note of the information and services that people have elected to offer through the Internet.

Well, considering that your textbook is loaded with Internet addresses that lead to interesting Web sites about the Internet and the World Wide Web itself, we were hard pressed to go one better – but we tried. Cranking up our array of search engines, we looked for obscure but significant sites and believe we've found some.

In the business-to-business sphere, we were surprised to discover that the global reach of the Internet was evident. Looking at the search string "electrical wholesalers," we suddenly found ourselves presented with sites for firms located in France – **http://www.sonepardic.com** – Sonepar Distribution, a firm with a worldwide presence, including subsidiaries in Canada and the United States; on a smaller scale, there was a site for an Irish firm – **http://www.schneiderelectric.ie/distributer.htm** and even one in Iceland – **http://www.volti.is/indexenska.htm** – but of course, you have to read Icelandic to do much with that one. Finally, we encountered old faithful, the firm originally founded as the supply unit for the Bell System to its outside customers, the American Gray and Barton Electric Company at **http://www.graybar.com**.

Then we went railroading, and found some biggies, among them French ALSTOM, which, in addition to producing heavy rolling stock for the TGV train (Tres Grande Vitesse – Very High Speed), is also involved in the development of the Supertrain, builds ships at its Chantiers de l'Atlantique and ALSTOM Leroux Naval locations, and seemingly has a finger in every transportation pie around. They're at **http://www.alstom.com**. We also discovered a German company, Contec Groupe, which specializes in switching apparatus, at **http://www.contecgroupe.com**, and finally another French firm, Faiveley at Saint-Ouen, that makes and distributes door assemblies for trains and similar equipment. They can be accessed at **http://www.faiveley.com/groupe**.

In the retain sphere, it really wasn't hard to find a few unusual yet interesting sites simply by searching the string "major retailers." We discovered a site at **http://www.bottomdollar.com** that acts like a bot, reporting the lowest prices from a significant array of vendors on all sorts of home entertainment and other electronics. We also stumbled on a brand new site for a firm called MVP, owned by John Elway, Michael Jordan, and Wayne Gretsky, which, as you might suspect, features an incredible assortment of sporting goods. Try **http://www.mvp.com** for this one. We also discovered CD World, at **http://www.cdworld.com** that features new and used CDs and claims to have over 500,000 items on hand at really low prices. And finally, there's Zale's, the jewelry store, except that it's also Gordon's, Bailey, Banks, and Biddle, and in Canada, People's Jewelry. The corporate Web site, where you can find out all about this stuff, is at **http://www.zalecorp.com**.

Sites verified January 29, 2000.

Chapter 5

Succeeding Using Relationship and Database Marketing

Chapter Outline

Use the following as a guide in taking notes.

I. Chapter Overview

    A. The Shift from Transaction-Based Marketing and Relationship Marketing

        1. Internal Marketing

II. What is Relationship Marketing?

III. Basic Foundations of Modern Buyer-Seller Relationships

    A. Promises in Relationship Marketing

        1. Making promises

        2. Enabling promises

        3. Keeping promises

IV. The Four Dimensions of Relationship Marketing

    A. Bonding – strong mutual dependencies

    B. Empathy – the ability to see things from both sides

    C. Reciprocity – give-and-take between parties

    D. Trust – reliance on another person's integrity

V. The Relationship Marketing Continuum

    A. The first level of relationship marketing – financial incentives

    B. The second level of relationship marketing – the social aspect

    C. The third level of relationship marketing – partnership

VI. Measuring Customer Satisfaction

    A. Understanding Customer Needs

    B. Obtaining Customer Feedback

Harcourt, Inc.

VII. Buyer-Seller Relationships in Consumer Goods and Services Markets

    A. The Rewards of Retaining Customers

    B. Affinity programs

    C. Frequent buyer and user programs

    D. Database marketing

VIII. Buyer-Seller Relationships in Business-to-Business Markets

    A. Building and maintaining business partnerships – Choosing business partners

    B. Types of partnerships

    C. Co-marketing and co-branding

IX. Links Between Buyers and Sellers in Business-to-Business Markets

    A. The Use of Databases

    B. Electronic Data Interchange

    C. National Account Selling

    D. Vendor-Managed Inventory

    E. Managing the Supply Chain

    F. Strategic Alliances

X. Managing Relationships for Superior Performance

    A. Assessing the Costs and Benefits

    B. Structuring Relationships: Strategic Implications

    C. Measurement and Evaluation Techniques

Name _____ Instructor _____

Section _____ Date _____

Key Concepts

The purpose of this section is to allow you to determine if you can match key concepts with the definitions of the concepts. It is essential that you know the definitions of the concepts prior to applying the concepts in later exercises in this chapter.

From the list of lettered terms, select the one that best fits in the blank of the numbered statement below. Write the letter of that choice in the space provided.

Key Terms

a. relationship marketing
b. affinity program
c. frequency marketing
d. database marketing
e. co-marketing
f. co-branding
g. electronic data interchange (EDI)
h. quick response
i. vendor-managed inventory (VMI)
j. supply (value) chain
k. lifetime value of a customer
l. transaction-based marketing
m. partnership
n. external customer
o. internal customer

_____ 1. Marketing effort sponsored by an organization such as an alumni association that solicits responses from individuals who share common interests and activities.

_____ 2. Computer software that analyzes marketing information, then identifies and targets messages toward specific groups of potential customers.

_____ 3. Computer-to-computer exchanges of invoices, orders, and other business documents.

_____ 4. Formal links between two or more companies to closely link their brand names together for a single product.

_____ 5. EDI strategy that reduces the time a retailer must hold merchandise in inventory, resulting in substantial cost savings.

_____ 6. Partnership between two or more businesses to jointly market each other's products.

_____ 7. The revenues and intangible benefits that a customer brings to the seller over an average lifetime less the amount the company must spend to acquire, market to, and service the customer.

_____ 8. Frequent buyer (or user) marketing program that rewards customers who purchase a good or service with cash or other rewards.

_____ 9. The development and maintenance of long-term, cost-effective relationships with individual customers, suppliers, employees, and other partners for mutual benefit.

_____ 10. Sequence of suppliers that contribute to the creation and delivery of a good or service.

_____ 11. Inventory-management system in which the seller determines – based on an agreement with the buyer – how much product the buyer needs.

_____ 12. Involves buyer and seller exchanges characterized by limited communications and little or no ongoing relationship between the parties.

_____ 13. An affiliation of two or more companies that assist each other in the achievement of common goals.

_____ 14. People or organizations that buy or use another firm's goods or services.

_____ 15. Employee or department within an organization that depends on the work of another employee or department to perform a job.

Name _____ Instructor _____

Section _____ Date _____

Self-Quiz

You should use these objective questions to test your understanding of the chapter material. You can check your answers with those provided at the end of the chapter.

While these questions cover most of the chapter topics, they are not intended to be the same as the test questions your instructor may use in an examination. A good understanding of all aspects of the course material is essential to good performance on any examination.

True/False

Write "T" for True or "F" for False for each of the following statements.

_____ 1. The financial incentive programs used at the first level of relationship marketing are attractive to users and tend to create long-term buyer-seller relationships because they are not easily duplicated by competitors.

_____ 2. Database technology helps a company identify current and potential customers with selected demographic, purchase, and lifestyle characteristics.

_____ 3. When a company integrates customer service and quality with marketing, the result is a transaction-based marketing orientation.

_____ 4. Since the Industrial Revolution, most manufacturers have traditionally focused their energies on making products, promoting them, and then hoping enough people will buy them to cover costs and earn profits.

_____ 5. The German radio station SWF3, a rock outlet, practices relationship marketing through its club, which produces newsletters for club members, hosts a club lounge at sponsored events, and puts on a weekend-long party which members can attend to meet their favorite on-air personalities.

_____ 6. Relationship marketing depends on the development of class ties between buyer and seller whether the buyers are individuals or other companies.

_____ 7. Most companies make promises to potential customers through internal marketing.

_____ 8. A customer who receives a product's promised benefits and is satisfied with them may well develop loyalty to the brand but probably will not recommend it to others.

_____ 9. A company that desires to successfully implement relationship marketing must provide itself with a structure that facilitates rather then hinders the provision of quality offerings.

_____ 10. Federal Express' decision to locate drop boxes in Kinko's stores is motivated by its desire to increase commercial business and Kinko's desire to decrease overhead cost.

_____ 11. Trust is the ability to see situations from the perspective of the other party to the situation.

_____ 12. Purchasers at the second level of relationship marketing become involved in true partnerships with vendors, developing a dependence that continues to grow over time.

_____ 13. Mutual interests or dependencies between the parties to a relationship must be strong enough to tie them together; this is called bonding.

_____ 14. Databases allow sellers to focus on their best current customers, measured both by the quantity they purchase and by the profitability of those sales.

_____ 15. College and university alumni associations are masters of the third level of relationship marketing.

_____ 16. One reason many consumers form continuing relationships is their desire to increase the number of choices available to them. This is why consumers patronize habitual stores and malls only about 20 percent of the time.

_____ 17. The most common reasons why consumers end relationships with vendors are boredom or dissatisfaction with the current provider or dislike for the feeling that they are locked into a relationship with one company.

_____ 18. The "average lifetime" of a customer relationship is independent of the industry involved or the characteristics of its products.

_____ 19. The problem with affinity programs is that they are limited only to the issuance of sponsored credit cards.

_____ 20. Frequency marketing programs are set up so that the more products or the more often one buys from a particular company the greater the rewards one earns.

_____ 21. Effective database marketing improves customer retention and referral rates, boosts sales volume, and reduces direct costs and marketing outlays.

_____ 22. In a way, database marketing has created a situation such that the world of marketing is returning to the old days of mass marketing, where sellers offered a standardized product to several homogeneous segments of the market at once.

_____ 23. The first priority in choosing a business partners is to locate firms that can add value to the relationship; the greater the value added, the greater the desirability of the partnership.

_____ 24. PC makers who put "Intel Inside" labels on their machines to show they've got an Intel Pentium processor are practicing co-marketing.

_____ 25. Seller partnerships in the business-to-business market set up long-term exchanges of goods and services in return for cash or other valuable consideration.

Multiple Choice

Circle the letter of the word or phrase that best completes each sentence.

26. One of the compelling reasons that have induced marketers to pursue relationships is that
    a. they have realized that they can remain prosperous only by a continuous process of identifying and attracting new customers.
    b. focusing on short-term, single exchanges implies a commitment to their customers.
    c. existing customers and suppliers can be counted on to remain loyal without efforts to retain them.
    d. they can develop a proper conflict resolution posture with customers in the event of trouble.
    e. retaining existing customers costs much less than acquiring new ones.

27. The individual who shops extensively each time he or she needs to buy a new automobile creates
    a. a set of circumstances which usually put the buyer in a transaction-based situation with a vendor.
    b. an ideal environment to develop a marketing relationship with an automobile dealer.
    c. a cooperative environment involving ongoing interactions between buyer and seller.
    d. added value in their marketing experience through the shopping process.
    e. an array of complex, enduring economic relationships between the vendor and the buyer.

28. Every marketing transaction involves a relationship between buyer and seller. In a transaction-based situation,
    a. extensive social relationships typically develop between buyer and seller.
    b. the relationship may be quite short in duration and narrow in scope.
    c. customer service and quality are usually integrated in the marketing effort.
    d. the effort to retain existing customers is well-developed.
    e. promises made and kept are the basis of the relationship.

29. Companies must follow through on the promises they make to potential customers by enabling those promises through
    a. internal marketing activities involving recruiting, properly equipping, and empowering employees.
    b. external marketing directed to parties outside the organization itself.
    c. extensive public relations activities aimed at the firm's many publics.
    d. warranties and guarantees attached to the basic physical product or related service activities.
    e. demonstrating their financial strength in the stock and bond markets.

30. Establishing mutual interests or dependencies between the parties to an exchange process strong enough to tie them together is called
    a. empathizing.
    b. creating trust.
    c. reciprocity.
    d. bonding.
    e. coercion.

31. One of the characteristics of the first (lowest) level of relationship marketing is that
    a. buyer and seller develop interactions on a social level through newsletters and club memberships.
    b. structural changes occur that make buyer and seller into true business partners.
    c. marketing efforts rely on pricing and other financial incentives to motivate customers to buy.
    d. customer service and communications are key factors at this stage.
    e. as buyer and seller work closely together, they develop a dependence on each other.

Harcourt, Inc.

32. The fact that consumers patronize their habitual stores and malls about 90 percent of the time is evidence of the truth behind the idea that
    a. many consumers seek to increase the range of choices available to themselves by shopping.
    b. many consumers are seeking ways to simplify both their business and personal lives.
    c. consumers feel they find more choices at these outlets than at any others.
    d. the habitually chosen stores are always the stores closest to the consumers' homes.
    e. consumers are insensitive to store choice – it's the product that matters.

33. The Claire Company, a leading supplier of hotel and restaurant equipment, requires that its sales representatives become very familiar with the operations of each of their customers. They make every effort to find special needs. The Claire Company is trying to develop
    a. a reciprocal relationship with each customer by becoming an exclusive supplier.
    b. an intelligence report on operations it can sell to its customers' competitors.
    c. a relationship based on mutual between the firms.
    d. a sense of empathy between the sales representatives and their customers.
    e. dependency on the part of their customers so the Claire Company can take advantage of them.

34. One of the major forces driving the push from transaction-based marketing toward relationship marketing is the realization that
    a. consumers dislike the feeling that they are locked into a relationship.
    b. to succeed, companies must develop loyal, mutually beneficial relationships with existing customers, suppliers, and employees.
    c. new customers generate more business for a firm than do old ones, so identifying and attracting new customers is the key to success.
    d. unhappy customers don't usually tell anyone of their experiences but happy ones brag about how well they relate to their suppliers.
    e. customers always get bored with the firms that currently supply their needs and change them without reason.

35. As an alumnus of good old Sag Harbor State U., you find yourself bombarded with offers to join the Cobra Club (the school mascot is a Cobra), an alumni organization. With your membership, you get a subscription to *Fangs,* the school's alumni magazine; a bumper sticker with a big snake on it; and your choice of a Sag Harbor VISA, MasterCard, or Discover Card. Sag Harbor State is trying to get you to join
    a. the school's frequent user program – after all, it took you six years to finish.
    b. their database of alumni – they're not sure you actually graduated or when.
    c. the third level of relationship marketing – it's like a secret society and members are very special.
    d. an affinity program based on your alumni status – the credit card offer is the tipoff.
    e. a subversive anti-government organization – the cobra symbol is a dead giveaway.

36. The last time you got your car washed at Safari Car Wash, you were given a card with a hole punched in the edge and told that when you'd had your car washed there five more times and acquired the corresponding holes in your card, the sixth carwash would be free. This is typical of
    a. a frequent user program.
    b. an affinity program.
    c. database marketing.
    d. reciprocity.
    e. empathetic behavior.

37. Which of the following is a typical use of database systems in relationship marketing?
    a. developing customer relationship profiles
    b. tracking buying patterns
    c. customizing product offerings and sales promotions
    d. personalizing customer service
    e. all of the above are typical uses of database systems

38. The entire sequence of suppliers that contribute to the creation and delivery of a product is called the
    a. inventory-management system for the product.
    b. the supply chain (or value chain) along which the product passes.
    c. alliance partnership designed to retain customers for the product.
    d. integrative membership association for the product.
    e. coordinative linkage of association.

39. One capability of databases as marketing tools is that their use allows a firm to
    a. more profitably target the mass market by producing a standardized product.
    b. avoid the expense of providing a custom product even to a potentially valuable customer segment.
    c. precisely identify real potential customers in crowds of less-qualified prospects.
    d. develop a product that disregards people's individual priorities about the features of a relationship.
    e. increase direct costs and marketing outlays.

40. An example of a lateral partnership in business-to-business marketing would be
    a. an arrangement for a long-term exchange of goods and services in return for value received.
    b. the relationship between the purchasing department of a firm and the manufacturing facility that assembles the parts it buys.
    c. a contractual relationship between a retail store and a law firm for the law firm to be the store's exclusive supplier of legal services.
    d. Ford Motor Company's agreement to produce an Eddie Bauer model of the Ford Bronco SUV.
    e. an organization creating extra value for members and encouraging stronger relationships.

41. The first priority of a firm in choosing a business partner for a marketing relationship is
    a. to find a firm that really needs help; the more desperate it is, the better partner it will make.
    b. to prevent a competitor from establishing a partnership relationship with another firm, regardless of how beneficial a partnership with the other firm might be.
    c. to locate a firm that can add value to the relationship through resources of cash, contacts, extra manufacturing capacity, technical know-how, or distribution capabilities.
    d. finding a firm with different skills and resources; the idea is to complement each other, not duplicate expertise.
    e. to broaden the range of involvement of the two firms; no particular purpose for the partnership should be considered.

42. When a firm commits to be the exclusive provider of certain types of goods for another firm, it has entered into
    a. a buyer partnership with that firm.
    b. an internal relationship with the other firm.
    c. a seller partnership with the buying firm.
    d. a lateral partnership with the buyer.
    e. a symbiotic partnership.

Contemporary Marketing

43. Product tie-ins such as the prominent appearance of a firm's products in a motion picture or the naming of a candy the "official candy" of major-league baseball are examples of
    a. co-branding.
    b. co-development.
    c. empathetic behavior.
    d. co-marketing.
    e. co-dependence.

44. The place in the delivery of customer service where the greatest risk of a negative outcome is likely is
    a. where customer interaction with the system occurs.
    b. in the shipping department where damage to products and packaging often occurs.
    c. in the order-processing arena where paperwork mistakes are so common.
    d. in the design phase when the product is first laid out on paper.
    e. at any time that the system is called upon to function.

45. If LuVel Creamery and Community Coffee Company were to get together to produce and distribute LuVel's Community "New Orleans Blend" Coffee and Chicory Flavored Ice Cream, they would be engaged in
    a. co-branding.
    b. co-marketing.
    c. collaboration.
    d. corporate constructionism.
    e. lateral partnership.

46. Electronic data interchange is most correctly described as
    a. the use of the telephone to place and confirm orders and invoices.
    b. computer-to-computer exchanges of invoices, orders, and other business documents.
    c. development of databases to allow members of the firm to check inventory levels.
    d. creation of an e-mail system to let employees exchange messages and letters.
    e. what happens when a bunch of hackers distribute a computer virus through the Internet.

47. In addition to lifetime value analysis, which of the following can be used to evaluate the success of relationship programs?
    a. the payback from the relationship (how long it takes to break even on customer acquisition cost)
    b. tracking rebate requests, coupon redemptions, credit-card purchases, and product registrations.
    c. monitoring complaints and returned products and analyzing why customers leave
    d. reviewing reply cards, comment forms, and surveys.
    e. all of these may be used to evaluate the success of relationship programs.

48. Partnerships between buyers and sellers in the business-to-business market
    a. may lead to higher prices between the two.
    b. often result in lowering quality standards.
    c. may present communications problems between partners.
    d. often lead to improved distribution.
    e. require business to be conducted primarily in person.

49. Making promises as part of relationship marketing may take place
    a. as part of a special sales promotion.
    b. in the physical design of a business facility.
    c. in the level of cleanliness maintained by a place of business.

Harcourt, Inc.

    d. in the operation of the service process a business provides.
    e. in any or all of the ways specified above.

50. The dimension of relationship marketing known as reciprocity is best exemplified by
    a. the care shown by Blimpies and Pasta Central combo restaurants to complement each other.
    b. the willingness shown by a sales representative to offer free related supplies if the buyer is willing to pay for new equipment sooner than called for by the invoice.
    c. the faith on the part of Central Foundry Company that the steel billets needed for a major production process will always arrive on time and to specification from National Steel Company.
    d. the offer of two Big Macs for the price of one at McDonald's.
    e. the offer of a University of Saskatchewan Visa Card to alumni as part of a "join the alumni association" campaign.

Contemporary Marketing

Name_____ Instructor _____

Section _____ Date _____

Applying Marketing Concepts

"The time has come," thought Willard Hornsby, "to upgrade the old computer yet again. Sometimes technology just moves too fast. I wish it would slow down just a little. This business of having to buy a new system every couple of years is a bit much." But reflecting on his experiences with computers over the years, Willard ultimately decided things hadn't been all that bad. He felt that he had really been lucky back in 1989 when he decided to buy his first machine by mail from Tiger Trap Computers – you know, the people with the orange and black stripes all over their shipping boxes.

They had been very easy to deal with from the very beginning. Of course, his first phone call to them had been sort of long, what with all the questions they'd asked about him – where he lived, what he did for a living, what he knew about computers and why he felt he needed one, and so forth. But now, all he had to do was pick up the phone, and there was someone there to help him. The minute he mentioned his name, they were able to talk to him about his needs and his problems. And they fixed what was wrong, too. Willard even had his own advisor, Larry, for whom he could leave messages and who would call him back if he couldn't take the call right away. Larry seemed to know exactly what he needed before he mentioned it. And he was such a regular guy, too – a real friend.

Willard even had his own Tiger Trap VISA card that he made a point of using on those occasions when he shopped at CompHUGE, the local computer store, for diskettes and other incidentals. Now that was NOT a fun place! All they seemed to want to do was to take your money and get you out the door. Service was not a part of their vocabulary, and the staff seemed all to have taken "surly lessons" at the same school for the unhelpful. Willard admitted he liked to use his Tiger Trap card there just because it seemed to irritate them so.

1. The people at Tiger Trap had probably asked Willard a lot of questions during that first phone call
   a. just because they were curious.
   b. so that his profile would become part of a database to be used for marketing purposes.
   c. because it's a requirement of the law that a mail order vendor must qualify all customers to make sure they are legally able to buy the goods being offered.
   d. to kill time. They probably weren't getting a lot of calls just then and needed something to do.
   e. to decide whether Willard was a real customer or a competitor trying to gather information.

2. Larry's ability to "know exactly what he needed before he mentioned it" is evidence that which of the dimensions of relationship marketing had been achieved?
   a. bonding
   b. reciprocity
   c. empathy
   d. trust
   e. faith

3. The Tiger Trap VISA card of which Willard is so proud is part of
   a. the database that Tiger Trap has on him.
   b. a plan by the firm to make him totally dependent on them for credit.
   c. part of an electronic data interchange program.
   d. the business partnership between him and Tiger Trap.
   e. an affinity program created by Tiger Trap for its customers.

4. The fact that Willard thinks of Larry as a real friend is evidence that
   a. bonding has taken place between the two men.
   b. a co-marketing relationship has developed between Willard and Larry.
   c. Tiger Trap uses an outside call-handling service to handle business like Willard's.
   d. there exists a strategic alliance between Tiger Trap and Willard.
   e. the relationship between them is reciprocal.

5. Willard's perception of the way they treat people at CompHUGE would lead one to believe that CompHUGE
   a. is still practicing transaction-based marketing.
   b. relies too much on its database and not enough on its people.
   c. makes and keeps promises.
   d. has an effective internal marketing program.
   e. trains its personnel well in the principles of empathy and bonding.

Johan Waldmueller wondered what his customers would think if they ever saw the headquarters of American Flange and Gear Corporation, his firm. The bare, fifteen-by-thirty foot room was certainly anything but impressive, except for the row of computer terminals along both walls and the large mainframe at one end of the room. But Johan was very proud of that room. From his point of view, it represented the "state-of-the-art" in customer service. Stored in memory on that mainframe were the specifications for every type of flange and gear commonly used on the North American continent. The specifications were cataloged for each type of industry that used them, and he could put product and user together in an instant.

When one of his customers needed a supply of flanges or gears, all they had to do was go online with him through his system of dedicated phone lines (they never slept) and type an inquiry directly into their terminal. A price and availability quote would immediately be flashed back, and often a purchase would be made on the spot.

Johan worked closely with some of his biggest customers. Several of his personnel, in fact, were responsible for only one account. Jack Menschke, for example, worked exclusively with the Jet Engine Division of General Electric Company, living in Cincinnati so he could meet with their people every day if need be.

One of the side benefits of an efficient, customer-oriented operation, Johan knew, was improved efficiency all around. Today he was going to generate an order for the Peterson Tool Corporation. They hadn't ordered anything, but he knew their stock of SID 3343 low-noise helical power-transfer gears (an excellent design of which Johan was duly proud) was low and he was authorized to ship as needed. He had ordered the new supply from Marmon-Herrington in Indianapolis last week so they would be ready to ship today. Johan got a steady flow of business from the automated online system, he kept his inventory to a minimum, and his customers seldom got caught short when a new or replacement flange or gear was needed.

Contemporary Marketing

6. Johan's ability to match customers with the products they need using his computer system indicates that
   a. his memory must be incredible; how many people do you suppose can do that?
   b. he is using database marketing; the information is stored in the computer.
   c. he has created an affinity program for his customers.
   d. his business is based on trust.
   e. he must have a high level of empathy with his customers.

7. That Johan's customers can get price quotes and order online means that he
   a. has reduced the number of his employees to a minimum.
   b. has no idea what his customers really want.
   c. has a reciprocal arrangement with most customers.
   d. uses electronic data interchange as part of his marketing program.
   e. is operating at the first level of relationship marketing.

8. Jack Menschke's role in Johan's firm is as
   a. his brother-in-law.
   b. one of its laziest employees, servicing only one account.
   c. a national account representative.
   d. one of the VMI personnel.
   e. an out-of-the-way troublemaker.

9. This shipment to Peterson Tool indicates that, for some accounts at least, American Flange and Gear
   a. operates a vendor-managed inventory program for that account.
   b. has some kind of scam going. Nobody accepts unordered goods.
   c. has a deep bond with someone there and can do as they please.
   d. has formed a strategic alliance with the sewerage department.
   e. is using an empathetic relationship to keep Tuscumbia going.

10. Johan's obvious awareness of the needs and capabilities of his suppliers and customers indicates that
    a. he has done it all in this industry and should know how it works.
    b. he is skilled at managing the supply chain.
    c. he has an individual relationship with all of them.
    d. he probably should expand into other fields.
    e. his success is due to his incredible memory.

Part 2 Managing Technology to Achieve Marketing Success

Name_____ Instructor _____

Section _____ Date _____

Surfing the Net

Keeping in mind that addresses change and what's on the Web now may have changed by the time you read this, let's take a look at some of the places on the Net that reflect aspects of relationship marketing. We are not endorsing or recommending any of these sources, merely making note of the information and services that people have elected to offer through the Internet.

You don't buy them very often, and the Toro Company knows that their snow blowers, lawn mowers, and garden tractors don't make very exciting copy, so their Web site offers more in the way of guidance, fitting a customer to particular products on the basis of an online questionnaire. Take a look at http://www.toro.com.

Their repair parts and service database is reputed to be superb – the Frigidaire people will put you in touch with the nearest dealer that has the part you need. Just access **http://www.frigidaire.com.** OK, so you're not a Frigidaire fan! Try **http://www.whirlpool.com** or **http://www.subzero.com** or even **http://www.crosley.com** to see what wonders the major home appliance industry has for us these days. Note that Crosley, absent for many years, is back. Their site includes a very interesting corporate history.

A sleeper! Simmons Mattress Company will interpret your dreams, tell you about sleep disorders, and even analyze how much sleep you owe yourself due to bad sleeping habits. Try **http://www.simmonsco.com** or, as an alternative, their competitor, Sealy Mattress Company at **http://www.sealy.com**

Talk about bonding! Several sites offer credit analysis for businesses. As a condition for establishing a relationship in that market, knowing your possible partner's financial condition is a must. Take a look at the site of Corporate Performance Systems at **http://www.cpshome.com** Need help getting together your credit program? Try contacting Associated Credit Managers, Incorporated, at **http://www.ascmi.net**

Buying lots of stuff that just HAS to be there tomorrow? Try one of these sites as a source. Need to make up with someone in a BIG way? Try **http://www.flowerbud.com** for all your major floral needs overnight. Not your style? Ben and Jerry's can handle it. They'll get that creamy treat to you overnight, no problem. Go to **http://www.benjerry.com** to order. Still not good enough? How about Broadway theatre tickets? The people at **http:// broadwayticketsales.tripod.com** can get those to you. If all else fails, how about a shrimp boil? You can have them overnight too, from **http://www.savannahshrimp.net**

Sites verified December 15, 1999.

Contemporary Marketing

Name_____ Instructor_____

Section_____ Date_____

Cases for Part 2

1. Where'd They All Go?

As you may have noticed, one of the components of each chapter of this Study Guide is a section titled "Surfing the Web," in which I have tried to include a number of Web sites of interest in one way or another to you as a new student of marketing. One of the things that has to be done in a book revision is to make sure that references to outside sources are correct, so part of the preparation of this Study Guide has been a complete review of the Web sites included in the "Surfing the Web" sections prepared for the Ninth Edition of this text. Imagine my astonishment when I discovered that at least half, and for some chapters many more than half, of the sites included in the Ninth Edition – which was developed in 1997 – were either (1) no longer accessible – just not there at all; (2) accessible, but no longer contained the material for which they were chosen in the first place; or (3) accessible, but under another name.

A count of site disappearances indicates that those sites that referred to specific retail outlets were the most likely to disappear entirely, while those of government bodies or professional organizations (like the American Institute of Certified Public Accountants) were the most likely to now appear under another name, usually much shorter than their former Usenet or Milnet name and preceded by the initials www. Interestingly, one site I accessed which bore the name of a very large consumer goods manufacturer proudly proclaimed itself NOT to be owned by that manufacturer and proceeded to attack that firm for "trying to get this site away from me."

a. Why do you suppose that the retailers' sites were the most likely to have disappeared entirely in the interim between editions of this text?

b. What would account for the relocation of many of the governmental and organization sites from their previous addresses to their current (www) locations?

c. What are the implications of the registration of a site with an obvious relationship to a particular firm to someone else?

2. *Was It the Warranty or the Way It Was Honored?*

It had been five years since Tom Beaufort had bought a new car, and for the first time in his life he was serious about buying the same make of car he currently owned from the same dealership. His present car had been, he thought, an excellent choice. Not only had it had all the features he was looking for, it didn't have a lot he didn't want. The dealership hadn't pressured him when he appeared in their showroom, and the salesman he spoke to had been knowledgeable and seemingly quite concerned about his desires and interests. The process of negotiating a bottom-line price had gone painlessly, with Tom paying what he believed to be a very fair price for the car. And surprise of surprises! When he picked up his new car from the dealership, it was immaculately clean, the gas tank was full, and every single button, knob, dial, and gadget worked exactly the way it supposed to! The mechanic who brought the vehicle out to Tom seemed genuinely proud to be presenting it to him, and commented on what a fine car he thought it was and what a great company made them.

The warranty on the vehicle was impressive. It included a five-year, 50,000-mile comprehensive warranty, seven-year free roadside assistance program, and a seven-year rust through warranty. Tom was a little worried about the warranty. How could they offer such generous terms? But his concerns vanished as, over the next three years, he put over 70,000 miles on the car with only one problem: at 49,800 miles, and when he was 500 miles from home, the radio quit working. He was afraid that when he got home, his dealer would refuse to fix the radio because the car would then have over 50,000 miles on its odometer. He was right! They did refuse to fix the radio – they gave him a brand new one instead. And they did it in 30 minutes.

Tom really enjoyed reading the car maker's quarterly magazine, with its features on care and maintenance, suggested trips, and even invitations to owner rallies and events. And the normal maintenance he had done at the dealership was done promptly, correctly, and at a reasonable price. The more he thought about it, the more he realized that his best move would be to buy a new car of same make and give old one to his son who had just turned eighteen and started his first job. The kid could put another 100,000 miles on it to match the 150,000 already there and if something went wrong the dealership would certainly fix it, and fix it right, for a reasonable price.

Questions

1. Does this case show evidence of commitment to relationship marketing on the part of the car's maker? If so, what is the evidence to suggest this?

2. Is there also evidence of the same sort of commitment on the part of the dealer? Explain.

3. Does Tom's behavior show evidence of the effects of relationship marketing?

3. Cyberbeta.com™: The Most Useful Useless Site on the Web©

Cyberbeta.com bills itself as "The Most Useful Useless Site on the Web" because it is devoted primarily to frivolous material – jokes, cartoons, drink recipes, news relevant only to computer fanatics, and similar stuff. However, when one links to the site one immediately notices a banner headline at the top that says "Click here for the best digital phone service on the planet!" with appropriate visual effects. Interspersed among the drink recipes and cartoons are other "Click here for" types of links. Each refers the Web surfer to a commercial site where a good or service may be purchased. The material on the site is essentially "clean," though an occasional bit of mildly risque humor may from time to time creep in. The commercial sites linked to cyberbeta.com, however, appear to have been carefully checked for legitimacy.

Viewers are encouraged to send their favorite jokes, drink recipes, and related humor to the site's Webmaster. If a person's material is used, they receive a cyberbeta.com coffee mug emblazoned with the site's name and logotype (a picture of a Greek letter Beta disguised as a robot.) Their e-mail address is entered into the webmaster's database and each week a lucky winner of a prize from one of the site's links is awarded to that person. The site hosts a chat room in which people who enjoy the site can share their own jokes, recipes, and other bits of news and gossip. The chat room is monitored for content, the objective being to keep what goes on there suitable for Web Surfers of any age.

Site users may even qualify for Cyberbetan citizenship by submitting three jokes, cartoons, drink recipes, or verifiable news items that appear on the site. In addition to their prize (after the first success, the prize for additional items changes to a desk clock for the second and a T-shirt for the third, both bearing the site logo and slogan), three-timers get a Certificate of Cyberbetan Citizenship and a Cyberbetan Passport impressively printed in three languages – English, Latin, and Armenian just to make it interesting and funny. In addition, their grant of citizenship is "mentioned in dispatches" for the following week on the site.

a. Is this site engaged in e-commerce? If so, how? If not, why not?

b. Could cyberbeta.com also be considered an e-marketing site?

c. Is cyberbeta.com practicing relationship marketing?

© and ™ 2000 by Terrence M. O'Connor (Used by Permission)

Creating a Marketing Plan: Getting Started

The information you will receive in this part will help you to complete Parts I.A. and I.B. of your marketing plan for Telabri Industries.

Episode Two

In Episode One, we learned of the decision by Terry, Laura, and Brian to get together and start a company called Telabri Industries. For reasons of simplicity, and because of their families, the three ultimately decided to return to their home, a city of some 1.3 million people located in the American Southwest. After careful consideration of their resources, they decided that they could not possibly afford to enter the highly competitive computer sales market, as there were already over 150 vendors operating locally. They also discovered that custom software was available from no fewer than 85 in-city sources. Having absorbed the marketing concept and wishing to match their abilities and resources with some untapped pool of demand, they cast about a little further and discovered that, at least as it looked on the surface, though 150 local firms sold computers, 85 developed software for them, and 60 companies were equipped to repair them, only about 35 firms in the area were involved in the creation and maintenance of Web sites. A few hours in the library revealed that the market for firms that could provide and maintain a presence for others on the Internet was expected to reach $15 billion in potential for the current year, increasing at a rate of some 14 percent per year into the foreseeable future. Of the $15 billion current potential in the Web site development and maintenance market, some $1.3 billion was expected to be derived from service to individuals, with the remainder coming from the business sector. It was further predicted that the market for site maintenance for businesses actively using the Web would grow at a rate of 33 percent per year, leading all other Internet-related service fields.

Environmentally, analysis revealed that a Web site development and maintenance company faced no special inhibitions in law; but that a business license would be needed and a sales tax account would have to be opened (sales taxes were collected on <u>any</u> physical goods sold, but not on pure services). There was, of course, competition in the local market, but it seemed to be divided along very specific lines: some firms worked only with very large companies and others did very little original work, simply adapting "canned" software for their customers. The local economy was simply a miniature of the national economy. Projections made for the national scene could be scaled down to fit the local. The influence of the social environment on the firm would be minimal, except of course that people who use the Internet extensively and whose businesses have a presence there tend to be affluent and leaders of the community. Finally, the technological environment offers perhaps the greatest risk and complication to Telabri Industries. Changes in technology could conceivably lead to something beyond the conception of current thought as far as the Web is concerned. In other words, the pace of change in this industry has been such that it may soon become possible to access the Internet without having a dedicated address, a Web site, or any of the currently necessary bells and whistles. Mitigating this possibility is the idea that the Internet is interactive, so that some means of locating people and firms must be maintained if the interaction is to occur.

A research project conducted by the partners acquired additional information about the local market. This information is summarized in Table P2-2.

Contemporary Marketing

Table P2-2: Characteristics of the Local Market

Total Population: 1,300,000
Proportion of National Population: 0.52%
Number of households: 335,000
Proportion of households owning computers: (Est.) 35.5%
Proportion of Households with Web sites (Est.) 5.0%

Businesses in the Local Market:

		By Number of Employees				
	Total	1-4	5-9	10-19	20-49	50 up
Central Area	23,521	12,597	4,548	2,976	2,059	1,341
Suburbs	2,374	1,294	481	278	186	135
Total	25,895	13,891	5,029	3,254	2,245	1,476
Percent Active on Internet (Est.)	35	10	12	20	40	60

The partners, who, by the way, are going to incorporate their firm for reasons of taxation and personal liability, have on hand at present $240,000 in cash. $60,000 of this is their own, and the remaining money has been borrowed from various friends, relatives, and a local bank.

Guidelines:

a. In the context of Part I.A. of the outline of the marketing plan, how would you characterize the likely nature of this firm?

b. On the basis of the information presented, complete Part I.B. of the marketing plan. Basically, the points to be considered should relate, first, to the segments available for penetration, which segments may appear feasible for these people, and which you think they should choose.

Part 3

Marketing Planning, Information, and Segmentation

One of the marketing manager's primary responsibilities is to create plans to facilitate the achievement of marketing objectives. Marketing planning focuses on relationships between vendors and customers. Marketing management addresses strategic issues through long-range planning and tactical issues in the planning of shorter-term programs.

Top managers are responsible for strategic planning; lower level managers have a greater degree of involvement with the development and implementation of tactical plans. Planning begins with objectives stated in the firm's mission statement. SWOT analysis identifies strengths, weaknesses, opportunities, and threats related to the firm. Central to marketing planning is identification of strategic windows – short periods of time when company resources optimally match environmental conditions. The concepts of the Strategic Business Unit, market growth/market share matrix, and market attractiveness/business strength matrix are useful planning tools. Spreadsheet analysis may also be helpful.

Forecasts of sales can be developed using quantitative or qualitative forecasting methods. A number of different techniques are available for either method. Companies using a top-down process develop their forecasts of company sales from forecasts of industry sales that are based on forecasts of Gross Domestic Product and economic indicators. Company and product sales forecasts are based on past performance and the marketing plan. Grass-roots forecasts, on the other hand, begin with sales estimates by each sales representative and are combined and aggregated until an overall projection can be made.

The purpose of marketing research is to provide useful information for marketing decision making. Many firms do their own marketing research, but additional marketing research suppliers include syndicated services, full-service research suppliers, and limited-service research suppliers. Marketing research activities fall into three main categories: scanning, risk assessment, and monitoring. The marketing research process consists of defining the problem, conducting exploratory research, formulating a hypothesis, designing the research method, collecting data, and interpreting and presenting results.

Generally, secondary data – either externally or internally generated – are used first in marketing research because they are less expensive and easier to acquire than primary data. Primary data collection must be based on a research design that assures that it is gathered without bias and is truly representative of the population from which it was taken. Hypotheses are tentative explanations of some specific event posed as concepts to be tested by research.

Research design involves decisions about how primary data are to be gathered (observation, experiment, or survey methods), and who is to collect them. Design decisions are usually based on the types of information needed and the resources and time available. Related to these decisions is the question of how to select the sample from the population. Probability sampling methods such as simple random sampling or nonprobability methods such as convenience sampling may be used. Presenting research information often requires a meeting of the minds between two very dissimilar people – the researcher and the executive who commissioned the research.

Marketing research generates some of the information needed by marketing managers, but a great deal of it should come from a marketing information system (MIS) appropriate to the needs of marketing managers. Marketing information systems are computer-accessible databases that managers may use to access important company and industry information, while marketing decision support systems (MDSSs) are interactive processes somewhat like computer games that allow the manager to explore alternative scenarios related to decision making and its results. MDSSs also help handle the flow of information needed by every firm. Data mining is a process of data analysis used to detect patterns of behavior in customer files so those patterns can be used to discover potential basis for relationship development.

A market is people or institutions with purchasing power and the authority and willingness to buy. Segmentation is the process of dividing the aggregate market (the whole thing) into smaller, relatively homogeneous groups. Segmenting the consumer market can be done geographically, demographically, psychographically, and/or based on people's relationships to products: by benefits sought, by usage rates, or on the basis of brand loyalty.

The market segmentation process involves five steps: identifying the process to be used; developing a relevant profile for each segment; forecasting market potential; forecasting market share; and selecting specific segments. Segments may be reached by using the strategies of undifferentiated marketing, differentiated marketing, concentrated marketing, and/or micromarketing.

Part 3 Marketing Planning, Information, and Segmentation

Chapter 6

Marketing Planning and Forecasting

Chapter Outline

Use the following as a guide in taking notes.

I. Chapter Overview – The marketplace changes continually in response to emerging consumer expectations, technological developments, competitor's actions, economic trends, and political-legal events, as well as product innovations and pressures from channel members.

II. What Is Marketing Planning?

    A. Strategic planning versus tactical planning

III. Planning at different organizational levels

IV. Steps in the Marketing Planning Process

    A. Defining the organization's mission

    B. Determining organizational objectives

    C. Assessing organizational resources and evaluating environmental risks and opportunities

        1. SWOT analysis

        2. The strategic window

V. Formulating a marketing strategy

    A. Strategic Implications: Implementing a strategy through marketing plans

VI. Tools for Marketing Planning

    A. Strategic business units (SBUs)

    B. Market share/market growth matrix

    C. Market attractiveness/business strength matrix

        1. Evaluating the matrix approach to planning

    D. Spreadsheet analysis

Harcourt, Inc.

VII. Sales Forecasting

    A. Qualitative forecasting techniques – Using subjective data to predict the future

        1. Jury of executive opinion

        2. Delphi technique

        3. Sales force composite

        4. Survey of buyer intentions

    B. Quantitative forecasting techniques – Application of objective data to prediction

        1. Market tests

        2. Trend analysis

        3. Exponential smoothing

    C. Steps in sales forecasting

        1. Environmental forecasting

        2. Industry sales forecasting

        3. Company and product sales forecasting

        4. Grass-roots forecasting

        5. New-product sales forecasting

Harcourt, Inc.

Part 3 Marketing Planning, Information, and Segmentation

Name_____ Instructor_____

Section_____ Date_____

Key Concepts

The purpose of this section is to allow you to determine if you can match key concepts with the definitions of the concepts. It is essential that you know the definitions of the concepts prior to applying the concepts in later exercises in this chapter.

From the list of lettered terms, select the one that best fits in the blank of the numbered statement below. Write the letter of that choice in the space provided.

Key Terms

a. planning
b. marketing planning
c. strategic planning
d. tactical planning
e. mission
f. SWOT analysis
g. strategic window
h. marketing strategy
i. strategic business unit (SBU)
j. market share/market growth matrix
k. market attractiveness/business strength matrix
l. spreadsheet analysis
m. sales forecast
n. jury of executive opinion
o. Delphi technique
p. sales force composite
q. survey of buyer intentions
r. market test
s. trend analysis
t. exponential smoothing
u. environmental forecasting

_____ 1. Forecasting method that introduces a new product or other marketing variable in a small test location to assess consumer reactions.

_____ 2. Enduring statement of the overall purpose of an organization.

_____ 3. Effort to anticipate future events and conditions and determine the courses of action necessary to achieve marketing objectives.

_____ 4. Limited period of time during which the "fit" between the key requirements of a market and the particular competencies of a firm are optimal.

_____ 5. Determining an organization's primary objectives, allocating funds, and initiating action to achieve those objectives.

_____ 6. An estimate of company sales for a specified future period.

_____ 7. A firm's overall program for selecting and satisfying a target market.

Harcourt, Inc.

_____ 8. Sales forecasting method that qualitatively predicts sales based on the combined estimates of the firm's salespeople.

_____ 9. Marketing planning tool that classifies a firm's products according to industry growth rates and market shares relative to competitive products.

_____ 10. Qualitative forecasting method that gathers and redistributes several rounds of anonymous forecasts that end when the participants reach a consensus.

_____ 11. Anticipating future events and conditions and determining the courses of action necessary to achieve organizational objectives.

_____ 12. Sales forecasting method that estimates future sales quantitatively through statistical analyses of historical sales patterns.

_____ 13. Portfolio analysis technique that rates SBUs according to the attractiveness of their markets and their organizational strengths.

_____ 14. Study of organizational resources and capabilities to assess the firm's strengths and weaknesses and scanning its external environment to identify opportunities and threats.

_____ 15. In a multi-product firm, a division built around related product groupings or business activities with specific managers, resources, objectives, competitors, and structure for optimal independent planning.

_____ 16. Projection of economic activity that focuses on the impact of external events and influences on the firm's markets.

_____ 17. Planning tool that uses a decision-oriented computer program to answer "what-if" questions posed by marketing managers.

_____ 18. Qualitative forecasting technique that combines and averages the sales expectations of various executives.

_____ 19. Defining implementation activities the firm must carry out to achieve its objectives.

_____ 20. Sampling opinions of groups of present and potential customers concerning their purchase intentions.

_____ 21. Quantitative forecasting technique that assigns weights to historical sales data, giving greater weight to more recent data.

Part 3 Marketing Planning, Information, and Segmentation

Name_____   Instructor_____

Section_____   Date_____

Self-Quiz

You should use these objective questions to test your understanding of the chapter material. You can check your answers with those provided at the end of the chapter.

While these questions cover most of the chapter topics, they are not intended to be the same as the test questions your instructor may use in an examination. A good understanding of all aspects of the course material is essential to good performance on any examination.

True/False

Write "T" for True or "F" for False for each of the following statements.

_____ 1. Strategic plans focus on adoption of courses of action necessary to achieve organizational objectives in the very short run – under a year.

_____ 2. A sales forecast cannot be used as a tool for marketing control because it does not produce standards against which to measure actual performance.

_____ 3. Middle-level managers, like regional sales managers, tend to focus their efforts on operational planning.

_____ 4. Organizational objectives are the starting point for marketing planning, guiding and supporting marketing objectives and plans.

_____ 5. SWOT analysis does not involve any consideration of organizational resources or environmental factors.

_____ 6. The explosive growth of Internet services has created a strategic window that lets smaller computer manufacturers compete with industry giants such as Microsoft and Intel.

_____ 7. Sales forecasts are typically prepared using only quantitative techniques.

_____ 8. Internal weaknesses in a company can create vulnerabilities within it – environmental threats to its organizational strength.

_____ 9. Corporate mission statements provide specific rules on which to base current management actions.

_____ 10. The SBU concept provides a method top executives can use to identify promising product

Harcourt, Inc.

Contemporary Marketing

lines that warrant investment of additional resources as well as those which should be pruned from the company's product portfolio.

_____ 11. As conceptualized in the market share/market growth matrix, "stars" generate considerable income while requiring little cash inflow to provide further growth.

_____ 12. Using the market attractiveness/business strength matrix, the firm's financial resources, its image, and its relative cost advantages are some of the market attractiveness criteria.

_____ 13. The survey of buyer intentions is one type of qualitative forecasting technique.

_____ 14. Because of its success in implementing its strategic marketing plan, Blockbuster Video's market share is up from 22 percent to 30 percent and a 40 percent market share is expected well ahead of the original five-year schedule.

_____ 15. An alternative to top-down forecasting is grass roots or bottom-up forecasting.

_____ 16. Quantitative forecasting techniques are more subjective than qualitative techniques because they are based on opinions rather than historical data.

_____ 17. The market share/market growth matrix identifies a firm's business units as cows, comets, cannibals, and cart horses – the four Cs.

_____ 18. Companies forecasting sales for a new product typically use consumer panels to obtain reactions to the products and to gauge probable purchase behavior.

_____ 19. The method of trend analysis gives reliable forecasts even when stable demand conditions and steady sales growth are not present.

_____ 20. Spreadsheet analysis helps planners to anticipate marketing performance given specified sets of circumstances.

_____ 21. Company and product sales forecasts typically begin with a detailed analysis of performance in prior years.

_____ 22. Matching an internal strength with an external opportunity produces a situation known as "vulnerability to constraints" for the organization.

_____ 23. Environmental effects can emerge both from within the organization and from the external environment – the World Wide Web, for example, has transformed the way people communicate and do business.

_____ 24. Surveys of buyer intentions are limited to situations in which customers are willing to reveal their buying intentions; they are also time-consuming and expensive.

_____ 25. The electronic spreadsheet is a flexible array of interrelated data that enables the manager to organize information in a standardized, easily readable format.

Part 3 Marketing Planning, Information, and Segmentation

Multiple Choice

Circle the letter of the word or phrase that best completes each sentence.

26. Strategic planning is best described as
    a. decisions related to the pricing of the firm's output for the current year.
    b. actions taken based upon review of monthly and quarterly sales data.
    c. determining primary objectives of an organization and adopting courses of action that will achieve them.
    d. planning designed to attack and systematically solve short-term company problems.
    e. the responsibility of middle-level managers within the firm.

27. Which of the following differentiates correctly between strategic and tactical plans?
    a. tactical – 10-year plan; strategic – next year
    b. tactical – activity implementation; strategic – broad in scope, long term in orientation
    c. tactical – top management responsibility; strategic--supervisory responsibility
    d. tactical – total company budgets; strategic unit or division budgets
    e. tactical – plans for new product development in the next 20 years; strategic--advertising plan for new product to be introduced next year

28. Which of the following is an example of strategic planning?
    a. Northern Telecom raises its rates in response to an increase announced by Pacific Bell.
    b. The Anaheim Mighty Ducks offer the first 15,000 fans into the arena for their next game a free padded seat cushion.
    c. Transtar International plans to phase out its tractor division over the next five years and to purchase several manufacturers of major household appliances to expand its product base.
    d. The May Company decides to switch the bulk of this year's advertising from television to newspaper ads.
    e. Panasonic offers a $10 rebate to everyone who purchases one of its cordless phones during the next month.

29. Electromotive Corporation is preparing its new strategic plan. Who, of the following people, should be given the greatest responsibility (and spend the most time) on this planning process?
    a. district sales managers
    b. the marketing research director
    c. the director of advertising
    d. sales representatives
    e. the vice-president of marketing

30. Marketing planning usually includes which of the following?
    a. a program for selecting a particular target market and then satisfying consumers in that market
    b. determining the basic overall goals or objectives of the firm for the next several years
    c. selection of appropriate production techniques for the firm's output
    d. deciding whether or not to reorganize the company and how to do it
    e. testing to ascertain whether products meet engineering-related standards

31. Which of the following statements is an example of use of the concept of the strategic window?
    a. Transcripts of the meetings of the board of directors are made required reading for middle-level managers.
    b. The law firm of Anderson, Villere, and Jones decides to open a labor relations department because several of the firm's partners have developed an interest in the area.

Harcourt, Inc.

c. Diamond Community Antenna Company (a cable TV service provider) has decided to expand its service from Diamond to the nearby town of Westphalia because it has done a research study which showed a need for the service. In addition, Diamond has the resources to provide the service.
d. The Gates Tire and Rubber Company has decided to produce and market hip boots because they feel there is a market for hip boots. The company does not have adequate resources, however, to fund the production and marketing of this new product line.
e. The Watrous Valve Company has decided to lower the prices of its products by 20 percent across the board.

32. Which of the following is not a planning tool specifically designed to assist in effective marketing planning?
a. the SBU concept
b. the market share/market growth matrix
c. spreadsheet analysis
d. the market attractiveness/business strength matrix
e. a jury of executive opinion

33. Quantitative forecasting
a. relies on subjective techniques to prepare its predictions.
b. is based on numerical data examined through statistical computations.
c. includes the Delphi technique, jury of executive opinion, and trend analysis.
d. can be highly judgmental since it is based on people's opinions.
e. may be categorized as composite or synthetic.

34. A business executive of your acquaintance tells you that she can't go to the basketball game next week because she will be involved in planning meetings at corporate headquarters helping put together her firm's next "five-year plan." She is probably
a. a top management member: they are usually the ones who do the strategic planning for the firm.
b. a middle manager: she's probably working on some tactical plan to be applied locally.
c. a supervisor: her job involves planning sales events and other special promotions.
d. an assembly-line worker who is there simply to make it look like management cares.
e. just trying to avoid going to that particular game.

35. American Kitchen Products, a firm that produces and sells kitchen implements to food processors, restaurants, hotels, and consumers, is trying to organize its businesses into Strategic Business Units. Which of the following questions should be used in deciding on how to create the SBUs?
a. Will defining this particular area of the business as an SBU focus managerial attention so they can respond effectively to changing consumer demand within limited markets?
b. Does this particular area of the business produce mechanically similar products using a coherent technological base?
c. Can this area of the business use the same production lines and distribution facilities to handle the products it sells and markets?
d. Do the entities to be brought under this SBU use the same raw materials drawn from the same sources?
e. Do the activities of the components of the proposed SBU use basically the same quality control personnel?

36. If the framework provided by the market growth/market share matrix is used as the guideline, a firm would be most likely to consider dropping a product which was classified as a
    a. cash cow.
    b. dog.
    c. star.
    d. question mark.
    e. skunk.

37. You are using the market share/market growth matrix approach to adjust your company's product portfolio. A usually correct action when using this approach is to
    a. eliminate all question marks; they're hopeless, anyway.
    b. invest heavily in promotion and production capacity for cash cows.
    c. find funds to finance the future growth of stars.
    d. continue to fund question marks under all conditions; they're bound to become stars.
    e. hold on to dogs for as long as possible; they might still make some money.

38. This type of forecast focuses on factors external to the firm that affect its markets. It is
    a. the long-term sales forecast.
    b. a sales force composite.
    c. a survey of buyer intentions.
    d. an environmental forecast.
    e. a market test.

39. Qualitative sales forecasting methods include
    a. trend projections based on the historical relationship of sales and time.
    b. surveys of buyer intentions of a representative group of potential and current customers.
    c. computer simulations of likely consumer reaction to a new product.
    d. test markets to gauge consumer responses to a new product under actual market conditions.
    e. input-output models of relationships between industries.

40. The Delphi technique of sales forecasting involves
    a. a mandatory visit to Delphi, Ohio, to learn the technique from the oracle.
    b. extrapolation of trend predictions of company sales to forecast industry sales.
    c. asking members of the sales force to estimate future sales based on their experience.
    d. reliance on juries of executive opinion internal to the firm for forecasts of product sales.
    e. seeking expert opinion from inside and outside the firm in a process that continues until a consensus has been reached.

41. "We create solutions to problems involving the leading-edge technology needs of major industrial corporations." This quote is an example of
    a. a mission statement.
    b. a strategic plan.
    c. an operational plan.
    d. a tactical appraisal of conditions.
    e. wishful thinking: it is obviously not attainable.

42. Which of the following is one of Ford Motor Company's identified strengths?
    a. a higher level of sales than its competitors
    b. a larger dealer network than other domestic auto makers
    c. an efficient production process featuring high labor productivity
    d. a conservative, non-innovative management team

Harcourt, Inc.

e. a lower rate of vehicles sold per dealership than other car manufacturers

43. When a firm possesses internal weaknesses or limitations that prevent it from taking advantage of opportunities, it is said to suffer from
   a. leverage.
   b. core competency.
   c. a problem.
   d. constraints.
   e. vulnerabilities.

44. The term SWOT as used in "SWOT analysis" stands for
   a. safety without overt threats.
   b. standards, work orders, and techniques.
   c. seasonal, weekly, and orderly transmission (of data).
   d. sequences and workovers of organization and territory.
   e. strengths and weaknesses, opportunities and threats.

45. One of the strategic business units in your company's portfolio is a cash cow. The best set of actions to take with that SBU would be to
   a. allocate substantial advertising money and new equipment to it to stimulate future growth.
   b. withdraw from this market by selling or closing the SBU as soon as possible.
   c. reallocate resources away from this marginal SBU; allow it to wither on the vine.
   d. maintain this status for as long as possible, using the funds generated by this SBU to finance the growth of other SBUs with higher growth potential.
   e. make a "go" or "no go" decision as soon as possible; then either get out of that market or aggressively pursue development of the SBU.

46. LOTUS 1-2-3, QuattroPro, and Excel are examples of
   a. spreadsheet software often used to help planners anticipate marketing performance.
   b. audit marketing systems used by accountants to test the financial stability of firms.
   c. decision-making tools designed on the basis of the Persian Messenger Rule.
   d. sales forecasting programs widely used in connection with the Delphi technique.
   e. qualitative sales forecasting techniques.

47. Of the following, which is true of the sales force composite?
   a. It often recognizes the impact of sales trends developing in single sales territories.
   b. If you're only going to use one way to forecast sales, this is the method to use.
   c. It shows the impact of major changes in marketing strategies quicker than any other method.
   d. Inaccurate results may result from low estimates by sales personnel concerned about their influence on quotas.
   e. It is time-consuming and expensive but has been successfully used to predict long-term events like technological breakthroughs.

48. Which of the following is a qualitative sales forecasting technique?
   a. market testing
   b. trend analysis
   c. exponential smoothing
   d. Delphi technique
   e. spreadsheet analysis

Part 3 Marketing Planning, Information, and Segmentation

49. An analysis of the historical relationship between sales volume and the passage of time forms the basis of the sales forecasting technique(s)
    a. of market testing and the sales force composite.
    b. called trend analysis and exponential smoothing.
    c. used in the Delphi method.
    d. which are qualitative and quasimodal in nature.
    e. called Stanforth's Rule.

50. Of the following, which would typically come first in the marketing planning process?
    a. the assessment of organizational resources
    b. evaluation of environmental risks and opportunities
    c. monitoring and assessing strategy based on feedback
    d. implementing strategy through operational plans
    e. determination of organizational objectives

Contemporary Marketing

Name_____ Instructor_____

Section_____ Date_____

Applying Marketing Concepts

Arnold Sandifer of Aquasil, Inc., was pleased with his company's prospects. The recent earthquakes in the far Pacific Rim had left a number of cities and towns on smaller islands and in coastal areas with damaged or destroyed seawater distillation plants. Aquasil rushed in its personnel to get some of the plants back on line as a humanitarian gesture, but Mr. Sandifer knew that many of the facilities which his personnel had repaired needed to be replaced soon – the repairs made were far from permanent. He knew he had the advantage over his two closest competitors in competing to sell the replacements. The competitors were Freshwater Proprietary, Ltd., from Great Britain, and Wetco, another U.S. firm.

Freshwater had recently run into some financial difficulties and was unable to send anyone into the area to help out or to solicit business. Wetco, despite making a good product and being financially sound, had only recently gotten into foreign markets and still made products with all U.S. type threads and fasteners – very different from the ISO metric fasteners used in the typical Asian application and hard to interface with existing plants. Aquasil was able to supply base units with either U.S. or ISO fittings and a wide range of special adaptors from inventory.

Mr. Sandifer was worried about one thing. He knew that his success doing business in the far Pacific depended on being associated with the right people locally – the ones with the most power and status. Prior to the earthquake, his firm had worked closely with the Nagumo/Chen Wa group and had been quite successful. Rumor had it, though, that the Nagumo/Chen Wa consortium, because of some unpopular political positions they had recently taken, might be eased out by the Kim Lees, who represented Austrawasser KG, a European manufacturer of saltwater distilleries.

1. Because of its ability to be there when needed and to supply the products to meet local interface needs. Aquasil finds itself
   a. with considerable leverage in the far Pacific Rim market.
   b. with a problem doing business on the far Pacific Rim.
   c. vulnerable to competitive pressure, particularly from Wetco.
   d. constrained by staff shortages.
   e. lacking a strategic window to develop its opportunity.

2. Freshwater Proprietary
   a. is vulnerable in the Pacific Rim.
   b. suffers from constraints in this market.
   c. has real problems with product quality.
   d. probably has as much leverage as does Aquasil.
   e. has shown more wisdom than any of its competitors so far; it is staying away until the dust settles.

3. Wetco's entry into the Pacific Rim market
   a. is hampered by a problem.
   b. is hampered by constraints.
   c. depends on its leverage in the market.

Harcourt, Inc.

d. seems particularly vulnerable.
   e. goes without saying.

4. Aquasil's relationship with the Nagumo/Chen Wa group
   a. could never constitute a problem for them.
   b. places a high level of constraint on them.
   c. may make them vulnerable, particularly if the Kim Lees accede to power.
   d. has no effect on the amount of leverage they are able to employ.
   e. is irrelevant to their marketing effort.

5. Every town in the region that has access to salt water already uses distillery equipment to produce fresh water from it. If Aquasil succeeds in dominating the market for replacement equipment, it will hold a very large share of the market, but the market probably will not grow very rapidly, if at all. From a market share/market growth matrix point of view, the Pacific Rim saltwater distillation market would appear to be
   a. a question mark.
   b. a cash cow.
   c. a dog.
   d. a star.
   e. a rocket.

The Tyrolische und Sudtyrolische Bergsbahn (Tyrolean and South Tyrolean Mountain Railroad or TSTB, for short) has been involved in an analysis of its operations in the context of the advent of EC-2000, the complete abolition of barriers to travel in Europe that occurred that year. Despite its name, TSTB is a diversified transportation company offering coordinated rail, autobus, and river and coastal steamship passenger and cargo service all through Northern Italy and much of western Austria. Aldo Vitterini, the firm's chief executive officer, is concerned about his firm's future. He is, in fact, considering moving his firm's headquarters from Innsbruck, Austria, to Bolzano, in Italy, to take advantage of the more advantageous banking laws there. He is also concerned that the appearance on the rivers of the area of vessels from Switzerland, Slovenia, and even Hungary may negatively impact his business.

6. If Signore Vitterini polls his ship captains, who serve as the authority over the ship each commands and are like vice-presidents of a land bound firm, concerning their thinking about the future of TSTB in the ship-borne cargo business, he will be using the forecasting technique known as
   a. a jury of executive opinion.
   b. the Delphi technique.
   c. a sales force composite.
   d. trend analysis.
   e. a survey of buyer intentions.

7. If, on the other hand, Signore Vitterini conducts a survey of potential users of his company's cargo-handling services and asks them about the likelihood of their use of those services in the near future and further asks them about the quantity of cargo they intend to ship, he will be using a
   a. market test.
   b. Sales force composite.
   c. survey of buyer intentions.
   d. Delphi technique.
   e. linear retrograde estimate.

8. If a detailed history of sales is used to project sales into the future, the chances are that
   a. a jury of executive opinion will be used.
   b. trend analysis or exponential smoothing will be used.
   c. a qualitative rather than a quantitative tool will be used.
   d. it will be in error; you can't project the past into the future.

The Haspling Publishing Company has been producing a broad line of books for over 100 years. Its product portfolio includes hardbound fiction for adult readers, books for younger readers, hardbound nonfiction, and even a line of trendy paperbacks aimed at male and female teenagers. The line of hardbound novels, which was the first line the company published beginning back in 1882 and is anchored by a stable of well-known, popular writers, remains a sound, steady performer in the marketplace, with a substantial share of a slowly growing but quite loyal market segment.

In recent years, the performance of the hardbound nonfiction line has been disappointing. Sales have been declining every year despite a determined effort by the company to offer an attractive, well-researched and topical product at a reasonable price. A recent analysis by the Haspling marketing team indicates that there has been an industry-wide reduction in the demand for nonfiction books and that Haspling's share of the market in this area has been shrinking as well..

The books for younger readers are the company's present pride and joy. The dominant entry in a rapidly growing segment, the "Haspling Heroes" stories for the 12-and-under crowd have proven themselves the company's big profit-producer for the new millennium. The results are still out on the teen paperbacks. Only recently introduced, they have not yet captured a large share of the market. Haspling management feels the line is an "in product" and will ultimately capture a substantial share of this rapidly growing market.

9. According to market share/market growth analysis, the "Haspling Heroes" are
   a. a cash cow.
   b. a star.
   c. a dog.
   d. a question mark.
   e. a duck.

10. Using the market share/market growth matrix as a base, Haspling's adult fiction line would be a
    a. dog.
    b. star.
    c. cash cow.
    d. question mark.
    e. dreamer.

11. Haspling's new line of teen paperbacks
    a. is obviously a loser and should be dropped as soon as possible.
    b. shows every evidence of being a question mark offering and should be carefully watched and nurtured.
    c. is undoubtedly a star right now and should be treated as such.
    d. will probably become a cash cow before it becomes a star.
    e. will never beat out the Hardy Boys and Nancy Drew.

12. If you had to make the decision to drop one of the Haspling lines of products right now, it would be
    a. the teen paperbacks; the market is too uncertain and the risk too great to stay in it.

Harcourt, Inc.

b. the adult fiction; resources could be better allocated to developing the teen paperback line.
c. the books for younger readers; sales have undoubtedly peaked and the end is in sight for this line.
d. the hardbound nonfiction; a declining share of a declining market makes this product a dog and a prime candidate for deletion.

Contemporary Marketing

Name_____ Instructor_____

Section_____ Date_____

Surfing the Net

Keeping in mind that addresses change and what's on the Web now may have changed by the time you read this, let's take a look at some of the places on the Net that reflect aspects of marketing planning and forecasting. We are not endorsing or recommending any of these sources, merely making note of the information and services that people have elected to offer through the Internet.

It's worth knowing about *Hoover's Business Profiles* of some 2,000 of the largest and fastest-growing public and private companies in the United States and the rest of the world. You have to subscribe to use this service, but the coverage of the competition is exhaustive. To inquire, access the Hoover Web site at **http://www.hoovers.com** If you don't want to fork over to use the Hoover's database, you might try a look at the *Fortune 500*. This refers to America's 500 largest corporations ranked by sales volume. You can also click for a company profile and other info. That's at **http://www.pathfinder.com/fortune/fortune500/index.html**

Among the research oriented publications to be found on the Net are *American Demographics* (**http://www.demographics.com/main.html**). You can review current articles from the magazine or even subscribe if you like.

If segmentation is your interest, try accessing this site, devoted to examination of all sorts of issues related to marketing segmentation. It's **http://nsns.com/MouseTracks/** Nearby, you can also find a list of marketing lists and links to all sorts of specialized topics in marketing. The address is **http://nsns.com/MouseTracks/tloml.html.**

Feeling really professional? The American Marketing Association, which many regard as the definitive organization for marketers worldwide, is online at **http://www.ama.org.** You can browse their publications, including the *Journal of Marketing,* decide which marketing conferences to attend, and there is even a section which offers support (moral, we assume, as opposed to financial) to students of the discipline.

Sites verified December 16, 1999.

Chapter 7

Marketing Research and Decision-Support Systems

Chapter Outline

Use the following as a guide in taking notes.

- I. Chapter Overview – Quality Decisions Depend on Quality Information
- II. The Marketing Research Function
    - A. Development of the marketing research function
    - B. Who conducts marketing research?
        1. Syndicated services
        2. Full-service research suppliers
        3. Limited-service research suppliers
    - C. Strategic implications of marketing research
    - D. Marketing research activities
        1. Customer Satisfaction Measurement Programs
- III. The Marketing Research Process
    - A. Define the problem
    - B. Conduct exploratory research
        1. Using internal data
    - C. Formulate a hypothesis
    - D. Create a research design
    - E. Collect data
    - F. Interpret and present research information
- IV. Marketing Research Methods
    - A. Secondary data collection
        1. Government data

2. Private data

3. Online sources of secondary data

B. Sampling techniques

C. Primary research methods

1. Observation method

2. Survey method

   a. Telephone interviews

   b. Personal interviews

   c. Focus groups

   d. Mail surveys

   e. Fax surveys

   f. Online surveys and focus groups

3. Experimental method

D. Conducting international marketing research

V. Computer Technology in Marketing Research

A. The Marketing information system (MIS)

B. The Marketing decision support system (MDSS)

C. Data mining

Name_____ Instructor_____

Section_____ Date_____

Key Concepts

The purpose of this section is to allow you to determine if you can match key concepts with the definitions of the concepts. It is essential that you know the definitions of the concepts prior to applying them in later exercises in this chapter.

From the list of lettered terms, select the one that best fits each of the numbered statements below. Write the letter of that choice in the space provided.

Key Terms

a. marketing research
b. exploratory research
c. sales analysis
d. marketing cost analysis
e. hypothesis
f. research design
g. secondary data
h. primary data
i. sampling
j. population (universe)
k. census
l. probability sample
m. simple random sample
n. stratified sample
o. cluster sample
p. nonprobability sample
q. convenience sample
r. quota sample
s. focus group
t. experiment
u. marketing information system (MIS)
v. marketing decision support system (MDSS)
w. data mining
x. customer satisfaction measurement (CSM) program

____ 1. Previously published data.

____ 2. Nonprobability sample selected from among readily available respondents.

____ 3. Arbitrary grouping that produces data unsuited for most standard statistical tests.

____ 4. Information-gathering procedure in marketing research that typically brings 8 to 12 people together to discuss a given subject.

____ 5. In-depth evaluation of a firm's sales.

____ 6. Searching through customer information files to detect patterns that guide marketing decision making.

____ 7. Probability sample constructed to represent randomly selected subsamples of different groups within the whole sample.

____ 8. Sample that gives every member of the population a known chance of being selected.

____ 9. Collection and use of information for marketing decision making.

Contemporary Marketing

_____ 10. Total group that researchers want to study.

_____ 11. Tentative explanation for some specific event.

_____ 12. Process of selecting survey respondents or other research participants.

_____ 13. Scientific investigation in which a researcher manipulates a test group and compares these results with those of a group that did not receive the manipulations.

_____ 14. Discussing a marketing problem with informed sources within the firm as well as outside it and examining information from secondary sources.

_____ 15. Evaluation of expenses for tasks like selling, billing, and advertising to determine the profitability of particular customers, territories, or product lines.

_____ 16. MIS component that links a decision-maker with relevant databases and analysis tools.

_____ 17. Collection of data on all possible members of a population or universe.

_____ 18. Basic type of probability sample in which every individual in the relevant universe has an equal opportunity to be selected.

_____ 19. Data collected for the first time.

_____ 20. Series of decisions that, taken together, comprise a master plan for conducting marketing research.

_____ 21. Nonprobability sample divided to ensure representation of different segments or groups in the whole sample.

_____ 22. A planned, computer-based system designed to provide managers with a continuous flow of information relevant to their specific decisions and areas of responsibility.

_____ 23. Probability sample in which geographical areas or clusters are selected and all of them or chosen individuals within them become respondents.

_____ 24. Measures customer feedback against customer satisfaction goals and developing a plan of action for improvement.

Part 3 Marketing Planning, Information, and Segmentation

Name_____Instructor_____

Section_____ Date_____

Self-Quiz

You should use these questions to test your understanding of the material in Chapter 6. You can check your answers with those provided at the end of the chapter.

While these questions cover most of the chapter topics, they are not intended to be the same as the test questions your instructor may use in an examination. A good understanding of all aspects of course material is essential to good performance on an examination.

True/False

Write "T" for True and "F" for False for each of the following statements.

____ 1. The first organized marketing research project was conducted by N. W. Ayer in 1879.

____ 2. Charles C. Parlin who got his start as a marketing researcher by counting soup cans in Philadelphia's garbage, became the manager of the nation's first commercial research department in 1911.

____ 3. The size and organizational form of the marketing research function is independent of the structure of the company doing the research.

____ 4. One of the drawbacks to using secondary data is that the information may be obsolete when the researcher gets it.

____ 5. The National Research Group (NRG) is a full-service research supplier that specializes in the motion picture industry.

____ 6. A check of license plates at a shopping center to determine where the cars came from would be secondary data for the firm that did the study.

____ 7. An organization that regularly provides a standardized set of research data to all its customers is called a syndicated service.

____ 8. Experimentation is the least-used of the primary data gathering methods because it is so difficult to take into account all the variables in a real-life situation.

____ 9. Risk assessment activities conducted by marketing researchers seek to discover how well past decisions are working out.

____ 10. The step in the marketing research process which we have called "marketing cost analysis" is also known as "sales analysis."

____ 11. Many research projects find it desirable to combine secondary and primary data to fully answer marketing questions.

Harcourt, Inc.

Contemporary Marketing

____ 12. Simple random sampling and cluster sampling are two types of nonprobability samples.

____ 13. Unlike other interview techniques, focus groups usually discourage a general discussion of a predetermined topic.

____ 14. A well-designed Internet-based marketing research project can cost less yet yield faster results than research done offline.

____ 15. Properly constructed, marketing information systems can serve as a company's nerve center, monitoring the marketplace continually and providing instantaneous information.

____ 16. An MIS takes the MDSS one step further by allowing managers to explore and make connections between varying information such as the state of the market or consumer behavior.

____ 17. When using the Census of Population as a data source, the BNAs and census tracts are important for marketing analysis because they highlight populations with dissimilar traits, examining diversity within political boundaries such as county lines.

____ 18. Information extracted from a Web site is almost always valid; the people posting data on a discussion forum and those producing Web pages are typically highly knowledgeable on the subject.

____ 19. The most important source of marketing data in the United States is the Federal government.

____ 20. The first step in the marketing research process is defining the problem.

____ 21. The observational method of gathering marketing research data has become more sophisticated through the use of technological advances.

____ 22. Telephone surveys suffer from low response rates because people are reluctant to provide even the most impersonal information about themselves.

____ 23. Some knowledgeable people believe that focus groups may not produce completely honest responses to questions, perhaps because the members of the group feel they have an image to maintain and need to identify with the other members of the group.

____ 24. Interviews conducted in shopping centers are typically called *mall calls*.

____ 25. Data to be used in a data mining operation is usually stored in a database called an "information gallery."

Multiple Choice

Circle the letter of the word or phrase that best completes the sentence or best answers the question.

26. Marketing research consists of collecting and using information to
    a. best employ new technologies in business.
    b. make marketing decisions.
    c. acquire testimonials from famous criminals.

d. decrease the cost of products.
   e. analyze sales information.

27. A recent survey of *Fortune* 200 firms found that they budget an average of
   a. 38 percent of gross revenues for marketing research activities.
   b. $350 thousand for the services of external marketing research activities.
   c. $11 million each per year for in-house marketing research departments.
   d. only $500,000 per year for marketing research versus $5 million for scientific research.
   e. $43.7 million per year to operate their vehicle fleets.

28. The type of marketing research organization that provides a standardized set of data on a regular basis to all its customers is the
   a. full-service supplier.
   b. industrial research supplier.
   c. contract research firm.
   d. syndicated service.
   e. none of the above.

29. The first task of the marketing researcher when undertaking a new project is to
   a. conduct exploratory research – perform a situation analysis.
   b. go to the library or some convenient bar for reflection on the matter.
   c. create an accurate definition of the problem.
   d. do a sales and cost analysis of the project as proposed.
   e. plan a research design.

30. The marketing research process ordinarily follows the sequence of
   a. problem definition, exploratory research, hypothesis, research design, data collection, interpretation and presentation.
   b. problem definition, interpretation and presentation, data collection, research design, hypothesis, exploratory research.
   c. problem definition, research design, hypothesis, exploratory research, data collection, interpretation and presentation.
   d. interpretation and presentation, problem definition, exploratory research, research design, data collection, hypothesis.
   e. interpretation and presentation, problem definition, exploratory research, research design, data collection.

31. Which of the following can be sources of secondary data?
   a. company sales records
   b. online databases available on the Internet
   c. industry sales figures published by a trade organization
   d. government publications such as the *Survey of Current Business*
   e. All of the above are sources of secondary data.

32. Compared to secondary data, primary data has the advantage of
   a. usually being less expensive to collect.
   b. providing richer, more detailed information.
   c. taking less time to get.
   d. being readily available from the U. S. government and other sources.
   e. possessing all of the above characteristics.

33. The purpose of a sales analysis is to
    a. eliminate accountants' jobs.
    b. analyze the company's achievement of market share objectives.
    c. evaluate such items as selling costs, warehousing, advertising, and delivery expenses.
    d. compare actual sales results with expected sales performance.
    e. acquire external secondary data to make decision-making more successful.

34. One of the most basic criteria for designing a research project is the assurance that
    a. the study will measure what it's intended to measure.
    b. the results are what the president of the company wants to see.
    c. budgetary constraints can be met even at the cost of accuracy.
    d. no one's job will be put at risk because of the study results.
    e. the measures used will be acceptable to the users.

35. Which of the following correctly matches the type of survey to the reason for choosing it?
    a. focus group–need to interview many people, one at a time, at very low cost.
    b. mall intercept–required to contact people where they work.
    c. mail survey–necessary to take advantage of very high response rates to efficiently gather data.
    d. personal interview–want to contact people living all over the world at the lowest possible cost.
    e. telephone interview–desire to gather small amounts of impersonal information cheaply and quickly.

36. Which of the following correctly matches the type of sample with an appropriate example?
    a. cluster sample – interview all residents of six city blocks chosen randomly from within Minneapolis.
    b. stratified sample – interview the first 35 men and the first 35 women who enter the Lakeside Shopping Mall.
    c. simple random sample – interview anybody you can find on the street who will speak to you.
    d. convenience sample – after randomly choosing the first name, call every tenth name in the telephone directory.
    e. quota sample – interview 100 students selected randomly from a list of all students.

37. The focus group is an example of
    a. an experimental research technique involving physical measurements of each subject.
    b. a type of interview research technique that doesn't ask questions but encourages discussion.
    c. an observational research technique using high-tech equipment to gather data.
    d. a method of collecting secondary personal data by reading people's mail.
    e. a method of assuring the accuracy of nonprobability samples by forcing participation.

38. Marketing information systems
    a. gather information only from within the organization using them.
    b. periodically monitor the marketplace and provide occasional information about it.
    c. store data for later use, though retrieving it may not be so easy.
    d. are components of the organization's overall management information system.
    e. rely on information stored in hard-copy form kept in filing cabinets.

39. Data mining
    a. is seldom used by firms in the health care and banking industries.
    b. meets corporate expectations an average of 70 percent of the time.
    c. often suffers from unreasonable expectations on the part of its users.
    d. stores its data in a humongous database called a *data depository*.

e. requires the use of a hard hat, safety glasses, and miner's lamp.

40. A simple random sample is
    a. a probability sample in which every item in the population has an equal chance of being selected.
    b. a probability sample arranged so that randomly selected subsamples of different groups within the population are represented in the sample.
    c. a probability sample in which areas are selected from which respondents are drawn.
    d. a nonprobability sample based on the selection of readily available respondents.
    e. a nonprobability sample designed so that each subgroup in the population will be represented in the sample in proportion to its representation in the population.

41. Among the challenges faced by marketing researchers in global markets are
    a. language issues involving the most effective means of communication.
    b. cultural issues related to capturing local citizens' interest without offending them.
    c. the possibility that data gathering methods used at home may not be successful elsewhere.
    d. conditions in the business environment such as political and economic condtions.
    e. all of the above may be challenges the global researcher may have to meet.

42. Marketing research that focuses on the assessment of current events falls into the class called
    a. scanning activities.
    b. risk assessment activities.
    c. monitoring activities.
    d. exploratory work.
    e. definitive research.

43. A marketing information system (MIS) consists of
    a. statistics, opinions, facts, and predictions categorized on some basis for storage and retrieval.
    b. a compilation of data potentially useful to the marketing manager in making decisions.
    c. a cardboard box into which the firm's records have been carefully packed so that in the event of the need for a quick getaway, they will be handy.
    d. a way of writing research reports so that they can be understood by the executives who must use them.
    e. a planned, computer based system designed to provide managers with a continual flow of information relevant to their decision areas.

44. O and A Research Services is an organization that contracts with clients to conduct complete marketing research projects having to do with consumer goods distribution in the Southeast. O and A is
    a. a syndicated service company.
    b. a captive research source.
    c. a full-service research supplier.
    d. a limited-service research supplier.
    e. either b or d.

45. The cardinal rule of presenting marketing research requires
    a. that it involve a complete discussion of its limitations.
    b. that it assist in decision making rather than being an end in itself.
    c. direction of the presentation toward other research specialists to avoid embarrassment.
    d. discussion of the technical details as a central part of the presentation.
    e. creation of a report that will impress management with the researchers' skill.

Contemporary Marketing

46. Cuadra Associates now offers as a quarterly publication
    a. the *Directory of Online Databases,* a quarterly list of many sources of online information.
    b. direct access to state trade offices in each state through its offices in state capitols.
    c. Internet access to many foreign businesses through InterNatNet.
    d. Small Business Development Centers all over the U. S. Run in collaboration with the State Department.
    e. *Overseas Business Reports*, an annual synopsis of marketing activity in 100 countries.

47. For sales analysis to yield meaningful results, the comparison of expected sales to actual sales must be based upon
    a. spot examination of specific sales events.
    b. the fevered imaginations of the individual sales representatives.
    c. whatever the sales manager thinks it should be based on.
    d. sales quotas based on a detailed sales forecast as the measure of expected sales.
    e. wishful thinking.

48. Which of the following is an example of a hypothesis?
    a. We sell 53 percent of the total quantity of this product sold in the world.
    b. Our sales force consists of 57 people, 14 of whom work in the field; the rest are support staff.
    c. Our president is an engineer; his brother, who serves as vice-president of finance, is an accountant.
    d. When buying a home, families first investigate the neighborhood; then they look for a house in the preferred neighborhood.
    e. Gianetti jeans are designed with the active woman in mind.

49. Of all of the sources of primary research data, the one which is the best means of obtaining detailed information about attitudes, motives, and opinions is
    a. observation.
    b. the mail survey.
    c. experimentation.
    d. the telephone interview.
    e. the personal interview.

50. If your supervisor in the marketing research department of the Southern States Life, Health, and Accident Insurance Company told you that he wanted you to take a probability sample such that the members of the sample were broke down into the age groups 18-35, 36-49, and over 49 in the same proportion that those ages were distributed in the population, you would take a
    a. simple random sample.
    b. stratified sample.
    c. systematic sample.
    d. convenience sample.
    e. quota sample.

Harcourt, Inc.

Name_____Instructor_____

Section_____Date_____

Applying Marketing Concepts

Lazslette Tchenyik, marketing research analyst for Remlap Biologicals, a national supplier of medical testing kits, was told to find out why "Ceekit," the company's new analytical product to detect the presence of Hepatitis C in human blood, wasn't doing as well as it they thought it should in the marketplace and to report back to the executive committee in two weeks.

She decided that the first thing to do was to gather primary data from all the 7,500 Remlap customers who'd bought "Ceekits" during the past year. Her main concern was to find out why the customers weren't making repeat purchases of the product. After reviewing bids from three outside marketing research suppliers, she chose the Filarion Company because its bid was the lowest. Ms. Tchenyik directed Filarion to design and conduct the study of all "Ceekit" customers without talking to any Remlap management personnel.

After the primary research study was commissioned, Ms. Tchenyik talked with Remlap's sales force and wholesalers to attempt to determine the cause of "Ceekit's" lackluster sales performance. Finally, Laszlette reviewed the records available in the company's marketing information system. These records included breakdowns of sales and marketing costs for "Ceekit" in each territory. This data is reproduced below.

TERRITORY

	East		West		North		South	
	Actual*	Quota*	Actual*	Quota*	Actual*	Quota*	Actual*	Quota*
Sales	$500	$400	$300	$200	$400	$300	$600	$500
Cost of Sales	300		180		120		180	
Gross Margin	200		120		280		420	
Marktg. Expenses	400	120	90	60	240	90	500	150
Contribution	(200)		30		40		(80)	

*thousands of dollars

Write "T" for True or "F" for False for each of the following statements.

_____ 1. Ms. Tchenyik was collecting primary data before examining the secondary data.

_____ 2. A census of customers was taken.

_____ 3. Outside marketing research organizations should conduct research projects without talking to the users of the research information.

_____ 4. Very few organizations purchase outside marketing research services.

_____ 5. Remlap should not need marketing research if its marketing information system is effective.

Circle the letter of the word or phrase that best completes each sentence.

6. The best way to gather the information Ms. Tchenyik wanted from customers in two weeks would be by means of
   a. observation.
   b. telephone interviews.
   c. personal interviews.
   d. focus group interviews.
   e. a mail survey.

7. The sales and expense analysis suggests that
   a. sales in all territories were below expectations.
   b. the East territory was the only problem market.
   c. marketing expenses were above expected levels in all territories.
   d. the sales force is incurring excessive travel and entertainment expenses.
   e. customers do not like the products.

8. Ms. Tchenyik's decision to do primary research before sales and expense analysis was based on the conclusion that answers about the causes of "Ceekit's" problems could be obtained from
   a. dealers.
   b. customers.
   c. the sales force.
   d. government publications.
   e. company management.

9. The results of her investigation should be
   a. discarded.
   b. reviewed by management and then discarded.
   c. stored in Remlap's marketing information system for future use.
   d. acted upon immediately.
   e. kept under lock and key.

10. The major reason why Ms. Tchenyik chose the Filarion Company is that
    a. it was the cheapest.
    b. it had the desired expertise.
    c. it was intellectually detached.
    d. it was a subsidiary of Remlap.
    e. the Filarion Company had done many similar projects for other companies.

Allen Banting, local services director for the Cogburn Consolidated Cable Communications Corporation (5C) system, was perturbed. He knew that the government charter under which his company provided cable television service to Mirkheim City required it to provide a "public access" channel to the community. Though the charter said that access to the production facilities and distribution system of Cogburn Consolidated Cable for purposes of producing and sending out public access programming should be free, there was nothing in the charter which said that the cable company could not sell commercial time on the public access channel. Mr. Banting wondered if selling commercial time on the 5C public access channel would be worthwhile. Since TV and radio stations and cable channels generally price their commercial time on the basis of the number of people who watch their shows, he knew he would have to get some estimate of how many people watched "Mirkheim at Home," as the 5C public access channel was known. He also felt that he should get the information as soon as possible, for he knew that Cogburn was soon scheduled to go before the city council to plead for a renewal of its charter to provide service, and even if it didn't prove possible to sell commercial time on the access channel, it would be good to have the information about "watchership" for the council hearings on renewal.

____ 11. Mr. Banting's project is in the nature of an exploratory study.

____ 12. Most of the data for this project must be gathered from primary sources.

____ 13. A major source of secondary information for this study would be Cogburn's logs of public access use of its production facilities.

14. The most appropriate definition of Mr. Banting's problem is
    a. He does not know how many homes are served by 5C's system.
    b. He does not know the size of the audience that watches "Mirkheim at Home."
    c. He does not know who is using the production facilities of 5C to produce shows for "Mirkheim at Home."
    d. He is unaware of the legal implications of "public access" television.

15. Since Mr. Banting needs his information in a short period of time, the best way to get it would be
    a. by use of the experimental method.
    b. through use of a mail survey.
    c. over the telephone; use telephone interviews.
    d. by stopping people on the street and asking them questions about "Mirkheim at Home."

16. Which of the following might be an acceptable hypothesis upon which Mr. Banting might develop his research?
    a. Viewers want to see more entertainment shows and fewer educational offerings on their public access channel.
    b. The quality of production for the public access channel is inferior to the quality of production on other channels.
    c. Public access television is a waste of time and should be disallowed as a disservice to the viewership.
    d. Public access television has a sufficiently large audience that advertisers would be willing to pay enough to use it to make it profitable for the cable company.

17. If Mr. Allen does decide to use primary research and to design a sample-based method, which of the following would you suggest to him is most appropriate?
    a. He should randomly sample customers from 5C's list of current subscribers.
    b. He should conduct in-depth interviews with highly placed executives at Cogburn to get the benefit of their expertise and knowledge about how people watch TV.

c. He should systematically draw a sample from the pages of the local telephone directory.
d. He should carefully analyze the location characteristics of Cogburn's subscribers and assume an audience from what he finds there.

Name_____Instructor_____

Section_____Date_____

Surfing the Net

Keeping in mind that addresses change and what's on the Web now may have changed by the time you read this, let's take a look at some of the places on the Net that reflect aspects of marketing research. We are not endorsing or recommending any of these sources, merely making note of the information and services that people have elected to offer through the Internet.

Secondary data on the Web. One way of finding information is by using a **search engine.** A search engine provides access to a database of many million Web sites. Some examples of search engines are *Excite,* at **http://www.excite.com.** Excite indexes over fifty million Web sites. These are made accessible by key word searches. Other search engines include *Alta Vista* at **http://www.altavista.digital.com,** *HotBot* at **http://hotbot.com**, and *Infoseek* at **http://infoseek.com**. Your Web Browser probably gives you a choice of several search engines to use. It is often interesting to conduct the same search on several of these just to see how their databases contain often quite different entries keyed to the same search string (that's the several words you enter to trigger the search). You may have already developed a preference for a particular search engine.

Dun and Bradstreet's Web Site is at **http://www.dnb.com.** This firm compiles data on firms all over the United States. Searches and registration are free, but should you want a Dun and Bradstreet report, the charge is $20.

Most major newspapers are on the Net. For the *Houston Chronicle,* try **http://www.chron.com/**. The *London Times* is at **http://www.the-times.co.uk**.

A number of professional research services may be accessed through the Web. Burke, Incorporated, parent company of Burke Marketing Research, has its site at **http://www.burke.com** and O and A Research is located at **http://oaresearch.com.** You might be interested to see how these firms of varying background, specialties, and style write their Web sites. Ipsos-ASI Marketing Research, a firm that specializes in copy testing, sponsors the Marketing Research Center at **http://www.asiresearch.com**. They offer links to the market research industry and an e-mail directory of research professionals.

Need secondary data? American Demographics, Inc., can be reached at **http://www.demographics.com**, at which site you can search the archives of their two magazines, *American Demographics* and *Marketing Tools.* And finally, Princeton University's Survey Research Center has a site at **http://www.princeton.edu/~abelson/ index.html** where one can find links to survey, poll, and other research sites.

Sites verified December 17, 1999.

Chapter 8

Market Segmentation, Targeting, and Positioning

Chapter Outline

Use the following as a guide in taking notes.

I. Chapter Overview – Understanding the Meaning of the Term "Market"

II. Types of Markets

III. The Role of Market Segmentation

    1. Criteria for Effective Segmentation

IV. Segmenting Consumer Markets

    A. Geographic segmentation

        1. Using geographic segmentation

        2. Geographic Information System (GIS)

    B. Demographic segmentation

        1. Segmenting by gender

        2. Segmenting by age

        3. Segmenting by Ethnic Group

        4. Segmenting by family life cycle

        5. Segmenting by household type

        6. Segmenting by income and expenditure patterns

        7. Demographic segmentation abroad

    C. Psychographic segmentation

        1. What is psychographic segmentation?

        2. VALS 2

        3. Psychographic segmentation of global markets

4. Using psychographic segmentation

D. Product-Related Segmentation

1. Segmenting by benefits sought

2. Segmenting by usage rates

3. Segmenting by brand loyalty

V. The Market Segmentation Process

A. Stage I: Identify market segmentation processes

B. Stage II: Develop a relevant profile for each segment

C. Stage III: Forecast market potential

D. Stage IV: Forecast probable market share

E. Stage V: Select specific market segments

VI. Strategies for Reaching Target Markets

A. Undifferentiated marketing

B. Differentiated marketing

C. Concentrated marketing

D. Micromarketing

E. Selecting and executing a strategy

VII. Market Segmentation: Strategic Implications

Name_____ Instructor_____

Section_____ Date_____

Key Concepts

The purpose of this section is to allow you to determine if you can match key concepts with the definitions of the concepts. It is essential that you know the definitions of the concepts prior to applying them in later exercises in this chapter.

From the list of lettered terms, select the one that best fits each of the numbered statements below. Write the letter of that choice in the space provided.

Key Terms

a. market
b. target market
c. consumer product
d. business product
e. market segmentation
f. geographic segmentation
g. Metropolitan Statistical Area (MSA)
h. Consolidated Metropolitan Statistical Area (CMSA)
I. Primary Metropolitan Statistical Area (CMSA)
j. geographic information system (GIS)
k. demographic segmentation
l. cohort effect
m. family life cycle
n. Engel's laws
o. psychographic segmentation
p. lifestyle
q. AIO statements
r. VALS 2
s. product-related segmentation
t. 80/20 principle (Praedo's Law)
u. target market decision analysis
v. undifferentiated marketing
w. differentiated marketing
x. concentrated marketing
y. micromarketing
z. positioning
aa. positioning map
ab. reposition

_____ 1. Marketing strategy that commits all of a firm's marketing resources to serve a single market segment.

_____ 2. Good or service purchased for use either directly or indirectly in the production of other goods and services for resale.

_____ 3. Specific segment of consumers most likely to purchase a particular product.

_____ 4. A group of people or institutions who possess sufficient purchasing power and the authority and willingness to buy.

_____ 5. Statements in a psychographic survey that reflect the respondent's activities, interests, and opinions.

Contemporary Marketing

_____ 6. Process of family formation and dissolution which affects market segmentation because life stage is the primary determinant of many consumer purchases.

_____ 7. Dividing an overall market into homogeneous groups on the basis of population location.

_____ 8. Dividing a consumer population into homogeneous groups based on characteristics of their relationships to a product.

_____ 9. Commercially available system for psychographic segmentation of consumers.

_____ 10. Freestanding urban population center.

_____ 11. Marketing strategy used by firms that produce only one product and market it to all customers using a single marketing mix.

_____ 12. Marketing strategy to target potential customers at basic levels such as by ZIP code.

_____ 13. Dividing consumer groups into homogeneous segments on the basis of characteristics such as age, sex, income level, and stage in the family life cycle.

_____ 14. Marketing strategy of changing the position a product holds in the consumer's mind relative to competing products.

_____ 15. Evaluation of potential market segments on the basis of relevant characteristics and prospects for satisfying business objectives.

_____ 16. Division of the total market into smaller, relatively homogeneous groups.

_____ 17. Concept that a small percentage of customers of a product can account for a large percentage of its consumption.

_____ 18. Major urban area within a CMSA.

_____ 19. Tendency for members of the same generation to be influenced by the same events occurring during their key formative years.

_____ 20. Three general statements on spending behavior: As a family's income increases, the percentage spent (1) on food increases; (2) on housing, household operations, and clothing remains constant; and (3) on other items increases.

_____ 21. A good or service purchased by the ultimate consumer for personal use.

_____ 22. Dividing a consumer population into homogeneous groups based on their psychological and lifestyle profiles.

_____ 23. Computer technology that records several layers of data on a single map.

_____ 24. Activities that reflect a person's needs, motives, perceptions, and attitudes.

_____ 25. Marketing strategy that emphasizes serving a specific market segment by achieving a certain position in buyers' minds.

_____ 26. Graphic illustration that shows differences in consumer perceptions of competitive products.

_____ 27. Strategy used by organizations that produce numerous products and use different marketing mixes to satisfy smaller market segments.

_____ 28. Major population concentration, including the 25 or so urban giants.

Contemporary Marketing

Name_____ Instructor_____

Section_____ Date_____

Self-Quiz

You should use these objective questions to test your understanding of the chapter material. You can check your answers with those provided at the end of the chapter.

While these questions cover most of the chapter topics, they are not intended to be the same as the test questions your instructor may use in an examination. A good understanding of all aspects of course material is essential to good performance on any examination.

Write "T" for True or "F" for False for each of the following statements.

_____ 1. The key to proper classification of goods and services is determining the purchaser and the reasons for the purchase.

_____ 2. Henry Ford was one of the pioneers in the segmentation of the U.S. automobile industry.

_____ 3. A market requires that there be people or institutions with purchasing power, authority, and the willingness to buy.

_____ 4. Light bulbs sold to lamp manufacturers to be sold with their lamps are business products. Light bulbs sold to consumers to replace light bulbs in their home fixtures are consumer products.

_____ 5. To segment a market effectively, the only requirements are that the segment must present measurable purchasing power and size and that it matches the marketing capabilities of the firm.

_____ 6. The traditional family consisting of two parents and their children living in one household declined from 50 percent of all U.S. households in 1970 to only 33 percent today.

_____ 7. New York, with its population of over 7 million people, is the world's largest city.

_____ 8. Between now and the year 2020, the states expected to experience the fastest population growth include Nevada, California, Hawaii, and Washington.

_____ 9. Huntsville, Alabama, with its population of 300,000, is an example of a Primary Metropolitan Statistical Area.

_____ 10. Market segmentation is the process of dividing the total market into smaller, relatively homogeneous groups.

Harcourt, Inc.

____ 11. Geographic market segmentation of consumers is useful when specific regional preferences for products and services exist.

____ 12. Geographic Information System software is still prohibitively expensive for all but the largest firms and organizations.

____ 13. One of the reasons demographic market segmentation is used is because vast quantities of demographic data are available.

____ 14. Generation Y refers to that group of children born between 1965 and the late 1970s who value the quality of personal life above that of work life.

____ 15. The most common approach to market segmentation in the consumer market is benefits segmentation.

____ 16. The significant events that a person experiences between the ages of about 23 to 29 tend to bind him or her to others of his or her generation. This is called the cohort effect.

____ 17. Despite the fact that its marketing costs will be higher, a firm may be forced to resort of differentiated marketing to remain competitive.

____ 18. Concentrated marketing – in which a firm devotes its efforts to profitably satisfying only one market segment – is also known as "niche marketing."

____ 19. In terms of the family life cycle, couples without children are good prospects for inexpensive furniture and small home appliances; expenditures on luxuries are unusual.

____ 20. The two key concepts underlying the VALS 2 typology are occupation and income.

____ 21. Product-related segmentation of the toothpaste market by benefits sought might produce segments concerned with receiving a low price, reducing tooth decay, enjoying the taste while brushing, or brightening the teeth.

____ 22. For census purposes, the term DINKs identifies unmarried people of opposite sexes sharing the same living quarters.

____ 23. One's lifestyle bears the mark of many influences such as one's needs, motives, perceptions and attitudes.

____ 24. One of the problems encountered in using demographic segmentation abroad is that some countries gather census data only irregularly, while others do not collect some of the demographic data commonly used as bases for segmentation in the United States.

____ 25. Segments which have been identified by psychographic analysis as having different lifestyles cannot be expected to behave differently from each other.

Contemporary Marketing

Multiple Choice

Circle the letter of the word or phrase that best completes the sentence or best answers the question.

26. Markets require people, a willingness to buy, purchasing power, and
    a. engineering personnel.
    b. authority to buy.
    c. a bargaining committee.
    d. descriptions of products.
    e. purchasing agents.

27. An in-depth analysis of customers in market segments identified as promising helps managers accurately match the customers' needs with the firm's marketing offers in which stage of the market segmentation process?
    a. Stage II
    b. Stage III
    c. Stage IV
    d. Stage V
    e. Stage VI

28. A basic reason why marketers elect to segment markets is because
    a. products often succeed by appealing to single, homogeneous markets.
    b. they need some means of solving the complex problem of finding buyers for their products.
    c. by identifying, evaluating, and selecting a target market to pursue, marketers are able to develop more efficient and effective marketing strategies.
    d. when the production line goes into operation, it can turn out the millions of items necessary to secure economies of scale.
    e. competition will find it difficult to determine what is going to happen next.

29. Under which of the following conditions may segmentation not promote marketing success?
    a. When it is possible to measure the market segment in terms of both purchasing power and size.
    b. When it appears feasible to promote effectively to the market segment.
    c. When the segment or segments of the market under consideration are large enough to be adequately profitable.
    d. When there are no apparent problems in providing the chosen segment or segments of the market with adequate service.
    e. When the firm cannot find a segment or segments that match its marketing capabilities.

30. A Consolidated Metropolitan Statistical Area (CMSA)
    a. must include two or more Primary Metropolitan Statistical Areas.
    b. is an urbanized county with a population in excess of 500,000.
    c. usually borders on nonurbanized counties.
    d. must be a freestanding urban area with a population of at least 50,000.
    e. cannot include more than 6 counties or 3 incorporated municipalities.

31. At present, the proportion of the population that can be expected to move in any given year is about
    a. one-fourth, down from one-third in recent years.
    b. one-fifth, the highest it has been in recorded history.
    c. one-sixth, but at one time it was one-fifth.
    d. one-ninth; we are not a very mobile population.

Harcourt, Inc.

e. one-tenth; urban dwellers are very reluctant to move.

32. A freestanding urban area with an urban center population of 50,000 and which has a total population of 100,000 or more would be defined by the U. S. government as a(n)
    a. PMSA.
    b. MSA.
    c. CMSA.
    d. SSMA.
    e. OGPU.

33. Which of the following is a psychographic variable?
    a. your opinion about conservative government
    b. the state in which you reside
    c. the rate at which you use a particular product
    d. your occupation, craft, or trade
    e. the number, ages, and genders of your children

34. The largest racial/ethnic minority in the United States at present is
    a. Asian-Americans.
    b. Hispanics.
    c. Pacific Islanders.
    d. African Americans.
    e. Acadian Americans.

35. A market segment based on the family life cycle concept is
    a. the high-income segment.
    b. people who buy new automobiles frequently.
    c. married couples without children.
    d. residents of large eastern metropolitan areas.
    e. Polish Americans.

36. Geographic Information Systems
    a. simplify the job of analyzing marketing information by placing data in a spatial format.
    b. present data in the form of a geographic map overlaid with digital data.
    c. can be used to identify favorable sites for new store locations.
    d. have now become feasible for even small firms because software is now available at much lower cost than before.
    e. All of the above statements are true.

37. According the Engel's laws, an increase in family income should bring
    a. more dollars expended for food.
    b. fewer dollars expended for housing.
    c. fewer dollars expended for education and recreation.
    d. no change in the percentage of income spent on housing and clothing.
    e. a higher percentage of income spent for more and better food.

38. The group of people born between 1946 and 1965 and who now account for nearly 42 percent of the U.S. population are the
    a. Seniors who control about three-quarters of the nation's total financial assets.
    b. Generation Xers who tend to be more egalitarian about gender roles than the general population.
    c. Y Generation, more racially diverse than the others and more computer literate.

d. Baby Boomers, many of whose behavior is not as expected by forecasters.
e. Cohorts, those who do as their fellow members of this generation do with little variation.

39. According to the VALS 2 typology, the action-oriented people who follow fashion and fads and spend much of their disposable income on socializing are the
   a. fulfilleds.
   b. believers.
   c. achievers.
   d. strivers.
   e. experiencers.

40. Marketers who want to aim their marketing mix at the segment of the population who are married couples both of whom have incomes and who have no children should target the group the Census calls
   a. MSAs.
   b. SSWDs.
   c. CMSAs.
   d. DINKs.
   e. POSSLQs.

41. A firm that targets as potential customers only neurosurgeons in the Chicago area who perform twenty or more of a specific procedure per year is using
   a. undifferentiated marketing.
   b. differentiated marketing.
   c. concentrated marketing.
   d. arbitrary segmentation.
   e. micromarketing.

42. Melrose Specialty Company has designed and markets to people who follow fashion closely, buy on impulse, and listen to rock music a special package of computer software specifically designed to help them shop on the Internet. Melrose has used
   a. geographic segmentation.
   b. psychographic segmentation.
   c. demographic segmentation.
   d. marginal segmentation.
   e. undifferentiated segmentation.

43. The stage of the segmentation process which involves examining competitors' positions in targeted segments and preparation of a strategy designed to serve these segments is that of
   a. developing a relevant profile for each segment.
   b. forecasting market potential.
   c. selecting specific market segments.
   d. forecasting probable market share.
   e. selecting market segmentation bases.

44. A firm which produces numerous products with different marketing mixes, each of which is designed to satisfy a segment of the market, is said to be practicing
   a. undifferentiated marketing.
   b. mass marketing.
   c. differentiated marketing.
   d. consolidated marketing.

e. concentrated marketing.

45. Which of the following is an appropriate example of the indicated type of market segment?
    a. geographic – people living within 1.5 miles of a particular shopping center
    b. psychographic – young married couples with children
    c. demographic – people looking for the lowest cost watch
    d. benefits sought – people interested in sports events
    e. demographic – people with a positive attitude toward education

46. American Airlines' "College Saavers" program, which the airline markets to student travelers through its Web site, is an example of
    a. differentiated marketing.
    b. concentrated marketing.
    c. undifferentiated marketing.
    d. micromarketing.
    e. melodramatic marketing.

47. Target market decision analysis is usually part of the stage of the market segmentation process involved with
    a. developing a relevant profile for each segment.
    b. forecasting market potential.
    c. selecting specific market segments.
    d. forecasting probable market share.
    e. determining the bases on which to identify markets.

48. The world's two largest cities in terms of population are
    a. New York City and Los Angeles.
    b. Tokyo and Mexico City.
    c. Beijing, China and Bangkok, Thailand.
    d. Rio de Janeiro, Brazil and Paris, France.
    e. New Delhi, India, and New Braunfels, Texas.

49. When a manufacturer creates a product such as Chevrolet's "Beau Jacques" pickup truck, which was sold in Louisiana some years ago (the same truck was sold in surrounding states as the "Gentleman Jim" model), it is using
    a. benefit sought segmentation.
    b. geographical segmentation.
    c. end-use application segmentation
    d. psychographic segmentation.
    e. arbitrary segmentation.

50. Within the broader classification of product-related segmentation, the classic example of this segmentation technique is airline frequent flyer programs. The technique has evolved into
    a. segmenting by benefits sought.
    b. segmenting by usage rates.
    c. segmenting by demographic characteristics.
    d. segmenting by psychographics.
    e. segmenting by brand loyalty.

Contemporary Marketing

Name_____ Instructor_____

Section_____ Date_____

Applying Marketing Concepts

The Wolverine Manufacturing Company has developed a line of disposable clothing. The clothing can be sold profitably for about half the price of conventional garments. The items are durable enough to withstand several washings if desired, but can be easily disposed of simply by treating them with a special chemical solution in which they dissolve. Due to the manufacturing processes involved, the materials of which the clothes are made can only be made in solid colors. Children are expected to be a major market for these clothes, so their parents will be the people with the authority and purchasing power to buy. The company expects the most interest in its products to come from parents of younger children whose rough treatment destroys clothes at a rapid rate. Executives at Wolverine also foresee a market for their product among individuals who like do-it-yourself projects but don't like to have old, oily, scruffy clothes lying around the house.

Write "T" for True or "F" for False for each of the following statements.

_____ 1. By definition, the real market for Wolverine's disposable clothing is younger children.

_____ 2. According to Engel's laws, the percent of income spent on clothing stays the same over all levels of consumer income.

_____ 3. The disposable clothing sold to people who want to use them for their do-it-your-self projects would be classed as commercial products.

Circle the letter of the word or phrase that best completes each sentence.

4. The Wolverine Manufacturing Company is selling disposable clothing as
   a. business products.
   b. consumer products.
   c. both business and consumer products.
   d. flammable products.

5. The segmentation method most appropriate to Wolverine's attempt to reach its primary market of small children is probably
   a. geographical, concentrating on the West where all the small children are.
   b. product-based, orienting toward brand loyalty.
   c. demographic, using the family life cycle as a basis.
   d. psychographic, targeting the DINKs.

6. If benefits-sought segmentation is used by Wolverine, it should direct its efforts toward people who want
   a. long-lasting durability.
   b. high fashion, stylish garments.
   c. convenience in use at reasonable cost.
   d. lowest overall (no pun intended) cost clothes.

Part 3 Marketing Planning, Information, and Segmentation

You have recently concluded a month-long visit to your company's main branch in the Eastern European country of Norsworthy, which shares many cultural values with nearby Malencontri. You were impressed with the differences among the various groups of people you met there. Many of your contemporaries (you're in your early thirties) seemed really into education and knowledge, taking self-improvement courses at every opportunity. Many were working on science and engineering degrees or certificates. Others, about the same age, were more mellow. Most of them were established professionals with some measure of success, and their homes and activities reflected their success, being well appointed and very comfortable.

You did notice, though, that many of the people you met, whatever their status in life, seemed very home oriented. They were generally well-educated and professionally active, often very well-respected, but liked to go home and be with their families rather than partying to all hours. Others of the citizens of Norsworthy, who leaned toward the female side in numbers, seemed to be steeped in tradition and spent much of their time at the office, often going back in at night to "do their duty" and complete a task if they felt they had left something undone at quitting time.

Using the results reported in the Roper Starch Worldwide study, how would you characterize each of the groups discussed above?

7. Your contemporaries who were heavily into education and technology would probably be classified by Roper-Starch as
   a. Devouts.
   b. Altruists.
   c. Apparatchiks.
   d. High pragmatics.
   e. Creatives.

8. Your mellower contemporaries are probably
   a. Devouts.
   b. Altruists.
   c. Strivers.
   d. High pragmatics.
   e. Fun seekers.

9. The group of people who were active professionally but home-oriented were probably
   a. Strivers.
   b. Altruists.
   c. Creatives.
   d. Intimates.
   e. Sustainers.

10. The people who seemed to be duty-oriented and more traditional would be classified as
    a. Strivers.
    b. Integrators.
    c. Devouts.
    d. Intimates.
    e. Sustainers.

Contemporary Marketing

Name_____ Instructor_____

Section_____ Date_____

Surfing the Net

Keeping in mind that addresses change and what's on the Web now may have changed by the time you read this, let's take a look at some of the places on the Net that reflect aspects of segmentation, targeting, and positioning. We are not endorsing or recommending any of these sources, merely making note of the information and services that people have elected to offer through the Internet.

How targeted can you get? The restaurant industry is an excellent example. There are Web sites for a number of fairly specialized restaurant chains on the Web. Consider Bagel Oasis at **http://www.bageloasis.com** or a California chain, The Fish Market, which can be reached at **http://www.thefishmarket.com**. If you like pretzels, try Kim and Scott's Pretzels at **http://www.great-pretzels.com**.

Among soft-goods retailers (that's firms that sell clothes), the Net offers a number of interesting possibilities. One site is operated by Casual Male, a big and tall men's chain. They're at **http://www.thinkbig.com**. Looking for women's clothing? No problem. Active Body, in Scottsdale, Arizona, offers wardrobe consultations for the active woman; Any Wear, on the other hand, claims to offer comfortable, stylish clothing designed to mix and match, and at reasonable prices, on their Web site. Try **http://www.activebody.com** for Active Body and **http://www.any-wear.com** for Any Wear.

Here's another classic example of a well-segmented market – the retail record industry. The nation's largest vendor of classical music, Allegro Corporation, is on the net at **http://www.teleport.com/~allegro**. You don't groove on the classics? Try Insomnia, the punk-oriented outlet that even has cutout bins where you might even find that really great *Runesong* album. Go for it at **http://www.insomnia.com**. Want to go a step further? If Reggae and Ska are your kettle of fish, why not try **www.reggaeexpress.com/wgi2.html** for an extensive selection of reggae, ska, and related musical styles.

Sites verified December 20, 1999.

Name_____ Instructor_____

Section_____ Date_____

Cases for Part 3

1. The O'Leary Glass Company

The O'Leary Glass Company is a medium-sized producer of drinking vessels located in Muncie, Indiana. The company produces three lines graduated by increasing size and somewhat different appearance: mugs, schooners, and flagons. Management has recently become concerned because sales have declined from $2,000,000 last year to $1,600,000 this year. In an effort to find the source or sources of the decline in sales, they have performed a sales and costs analysis of company field operations. The firm maintains three regional sales forces: the northern force, the central force, and the southern force, each of which calls on sixteen of the contiguous states. The northern force also handles Alaska and the Aleutian Islands, the central force represents the company in the Hawaiian Islands and other U.S. Pacific territories such as Guam and American Samoa, and the southern force handles Puerto Rico and the Virgin Islands. The results of the company's sales and cost analysis appear in Table P3-1.

Table P3-1: The O'Leary Glass Company

Sales Performance By Sales Force Area: Last Year versus This

Area: Year:	Northern Last	Northern This	Central Last	Central This	Southern Last	Southern This	Total Last	Total This
Sales*	$1000	$1160	$600	$200	$400	$240	$2000	$1600
Cost of Sales	600	920	360	120	240	120	1200	1080
Gross Margin	400	240	240	80	160	120	800	440
Marketing Expenses	280	200	200	20	120	20	600	240
Area Contrib.	$120	$40	$40	$60	$40	$100	$200	$200
Product Sales by Area								
Mugs	$300	$500	$100	$100	$100	$100	$500	$700
Schooners	200	600	300	80	0	120	500	800
Flagons	500	60	200	20	300	20	1000	100
Totals	$1000	$1160	$600	$200	$400	$240	$2000	$1600

*All numerical values are in thousands of dollars (x 000)

Questions

Having examined the information contained in Table P3-1, answer the following questions.

a. What are the problems facing the O'Leary Glass Company?

b. What other information, if any, would you need prior to suggesting action to correct the problems?

2. The Four Wise Men[1]

Once upon a time, in a far and distant land, there lived four wise and learned men who were, unfortunately, blind.

And one day there came unto them a traveler who had been to an even more remote land where he had acquired a handsome elephant. Now this stranger knew that the four wise men had the ear of the king and if they would but go to his majesty and extol the virtues of his wondrous beast, his fortune would assuredly be made. Accordingly, he appealed to the wise men to come and examine his new acquisition so they could go forth and tell the king what they found the animal to be like. The wise men agreed, but being wise, they did not wish to hear a sales talk from the elephant's owner. He was allowed to leave with the elephant only a voiceless mahout to hold the animal's rein while the wise men conducted their examination. The wise men, meanwhile, had agreed to keep their own counsel (mouths shut) about their opinions of the new animal, even among themselves.

The first wise man approached the elephant, and, feeling about, encountered the animal's facile and active trunk. Grasping it and feeling it writhe about in his hands, he thought, "A-ha; this animal is very much like a snake." And so thinking, he withdrew and allowed the second wise man to approach the animal.

---

[1] This story, in one or another of its many forms, appears either in the *Rubyiat* of Omar Khayam or the *Tales of a Thousand and One Nights*, or possibly in both.

The second wise man promptly collided with one of the elephant's massive legs. Feeling the rough, craggy skin of the animal and the huge girth of its leg, this wise man thought, "So! This animal is very much like a tree." The third wise man, after nearly being knocked from his feet by the flapping movement of the elephant's ear and feeling its leathery yet plastic texture, concluded that elephants must be some species of giant bat. The fourth wise man, encountering the tail of the animal, concluded, "This animal must surely be some kind of giant cat."

And each wise man, thinking his own thoughts, left the elephant's stall to report to the king.

Questions

a. If the elephant as a whole described the population the four wise men were to sample, how representative of that population do you suppose their four samples are?

b. What sort of sample did each wise man take? Answer in the context of the descriptions of sampling methods in your text.

c. What changes in the method of sampling and the analysis of the information gained from the samples would you advise the wise men to use the next time they are called upon to describe some innovation to the king (provided their credibility and their heads survive this experience).

3. U. S. Grain Exports to Europe: The Data Looks Good But How About the Interpretation?

As part of an assignment for the United States Department of Commerce, a marketing researcher interviewed officials of grain importing and processing firms in several European countries. These interviews, which were completed during the late 1990s, were designed to field-test two survey questionnaires which it was hoped would improve the process of evaluation of the success of U.S. efforts to export grain to Europe.

Many of the European officials with whom the researcher discussed the questionnaires took advantage of the opportunity to complain about a problem with which they were concerned. They lamented what they reported was the deteriorating quality of U.S. grain shipments to their part of the world. Their specific complaints were that the shipments contained excessive quantities of dirt and other foreign matter. The researcher was urged to report this problem to U.S. officials in order to reinforce the foreign officials' previous requests that the quality of grain shipments be brought up to U.S. domestic standards.

Before departing for home, the researcher discussed the problem with an official at the U.S. Embassy in the country from which he was leaving. The embassy staff member replied, "Oh, you've got to watch out for these buyers; they're shrewd. The grain they're receiving now was bought under cash grain contracts for future delivery at prices that are higher than the spot market price today. In other words, because they agreed several months ago to the price and terms of the deal to buy the grain they're getting now, they've got to pay more for it than if they bought it today. They're just looking for an excuse to get out of these costly contracts. Don't worry about their complaints. It happens often that when grains have been contracted for future delivery at a high price and the market falls, we get lots of complaints about quality. We have to be careful to separate <u>real</u> quality problems from attempts to deal with market fluctuations."

Not long after the researcher's return to the United States, newspapers broke the first story about the bribery of grain inspectors at a major U.S. port; two months later, a similar situation was reported in another domestic location. It should be noted, however, that grain inspectors would be well aware that the likelihood of detection of substandard shipments would be much higher at ports in advanced industrialized countries than would be the case in a developing nation. It would be much more risky to take a bribe for upgrading shipments to Europe than to some third world countries.

Questions

a. Is this a common type of problem – field-level interpretation and filtering of information (like the embassy official's interpretation of the grain buyers' complaints) – affecting the adequacy of the home office data base?

b. What might have been done by the embassy official in Europe to determine whether the problem was real or the European buyers were trying to take advantage of a situation which probably affected primarily third-world destinations?

c. What control measures might be incorporated into a marketing information system to protect against the possibility of field-level misinterpretation and filtering of data flow?

4. Kaufsaale AG: München Neuhauser-Strasse, Nürnberg, Augsburg, Weihanstephan

Johan Spiegelmann, Managing Director of Kaufsaale AG, a major Bavarian department store chain, is examining the performance of several of his firm's branches. München Neuhauser-Strasse, the company's flagship store, remains one of its best and most consistent performers, increasing its share of the growing Munich market at a rate greater than that of the competition. It now holds 44 percent of downtown department store sales, up from 41 percent two years ago. Given that Munich city trade is up by 14 percent during the same period, Johan feels very good about the store. He is not so comfortable about the stores in Nuremberg and Augsburg, though. Opened with much fanfare just a year ago, the store in Nuremberg, Bavaria's second largest city and a growing tourist and manufacturing center, is off to a slow start. Johan realizes it faces competition from two well established locally owned stores, but feels that ultimately it will move ahead of them and become dominant in the market. In Augsburg, things don't look so hopeful. The once thriving truck-manufacturing city has been suffering for years from the depression in heavy vehicle prices caused by intense competition from Asian-built products. Population is down, incomes are down, and the Kaufsaale store is losing trade to Albrecht's – the Bavarian version of Wal-Mart. Finally, Johan looks at the figures for the store in Weihanstephan. The firm's oldest store opened in 1318, the Weihanstephan store still has on the tips of its third-floor dormers bronze models of the sailing ships that used to bring it the goods that it sold. A solid, steady performer, thought Johan. It's true that Weihanstephan isn't growing very fast, but its people are very loyal to Kaufsaale. The store there continues to hold onto its comfortable market share.

Question

Using the market growth/market share matrix, characterize each of the four Kaufsaale AG stores discussed, and advise Mr. Spiegelmann concerning how they should be treated. Which should receive substantial resource commitments and which not, and why?

5. City Center Cultural Complex

Janelle Van Dortmund, Executive Director of the City Center Cultural Complex in Springfield, is working on a five-year marketing plan. Part of the planning process involves deciding whether the complex should adopt an undifferentiated marketing strategy, a concentrated strategy, or a differentiated strategy. The Cultural Complex has been in existence for some ten years, and its entire history has been one of financial struggle.

The problem lies, in part, in the fact that within ten miles of the Cultural Complex there are two other, similar facilities with very distinct images. *Country Heritage, USA,* appeals to people with an interest in music, art, and crafts activities typical of the development of this country as a rural, individually oriented nation of small farmers and dwellers in small towns. *The Twenty-first Century*, on the other hand, features cultural activities of the most modern sort, from exhibits of the most modern of innovative art to concerts by orchestras and groups so innovative that their names change weekly. Ms. Van Dortmund is well aware that audience studies conducted at cultural centers all across the country have shown that people have very definite likes and dislikes in their cultural pursuits; culture is a very personal thing.

Approximately 20 percent of the residents of Springfield participate in cultural activities of one sort or another on a regular basis. The population has remained stable over the last ten years and will probably not vary much over the next five.

Question

What marketing strategy would you recommend to Ms. Van Dortmund? Should she adopt a concentrated, differentiated, or undifferentiated strategy? Explain your choice.

Creating a Marketing Plan

The information you will receive in this part will help you to complete Part I.C. of your marketing plan for Telabri Industries, Incorporated.

Episode Three: Who's Out There?

Having performed the appropriate rituals and filled out the proper forms, Telabri Industries was now duly and properly incorporated as a Subchapter S corporation under the laws of the state in which it was domiciled. The officers of the corporation were Laura Claire, President; Brian McPatrick, Executive Vice President for Web site development; and Terrence Michaels, Executive Vice President for Web site maintenance and security. Having gotten themselves organized, the three partners decided they needed more information about the nature of the competitive environment if they were to reduce the risk of business failure. They accordingly turned to that standard research volume which the telephone company thoughtfully provides to all of us – but which few of us use to its logical extent – the *Yellow Pages*. Searching through the current *Yellow Page* listings for New Essex, their home city, they discovered 34 firms listed under "Computers – Internet-related services." A telephone survey of these 34 firms revealed that the telephones of two were no longer in service, three were actually located in cities well away from the New Essex metropolitan area, and five actually only serviced computers and modems but didn't develop sites or maintain them. This left 21 firms remaining active in the market as direct competitors of Telabri.

The partners were aware, however, that a number of computer sales firms might have some involvement in Web site development and maintenance. Accordingly, they checked their *Yellow Pages* once again, and determined that, of the 164 firms which survived the same sort of culling process as outlined above, 121 (75%) offered some Web development service, but only 102 (62%) evinced interest in site maintenance, and only 29 did either of these activities for people who were not what they called "regular customers."

Forty-one computer vendors (25%) indicated that they did not do Web-related work, and 24 of these indicated that they did not make any recommendations to their customers about who they could get to create Web sites for them. The 60 "service-and repair" firms in the area were contacted, and none of them offered services to provide a Web presence to customers. None of the 21 companies that were known to be Web site development firms received more than one recommendation from a computer vendor.

The partners, who conducted the two surveys themselves, remarked to each other on an aspect of their work that the raw statistics didn't reveal. As Brian put it, "These computer store people don't seem to care about the Web site market at all. In fact, one guy I called said he knew his firm <u>sold</u> computers, but he wasn't sure about "that Internet thing." Laura responded with, "You know, I noticed that even when I was talking to the places that didn't sell computers; you know, the "service and repair" companies. At eight of the firms I talked to, and I did all the service and repair places, they put me on "hold" when I asked if they developed or maintained Web sites."

"You know something else," piped up Terry, "there are over fifty display ads in the "Computers – Dealers" section of the *Yellow Pages*, but only two displays in the "Internet-related services" section. I wonder why that is?" (A display ad is an ad, usually in a box with pictures and copy text, unlike the usual plain listing in the *Yellow Pages*, and you have to pay extra for it.)

Guidelines:

There are both an objective and a subjective component to the analysis of competition. Apply both quantitative and qualitative analysis to the information presented above to complete part I.C. of your marketing plan.

Part 4

Customer Behavior

A key consideration in the design of marketing mixes is the behavior of consumers. The acts of consumers as they obtain and use products and services depend on personal and interpersonal influences. The family, reference groups, social classes, opinion leadership, and culture are important interpersonal determinants of consumer behavior. Cultural influences are particularly important for international marketers. In the domestic market, understanding subcultures is necessary.

Important personal determinants of consumer behavior are needs, motives, perception, attitudes, and learning. Consumers do not act until they realize they have a need. Motivation depends on which needs have already been satisfied, as is developed in Maslow's hierarchy, and the consumer's perception of those stimuli that have passed through perceptual screens. Attitudes are enduring evaluations, emotional feelings, or action tendencies to an attitude object. Marketers often seek to change attitudes through altering their affective, behavioral, or cognitive components. The amount of time and effort spent on consumer decision making varies for the three categories of (1) routinized response behavior, (2) limited problem solving, and (3) extended problem solving.

The business market is made up of four components: (1) the commercial market, (2) trade industries (wholesalers and retailers), (3) government organizations, and (4) institutions. The business market is typically segmented demographically, by customer type, by end-use application of bought goods, and/or by purchasing situation. Several characteristics differentiate business markets from consumer markets. These include geographic concentration, a relatively small number of buyers, a formal decision-making process, and a unique classifying system – the new North American Industrial Classification System (NAISC). Demand in organizations is different from consumer demand due to such influences as derived demand, volatile demand, joint demand, and inventory adjustments.

Multiple buying influences – environmental, organizational, and interpersonal – are common in organizational purchasing because many individuals may be involved in the purchase of a single item. In addition, the question of whether a firm makes, buys, or leases products may have to be answered. Outsourcing – buying from other firms goods and services formerly produced in-house – has become an issue in the business market. Organizational buying is an eight-step process. The buying center concept is vital to the understanding of business buying behavior. Government, institutional, and international markets each offer their own set of challenges to the marketer seeking to serve them.

Harcourt, Inc.

Chapter 9

Consumer Behavior

Chapter Outline

Use the following as a guide in taking notes.

I. Chapter Overview – People Are Motivated by Personal and Interpersonal Factors

II. Interpersonal Determinants of Consumer Behavior

    A. Cultural influences

        1. Core values in U.S. culture

        2. An international perspective on cultural influences

        3. Subcultures – cultures within a larger culture

    B. Social influences

        1. The Asch phenomenon

        2. Reference groups

        3. Social classes

        4. Opinion leaders

    C. Family influences

        1. Children and teenagers in family purchases

III. Personal Determinants of Consumer Behavior

    A. Needs and motives

        1. Maslow's hierarchy of needs

    B. Perceptions

        1. Perceptual screens

        2. Subliminal perception

    C. Attitudes

          1. Attitude components

          2. Changing consumer attitudes

          3. Modifying the components of attitude

    D. Learning

          1. Applying learning theory to marketing decisions

    E. Self-concept theory

IV.   The Consumer Decision Process

    A. Problem or opportunity recognition

    B. Search

    C. Evaluation of alternatives

    D. Purchase decision and purchase act

    E. Postpurchase evaluation

    F. Classifying consumer problem-solving processes

          1. Routinized response behavior

          2. Limited problem solving

          3. Extended problem solving

V.   Consumer Behavior: Strategic Implications

Part 4 Customer Behavior

Name_____ Instructor_____

Section_____ Date_____

Key Concepts

The purpose of this section is to allow you to determine if you can match key concepts with the definitions of the concepts. It is essential you know the definitions of the concepts prior to applying the concepts in later exercises in this chapter.

From the list of lettered terms, select the one that best fits each of the numbered statements below. Write the letter of that choice in the space provided.

Key Terms

a. customer behavior
b. consumer behavior
c. culture
d. subculture
e. norm
f. status
g. role
h. Asch phenomenon
i. reference group
j. opinion leader
k. need
l. motive
m. perception
n. perceptual screen
o. subliminal perception
p. attitude
q. learning
r. drive
s. cue
t. reinforcement
u. self-concept
v. evoked set
w. evaluative criteria
x. cognitive dissonance

_____ 1. Number of brands that a consumer actually considers before making a purchase decision.

_____ 2. Process by which consumers and business buyers make purchase decisions.

_____ 3. Relative prominence of any individual in a group.

_____ 4. Behavior that members of a group expect of an individual who holds a specific position within it.

_____ 5. Group with which an individual identifies enough that it dictates a standard of behavior for him or her.

_____ 6. Receipt of information at a subconscious level.

_____ 7. Meaning that an individual creates by interpreting a stimulus.

_____ 8. A strong stimulus that impels action.

Harcourt, Inc.

155

Contemporary Marketing

_____ 9. Features that a consumer considers in choosing among alternatives.

_____ 10. Buyer behavior of ultimate consumers.

_____ 11. One's enduring favorable or unfavorable evaluation, emotional feeling, or pro or con action tendency.

_____ 12. Inner state that directs a person toward the goal of satisfying a felt need.

_____ 13. Reduction in drive that results from an appropriate consumer response.

_____ 14. Values, beliefs, preferences, and tastes that are handed down from generation to generation.

_____ 15. Subgroup of a culture with its own distinct modes of behavior.

_____ 16. Occurrence first documented by the psychologist after which it is named that illustrates the effect of a reference group on individual decision making.

_____ 17. Discrepancy between a desired state and the actual state; lack of something useful.

_____ 18. Object existing in the environment that determines the nature of the response to a drive.

_____ 19. Postpurchase anxiety that results when an imbalance exists among an individual's knowledge, beliefs, and attitudes.

_____ 20. The real self, self-image, looking glass self, and ideal self; mental conception of one's self.

_____ 21. Value, attitude, or behavior that a group deems appropriate for its members.

_____ 22. Consumers' mental filtering process through which marketing messages must pass to gain attention.

_____ 23. Individual within a group who serves as an information source for other group members.

_____ 24. Changes in behavior, immediate or expected, that occur as the result of experience.

Part 4 Customer Behavior

Name_____ Instructor_____

Section_____ Date_____

Self-Quiz

You should use these objective questions to test your understanding of the chapter material. Check your answers with those provided at the end of the chapter.

While these questions cover most of the chapter topics, they are not intended to be the same as the test questions your instructor may use in an examination. A good understanding of all aspects of course material is essential to good performance on any examination.

True/False

Write "T" for True and "F" for False for each of the following statements.

____ 1. The basic core values of a culture – such as the work ethic in America – do not change.

____ 2. The three largest and fastest-growing ethnic subcultures in the United States are African Americans, Hispanics, and Asians.

____ 3. American products are not immune from criticism in the rest of the world. Europeans, for example, dislike American milk chocolate, which they consider to be sour and waxy.

____ 4. The interpersonal determinants of consumer behavior include attitudes, learning, and perception.

____ 5. Asian Americans are a homogeneous group because their origins are a number of different cultures and many retain their own languages, religions, and value systems.

____ 6. It has been demonstrated, especially in the case of the Hispanic subculture, that the degree of acculturation has little effect on consumer behavior.

____ 7. The formula $B = f(I,P)$ may be interpreted to mean that the behavior of consumers (B) is a function of the interaction of interpersonal determinants (I), such as attitudes, learning, and perception, and personal determinants (P), like reference groups and culture.

____ 8. The Asch phenomenon suggests that most consumers tend to adhere in varying degrees to the general expectations of any group they consider important to themselves, often without being aware of the motivation.

____ 9. Consumers may be influenced by groups they belong to, groups they desire to associate with, and by groups with which they do not want to be identified.

____ 10. Information sometimes flows from mass media such as radio, newspapers and television to opinion leaders, and then from opinion leaders to others, but this is not the only case in which opinion leadership may occur.

Harcourt, Inc.

_____ 11. Asian Americans tend to be less brand conscious than members of other subcultures.

_____ 12. Studies of family decision making have shown that households with two wage earners are more likely than others to exhibit joint purchasing decision making.

_____ 13. One's role in a group is the relative position that one occupies in that group.

_____ 14. The primary determinants of a person's social class are the person's income, level of education, family background, and type of dwelling in which he or she resides.

_____ 15. Opinion leaders are found within all segments of the population and tend to act as opinion leaders for specific goods and services based on their knowledge of and interest in those products.

_____ 16. Alone and with their parents, children average more than 200 visits to stores per year.

_____ 17. Within the household, syncratic decision making occurs when an equal number of decisions is made independently by each partner.

_____ 18. Closure – the human tendency to perceive a complete picture from an incomplete stimulus – helps marketers to create a message that stands out and breaks through perceptual screens.

_____ 19. Motives are inner states of tension that direct a person toward the goal of satisfying a felt need by taking action to reduce the tension and return to a condition of equilibrium.

_____ 20. A person who flies "First Class" on Virgin Atlantic Airlines so that he or she will be admired and respected by his or her friends is satisfying a need to be accepted by people and groups important to the individual, according to the hierarchy of Abraham Maslow.

_____ 21. The affective component of attitude refers to the individual's information and knowledge about an object or concept.

_____ 22. When a marketer attempts to apply *shaping* to achieve a desired consumer behavior, both promotional strategy and the product itself play a role in the process.

_____ 23. One's self-concept grows only out of the interaction of interpersonal influences that affect one's behavior.

_____ 24. The statement "My friends see me as an outstanding coach and manager," is an example of the component of self-concept known as the ideal self.

_____ 25. The marketing of products such as smoke detectors, insurance, burglar alarms, and safes for valuables appeals to the need for safety characterized by Maslow's hierarchy.

Multiple Choice

Circle the letter of the word or phrase that best completes the sentence or best answers the question.

26. Customer behavior includes
    a. the design of marketing strategies and business practices.
    b. the study of organization theory and practice.
    c. analysis of pricing policies and procedures.
    d. looking at how goods get from the producer to the marketplace.
    e. the way people purchase goods and services for personal use or for use by a business.

27. The typical lifestyle of the U.S. Southwest emphasizes casual dress, outdoor entertaining, and active recreation. This is an example of
    a. how climate and weather affects the way people do things.
    b. the effect of genetic predispositions – Southwesterners naturally prefer the outdoors.
    c. how a subculture develops its own distinctive mode of behavior.
    d. the result of a lack of education about how things should be done.
    e. the youth of the market in the Southwest.

28. Which of the following generalizations about the African-American, Hispanic, and Asian-American subcultures in the U.S. is correct?
    a. There are over 40 million Hispanics now living in the United States.
    b. The African-American population is less conservative in its investments than other groups.
    c. The Asian subculture in the United States is marked by its diversity, actually including more than two dozen different ethnic groups.
    d. Neither African-Americans nor Hispanics tend to be younger than other groups in U.S. society.
    e. The average Hispanic household is smaller than that of the average non-Hispanic.

29. For a reference group to significantly influence a person's behavior
    a. the person must belong to the group.
    b. the group must be composed of opinion leaders.
    c. the product purchased must be in common use; it must not be conspicuous or different.
    d. the product purchased must be one that can be seen by others.
    e. the person has to have daily physical or electronic contact with the group.

30. When they decide to purchase a product that's new to them, consumers
    a. usually have no clue and go straight to a store to get help from a sales rep.
    b. often rely for information on opinion leaders who can share their experiences and opinions by word of mouth.
    c. seek out professional experts on the product to get the most reliable information about what's current.
    d. probably buy a specialized shopper's guide and read every ad and product review.
    e. put it off for a while, knowing that as time goes along, they'll become more knowledgeable about the product and can make a better decision.

31. Self-help cassette tapes which feature relaxing music or the sound of the ocean audible only at a conscious level and, at a level imperceptible to the ear, messages such as "Quit smoking," or "Work smarter, not harder," use

a. perceptual screening to keep out the lower-level messages; the ocean sounds, however, are very nice.
b. the concept of subliminal perception to impress the desired message on the listener's subconscious; such messages, however, have little real effect.
c. our need, according to Maslow, for self-actualization to cause us to take some desired action.
d. selective perception as a cue which allows us to choose to listen to the music or the lower-level message.
e. the Asch effect as a basis for their operation.

32. A cue is
    a. any object in the environment that determines the nature of the response to a drive.
    b. the individual's reaction to motives and drives.
    c. changes of behavior which come about as the result of experience.
    d. the reduction in drive that results from an appropriate response to it.
    e. the process by which consumer decisions change over time.

33. Which of the following is a correct description of a specific need?
    a. safety need – purchase of a bulletproof vest for protection from physical harm
    b. social need – joining an exclusive club to achieve recognition and respect
    c. self-actualization need – taking a sea cruise to be with your friends
    d. physiological need – enrolling in an adult education class to develop unrealized potential
    e. esteem need – enrolling in a local health club to increase personal longevity

34. Which of the following is a good way to ensure that customers will receive an advertising message?
    a. Decrease the size of ads in newspapers and magazines – increase their "boutique" nature.
    b. Use black and white rather than full-color in newspaper ads.
    c. Create ads that leave it to the imagination of the reader or viewer to fill in missing words or to complete the concept – rely on closure to get the message across.
    d. Make the presentation less intense – avoid the use of virtual reality devices.
    e. Do everything you can to circumvent word-of-mouth promotion – it never helps.

35. Which of the following is an example of a comment reflecting the cognitive component of attitude?
    a. "I just LOVE going to Foodie's Kitchen to buy take-out. It always smells SO good!"
    b. "I intend to buy a new red BMW when I get my next promotion."
    c. "Light blue is my favorite color."
    d. "It must be a good movie – the stars are my favorites."
    e. "The best food value for the money is at Rouse's Supermarkets."

36. Jahn Hankammer ate dinner at the Bon Ton Café because he wanted to use the 20% discount coupon that he had clipped from a newspaper ad. He was so impressed with the food and the service that he plans to return to the Bon Ton tomorrow night. Which of the following is a correct description of a component of the process of learning in this example?
    a. drive – newspaper coupon
    b. response – clip coupon
    c. drive – cheap price
    d. reinforcement – quality food and service
    e. drive – desire for money

37. "Be all that you can be – in today's Army" is the U. S. Army's appeal to you to make your
    a. real self more like your ideal self.

b. looking-glass self more like your real self.
   c. utopian self more like your looking-glass self.
   d. ideal self more like your utopian self.
   e. none of the above.

38. Which of the following correctly describes a stage in the consumer decision making process?
    a. postpurchase evaluation – read newspaper ads to find dealers who sell the desired product.
    b. problem or opportunity recognition – discover that any of several brands would be satisfactory for your intended use.
    c. search – buy the desired product at the nearest store.
    d. alternative evaluation – create a set of evaluative criteria with which to analyze possible choices.
    e. purchase act – discover that you don't have any toothpaste.

39. The marketing implications of cognitive dissonance are that
    a. buyers do not re-evaluate their purchases after they've paid their money.
    b. the postpurchase evaluation process only occurs for products of low dollar value.
    c. it may be desirable for the vendor to provide information that supports the chosen alternative.
    d. dissatisfied customers do not change their behavior in the future.
    e. consumers will be dissatisfied regardless of the quality or price of the product.

40. Which of the following would be a likely factor on which a subculture might be based?
    a. the average age of a group of people – teenagers, for example, versus retired persons
    b. the type of location in which a group of people live – rural versus urban dwellers
    c. religious affiliation of a group of people – Catholics versus Methodists
    d. the national origin of a group – Guatemalans versus Hondurans
    e. All of the above may be bases for a subculture.

41. In the consumer decision process,
    a. the most common cause of problem recognition is usually a change in the consumer's financial status.
    b. subjective impressions of a product should have no role at any level.
    c. the alternatives are narrowed to a single option after the choice of purchase location is made.
    d. the search identifies alternative brands for consideration and possible purchase.
    e. consumers are seldom satisfied even if the purchase exceeds their every expectation.

42. You are attending a party at the home of a friend and are introduced to Lieutenant Commander Cheryl Harrison of the U.S. Navy. From this introduction, you know
    a. Commander Harrison's role within an aspirational group.
    b. Commander Harrison's status within a membership group.
    c. Commander Harrison's social class position in society.
    d. Commander Harrison's role within a dissociative group.
    e. Very little about the Commander; certainly none of the above.

43. Being an opinion leader
    a. goes with the territory – A person who is an opinion leader in one situation will probably be an opinion leader in all situations.
    b. is product and service specific. Knowledge of and interest in the item under consideration motivates leadership.
    c. tends to induce one to delay purchasing new products so as not to make mistakes which will be visible to your followers.

Harcourt, Inc.

d. is generally a role that goes with high visibility and upper social class status.
e. means that your followers expect you to take information from them and to use that information to make decisions for them.

44. When the flow of information about products, retail outlets, and ideas passes from the mass media to one layer of opinion leaders and then to another layer of opinion leaders before it reaches the general public,
    a. you have an example of a "Texas two-step" process of communication.
    b. the flow is what is known as "direct."
    c. the process can be characterized as a "hypodermic needle" communications system.
    d. you have a typical "multistep flow of communications."
    e. none of the above is a good description of what's happening.

45. In the consumer decision process, the gathering of information related to the attainment of a desired state of affairs is part of
    a. the stage of problem or opportunity recognition.
    b. attitude modification – changes that have to take place before action results.
    c. the third step in the decision process – evaluation of alternatives.
    d. the purchase decision – actually committing resources to one's choice.
    e. the search process – identifying alternative means of solving the problem.

46. When an individual joins an elite country club, buys a "prestige" automobile, or takes a course in opera appreciation to know more than others about the subject, he/she is probably seeking to satisfy his/her
    a. social needs.
    b. safety needs.
    c. esteem needs.
    d. self-actualization needs.
    e. physiological needs

47. If a marketer were to seek to shape a consumer's response pattern to the marketer's product by reinforcement, a good program to follow might be
    a. first, to distribute cents off coupons of moderate value; then, if a purchase resulted, to include in the bought goods a higher value coupon.
    b. first, to distribute free samples of the product accompanied by a substantial cents off coupon; if a purchase resulted, to include in the bought goods a coupon of lower value.
    c. first, to advertise the product heavily to the target market; then, if a purchase resulted, offer free merchandise by mail to responding buyers.
    d. first, to redesign the product package; then, promote heavily to a new, untapped market segment.
    e. first, to require of all retailers who wished to stock the product that they buy at least ten cases in their first order; then, insist that stock levels be maintained at least at that level in all subsequent orders.

48. When a group defines the values, attitudes, and behaviors that it deems appropriate for its members, it has set the group's
    a. norms.
    b. status criteria.
    c. role relationships.
    d. proprietary values.
    e. membership.

49. In the problem-solving process, the "evoked set" includes
    a. those brands and types of product which the consumer actually considers in making a purchase decision.
    b. only those brands and types of product suitable for the desired purpose with which the consumer may have had previous experience as a user.
    c. all brands and types of product which may be capable of satisfying the perceived need, whether known to the individual or not.
    d. only one product – the one that's ultimately chosen by the consumer.
    e. a listing of the various problems which the consumer seeks to solve along with some scheme to prioritize them.

50. Mel Jacobs has decided it's time to buy a refrigerator. To help him in his efforts, he has bought several issues of *Modern Home Appliance* magazine, visited several appliance stores, and carefully read all the sales literature with which they have provided him. He is ready to make his choice from the four models that he believes meet his needs. Mel's problem-solving behavior exemplifies
    a. routinized response behavior.
    b. limited problem solving.
    c. extreme problem solving.
    d. extended problem solving.
    e. outrageous problem solving.

Contemporary Marketing

Name_____   Instructor_____

Section_____   Date_____

Applying Marketing Concepts

Aldo Ludovico was glad, in a way, to be coming home. After eight years away, first at college in the northeast, then for graduate study at a large southern university, it was nice to know he'd soon be seeing his parents, grandparents, and great-grandparents again. To himself he admitted, though, that he was going to have to readjust to his family's way of doing things. During his years away from home, he'd gotten used to doing things pretty much his own way, keeping his own hours, and making decisions for himself. He knew that some of that would have to change if he wanted to stay on good terms with the Ludovico clan.

One of the first things that he knew was going to cause difficulty was his intention to have his own apartment near the medical facility where he was to be employed. Aldo was concerned that great-grandfather Giuseppe might want him to live at Villa Ludovico "just for a while" so that the family could reintroduce him to the local Italian-American community. Aldo knew that, even if great-grandfather Giuseppe Ludovico approved of his decision to live away from the family center, he was going to want to go with Aldo (possibly even bringing along a number of other members of the family) when he went apartment hunting. And Aldo was concerned that his great-grandfather would try and bargain with the landlord over the rent or as to who would pay the utilities. Aldo had seriously considered taking a position far away from home, being quite concerned about the levels of influence he was sure his family was going to bring to bear on him, but he had always felt comfortable in Napa Valley and, after all, there certainly were a lot more young Italian-Americans there than there had been in Pottstown or Atlanta.

Wondering a little bit about how long it would take for him to brush up on his Italian so he could keep up and hold his own in his family's mile-a-minute conversations and then breathing a small sigh, Aldo gathered up his possessions and left the plane.

Write "T" for True or "F" for False for each of the following statements.

_____ 1. Part of Aldo's interest in the number of Italian-Americans in Napa Valley may have had something to do with the fact that Italian-Americans like to operate in an environment that preserves their ethnic identity.

Circle the letter of the word or phrase that best completes the sentence or answers the question.

2. Aldo's thoughts about there being "more young Italian-Americans in Napa Valley than in Pottstown or Atlanta" reflects the idea that
    a. Italian-Americans who live in the east and south have tended to be assimilated into the general population.
    b. Aldo thought of himself as an Italian-American and wished to remain related to that culture.
    c. Aldo didn't really know where to look to find persons of his own ethnic group. Pottstown and Atlanta have large ethnic Italian populations.
    d. Aldo was such an unusual young man, having a much higher level of education than is typical of Italian-Americans.

3. Aldo's worries about apartment shopping stemmed from the Italian custom(s)
   a. of shopping as a family group.
   b. of allowing buying decisions to be made by a family elder.
   c. of bargaining over almost any purchase.
   d. all of the above were part of his concern.

4. Aldo realized he'd have to brush up on his Italian because
   a. his family, like many Italian-American families, spoke the language at home and when dealing with other ethnic Italians.
   b. it's always a good idea to have working knowledge of a second language.
   c. he knew that his work would require him to use Italian a lot.
   d. Italian is such a complex language that it must be used constantly or you forget it.

For several years, Max O'Reilly has been a successful amateur golfer. Ranked seventh in his home state, he had long favored PingPro Pilot clubs. Recently, though, he had been having problems with his old clubs (he was growing and they weren't) and had decided to invest in a new set. Though he wasn't fabulously wealthy, his standing in the sport meant that he felt that he had to buy the best equipment for this special activity, so he started looking for the best clubs money could buy.

He spoke with friends at his country club about their preferences in clubs and became convinced that he would be more credible on the course and would have a psychological advantage if he switched to Syracuse Augusta clubs. Max's brother, golf pro at a nearby club, opposed the change because he thought the Syracuse clubs weren't as durable as the PingPro. Max continued to read golf magazines, talk to friends, and check advertisements for the Syracuse line. Ultimately, he decided to buy the Augusta set.

Next, he had to decide where to buy his new golf clubs. The alternatives available were two local dealers and a mail-order firm located only 100 miles away in Capital City. All three of these dealers stocked the clubs Max wanted, but the mail-order house's price was substantially lower than the other two outlets. Max finally ordered his golf clubs from the mail-order house, "Proclub Golf."

The following week, Max's clubs arrived. He immediately drove over to the country club to show his brother his new acquisition and convince him he'd made the right decision. Unfortunately, on the fourth hole of the front nine, the head of Max's beautiful new three-wood took off after the ball. Max began to feel doubtful about his purchase. Standing there in front of his brother holding his brand-new – but headless – club, he would have liked to tell "Proclub Golf" what to do with their clubs – keep 'em!

Write "T" for True or "F" for False for each of the following statements.

_____ 5. Max was mainly concerned with his ideal self.

_____ 6. Need arousal occurred in Max because of dissatisfaction with the clubs he already owned.

_____ 7. Max bought his new clubs because of subliminal perception.

_____ 8. Max is probably a member of the lower class.

_____ 9. Max's search for alternatives was affected by both personal and interpersonal factors.

Contemporary Marketing

Circle the letter of the word or phrase that best completes the sentence or answers the question.

10. Max's decision to buy the Augusta clubs because of his friends' influence helped satisfy which of the following level of needs?
    a. physiological
    b. safety
    c. social
    d. esteem
    e. self-actualization

11. If Maslow's theory of needs is true for Max, he has at least partially satisfied which of the following levels of needs?
    a. physiological
    b. safety
    c. social
    d. all of the above.
    e. none of the above.

12. For this purchase, the most important influence on Max was the
    a. social class.
    b. reference group.
    c. culture.
    d. attitude.
    e. family.

13. Max's postpurchase doubt about his purchase is an example of
    a. cognitive dissonance.
    b. subliminal perception.
    c. psychotic imbalance.
    d. psychographic influence.
    e. status loss.

14. Max may have learned not to buy Syracuse clubs because
    a. reinforcement did not take place.
    b. no drive was present.
    c. his response was inconsistent with his drive.
    d. the cues were correct.
    e. he could find a better price elsewhere.

Part 4 Customer Behavior

Name_____ Instructor_____

Section _____ Date_____

Surfing the Net

Keeping in mind that addresses change and what's on the Web now may have changed by the time you read this, let's take a look at some of the places on the Net that reflect aspects of consumer behavior. We are not endorsing or recommending any of these sources, merely making note of the information and services that people have elected to offer through the Internet.

Tired of letting someone else drive? Learn to fly using information you can get at **http://www.avhome.com/fschools.html**. This site features an extensive list of flight schools of all sorts, from colleges and universities with flight programs to independent local firms that will teach you how to soar in the cerulean blue. That one not good enough for you? Try **http://www.aopa.org/learntofly/startfly/**, a site maintained by the Aircraft Owners' and Pilots' Association. This site offers a lot of advice on the right way to go about learning how to fly.

Been ripped off on the Web? There is a site devoted to complaints. It's at **http://www.abuse.net** and lets you complain about any Web site you feel has caused you a problem, whether by misrepresentation or fraud or even just plain bad taste. Need to vent your spleen about someone or something in cyberspace? That's the place to go.

Remember the Swedish Chef on The Muppet Show? Apparently lots of people do, and he's alive and well at **http://www1.mhv.net/~guito/chef2.htm** There's no accounting for taste, and here's a classic example. This site is devoted to news and comment on the well-loved character. As if that weren't enough, you can even access "encheferizer" software that turns normal English into "chefspeak" by going to **http://www.rinkworks.com/dialect**. This site also features translators that will turn normal English into several other dialects as well.

Love junk food? Get in touch with The Twinkies Project. This hilarious site deals with the results of scientific (?) testing of these little goo-filled cakes. Bring your own milk when you try **http://www.twinkiesproject.com**.

Need a car – or better yet, a price on one? There are several sites that offer all sorts of information, deals, financing, and other features related to buying a new car. Try **http://www.carbuyer.com** for all the basics. An alternative is **http://carseverything.com**. If you're interested in buying a used car and want to know how to spot a bad deal, check out **http://www.e-lemon-aider.com**. These people sell a video tape on what to look for in a used car, but their Web site offers a lot of information for free as well.

Sites verified December 27, 1999.

Harcourt, Inc.

Chapter 10

B2B: Business-to-Business Marketing

Chapter Outline

Use the following as a guide in taking notes.

I. Chapter Overview – Participants in the Business Market: B2B Defined

II. The Nature of the Business market

    A. Components of the business market: trade, resellers, government, institutions

        1. B2B Markets – The Internet Connection

    B. Differences in foreign business markets

III. Segmenting business-to-business markets

    A. Demographic segmentation

    B. Segmentation by customer type

        1. NAICS

    C. Segmentation by end-use application

    D. Segmentation by purchasing situation

IV. Characteristics of the B2B Market

    A. Geographic market concentration

    B. Sizes and numbers of buyers

    C. The purchase decision process

    D. Buyer-seller relationships

    E. Evaluating international business markets

V. Business Market Demand

    A. Derived demand

    B. Joint demand

    C. Volatile demand

Contemporary Marketing

        D. Inventory adjustments

VI.   The Make, Buy, or Lease Decision

        A. The rise of outsourcing

            1. Why Outsource?

        B. Problems with outsourcing

VII.   The Business Buying Process

        A. Influences on purchase decisions: environmental, organizational, interpersonal

            1. Environmental Factors

            2. Organizational Factors

            3. Interpersonal Influences

        B. The eight-stage model of the organizational buying process

        C. Classifying business buying situations

            1. straight rebuy

            2. modified rebuy

            3. new-task buying

            4. reciprocity

        D. Analysis tools: Value and vendor analysis

VIII.   The Buying Center Concept

        A. Buying center roles

        B. Marketing to buying centers: Strategic Implications

        C. International buying centers

IX.   Developing Effective Business-to-Business Marketing Strategies

        A. Challenges of government markets

            1. Government Purchasing Procedures

            2. Online with the Federal Government

Harcourt, Inc.

B. Challenges of institutional markets

C. Challenges of international markets

D. Strategies for marketing to both business purchasers and final users

Contemporary Marketing

Name_____   Instructor_____

Section_____   Date_____

Key Concepts

The purpose of this section is to allow you to determine if you can match key concepts with the definitions of the concepts. It is essential that you know the definitions of the concepts prior to applying the concepts in later exercises in this chapter.

From the list of lettered items, select the one that best fits each of the numbered statements below. Write the letter of that choice in the space provided.

Key Terms

a. business-to-business marketing
b. B2B
c. commercial market
d. trade industry
e. resellers
f. customer-based segmentation
g. North American Industrial Classification System (NAICS)
h. end-use application segmentation
i. global sourcing
j. derived demand
k. joint demand
l. sole sourcing
m. outsourcing
n. multiple sourcing
o. systems integration
p. straight rebuy
q. modified rebuy
r. new-task buying
s. reciprocity
t. value analysis
u. vendor analysis
v. buying center
w. team selling
x. bid
y. specifications
z. remanufacturing

_____ 1. Written description of a needed good or service.

_____ 2. Takes place when goods that were formerly produced in-house are acquired from outside vendors.

_____ 3. Participants in an organizational buying action.

_____ 4. The use of other associates to assist a sales representative's selling efforts aimed at dealing with a buying center.

_____ 5. Centralization of the procurement function within an internal division or as a service of an external supplier.

_____ 6. A first-time or unique purchase situation that requires considerable effort by decision makers.

_____ 7. Written sales proposal from a vendor.

____ 8. Demand for one business product that depends on the demand for a second business product that is required to use the first.

____ 9. Dividing a business-to-business market into homogeneous groups based on buyers' product specifications.

____ 10. Purchasing a firm's entire requirement of a product from a single vendor.

____ 11. Contracting to purchase goods and services from suppliers worldwide.

____ 12. Marketing intermediaries operating in the trade sector of the business-to-business market.

____ 13. The demand for a business product that results from the demand for a consumer product of which it is a part.

____ 14. Popular abbreviation for the business-to-business market.

____ 15. Purchase decision situation in which the purchaser is willing to reevaluate available options for repurchasing a good or service.

____ 16. Segmentation of a business-to-business market based on how industrial purchasers will use the product.

____ 17. Replacement for the Standard Industrial Classification (SIC) now used by NAFTA countries to categorize the business market into detailed segments.

____ 18. Individuals and firms that acquire products (goods and services) to support production of other products whether directly or indirectly.

____ 19. Production process which restores worn-out products to like-new condition.

____ 20. Policy of extending purchasing preference to suppliers who are also customers.

____ 21. Assessment of supplier performance in areas such as price, back orders, timeliness of deliveries, and attention to special requests.

____ 22. Recurring purchase decision in which the customer repurchases a good or service that has performed satisfactorily in the past.

____ 23. Spreading purchases among several vendors.

____ 24. Purchase by organizations of goods and services to support production of other goods and services, for use in daily company operations or for resale.

____ 25. Systematic study of the components of a purchase to determine the most cost-effective way to acquire the needed goods or services.

____ 26. Retailers or wholesalers that purchase products for resale to others.

Contemporary Marketing

Name_____   Instructor_____

Section_____   Date_____

Self-Quiz

You should use these objective questions to test your understanding of the chapter material. You can check your answers with those provided at the end of the chapter.

While these questions cover most of the chapter topics, they are not intended to be the same as the test questions your instructor may use in an examination. A good understanding of all aspects of the course material is essential to good performance on any examination.

True/False

Write "T" for True or "F" for False for each of the following statements.

_____ 1. The commercial market is the largest segment of the business market.

_____ 2. The highest level of industrial concentration in the United States is in the states of the Middle Atlantic region.

_____ 3. Because of the professionalism and expertise of business buyers, the typical business purchase requires less time than is the case with consumer purchasing.

_____ 4. The buying center is a formal group within an organization charged with the responsibility for all purchasing by that organization.

_____ 5. Gatekeepers control the information that all buying center members will review.

_____ 6. The Census of Manufactures and the Census of Retailing and Wholesaling are conducted every ten years by the federal government.

_____ 7. Because the federal government's fiscal year runs from October 1 through September 30, many agencies hoard their funds to cover unexpected expenses and when the need for the funds doesn't arise find themselves with money to spend in late summer.

_____ 8. The NAICS improved on the SIC by creating new service sector classifications to better reflect the economy of the year 2000 and beyond.

_____ 9. Capital items purchased by organizational buyers typically include things such as paper clips, pencils, and related business supplies.

_____ 10. Under a government cost-reimbursement contract, buyer and seller agree to a firm price before the contract is signed.

_____ 11. Demand in the business market is often linked to demand in the consumer market.

Harcourt, Inc.

_____ 12. The business buying process is more complex than the consumer decision process because, among other considerations, it involves many people with complex interactions between them and the organization's goals.

_____ 13. Value analysis would support the use of the material Kevlar for aircraft components because it weighs less than the metals it can replace, creating significant fuel savings.

_____ 14. Most business goods can be made internally by the firms that need them; indeed, this is the most common source for such goods.

_____ 15. The North American Industrial Classification System, because it lacks detail, is of little use for segmenting markets and identifying new customers.

_____ 16. Acquiring and analyzing supplier proposals is the fifth stage of the organizational buying process.

_____ 17. Just-in-time II (JIT II) inventory policies involve suppliers placing representatives at the customer's facility to work as part of an integrated, on-site customer-supplier team.

_____ 18. The South Atlantic Coastal part of the United States – the Carolinas, Georgia, and Florida – leads the nation in industrial concentration.

_____ 19. Systems integration disperses the procurement function throughout the firm or organization so as to be nearer the point of need.

_____ 20. Selecting an order routine, the activity in which buyer and vendor work out the best way to process future purchases, is the last stage of the organizational buying process.

_____ 21. Marketers who want to ensure continuing straight rebuys should concentrate on maintaining good relationships with buyers by providing excellent service and delivery performance.

_____ 22. The commercial market includes manufacturing firms, farmers and members of other resource producing industries, construction contractors, and providers of such services as transportation, public utilities, finance, insurance, and real estate brokerage.

_____ 23. Though the number of buyers in any segment of the business market is usually quite large, geographical concentration makes it easy to serve them all.

_____ 24. In a buying center situation, people in the decider's role supply information for the evaluation of alternatives or set buying specifications.

_____ 25. The trade industries include retailers and wholesalers that purchase for resale to others.

Multiple Choice

Circle the letter of the word or phrase that best completes the sentence or answers the question.

26. The business-to-business market is also known as
    a. trade or reseller industries.
    b. the organizational market.

c. the government market.
d. the institutional market
e. the commercial market

27. Which of the following is not a component of the business market?
    a. the commercial market
    b. trade industries
    c. government organizations
    d. consumer services
    e. institutions

28. The truck has become the vehicle of choice for the consumer, largely because of the popularity of sport utility vehicles. As a result, sales of the larger tires required for these vehicles have increased significantly. This is an example of what phenomenon?
    a. derived demand
    b. joint demand
    c. demand variability
    d. inventory adjustments
    e. specific demand

29. Because business buyers are geographically concentrated, relatively few in number, and the purchase decision process they use is so complex,
    a. the marketing channel for industrial goods is typically much longer than for consumer goods.
    b. wholesalers are more frequently used to handling their business than they are in the consumer goods field.
    c. the relationship between buyers and sellers is more intense than consumer relationships and they require better communications among the organizations' personnel.
    d. advertising plays a much larger role in the industrial market than it does in the consumer market.
    e. personal selling is seldom used as the promotional tool of choice by vendors to this market.

30. The largest single source of statistics to estimate the sizes and characteristics of business markets is
    a. advertising.
    b. trade listings.
    c. the federal government.
    d. a buying center.
    e. distributors' guides.

31. Which of the following properly defines the NAICS Code for U.S. firms engaged in the reproduction of software?
    a. 33461
    b. 334
    c. 33461
    d. 334611
    e. 33

32. CableBox, Inc., the hypothetical manufacturer of cable signal decoders mentioned in your text, has based its products on analog technology for the last ten years. If it were suddenly to decide to change over to digital technology, its decoders would have to be massively redesigned for the new technology. The buying situation for components would then probably change from
    a. modified rebuy to straight rebuy conditions.
    b. straight rebuy to modified rebuy conditions.

c. modified rebuy to new-task buying conditions.
d. straight rebuy to new-task buying conditions.
e. new-task buying to modified rebuy conditions.

33. Which of the following would you expect to have no effect on an organizational buyer's purchase process?
    a. the complexity of the decisions which must be made
    b. the existence of competing proposals
    c. the formality and professionalism of the purchasing process
    d. the necessity to meet technical requirements and specifications
    e. All of the above would have some effect on the purchase process.

34. Vendor analysis may be defined as
    a. securing needed products at the best possible price.
    b. using a professional buyer to systematize purchasing.
    c. examining each component of a purchase in an attempt either to delete the item or replace it with a more cost-effective substitute.
    d. convening a committee which will be charged with all the buying responsibility for the firm.
    e. evaluating suppliers' performance in categories such as price, back orders, delivery time, and attention to special requests.

35. A competitor seeking to win over another vendor's straight rebuy customers by converting the straight rebuy situation to a modified rebuy should
    a. raise issues that will make customers reconsider their purchasing decisions.
    b. work to sell other accounts; these accounts are in the other vendor's bag.
    c. hope that the other vendor will maintain a high standard of delivery and service; this bores customers and makes them more likely to listen to other vendors.
    d. try and convince the customers that the buying situation is entirely new or completely unique.
    e. recognize that a paper clip is a paper clip and try to sell the customers other products.

36. In the buying center, the role filled by the individual who decides which salespeople will be allowed to see the engineers responsible for developing specifications is the
    a. user.
    b. gatekeeper.
    c. decider.
    d. influencer.
    e. buyer.

37. Most government purchases, by law, must be made on the basis of
    a. the availability of the most graft to the greatest number.
    b. book value of the item needed.
    c. estimates prepared by government personnel.
    d. cost/benefit studies of the goods required.
    e. bids – written sales proposals from vendors.

38. The firm's purchasing department and its staff of professional buyers
    a. are responsible for procuring needed products regardless of the price.
    b. do not incorporate periodic buying decisions with other activities.
    c. devote some of their time and effort to determining needs, evaluating supplies, and making purchase decisions.
    d. treat purchase decisions for capital items exactly as they treat those for expense items.

e. avoid using systematic procedures; keep suppliers confused about what's going to happen next.

39. Which of the following is typically a part of the fourth stage of the organizational buying process?
    a. recognition of a problem, need, or opportunity
    b. search for and identification of potential suppliers
    c. determination of characteristics of and quantity of a needed good or service
    d. selecting an order routine
    e. acquisition and analysis of proposals

40. Which of the following characteristics is most typical of the business-to-business market?
    a. a more formal, professional, and complex decision process
    b. geographic dispersion of members of the market
    c. large number of buyers of a given class of goods
    d. purchases are never made for resale, only for use in production
    e. public benefit is primary motivation of the market

41. As a general rule, a significant difference between domestic buying centers and the buying centers of foreign companies is that the foreign buying center
    a. tends to have members who are more difficult to identify than is the case in the U.S.
    b. will usually be operated by staff, rather than line, personnel.
    c. is often much smaller than is usually the case in the U.S.
    d. is seldom affected by cultural differences in decision making.
    e. is usually unresponsive to political and economic trends.

42. Which of the following organizations would be considered a member of the institutional sector of the business market?
    a. Metropolitan Life and Casualty Insurance Company of New York
    b. First American Bank of Destrehan
    c. The American Red Cross, South Alabama Chapter
    d. National Stock and Bond Trading Corporation of St. Louis
    e. Rubenstein Brothers Men's Clothing Store, New Orleans

43. Which of the following is typical of the buying practices that have been evident in the federal government market during the last several years?
    a. Extensive corruption because each agency maintains its own procurement department
    b. Greater difficulty in meeting specifications because of the executive order which requires that all vehicles owned by the federal government have some military usefulness in the event of war
    c. Allocation of resources to departments which have shown the greatest ability to spend their budget allotment
    d. Development of unit-system costing techniques to reduce the cost of particular government operations
    e. The influence of social goals such as minority subcontracting programs

44. As evidence of the importance of the Internet in business-to-business marketing, it should be realized that
    a. though the bulk of e-commerce is consumer-based, almost 15 percent of business-to-business sales occur on the Internet.
    b. a far larger number of e-commerce vendors are targeted to consumers than to the business-to-business market, yet business customers account for at least 20 percent of their sales.
    c. about 70 percent of all Internet sales are business-to-business transactions, and estimates note that by the year 2003 the Internet will generate almost 10 percent of all B2B sales.

d. the Internet accounts for a much larger volume of business than consumer sales.
e. were it not for government interference, the Internet would account for at least 50 percent of B2B sales.

45. The most complex category of business buying is
    a. new-task buying.
    b. reciprocal arrangements with other firms.
    c. straight rebuys
    d. modified rebuys.
    e. value analysis.

46. A good definition of the business-to-business market should include
    a. recognition that nonprofit organizations are not and cannot be members.
    b. a managerial philosophy oriented toward heavy industry.
    c. the condition that its primary need is meeting the internal demand of the firm.
    d. recognition of the informal nature of its structure and context.
    e. mention of retailers and wholesalers as an integral part of the market.

47. Heldamen Engineering Corporation designs and builds railroad bridges. It has developed a close working relationship with Tennessee Coal and Iron Corporation, one of its suppliers, because TC&I has developed an assortment of steel shapes specifically designed for railroad bridge construction. From this evidence, it can be concluded that TC&I probably segments its market by
    a. using demographics or the type of purchasing situation encountered.
    b. breaking it down into foreign and domestic segments.
    c. analyzing the customer type or purchasing situation encountered.
    d. customer-based or end-use application methods.
    e. analysis of sales made through the Internet.

48. Which of the following would be an example of a member of the trade industries?
    a. The Texas Highway Patrol (State law enforcement agency)
    b. The Missouri School of Mines (an engineering school)
    c. National Metal Stamping Co. (produces steel parts for automobiles)
    d. Ernest F. Ladd Memorial Stadium (a city-owned football stadium)
    e. Lumber Products Company (wood products wholesale and retail)

49. A large change in the demand for a business good that results from a relatively small change in demand for a consumer good
    a. is an example of the volatile nature of business demand based on the accelerator principle.
    b. is very unusual and is symptomatic of supply-chain breakdown. Such conditions seldom exist.
    c. occurs because many business products are subject to conditions of joint demand.
    d. reflects the demands being made on producers by JIT inventory policies.
    e. is called reciprocal reaction to market fluctuations.

50. The practice of extending purchasing preference to firms that are also customers is called
    a. value analysis.
    b. reverse reciprocity.
    c. reciprocity.
    d. professional purchasing behavior.
    e. international trade.

Contemporary Marketing

Name_____   Instructor_____

Section_____   Date_____

Applying Marketing Concepts

Joe House, director of marketing for Kalamat Foernero Company, a meatpacking firm, was pondering two reports that had just arrived in his office. Both were somewhat disturbing because they told him that his firm had lost two major sales to competition that he thought was at least a little bit less than fair. In the first instance, Kalamat had lost out on a contract to supply beef cuts to Lowenhaupt Restaurants because Lowenhaupt had decided to buy from Midwestern Packing Company. Mr. House felt that the decision had been based, not on the quality of Midwestern's product, but on the fact that Midwestern had a substantial interest in Seldon Travel Brokers, a firm that used Lowenhaupt restaurants extensively to provide meals to its tour groups. In the second case, it appeared that Kalamat Foernero had lost out to a Canadian firm on a U. S. Army contract to supply MRE (Meals-ready-to-eat) ration products because the Canadians could supply the needed MREs at a lower price. The Army ignored Kalamat's arguments that the Canadian product would cost substantially more in the long run because of losses in storage because it had a shorter shelf life than that of Kalamat Foernero's product and would become unuseable sooner.

Write "T" for True or "F" for False for each of the following statements.

_____ 1. In all likelihood, Kalamat Foernero had to supply a written sales proposal or bid for the Army contract.

_____ 2. The two episodes outlined involved purchases by members of the commercial and government segments of the organizational market.

Circle the letter of the word or phrase that best completes the sentence or best answers the question.

3. The case of Lowenhaupt favoring Midwestern Packing over Kalamat Foernero was most probably caused by
   a. bribery.
   b. reciprocity.
   c. derived demand.
   d. threats of force or violence.
   e. global sourcing.

4. The NAICS general code for Lowenhaupt Restaurants would probably be
   a. 11; agriculture, forestry, hunting, and fishing.
   b. 42; wholesale trade.
   c. 44-45; retail trade
   d. 48-49; transportation and warehousing.
   e. 72; accommodation and food services.

5. The main reason Kalamat Foernero lost the Army contract was because
   a. price was too high.
   b. their product was of inferior quality.
   c. the Army thought they might be an uncertain source of supply.

Part 4 Customer Behavior

   d. they were unable to provide the needed service.
   e. somebody got bribed.

6. Kalamat Foernero might have gotten the Army contract if
   a. international politics hadn't tainted the decision.
   b. it had pressed the issue of foreign ownership of the Canadian firm.
   c. the Canadian product hadn't been vastly superior in quality.
   d. Midwestern Packing hadn't interfered with the sale.
   e. The Army hadn't heard about the Middledale incident.

Honda, like most Japanese automobile manufacturers, makes extensive use of components made by other firms: electrical equipment from Fujitsu and Toshiba; cooling system and air conditioning components from Nippondenso and Harrison companies; brake parts from Mitsubishi and Japan Brake; tires from Yokohama Tire Company; and turbosuperchargers from both Garret and Airboost. They have even been known to buy whole vehicles from other manufacturers, such as Isuzu. A given Honda may contain parts from as many as fifty different manufacturers.

7. If consumer demand for Honda products declined, demand for Yokohama tires would also decline. This is a case of
   a. reciprocity.
   b. joint demand.
   c. derived demand.
   d. variable supply.
   e. inventory failure.

8. In deciding to buy components from outside suppliers rather than make them themselves, and in choosing the sources from which those parts would be bought, Honda probably bases their decision on
   a. value analysis.
   b. vendor analysis.
   c. a combination of value analysis and vendor analysis.
   d. their desire to be innovative and to be leaders in automotive engineering technology.
   e. their need to keep the price of their cars down.

9. Suppose that Honda management had decided that a two-month inventory of parts was not enough to have on hand to assure that production would continue if the availability of air conditioner compressors was curtailed and increased its stock-on-hand to four months' worth. This would be an example of
   a. an inventory adjustment.
   b. conservative thinking.
   c. demand variability.
   d. derived demand.
   e. reciprocity.

10. The NAICS for Honda Motor Company would have been between
    a. 11-19; agriculture, forestry, fisheries, hunting.
    b. 21-23; mining.
    c. 31-33; manufacturing.
    d. 48-49; transportation and warehousing.
    e. 81-94; services except public or as otherwise noted.

Contemporary Marketing

Name_____   Instructor_____

Section_____   Date_____

Surfing the Net

Keeping in mind that addresses change and what's on the Web now may have changed by the time you read this, let's take a look at some of the places on the Net that reflect aspects of business-to-business marketing. We are not endorsing or recommending any of these sources, merely making note of the information and services that people have elected to offer through the Internet.

Interested in risk on a global level? You can get into investigating international trade at the Global Trade Center at **http://www.tradezone.com/tz/.** Find out what's involved in dealing in everything from falafel to spaghetti in the world market.

Government Business? Browse the *Commerce Business Daily* and see what it's like to consider becoming a supplier of government. The Web site's at **http://www.ld.com/cbd/today/**.

How's Asian business doing? Try the Web site of Nihon Keizai Shimbun (Japan Business News). The English language version of this major firm's news service – they're the people who do the Nikkei Index, Japan's equivalent of the Dow-Jones – is on the Web at **http://www.nikkei.co.jp/enews.** If you prefer a domestic source, try the business section of the *New York Times* at **http://www.nytimes.com/.** Alternatively, you can check practically any business situation at *The Wall Street Journal,* **http://www.wsj.com.**

A general overview? We can't leave out the U. S. Commerce Department's Web site at **http://www.doc.gov.** Numerous subagencies are available at this address that do all sorts of things having to do with business. This is the Department's main Internet Site with links to numerous other sites.

Sites verified December 30, 1999.

Part 4 Customer Behavior

Name_____   Instructor_____

Section_____   Date_____

Cases for Part 4

1. Bledsoe Creative (A Derwenter Company)

Bledsoe Creative, a member of the highly technical Derwenter Group, has developed a new interactive software program for teaching mathematics to children from first to eighth grade that offers a significant improvement in ease of use and effectiveness over products previously available. Their immediate problem is to decide on an appropriate target market so as to maximize profits. The company has been able to acquire a substantial amount of information to aid in making the decision.

The two variables usually used by firms selling this sort of product are family income and number of children in the home in the relevant grade levels. The levels of income used are low (up to $29,999 annual income), medium ($30,000 to $60,000 annual income) and high (more than $60,000 annual income). The categorization of number of children is: one child; two or three children; four or five children; six or seven children; more than seven children.

Four other firms sell products that could be considered similar to Bledsoe's. A sample of the members of each of the income/number of children segments was selected and each member of the sample was asked to try Bledsoe's product and each the four competitive products for a week. These people were then asked to express their preference for the five products by ranking the most preferred as 1 and so on. The average rank assigned to MathQuick (the interim name assigned to the Bledsoe product) is shown in Table P4-1.

Table P4-1: Relative Preference for MathQuick

Income	Number of Children in the Home				
	One	2 or 3	4 or 5	6 or 7	More than 7
Low	5	5	5	5	5
Medium	3	4	2	3	3
High	1	2	3	4	5

The estimated total unit sales for MathQuick's competitors for last year are shown in Table P4-2.

Contemporary Marketing

Table P4-2: Last Year's Sales (in Thousands of Units) for Four Competitive Products

Income	Number of Children in the Home				
	One	2 or 3	4 or 5	6 or 7	More than 7
Low	10,000	8,000	20,000	10,000	2,000
Medium	14,000	12,000	16,000	14,000	10,000
High	6,000	6,000	10,000	12,000	6,000

Finally, the company has estimated the costs of producing one million copies of MathQuick and marketing it to each segment. The selling price has been set at $25 per copy. The cost breakdown is shown in Table P4-3.

Table P4-3: Production and Distribution Costs for Each Segment (in $ millions)

Income	Number of Children in the Home				
	One	2 or 3	4 or 5	6 or 7	More than 7
Low	$6.6	$5.5	$13.2	$4.4	$5.5
Medium	4.4	5.5	12.1	3.85	7.92
High	4.95	5.5	13.75	3.3	8.25

The rankings shown in Table P4-1 are used to determine which of the choices within a category will be ranked highest as a choice possibility. A higher rank automatically results in a choice preference.

Questions

a. Given this information, which target market should the firm choose?

b. What additional information do you feel is necessary to make this target market decision?

c. It may be difficult to actually get the data in quantitative form as presented in these three tables. Which of the information would be the most difficult to gather? The easiest?

2. Southway Homes, Incorporated

Southway Homes, Inc., is in the process of subdividing a tract of land straddling the border between North and South Carolina– so part of it's North South Carolina and the other part's South North Carolina, or something like that. Although the area is essentially rural in nature, it is located within ten miles of a city of 100,000 and within 60 miles of Greensboro, whose population is now over 1 million. The company desires to focus in on a target market but is unsure of the consumer characteristics to use in its segmentation.

Southway has hired a newspaper-clipping firm to provide information about recent advertising by other property developers. Typical headlines taken from recent ads for similar single-family, detached dwelling developments read: "Country-Style Living with Every Modern Convenience," "The Home-Buying Opportunity of the Year FOR ONLY $2,500 DOWN!" and "Total Privacy and a Carefree Lifestyle."

The decisions Southway wants to make include the precise location of the dwellings within the subdivision; whether or not to include recreational features such as a golf course and swimming pool; whether or not to include a small shopping center in its development plans; the size of home (in square feet) to build; and what sorts of exterior design plans to adopt for the homes that it will build.

Question

What characteristics do you think Southway Homes should use when determining the target market?

3. John Huddleston, Househusband

John Huddleston was beginning to wonder if he had truly become a househusband. Though fully employed, the nature of his work (he was a sales engineer for a manufacturer of milling machines in an area of the country densely covered by factories) was such that, unless an emergency occurred, he could schedule his calls at his own convenience. His wife, who was a commodities broker for a large, Chicago-

Contemporary Marketing

based commodity trading house, absolutely, positively had to be in the office when the Chicago Board of Trade opened at 8:00AM, and usually couldn't get away until at least two hours after it closed at 2:00PM. (The Chicago Board of Trade is the equivalent of the New York Stock Exchange for Commodities – trading in wheat, frozen orange juice, pork bellies, and the like.)

This put most of the household chores squarely on John. It was he who woke the kids in the morning, made them breakfast, and drove them to school, his wife having long since left for work. He shopped at the supermarket between calls on customers, and if he had a slack day on his hands, often did laundry and cooked meals. When 3:00 in the afternoon rolled around, John picked up the kids at school, took them to Little League or soccer practice, and got dinner on the table before Susan, his wife, stumbled in the door.

In the evenings and on weekends, husband, wife, and kids pitched in and kept things on an even keel, Susan often cooking and freezing several days' worth of meals on an assembly line basis. Recently, however, there had been less emphasis on cooking and more on all of them having family fun together whenever possible. John was the first to admit, though somewhat sheepishly, that this had become possible because his cooking had become good enough to rival that of his wife's.

John was a happy man; there was no doubt of that in his mind. But he did wonder on occasion if he had become a classic "househusband"?

Questions

a. In what ways does John Huddleston's situation mirror the changes that have taken place in our society in the last 30 years?

b. Of what significance to marketers are scenarios such as the one represented by John as a consumer?

c. How have the changes evidenced in this case affected the segmentation process for consumer goods?

Creating a Marketing Plan

The information you will receive in this part will help you to complete all of Part II of your marketing plan for Telabri Industries, Incorporated.

Episode Four: Where Do We Go From Here?

As episode four begins, we find our young entrepreneurs discussing their long-term plans for the company. They are examining their resources, and attempting to match the potential in the marketplace to their abilities and potentials. They quickly recognize that the potential for the kind of service they plan to offer is quite substantial. If the information they have is correct, then the potential in the local market could be as much as $78,000,000 this year, growing at a rate of somewhere between 14 percent and 33 percent per annum. Their resources, on the other hand, are limited to the $240,000 they have saved or borrowed, plus their own education and talents.

Meanwhile, there are already 21 potentially active competitors in the market, with some 102 others who might someday pose a threat. On the other hand, many of these potential competitors displayed little marketing "savvy" to the partners when they conducted their market survey.

Laura was the first to speak. "Listen, guys," she said, "we have to set some kind of goals for ourselves or we won't have anything to work toward. What do you say we start with the long run and work our way back to the present? I figure that, if we play our cards right, we can get at least 1 percent of the market in five years. What do you think? That would be at least $1,131,000 in volume by then. Do you think we can get that big a market share? We'd have to do at least $375,000 this year and grow by at least 30 to 35 percent a year to get there in five years."

"Do you think that's aiming high enough?" asked Terry. "We've got to get this operation going, which we know is going to cost at least $200,000 if we do it right. We're sure to lose money unless we get a pretty big chunk of the market pretty quick."

"On the other hand," said Brian, "if we aim too high and don't achieve our goals, we may think we've failed when we're really doing well. I figure that we'd be better off looking at bottom line profits rather than share of the market. I think we ought to look to make at least 10 percent profit on sales."

"Look," said Laura, "I'll agree with both of you. I sure hope we can latch onto 1 percent of this market. I hope we can make 10 percent on sales. But remember, we have to do this the customer's way I think we should be available 24 hours a day, seven days a week. That should give us a real advantage over the other companies in the market. Sure, it'll cost a little more at first, but we'll build customer loyalty and probably generate more up-front money from maintenance contracts that way. Besides, I think we're all being too conservative. Remember, we're going <u>after</u> this market, not just giving it lip service.

We really should expect to lose money for the next couple of years. But we'll be offering people what they need, and it's sure to pay off in the long run."

Guidelines:

a. Where are Laura, Terry, and Brian getting the figures they are using in these discussions?

b. Remember that a lot of what happens depends on how actively our heroes pursue their business. Enthusiasm and dedication do count if the market offers sufficient potential in the first place. Summarize their objectives and complete Parts II.A., II.B., and II.C. in your marketing plan.

Part 5

Product Strategy

Products are bundles of physical, service, and symbolic attributes designed to satisfy wants. Products may be classified as either business or consumer products. Consumer products are usually referred to as convenience, shopping, or specialty products. Business products are classified into the six categories of installations, accessory equipment, component parts and materials, raw materials, supplies, and business services.

Product lines are a series of related products. They serve to promote optimal use of resources and enhance a firm's market position. The firm's products mix is its assortment of product lines and individual products.

Firms introducing new products must concern themselves with the stages through which the product will pass from the time it is introduced until it is removed from the market. The product life cycle, with its five stages of introduction, growth, maturity, decline, and death, is a major concept involved in the marketing process. It is important to understand techniques to extend a product's life by extending its product life cycle.

Very important to product strategy decisions are the availability and use of brands, brand names, symbols, trademarks, labeling, and packaging by companies to identify and differentiate their products. The growth of generic, captive, and private brands is a significant topic for today's marketer. Brand extensions, co-branding, and brand licensing have assumed new importance in this field. Consumer knowledge and acceptance of brands also constitute major considerations in the formulation of strategy. In today's litigious society, trademark protection and product safety have become important components of strategic decision making. The adoption process consumers follow in their acceptance of a new product and factors affecting its speed of acceptance must receive attention by marketers if new products are to be successful.

New product planning is an ongoing activity subject to a number of influences that affect the decision to develop a line of products rather than concentrate on a single product. The stages in the new product development process and four methods of organizing for new product development should be reviewed to ensure a thorough knowledge of this subject. Criteria for the deletion of existing products from the product line are also significant.

Defining services requires knowledge of the goods-services continuum. Services are essentially intangible, inseparable from their provider, perishable, difficult to standardize, of highly variable quality, and the buyer may participate in their development and distribution. There is often a gap between the service received and the consumer's expectation of what that service should have been like. A number of classification systems for services have been proposed. Industries providing services are known as tertiary industries.

The marketing of services is subject to the same environmental influences as is the marketing of goods. Services are subject to outsourcing, especially to foreign providers with lower cost structures. Creation of a marketing mix by service providers is somewhat more difficult than is the same task for goods vendors.

Chapter 11

Product Strategies

Chapter Outline

Use the following as a guide in taking notes.

I. Chapter Overview – Product and Service Strategies are Complex Issues

II. What Is a Product?

III. What Is a Service?

    A. Importance of the service sector

IV. Importance of Quality

    A. The Role of Benchmarking

V. Classifying Goods and Services for Consumer and Business Markets

    A. Types of consumer products

        1. Convenience products: impulse items, staple goods, emergency items and services

        2. Shopping products

        3. Specialty products

    B. Applying the Consumer Products Classification System

    C. Types of business products

        1. Installations

        2. Accessory equipment

        3. Component parts and materials

        4. Raw materials

        5. Supplies

        6. Business services

VI. The Marketing Environment for Service Firms

Contemporary Marketing

    A. The economic environment for services

    B. The socio-cultural environment for services

    C. The political-legal environment for services

    D. The technological environment for services

    E. The competitive environment for services

        1. Competition from government

        2. Outsourcing in the service sector

VII. Development of Product Lines

    A. Desire to grow

    B. Optimal use of company resources

    C. Enhancing the company's position in the market

VIII. The Product Life Cycle

    A. Introductory stage

    B. Growth stage

    C. Maturity stage

    D. Decline stage

    E. Strategic implications of the product life cycle concept

        1. Extending the Product Life Cycle

            a. Increasing frequency of use

            b. Increasing the number of users

            c. Finding new uses

            d. Changing package sizes, labels, or product quality

    F. Product deletion decisions

IX. The Product Mix

    A. Product mix decisions

Harcourt, Inc.

B. Marketing mix strategies for services

   1. Service strategy

   2. Pricing strategy for services

   3. Distribution strategy for services

   4. Promotional strategy for services

Contemporary Marketing

Name_____   Instructor_____

Section_____   Date_____

Key Concepts

The purpose of this section is to allow you to determine if you can match key concepts with the definitions of those concepts. It is essential that you know the definitions of the concepts prior to applying the concepts in later exercises in this chapter.

From the list of lettered terms, select the one that best fits in the blank of the numbered statement below. Write the letter of that choice in the space provided.

Key Terms

a. product
b. service
c. goods-services continuum
d. convenience product
e. shopping product
f. specialty product
g. installation
h. accessory equipment
i. industrial distributor
j. component parts and materials
k. raw material
l. supplies
m. MRO item
n. business service
o. product line
p. tertiary industry
q. productivity
r. product mix
s. line extension
t. product life cycle
u. total quality management (TQM)
v. ISO 9000
w. benchmarking

_____ 1. An intangible task that satisfies consumer or business user needs.

_____ 2. Product with unique characteristics that cause the buyer to prize it and make a special effort to obtain it.

_____ 3. Business supplies categorized as maintenance items, repair items, or operating supplies.

_____ 4. Capital investment of a business, such as a new factory or heavy machinery, that typically is expensive and relatively long-lived.

_____ 5. Product, such as a farm product (wheat, cotton, soybeans) or natural product (coal, lumber, iron ore), used by business in producing a final product.

_____ 6. Wholesaling marketing intermediary that sells small accessory equipment and operating supplies.

_____ 7. Intangible product a firm buys to facilitate its production and operating processes.

_____ 8. Finished business products also known as fabricated parts and materials that become part of a final product.

_____ 9. Four stages through which a successful product passes: introduction, growth, maturity, and decline.

_____ 10. Product purchased only after the consumer compares competing offerings from competing vendors on characteristics such as price, quality, style, and color.

_____ 11. Capital item, usually less expensive and shorter-lived than an installation, such as a laptop computer.

_____ 12. Introduction of a new product that is closely related to other products in the firm's existing line.

_____ 13. Regular expense items necessary in the firm's daily operation, but not part of the final product.

_____ 14. Bundle of physical, service, and symbolic attributes designed to enhance buyer want satisfaction.

_____ 15. The ratio of output to input of goods and services for a nation, industry, firm, or even individual worker.

_____ 16. Good or service that the consumer wants to purchase frequently, immediately, and with a minimum of effort.

_____ 17. Device that helps marketers to visualize the difference and similarities between goods and services.

_____ 18. A series of related products.

_____ 19. Industry that rises into prominence in the third stage of an economy's development.

_____ 20. A company's assortment of product lines and individual offerings.

_____ 21. Involves all employees in continually improving product and work processes to achieve customer satisfaction and performance.

_____ 22. Set of standards for quality management and quality assurance.

_____ 23. When an organization continuously compares and measures itself against the leading firms in an industry.

Contemporary Marketing

Name_____   Instructor_____

Section_____   Date_____

Self-Quiz

You should use these objective questions to test your understanding of the chapter material. You can check your answers with those provided at the end of the chapter.

While these questions cover most of the chapter topics, they are not intended to be the same as the test questions your instructor may use in an examination. A good understanding of all aspects of the course material is essential to good performance on any examination.

True/False

Write "T" for True or "F" for False for each of the following statements.

_____ 1. A broad definition of the word product focuses on the physical or functional characteristics of a good or service.

_____ 2. Consumer perceptions of a service provider become their perceptions of the service itself because the service is inseparable from its provider.

_____ 3. Products marketed to consumers who may not yet recognize any need for them are called *unsought* products.

_____ 4. One characteristic that distinguishes services from goods is the fact that buyers seldom play a role in the development and distribution of services.

_____ 5. Producers of specialty products often intentionally limit the range of outlets that carry their products.

_____ 6. Price and value are important factors in the purchase of heterogeneous shopping products, while style, color, and fit are more significant in the purchase of homogeneous shopping products.

_____ 7. Heterogeneous shopping products are shopping products whose brands the consumer considers essentially similar to each other.

_____ 8. Services represent nearly 80 percent of all jobs in the U.S.

_____ 9. The classification system for business products emphasizes product uses rather than consumer buying behavior.

_____ 10. Operating supplies can be considered the shopping products of the business market.

_____ 11. Most raw materials are graded based on set criteria, thus assuring purchasers that they will receive products that meet a standard of uniform quality.

Harcourt, Inc.

Part 5 Product Strategy

_____ 12. When bought by a firm, leasing and rental of equipment and vehicles, insurance, and legal counsel are examples of business services.

_____ 13. Component parts and materials seldom receive additional processing before becoming part of a finished good.

_____ 14. Supplies are often called MRO items because they include Marked Rebuilt Options.

_____ 15. The average American worker now works the equivalent of a month less per year than was the case thirty years ago.

_____ 16. The product life cycle concept applies to products or product categories in an industry rather than individual product brands.

_____ 17. During the introduction phase of the product life cycle, large profits are common as the public becomes acquainted with the product's merits and begins to accept it.

_____ 18. The width of a product mix refers to the number of products a firm sells.

_____ 19. One strategy for extending the product life cycle is to increase the overall market size by attracting new customers who previously have not used the product.

_____ 20. Marketers typically face the decision of pruning their product lines during the late growth and early maturity stages of the product life cycle.

_____ 21. Packaging and labeling decisions for service providers are limited because of the intangible nature of their products.

_____ 22. One way in which a service firm can extend its service mix is by adding new services.

_____ 23. The customer's perceived value of a service is seldom a consideration in deciding what price to charge for it.

_____ 24. A line extension develops individual offerings that appeal to different market segments while remaining closely related to the existing product line – like a low-fat version of a popular candy bar.

_____ 25. Price is often a deciding factor in the purchase of raw materials since it is negotiated on a purchase-by-purchase basis between buyer and seller.

Multiple Choice

Circle the letter of the word or phrase that best completes the sentence or best answers the question.

26. From a marketer's point of view, what people really buy when they purchase any product is
    a. a group of physical or functional characteristics.
    b. satisfaction of a want rather than a physical object.
    c. often nothing more than advice.
    d. something they cannot do for themselves.
    e. an absolute necessity for the maintenance of life and limb.

Harcourt, Inc.

Contemporary Marketing

27. One of the characteristics that distinguishes services from goods is
    a. tangibility. Services can be tested prior to purchase.
    b. separability. It is the service, not the service provider, that is important to the buyer.
    c. perishability. Services can't be held in inventory.
    d. standardization. It's easier to standardize services than goods.
    e. stable quality. Once service quality levels have been set, they are easy to maintain.

28. Consumer products that are purchased only after making comparisons of competing products in competing stores on the basis of such features as brand name, style, fit, and color are known as
    a. homogeneous shopping products.
    b. impulse products.
    c. specialty products.
    d. heterogeneous shopping products.
    e. demand products.

29. Specialty products would typically include
    a. soft drinks and beer for a picnic.
    b. bread, milk, and gasoline, especially when you're running low on any of these.
    c. clothing, furniture, and appliances such as refrigerators and washing machines.
    d. Rolex watches and Land Rover vehicles.
    e. candy, cigarettes, and newspapers.

30. Which of the following characteristics describes specialty products?
    a. They are often purchased on the spur of the moment.
    b. Such items usually are bought in response to unexpected and urgent needs.
    c. They are bought only after extensive comparison of competing offerings.
    d. Location can make all the difference between the choice of one product and another.
    e. Buyers refuse to accept substitutes for the desired products and know exactly what they want.

31. The goods-services continuum provides
    a. information on the ignorance of the average consumer about the things he/she buys.
    b. a broader definition of the term "products."
    c. a means of visualizing the differences and similarities between goods and services.
    d. a measure of the tangibility of services.
    e. an estimate of the perceived value of a product.

32. Today, consumers may even go so far as to hire leisure consultants to advise them on what to do with their spare time. This is a symptom of the
    a. changes which have taken place in the socio-cultural environment in recent years.
    b. economic well-being which allows us to let others do the groundwork for even our pleasures.
    c. astonishing growth of technological capacity that makes leisure choices so numerous.
    d. regulatory environment that forces us to make sure that our spare time activities are legal.
    e. rise of extreme competition for the leisure dollar which funds the consulting industry.

Part 5 Product Strategy

33. This term describes the stage of the product life cycle during which sales volumes rise rapidly as new customers begin to buy the product and previous users rebuy. Word of mouth and mass advertising induce hesitant buyers to make trial purchases.
   a. experimentation
   b. growth
   c. introduction
   d. maturity
   e. decline

34. The major obstacle to implementing the convenience, shopping, and specialty product classification of consumer goods is that
   a. many products are so different that they fall totally outside the scope of the classification.
   b. the system cannot be used in terms of the majority of buyers; it must be applied to a specific individual.
   c. some products fall into the gray areas between categories; they cannot be fitted neatly into one or another of the classifications.
   d. consumers differ in buying patterns; an item that's a shopping good for one person may be a specialty good for someone else.
   e. the system no longer works; human behavior has changed so radically during the last ten years that the system is out of date.

35. The category of industrial goods whose purchase may involve negotiations lasting over a period of several months, the participation of a large number of decision makers, and the provision of technical expertise by the selling company is
   a. installations.
   b. accessory equipment.
   c. raw materials.
   d. component parts and materials.
   e. supplies of various types.

36. The distribution strategy for services typically features a simpler, more direct channel than is the case for goods. This difference results largely from
   a. the inseparability of services from their supplier.
   b. the essential intangibility of services.
   c. the high level of service standardization.
   d. variation in service quality from vendor to vendor.
   e. the blurring of the distinction between services and goods.

37. Operating supplies are often called "MRO items." The letters MRO stand for the words
   a. manufacturing, research, and organizational.
   b. multiple, random, and obvious.
   c. many, ridiculous, and outstanding.
   d. manual, required, and out-of-stock.
   e. maintenance, repair, and operating supply.

38. In the business market, supplies might be called the
   a. specialty products.

b. shopping products.
c. accessory equipment.
d. convenience products.
e. raw materials.

39. In the industrial market, finished goods that become part of the final product are called
    a. accessory equipment.
    b. mechanical attachments.
    c. maintenance items.
    d. repair items.
    e. component parts and materials.

40. The firm's objective in the introductory stage of the product life cycle is to
    a. extend the cycle as long as possible.
    b. improve warranty terms and service availability.
    c. emphasize market segmentation.
    d. stimulate demand for the new market entry.
    e. price competitively.

41. Efforts to extend the product life cycle should begin
    a. toward the end of the introductory stage.
    b. toward the middle of the growth stage.
    c. early in the maturity stage.
    d. in the latter part of the maturity stage.
    e. as the product enters the decline stage.

42. Kraft Foods' promotion of Jell-O sales by offering customers free gelatin molds with various holiday themes is an example of extending the product life cycle by
    a. increasing frequency of use of the product.
    b. finding new uses for an existing product.
    c. increasing the number of users of Jell-O.
    d. changing package size, label, or product quality.
    e. physically modifying the product for a new market.

43. Arm & Hammer has been successful at extending the life cycle of its baking soda by
    a. getting people to use the product more often – the famous "bake a batch of biscuits" campaign.
    b. excelling at finding new uses for the product – as deodorizer, laundry freshener, household cleaner, and antacid, for example.
    c. constant product improvement – the product, once only 97.6 percent pure, is now 99.97 percent pure baking soda.
    d. increasing the number of users of the product by broadening its advertising base.
    e. broadening the product line by offering a whole array of different package sizes right up to a 150 pound drum for heavy users.

44. PepsiCo has two main product lines: soft drinks and snack foods. American Brands has five: tobacco products, distilled spirits, office products, home improvement items, and golf and leisure goods. From this information we can say that PepsiCo's product mix is
    a. narrower than American Brands'.
    b. longer than American Brands'.
    c. less consistent than American Brands'.

d. the older of the two.
e. deeper than American Brands'.

45. Promoting oatmeal as a cholesterol reducer, wax paper as a food covering for microwave cooking, and mouthwash as an aid in preventing gum disease are examples of extending a product's life cycle by
   a. increasing the product's frequency of use.
   b. increasing the number of people who use the product.
   c. changing the package size, label, or product quality.
   d. creating a new product service component for the firm.
   e. finding new uses for the product.

46. One of the problems of having a very large – wide, long, and deep – product mix is that
   a. it becomes impossible to achieve economies of scale.
   b. there is no cushion to fall back on if one line in the mix fails.
   c. little choice is provided for consumers who want something different
   d. some valuable segments of the market may remain unserved.
   e. retailers may not carry the full range of products and consumers may be overwhelmed by the array of choices.

47. Introducing a new product that appeals to a different market segment while remaining closely related to the existing product line – like a coffee company's introduction of a caffeine-free product – would be
   a. cannibalization of the existing line.
   b. corporate diversification.
   c. line extension.
   d. product evaporation.
   e. line complementation.

48. Products such as life insurance and funeral services, which are marketed to people who have not yet recognized any need for them, may be categorized as
   a. specialty products.
   b. homeopathic shopping products.
   c. convenience products.
   d. unsought products.
   e. monolithic shopping products.

49. In the business market, accessory equipment
   a. is often sold through industrial distributors.
   b. ultimately become part of the finished product of another producer.
   c. are marketed directly from manufacturers to users.
   d. are graded according to set criteria to facilitate purchase of products of known quality.
   e. are often referred to as AKC items.

50. A company with a line of products – as opposed to a single product – often
   a. suffers from a lack of identity because of the confusion about what it makes.
   b. makes itself more important to both consumers and marketing intermediaries.
   c. increases the average production and marketing costs of each product.
   d. reduces the firm's benefit from the expertise of its personnel.
   e. finds itself in exactly the same competitive position as a firm with a single product.

Contemporary Marketing

Name_____ Instructor_____

Section_____ Date_____

Applying Marketing Concepts

Leroy Allred was very busy. It was a nasty day outside, and the bad weather had stimulated him to analyze his company's sales records. He was both pleased and confused by what he saw there. Leroy's firm, Sand Mountain Enterprises, manufactured products that were used by both consumers and industry. From their new plant in Boaz, Alabama, they shipped "Sand Mountain Sandals," a line of distinctive high fashion casual footwear, all over the United States. The sandals were in such demand, Leroy knew, that people would literally drive a hundred miles to a store that sold them to buy a pair. The firm's other footwear line, a sturdy service shoe widely supplied by industrial firms to employees who worked at certain plant processes, had long been a satisfactory performer in the marketplace.

One of the firm's hard lines, the SandMan Chiropractic Chair, seemed to have fallen on hard times. Developed five years before, sales on this item had grown slowly for three years, then rapidly for another two years. Now, however, things were not so rosy. Competitors had begun to appear and Leroy felt that prices and profits from the chair were being squeezed by their activities. The other hard line in the Sand Mountain stable, the SandOff Precipitator, a device used to remove dust and grit from raw vegetables in canning and freezing plants and also by police forensic laboratories to extract dust samples from clothing, carpet, and similar locations to be tested as evidence in criminal cases, continued to do well. Leroy was glad he'd had the good luck to realize that police labs could use the precipitator just when the vegetable-based market for the thing seemed to be peaking out. He wondered if perhaps he could do the same thing with the chiropractic chair. So far, most chair sales had been made to chiropractors and physical therapists for use in treating their patients, but Leroy knew that the chair could also be used as a very convenient and comfortable work station for people doing clerical work because of all the adjustments that could be made to it. He began to think about the possibilities.

1. Into which category of consumer goods could "Sand Mountain Sandals" best be placed?
    a. convenience
    b. homogeneous shopping
    c. heterogeneous shopping
    d. specialty
    e. impulse

2. Sand Mountain's line of service shoes are probably treated by industry as
    a. installations.
    b. shopping goods.
    c. accessory equipment.
    d. supplies.
    e. raw materials.

3. The SandMan chair is in which stage of the product life cycle?
    a. introduction
    b. growth
    c. maturity
    d. decline
    e. death

Harcourt, Inc.

4. Leroy's deliberations about development of the SandMan chair into a workstation for clerical employees
   a. reveal his desperation; the idea is obviously ludicrous.
   b. have definite possibilities; it would extend the product life cycle by finding a new use for the product.
   c. would offer the possibility of extending the product life cycle by adding new users to the product's existing market.
   d. could conceivably extend the product life cycle by increasing the frequency with which the chair is used.
   e. Would have to be approved by the vendor first.

5. From Sand Mountain Enterprises' point of view, their new plant is
   a. a specialty product.
   b. an installation.
   c. accessory equipment.
   d. a convenience product.
   e. none of the above.

6. Leroy's development of the police laboratory market for the SandOff Precipitator was
   a. a good example of extending the product life cycle by finding new users for the product.
   b. pure luck; he couldn't do that again in a thousand years.
   c. an example of product life cycle extension through a change in product packaging or quality.
   d. a very astute example of how a product can be changed from a shopping good to a specialty good by advertising.
   e. A coincidence of being in the right place at the right time.

John Alberts is a landscape architect who has been in practice some fifteen years. His clients are primarily large business firms, among them Integrity Outdoor Advertising Company, one of the nation's largest owners of billboards and other outdoor advertising displays. John is somewhat concerned because his contract with Integrity will expire soon, and he knows that he will be facing competition to continue the beautification of the land surrounding the company's billboards all over the Southeast. He knows that the executives of the company are very happy with his work, and he feels that they think of him as "their" architect. The other firms competing for the contract have sent in "sales teams" to try and convince Integrity to do business with them, and each executive has mentioned to John what a turnoff the presentations have been, dealing primarily with costs and only marginally with aesthetics. This has made him feel better, because he knows his prices are competitive, and the plantings he has provided to Integrity to carry out his designs have been only the best stock. Despite this, he knows he's going to have to be prepared to offer his very best as the renewal date approaches.

7. Clients who rent Integrity's billboards on which to mount their display panels are purchasing
   a. a pure service or something very close to it.
   b. something which is predominantly a service with some goods included.
   c. something which mixes products and services in roughly equal proportions.
   d. something which is predominantly a product with a somewhat smaller service component.
   e. a pure good.

8. Given that Mr. Alberts provides the plantings which are used in his work of beautifying Integrity's billboard locations, his position on the goods-services continuum is
   a. at the service end; what he does is a pure service.

b. certainly not a pure service, though service is a large part of his product; he is dealing in goods as well.
c. well toward the goods end of the continuum; his services are a minor part of the total offering he's providing.
d. at the goods end; his product is purely goods.
e. at both ends; the services he provides are totally separate from whatever goods may be involved.

9. John is hoping to retain the contract because he feels that he is in a position to provide the one thing that the other competitors don't seem to have,
    a. size and scale of operations.
    b. effective sales personnel who can really hammer home a concept.
    c. the ability to do the job the company wants done.
    d. the ability to cut costs at every opportunity, doing an acceptable job at the lowest expenditure.
    e. a personal relationship with company executives and their trust in his relationship with them.

10. Judging by what you know of John's clients, how would you categorize the nature of his services?
    a. They are directed toward the business market and are an adjunct service.
    b. They are directed to the consumer specialty-goods market.
    c. They are business oriented and provide personnel services.
    d. They are directed to the consumer shopping-goods market.
    e. They are consumer based and are performed by unskilled workers.

11. John's recognition that he's going to have to "be prepared to offer his very best" as the end of his current contract draws near implies
    a. that he feels he's going to have to bribe Integrity officials to secure renewal of his relationship with them.
    b. that he hopes to hit them with his very best designs just before his contract runs out.
    c. that John knows that he's going to have to negotiate with the Integrity people to secure a renewal of his contract.
    d. that John feels there's little hope his contract will be renewed.
    e. that he hasn't done a very good job for Integrity in the past.

Sally Smith, owner of Sally Forth, Inc., is assessing the progress of her new business venture, shopping for people who don't have time to shop for themselves. A phone call to Sally Forth with a request that a birthday present be bought for a six-year-old nephew and sent to the child's address can be fulfilled the same day the request is made. Sally Smith is quite pleased; she has had to hire five additional shoppers to handle the avalanche of requests for things that people need to buy but can't find time to go out and get. The 30 percent surcharge over the cost of any merchandise purchased doesn't seem to bother many of the people who call to request the service, either.

12. Sally Forth provides
    a. a consumer convenience service.
    b. a core task business service.
    c. a consumer specialty service.
    d. a business personnel service.
    e. an adjunct business service.

13. The need for a service like Sally Forth grows out of changes in the
    a. economic environment.
    b. social/cultural environment.

c. political/legal environment.
   d. technological environment.
   e. competitive environment.

14. Which of the following aspects of the political-legal environment do you think would have the greatest effect on Sally Forth?
   a. State and local regulatory agencies
   b. Actions of the Securities and Exchange Commission
   c. The Federal Communications Commission
   d. Deregulation of freight rates by the railroad commission
   e. A change in customs rates and procedures

Contemporary Marketing

Name_____   Instructor_____

Section_____   Date_____

Surfing the Net

Keeping in mind that addresses change and what's on the Web now may have changed by the time you read this, let's take a look at some of the places on the Net that reflect aspects of product strategy. We are not endorsing or recommending any of these sources, merely making note of the information and services that people have elected to offer through the Internet.

There are so many Web sites that present product and service strategies that it has been extremely difficult to pick just a few for you to investigate. So I picked a lot of them for you to investigate!

Like ice cream? There's always Ben and Jerry's. Their Web site is at **http://www.benjerry.com** and is themed to the season or even the day if it's a major holiday. Duracell Batteries has an education-oriented site at **http://www.duracell.com.** Their major competitor, the Eveready Energizer, is at **http://www.energizer.com**, where you can order pink bunny stuff if you really like the durable little devil. For snack food junkies, Frito-Lay is out there at **http://www.fritolay.com.**

Sauce on the Web? It's Ragu at **http://eat.com.** For fun and games you might pick the Fox network at **http://www.foxnetwork.com** or Sega at **http://www.sega.com.** Magnavox lives at **http://www.magnavox.com,** and for those Kodak moments, go for **http://www.kodak.com**.

Feeling active? The Professional Association of Diving Instructors can be reached at **http://www.padi.com**, New Balance Shoes at **http://www.newbalance.com,** and Ping golf clubs at **http://www.pinggolf.com.**

Want to join? Information on membership in the American Business Women's Association is available at **http://www.abwa.org.** Alternatively, the American Astronomical Society can be reached at **http://www.aas.org.**

Thinking about getting an engineering degree overseas? Well, all sorts of interesting stuff about Bradford University in West Yorkshire, England, on their Web site at **http://www.brad.ac.uk.** It features an interesting overview of this school that began as a training institute for the textile industry 150 years ago. One of their more interesting programs is their "sandwich" degree – it's what we would call a co-op program. They're quite service-oriented.

New Orleans is my favorite city! And there's good stuff about it and Cajun Louisiana (also known as Acadiana) in the Gumbo Pages at **http://www.webcom.com/~gumbo/welcome.html.** The best part of this site is the link to some good Cajun and Creole recipes that'll light up your life. Interested in current goings-on in the city itself? Try **http://www.nola.com** for a site run in collaboration with the *Times-Picayune* newspaper updated daily.

Sites verified January 2, 2000.

Harcourt, Inc.

Part 5 Product Strategy

Chapter 12

Brand Management and New Product Planning

Chapter Outline

Use the following as a guide in taking notes.

I. Chapter Overview – Building and Maintaining Product Identity and New-Product Planning

II. Managing Brands for Competitive Advantage

    A. Brand loyalty – recognition, preference, and insistence

    B. Types of brands

        1. Manufacturer's brands versus private brands

        2. Captive brands

        3. Family and individual brands

    C. Strategic implications of brand equity – differentiation, relevance, esteem, and knowledge

        1. The role of brand managers

III. Product Identification

    A. Brand names and brand marks

    B. Trademarks

        1. Protecting trademarks

        2. Trade dress

        3. Developing global brand names and trademarks

    C. Packaging

        1. Protection against damage, spoilage, and pilferage

        2. Assistance in marketing the product

        3. Cost-effective packaging

        4. Labeling – Green labeling and the Universal product code

Harcourt, Inc.

Contemporary Marketing

IV. Brand Extensions, Brand Licensing, and Co-Branding

    A. Brand licensing

V. New-Product Planning

    A. Product development strategies

    B. The consumer adoption process

    C. Adopter categories

        1. Identifying early adopters

        2. Rate of adoption determinants

    D. Organizing for new-product development

        1. New product committees

        2. New product departments

        3. Product managers

        4. Venture teams

VI. The New Product Development Process

    A. Idea generation

    B. Screening

    C. Business analysis

    D. Development

    E. Test marketing

    F. Commercialization

VII. Product Safety and Liability

Harcourt, Inc.

Name_____ Instructor_____

Section_____ Date_____

Key Concepts

The purpose of this section is to allow you to determine if you can match key concepts with their definitions. It is essential that you know the definitions of the concepts prior to applying the concepts in later exercises in this chapter.

From the list of lettered terms, select the one that best fits each of the numbered statements below. Write the letter of that choice in the space provided.

Key Terms

a. brand
b. brand recognition
c. brand preference
d. brand insistence
e. generic product
f. manufacturer's brand
g. private brand
h. captive brand
i. family brand
j. individual brand
k. brand equity
l. brand manager
m. brand name
n. brand mark
o. generic name
p. trademark
q. trade dress
r. label

s. Universal Product Code (UPC)
t. brand extension
u. brand dilution
v. brand licensing
w. co-branding
x. product positioning
y. cannibalization
z. adoption process
aa. consumer innovator
ab. diffusion process
ac. product manager
ad. venture team
ae. task force
af. concept testing
ag. product liability
ah. test marketing

____ 1. Responsibility borne by manufacturers and marketers for injuries and damages caused by their products.

____ 2. Brand name that identifies several related products.

____ 3. Series of stages through which consumers decide whether or not to become regular users of a new product. Includes awareness, interest, evaluation, trial, and rejection or adoption.

____ 4. Initiative to measure consumer attitudes and perceptions of a product idea prior to actual development.

____ 5. Interdisciplinary group temporarily assigned to work through functional departments in examining new-product issues.

Contemporary Marketing

_____ 6. Loss of sales of a current product due to competition from a new product in the same product line.

_____ 7. Consumers' perceptions of a product's attributes, uses, quality, and advantages and disadvantages in relation to those of competing brands.

_____ 8. A unique brand name that identifies a specific offering within a firm's product line to avoid grouping it under a family brand.

_____ 9. Trial introduction of a new product supported by a complete marketing campaign to a selected city or television coverage area typical of the total market.

_____ 10. Application of a popular brand name to a new product in an unrelated product category.

_____ 11. The loss in brand equity that occurs when a firm introduces too many brand extensions.

_____ 12. A brand to which the owner claims exclusive access.

_____ 13. Descriptive part of a product's package listing the brand name or symbol, name and address of manufacturer or distributor, composition and size of product, and recommended uses.

_____ 14. Item characterized by a plain label, little or no advertising, and no brand name.

_____ 15. The practice of combining two strong brands, perhaps owned by different companies, to sell a product.

_____ 16. Stage of brand acceptance at which the customer will select one brand over competitive offerings based on previous experience with it.

_____ 17. Bar code on packages that provides information read by optical scanners.

_____ 18. National brands that are sold exclusively by a retail chain.

_____ 19. Added value that a certain brand gives to a product.

_____ 20. Marketing professional who plans and implements marketing strategies and tactics for a brand.

_____ 21. Symbol or pictorial design that identifies a product.

_____ 22. A brand name that has become a generally descriptive term for a class of products.

_____ 23. New product development organization bringing together specialists from different functional areas.

_____ 24. An initial purchaser of a new product.

_____ 25. The sequence of acceptance of new products by the members of a community or social system.

____ 26. Stage of brand acceptance at which the customer refuses all alternatives and will search extensively for the desired good or service.

____ 27. A brand name placed on products marketed by wholesalers and retailers.

____ 28. Marketing professional who determines objectives and marketing strategies for an individual product or product line.

____ 29. Name, term, sign, symbol, design, or some combination of these used to identify the products of a firm.

____ 30. The stage of brand acceptance at which the customer is aware of a brand but does not prefer it to competing brands.

____ 31. Visual cues used in branding to create an overall look.

____ 32. Brand name owned by a manufacturer or other producer.

____ 33. The practice of allowing other companies to use a brand name in exchange for payment.

____ 34. Part of a brand consisting of words or letters that form a name used to identify and distinguish a firm's offerings.

Contemporary Marketing

Name_____   Instructor_____

Section_____   Date_____

Self-Quiz

You should use these objective questions to test your understanding of the chapter material. You can check your answers with those provided at the end of the chapter.

While these questions cover most of the chapter topics, they are not intended to be the same as the test questions your instructor may use in an examination. A good understanding of all aspects of the course material is essential to good performance on any examination.

True/False

Write "T" for True or "F" for False for each of the following statements.

_____ 1. A brand mark is a symbol or pictorial design; it is the part of the brand that cannot be vocalized.

_____ 2. A product's brand name should give buyers the correct connotation of the product's image.

_____ 3. High brand equity may inhibit expansion into new markets because of the financial disadvantage the equity places on the product.

_____ 4. The unique shape of the bottle in which Michelob beer is sold constitutes part of its trade dress.

_____ 5. During the stage of brand acceptance called brand recognition, consumers will choose a product over its competitors if it is available.

_____ 6. Trade names and trademarks should not be confused; a trade name identifies a company while a trademark identifies a company's products.

_____ 7. Individual brands cost more to market than family brands because a new promotional campaign must be developed to introduce each new product to its target market.

_____ 8. Brand names which become generic, such as *aspirin* and *kerosene*, result in a strengthening original owner's exclusive claim to them.

_____ 9. In the Young & Rubicam approach to brand equity valuation, the term relevance refers to a brand's ability to stand apart from competitors.

_____ 10. Captive brands are brands bearing a manufacturer's or designer's name which are available exclusively from a single retail chain such as K-Mart or Target.

_____ 11. In the past, the label was an integral part of a typical package. Today it has become a separate element that is applied to the package at a later date.

____ 12. The Fair Packaging and Labeling Act requires that nutritional labels on foods list the amounts of fat, sodium, dietary fiber, and calcium in typical servings.

____ 13. If a newly introduced product takes sales away from an existing product in the same line, it is said to be cannibalizing the line.

____ 14. The Trademark Dilution Act of 1995 makes it more difficult to defend a trademark by requiring proof that a trademark violator knew it was in violation for a trademark owner to prevail in court.

____ 15. "Line extension" refers to the strategy of attaching a popular brand name to a new product in an unrelated product category.

____ 16. As its existing offerings enter the maturity and decline stages of the product life cycle, a firm must add new items to continue to prosper.

____ 17. A market development strategy concentrates on developing new products for new markets.

____ 18. In general, the more complex an innovative product is, the more slowly it will be adopted by consumers.

____ 19. In the new product development process, the business analysis stage separates ideas with commercial potential from those that cannot meet company objectives.

____ 20. Test marketing consumer durables, one of the most common applications of the technique, is often a long, drawn-out affair because of the high risk of loss if the testing is not thorough enough.

____ 21. Parallel product development programs have been encouraged by the desire of many firms to keep pace with rapidly changing technologies, shifts in consumer preferences, and competitive pressures.

____ 22. New product committees tend to reach decisions slowly and maintain conservative views, sometimes compromising so the members can return to their regular responsibilities.

____ 23. In the adoption process, consumers must first evaluate the product before they can become truly aware of it.

____ 24. Packaging plays a very small role in providing safety through protection against tampering; after all, most products aren't used until after they have been removed from the package.

____ 25. Beyond making sure that their products will do the job they have been advertised to do, even if there is some risk of harm involved in that use, manufacturers and marketers have no responsibility for injuries and damages caused by their products.

Contemporary Marketing

Multiple Choice

Circle the letter of the word or phrase that best completes the sentence or answers the question.

26. Once a product has moved from the unknown to the known category in the minds of consumers, it can be said to have achieved brand
    a. recognition.
    b. visibility.
    c. preference.
    d. elevation.
    e. insistence.

27. When a company uses a unique brand name for each of the products in a line, it is practicing
    a. institutional branding.
    b. individual branding.
    c. national branding.
    d. private branding.
    e. family branding.

28. Which of the following is more true of family branding than of individual branding?
    a. A promotional outlay typically benefits only one product in the line at a time.
    b. It is more difficult to introduce a new product to retailers and consumers.
    c. The approach should be used for products that are dissimilar in use and share few market characteristics.
    d. These brands cost more to market because of the need to develop a new promotional campaign to introduce each new product.
    e. Consumers who have a good experience with one of the firm's products will be more likely to purchase another.

29. When a firm's product development orientation is toward finding new markets for existing products, it is practicing a strategy of
    a. product positioning.
    b. market penetration.
    c. product development.
    d. market development.
    e. product diversification.

30. When a single individual sets product prices, develops advertising and sales promotion programs, and works directly with the sales force of a product, you have a
    a. captive branding strategy in force for that product.
    b. very volatile brand equity arrangement.
    c. product or brand manager structure for new-product development.
    d. distinct possibility of cannibalization by other products.
    e. product diversification strategy in place.

31. The most common organizational arrangement for new-product development is the
    a. new-product department.
    b. single-layer discovery system.
    c. the idea-generation concept.
    d. the venture team arrangement.

e. new-product committee.

32. Which of the following is a good example of using a package to assist in marketing a product?
    a. packaging beer in brown or green bottles or cans of standard shapes and sizes
    b. providing tamper-resistant seals on food and medicine containers
    c. combining colors, sizes, shapes, graphics, and typefaces used in packaging to create a distinctive trade dress which sets the product apart from competitors.
    d. designing the package so that the product will not be deformed or crushed in shipment or damaged by high levels of humidity
    e. choosing from among alternative package designs the one which will adequately protect the contents at least cost

33. Which of the following is a drawback to test marketing?
    a. Competitors who learn about the test marketing project may disrupt its findings.
    b. After the test has been going on for a few months, the firm can estimate the product's likely performance in a full-scale introduction.
    c. If the test is carefully controlled, consumers will not be aware that it is taking place.
    d. The test market should be of manageable size; that it, it need not be very large.
    e. Test market locations are typically chosen to have populations that share the same age, education, and income characteristics as the chosen target market segment.

34. The concept that manufacturers and marketers are responsible for injuries and damage caused by their products is called
    a. corporate social responsibility.
    b. the premise of extended warranty.
    c. customer relations.
    d. the rule of individual responsibility.
    e. product liability.

35. Brands owned by manufacturers and used to identify their products, such as Campbell's soups and Levi's jeans, are known as manufacturers' brands or
    a. national brands.
    b. private brands.
    c. individual brands.
    d. global brands.
    e. extended brands.

36. The practice of authorizing other companies to use a seller's brand name in return for payment of a royalty is known as
    a. brand licensing.
    b. line extension.
    c. brand dilution.
    d. co-branding.
    e. brand extension.

37. According to Young & Rubicam's *Brand Asset Valuator*, the dimension of a brand's personality that refers to a combination of perceived quality and consumer perceptions about its growing or declining popularity is
    a. stability.
    b. evaluation.
    c. esteem.

Harcourt, Inc.

d. knowledge.
e. relevance.

38. Of the following proposed brand names, which would be most likely to receive trademark protection under U.S. law?
    a. Grade A Milk
    b. Suntan Lotion
    c. O'Reilly's Irish Stew
    d. Grocery Store Foods
    e. 93 Octane Gasoline

39. Generic products
    a. often bear flamboyant brand names and flashy labels.
    b. increase market share during economic downturns but subside when the economy improves.
    c. are designed to mimic brands with high consumer recognition and steal sales from them.
    d. were first made available in the U.S. in 1966 and have been successful ever since.
    e. account for over half the sales of certain types of goods.

40. The right of exclusive use granted to the owner of a brand by trademark registration
    a. includes any pictorial designs used in the brand.
    b. covers the brand name of the product.
    c. includes brand name abbreviations such as "Coke" for "Coca-Cola."
    d. preserves the brand owner's right to slogans such as "It's Miller Time."
    e. extends to all of the conditions mentioned above.

41. The main purpose of oversized packaging, such as the plastic or paperboard trays in which prerecorded audio tapes and CDs are often displayed and sold, is to
    a. provide extra physical protection to the contents.
    b. prevent spoilage of the product by tampering.
    c. assist in the marketing of the product by providing convenience of access to it.
    d. reduce theft by making the product too bulky to fit conveniently into a pocket or purse.
    e. be a cost-effective way of facilitating goods handling.

42. That part of the product development process which is designed to determine consumer reactions to a product under normal conditions is called
    a. idea generation.
    b. concept testing.
    c. test marketing.
    d. business analysis.
    e. screening.

43. The stage of brand loyalty during which consumers refuse to accept substitutes for a desired brand, searching for it extensively if it is not immediately available, is called brand
    a. preference.
    b. insistence.
    c. aggravation.
    d. realization.
    e. recognition.

44. The Universal Product Code

a. allows consumers to determine how long it has been since a product they are buying was produced.
b. is a symbol displayed on many packages certifying that the product is manufactured to "universal standards."
c. is a law that specifies that the labels on packages all over the world contain the same type and quantity of information.
d. is a numerical code read by optical scanners that print the item's description and its price on the cash register receipt.
e. is a standard of ethics for manufacturers of consumer goods that sets forth their customer relations policy.

45. The approach to new-product development which assigns teams of design, marketing, manufacturing, sales, and service people to carry out development projects from idea generation all the way through to commercialization, often performing more than one step in the development process at a time, is
   a. phased development.
   b. the Critical Path Method.
   c. the Program Evaluation and Review Technique.
   d. parallel product development.
   e. sequential scheduling.

46. The original, historical objective of packaging was
   a. as a tool to assist in marketing the product.
   b. to offer physical protection for the product.
   c. to be cost-effective.
   d. to establish an "identity" for the product.
   e. to provide convenience in storage, use and disposal.

47. The federal agency created by this law has assumed jurisdiction over the safety of every consumer product category except food, drugs, and other products already regulated by other agencies. The law is
   a. the Toxic, Flammable, and Explosive Substances Act of 1995.
   b. the Fair Packaging and Labeling Act of 1966 as amended in 1989.
   c. the Omnibus Product Safety Standards Act of 1987.
   d. the Consumer Product Safety Act of 1972.
   e. the Magnusson-Moss Consumer Products Warranty Act of 1973.

48. The primary reason why long-lived durable goods are seldom test marketed is because
   a. the act of test marketing communicates company plans to competitors prior to introduction of the product.
   b. test market locations are so difficult to find.
   c. competitors who learn about the test market often cut prices in the test area, distribute cents-off coupons, or take other actions to disrupt the experiment.
   d. firms are afraid their competitors will "pirate" their ideas and rush into production with copycat products.
   e. of the major financial investment required for their development, the need to establish a distribution network for them, and the parts and servicing required.

49. Which of the following was a brand name but has become generic through common usage over the years?
   a. Linoleum

b. Jell-O
c. Xerox
d. Hoover
e. Frigidaire

50. Creating a package that features a handy pour spout as an integral part of the design assists marketing of the product by
    a. producing a package that can be easily reused.
    b. making the product more convenient to use.
    c. establishing the product's identity through package design.
    d. producing a package which is cost-effective.
    e. protecting the product against damage, pilferage, or spoilage.

Part 5 Product Strategy

Name_____   Instructor_____

Section_____   Date_____

Applying Marketing Concepts

Riverside Candy Company has been in business for over fifty years. The company was founded in 1936 to manufacture and distribute Riverside Ramps, a hard caramel confection in bar form that the company still carries in its product mix. Over the years, the company has added to its line of candies, and now sells Riverside Rollers, round, hard candies, Riverside Ripples, a bar candy with alternating vanilla/chocolate stripes, and Riverside Rapids, a fast-dissolving candy specially designed for use by joggers and runners "for quick energy on the go."

Each Riverside candy item is packaged in a distinctive brown and cream wrapper featuring the Riverside trademark.

Circle the letter of the word or phrase that best completes the sentence or best answers the question.

1. The type of branding which Riverside has traditionally used is
   a. individual branding.
   b. family branding.
   c. dealer branding.
   d. generic branding.
   e. indeterminate branding.

2. Just recently, Riverside was approached by a large supermarket chain that wants to buy Riverside Rapids to be packaged in their own wrappers and sold under their name. The supermarket brand is a
   a. generic brand.
   b. national brand.
   c. individual brand
   d. family brand.
   e. private brand.

3. Riverside has received an offer from the Fuchida Leisure Foods Company of Tokyo. They want to produce candy products using Riverside's recipes and bearing Riverside's brand in Japan, where a craze for American food (sort of like the Sushi craze here) is underway. They will pay Riverside for the use of their name and a certain sum for each unit of product made. If Riverside agrees, they will have
   a. implemented a market penetration strategy.
   b. begun a product positioning sequence.
   c. given Fuchida a brand license.
   d. decided to actively pursue market development.
   e. diversified their product mix.

Harcourt, Inc.

Contemporary Marketing

4. Though it is reasonably unlikely that such a thing would ever happen, suppose that some of Riverside's Rollers suddenly began exploding while on store shelves and in consumers' homes. Which federal agency do you suppose would show the greatest interest?
   a. Federal Energy Regulatory Commission
   b. Bureau of Alcohol, Tobacco, and Firearms
   c. Consumer Product Safety Commission
   d. Directorship of the Federal Reserve System
   e. Nuclear Regulatory Commission

5. If Riverside decided to branch out into the production of flavored syrups for use by sellers of sno cones and decided to create a new brand, such as "Best Taste," for that line, it would be
   a. developing a new family brand for the syrup line.
   b. individually branding the syrups.
   c. making a serious mistake; users of Riverside candies aren't going to be interested in sno cone syrups.
   d. in violation of the law; each food product must bear the brand name most closely associated with its maker.

"OK, people, settle down," Sam Delaney called the group gathered in the conference room at Trunnion Industries to order. "We've got a lot to do today. This is our third meeting this year, and we've got four items on the agenda. First, as some of you know, Mel Oustalet will be replacing Leslie Hussman as our engineering member until Leslie gets back from leave. If you haven't heard, it's a boy! Leslie's just fine and so is the baby. Next, I've got three new concepts I want you to take with you and look over." He handed out large brown envelopes to six of the other seven people in the room. "You'll find the preliminary appraisal forms for each idea attached to their descriptions."

Gesturing toward the person who didn't get an envelope, he continued. "I'd like to introduce Mia Cascabel to all of you. She'll be handling the New Era line when we introduce it next month. I've given her all the information we generated during our deliberations, but she may need to talk to some of you about details as we get closer to the intro date."

Everyone shook hands with Mia across the table and she excused herself to go back to her office. Sam started handing out slim volumes of paper bound in green to each person remaining. "Here are the preliminary results from Hannover City. As you can see, models K-30 and K-31 are doing well, but K-32 isn't really selling.

"Well, Sam, that's sort of what we expected from our earlier research, isn't it?" said a tall man halfway down the table.

"Yes, Jack," replied Sam.

"I'd be inclined to recommend we drop the K-32," said Jack, who was from manufacturing. "It's got too many bells and whistles, anyway."

"How do the rest of you feel?" asked Sam, scanning the table. Everyone was in agreement, as nodding heads indicated. "Good, then it's done. Our next meeting will be next week, same time, same place. Thank you all." They filed out from the room.

Harcourt, Inc.

6. The above is most probably a transcript of a meeting of Trunnion Industries'
   a. flight products venture team.
   b. new product department.
   c. new product committee.
   d. separately funded delivery department.

7. The members of the group were given the documents in the brown envelopes so they could
   a. begin the process of idea generation.
   b. examine them and give their input to the screening process.
   c. do a business analysis on the information in the envelopes.
   d. test market the information in the envelopes.
   e. commercialize the information given them.

8. Mia Cascabel is very likely
   a. the product manager for the New Era line.
   b. a visitor to company headquarters.
   c. a research analyst whose work the firm has used.
   d. nobody important.
   e. somebody important, but why she's important is a secret.

9. The "results from Hannover City" probably had to do with
   a. some preliminary concept testing Trunnion was doing.
   b. a jury of executive opinion done at company headquarters.
   c. a survey of several thousand consumers.
   d. the results of test marketing a new product line.
   e. deciding whether or not to drop an old line.

Alcide Rabalais didn't know whether to be happy or sad. "Oo-eee," he thought as he drove along the banks of Bayou LaFourche on his way home to Golden Meadow, "so many t'ings to do, so little time!" He wondered if he would ever have gotten into the fiberglass pirogue business if he had known how much work it was going to be. (A pirogue is a small, flat-bottomed boat, usually paddled or poled, uniquely suited to shallow water and widely used by fishermen and hunters.)

Alcide's product had been remarkably successful, not only because it was more durable than the traditional wooden pirogue, but also because he finished each boat in a special and unique camouflage pattern of his own design that had proven extremely effective in concealing them among swamp grass and hummocks. His name for the boats, "La Petite Liberté" (The Small Freedom), and the associated artwork consisting of a picture of a duck and a redfish in silhouette against a white circle, both of which he applied to the bow of each craft, also set his product apart. He had just received news from his attorney (and cousin), Placide Bordelon, that his application for registration of all of these with the government had been approved. Alcide had also just received a letter from Hippolyte Couvillon, a resident of Thibodaux and maker of trolling motors especially adapted for use on pirogues (and a distant cousin), about the idea of building a pirogue with a built-in trolling motor that would bear both the Petite Liberté name and Couvillon's own Electrovitesse nomenclature. He was also thinking about whether he should change the name of his company, Larose Fiberglass Works, to something related to boat building. Alcide decided he would deal with these issues after he had a cup of café au lait and a croissant.

10. Alcide's use of "La Petite Liberté" in relation to his boats constitutes a
    a. brand mark.
    b. brand name.

c. corporate name.
d. generic name.
e. trade suit.

11. The duck and redfish used by Mr. Rabalais to identify his boats is a
    a. trademark.
    b. brand name.
    c. dress name.
    d. generic mark.
    e. brand mark.

12. The combination of name, picture, and camouflage pattern for which Mr. Rabalais has secured registration would constitute
    a. a trade name.
    b. a brand name.
    c. a generic mark.
    d. a trademark.
    e. a brand mark.

13. Taken by itself, Alcide's unique camouflage pattern is probably an example of
    a. trade dress.
    b. a generic mark.
    c. an infringement.
    d. a logotype.
    e. a type style.

14. The letter from Hippolyte Couvillon has to do with the idea of
    a. brand licensing.
    b. co-branding.
    c. generic naming.
    d. collusion.
    e. brand management.

15. Larose Fiberglass Works is
    a. a trade name.
    b. a brand name.
    c. based on Alcide's wife's maiden name.
    d. a product identification.
    e. a measure of brand equity.

Part 5 Product Strategy

Name_____   Instructor_____

Section_____   Date_____

Surfing the Net

Keeping in mind that addresses change and what's on the Web now may have changed by the time you read this, let's take a look at some of the places on the Net that reflect aspects of new product introduction. We are not endorsing or recommending any of these sources, merely making note of the information and services that people have elected to offer through the Internet.

What's in a Cola – *Jolt* Cola, that is? Here's a product that's not yet available everywhere that you might want to look up. Why? Because its major selling point is that it's loaded with caffeine and compares itself with coffee, tea, and even caffeine tablets on this count. Go online with them at **http://www.joltcola.com** if the premise piques your curiosity. This site is a page of a larger site at **http://www.wetplanet.com** that features a number of novel soft drinks.

Interested in the pharmaceuticals market? There are a number of pharmaceuticals firms on the Net, both ethical houses (they make prescription medications) and proprietors (they make over-the-counter products). Some announce new-product introductions though their Web sites. Pfizer (**http://www.pfizer.com**) and Upjohn-Pharmacia (**http://www.upjohn.com**) are there representing the makers of ethical pharmaceuticals and Warner-Lambert (**http://warner-lambert.com**) represents the proprietary side. Bristol-Myers Squibb (**http://www.squibb.com**) owns a site showing its involvement with both ethical and proprietary products. Bristol-Myers Squibb also has a site at **http://www.womenslink.com** that outlines their involvement in women's health.

What's new in the automotive world? The automakers would like us to believe everything is. Check it out for yourself! The following should be self-explanatory: **http://www.bmwusa.com; http://www.chryslercars.com; http://www.ferrari.it; http://www.ford.com; http://www.isuzu.com; http://www.lexuscar.com; http://nissanmotors.com; http://www.gm.com** The Ford site is particularly interesting because it covers all their marquees: Ford, Mercury, Lincoln, Mazda, Jaguar, Volvo, and Aston-Martin. If I've missed your favorite, I'm sorry. Lots of other car companies have Web sites that I didn't mention. See if you can ferret them out. Good luck!

Sites verified January 5, 2000.

Harcourt, Inc.

Contemporary Marketing

Name_____ Instructor_____

Section_____ Date_____

Cases for Part 5

1. Ontario Chemicals and Coatings, Ltd.

Louis Sherbrooke, product manager for Ontario Chemicals and Coatings (OCC), was wondering what to do with one of the firm's new products, Tempadhere. Tempadhere, an adhesive designed for use as a temporary "tacking agent" to hold large sheets of steel in alignment for final assembly by welding, had recently been developed by OCC. It was, in fact, a by-product of one of OCC's major chemical processes. The product had tremendous holding power, which was its major advantage over other tacking agents used in the metal fabrication industry.

The product had been on the market only a couple of weeks when complaints began to pour in from dissatisfied users. The apparent problem was that the product worked too well! Users found that it was extremely difficult to remove Tempadhere from their weldments once fabrication had been completed, interfering with further processing and assembly. "Well, it looks like we're going to have to pull Tempadhere off the market," said Richard Hartmann, vice-president of production for OCC. "Surely we can find other uses for such a product."

Question

What was this company's definition of a product? How does this differ from the definition with which you have become familiar in this course?

2. Tres Bien Toys

Tres Bien Toys are high quality products made in France and marketed throughout Europe. They feature meticulous attention to detail and are made of the highest quality materials. Much care is spent on the design of the toys to assure that they are fun to play with and safe to use. They are usually sold in specialty toy stores and in a few of the best department stores.

Part 5 Product Strategy

Since prices in toy shops are normally higher than prices in the usual toy outlets, big people who shop in toy shops are usually more interested in quality and service than in price. Research evidence gathered by Tres Bien suggests that most people who have made a purchase of a Tres Bien toy continue to buy the Tres Bien brand when they purchase toys in the future.

Question

What kind of consumer goods are represented by the Tres Bien line of toys? What evidence leads you to believe this?

3. Herscholdt-Newman Products Company

Recent years have seen a number of financial crises at Herscholdt-Newman Products (H-N) because the company seems to be unable to introduce new products in timely fashion. Competitors always seem to introduce the innovations and H-N ends up copying these products. By the time H-N has a product ready to go into the marketplace, competitors are already well established with their innovations and H-N is forced to compete mainly on a price basis.

In the past, Pierre Printemps, the company's president, had depended on the sales and production staffs to come up with new product ideas. Those who had ideas got temporary relief from some of their other duties to see their ideas through actual development and marketing.

This procedure caused problems. Not only did it move workloads around, it also resulted in no one having the ultimate responsibility for developing new products. Pierre knows something must be done soon, so he is trying to create a better way to assign the responsibility for new product development within his organization.

Question

How can Mr. Printemps assure that someone is responsible for developing new products?

4. Center Point Tool Company[1]

In October of 1998, Center Point Tool Company, in cooperation with the U.S. Product Safety Commission, announced a voluntary recall and replacement of the plastic housings of its EZB brand "Portabench," "Carryon," and "Woodworker" portable work benches because the plastic frame might break during use.

---

[1] The company and the product are fictitious. The statement from the CPSC, however, is typical of statements issued by them on a number of occasions.

Harcourt, Inc.

Center Point had received 110 complaints that the bench frame, which was composed of two pieces of molded plastic joined by a glue joint across the middle of its shorter major dimension, had broken in half without warning while being used, causing the user to lose his or her balance and fall. Forty of these incidents resulted in minor injuries such as cuts, scrapes, and bruises. There had been no serious or life-threatening injuries as a result of the product's failure.

Over 100,000 of these portable workbenches, produced and distributed to retailers between March 1994 and May 1996, had been sold nationally for approximately $75 each. The defective products had been produced prior to June 1996 by the EZB unit of Center Point Tool. Only benches with control numbers (stamped on the frame) of 48893 or less were affected.

Consumers were warned to <u>immediately</u> stop using the products and retailers were warned to remove affected product that might remain on hand from sale. A toll-free number was provided for questions concerning replacement of the product and identification of potentially defective items.

A statement from the Consumer Products Safety Commission, attached to the recall document, read in part, "an estimated 325 million potentially hazardous products have been called back from the marketplace and consumers since 1973 (when CPSC was created). Most of these were voluntarily recalled by manufacturers, who established programs to repair or replace the products, or to refund the purchase price."

Questions

a. What is the significance of the voluntary recall of these products by Center Point Tool? Relate product liability to the recall.

b. How significant do you suppose pressure brought to bear by the CPSC was in causing Center Point to issue the recall?

5. Corporate Health Services

Ovid Reilly is thinking of leaving Corporate Health services and setting up his own medical clinic. For the past seven years, Dr. Reilly has been the medical director and examining physician for Corporate Health, which specializes in examining managerial personnel of local businesses.

These examinations are usually carried out in the manager's office. Some firms have their executives examined every two years as a matter of course, others when they are applying for an increase in life or medical insurance benefits for their employees.

Over the last seven years, Dr. Reilly has gotten to know a number of the high-level executives of numerous local firms and feels that they would come with him rather than remain with Corporate Health if he should leave. He knows, though, that Corporate Health is a large firm with a good local and regional reputation in this somewhat specialized field. He is wondering whether the move that he is contemplating would be a wise one.

Questions

a. What are some of the characteristics of the market for services that make Dr. Newman's idea potentially viable?

b. What are some of the characteristics of the market for services that make Dr. Newman's idea potentially risky?

Contemporary Marketing

6. Seagull Computer Corporation

Seagull Computer Corporation was started in 1991 in Sam Seagull's garage in West Charlotte, North Carolina. In the beginning, the majority of Sam's customers were people who had read his ads in publications like *Computer Shopper* and *PC Source* magazines and ordered by mail. The first year's sales totaled $100,000, which represented 41 units. Sam was one of thousands of direct-selling micro computer assemblers in the United States, most of which produced "IBM clones." These are machines that emulate the behavior of an IBM PC but are typically sold at a lower price.

Sam's computers were and are no exception. In fact, they are about as undistinguishable from other clones as peas in a pod in terms of design, features, and price. Sam decided, however, that he was going to be like Marshall Field and not just give lip service to the idea that "the customer is always right," but make sure that his customers were. Sam installed a 24-hour a day WATS line staffed with trained computer users, not technicians (though those were available as backup if the users couldn't help.) This line, called the "Flightline," would answer any question from any Seagull purchaser about any problem they might be having with their machine. The Flightline operators would bend over backwards to be of assistance, even repeating procedures step-by-step over and over if necessary. If the problem proved to be a bad part, a new one was sent out immediately by Federal Express or the customer was advised where to take their unit for repair, depending on their wishes and the terms of their warranty. Though it wasn't publicized, Seagull often made good on components on which the warranty had expired or helped customers by assembling special cables to interface with other equipment for them – free of charge. Meanwhile, Seagull Computers continued to be built with good-quality components and at a level of technology compatible with that of the industry as a whole. Though Sam continued to advertise as before, many new customers said they had been sold by people who already owned Seagull computers.

1998's sales were $1,220,000,000 (590,000 units) and the firm hired its 2000th employee on May 14. Sam Seagull expressed pleasure at his company's success by throwing a major party for employees, customers, and the community.

Questions

a. Where would you position Seagull Computer Corporation on the goods/services continuum? Justify your answer.

b. Outline the segmentation strategy you believe this firm to be using.

Creating a Marketing Plan

There is no Episode of Creating a Marketing Plan for this Part.

Part 6

Distribution Strategy

Distribution strategy involves moving goods and services from producers to customers, and is an important marketing concern. Marketing channels and logistics processes are the means by which this happens

A marketing channel performs four functions: (1) it facilitates exchange by cutting the number of marketplace contacts needed to acquire goods; (2) it adjusts for discrepancies in the market's assortment of goods and services; (3) it standardizes exchange transactions; and (4) it facilitates searches by buyers and sellers. It may be short, simple, and direct or long, complex, and indirect. Some channels have no marketing intermediaries in them, while others have several. Dual channels are often used to match product availability to the needs of users. "Reverse" channels have had to be developed to handle product recalls, warranty service, and returnable containers.

Channel strategy decisions begin with selection of a marketing channel. The selection is based on market factors, product factors, organizational factors, and competitive factors. Products may be made available through channels providing intensive, selective, or exclusive distribution. The battle for channel captaincy – a dominant position in the channel – has resulted in development and resolution of a number of types of channel conflicts. Now, in addition to the traditional, loosely organized channel, there are three classes of vertical marketing systems (VMS) which can be used. These three types include the corporate, administered, and contractual VMSs.

Logistics is the mechanism that facilitates the operation of marketing channels. It is not enough that title is transferred from manufacturer to wholesaler to retailer, it is also necessary that product move from source to ultimate user. Logistics operates, usually through facilitating agencies, to move, store, and keep track of the product as it transits from producer through the channel of distribution to the ultimate user. These functions must be performed in a timely, efficient, and effective manner.

The objective of logistics is to achieve a stated level of customer service at least total overall cost. The physical distribution manager chooses from among alternative transportation, warehousing, inventory control, order processing, and packaging and materials handling methods to achieve this objective. Suboptimization is to be avoided.

The major modes of transportation are the railroads, motor carriers, pipelines, water carriage, and air carriage. Intermodal and multimodal arrangements add versatility to the system. A given carrier may be a common, contract, or private carrier. Each type of carrier survives because of certain unique capacities it has that no other carrier has. The last twenty years have seen a substantial deregulation of the transportation industry, resulting in greater flexibility in the choice of modes and carriers. Actual cargo carriers are assisted in their work by freight forwarders, firms that handle the paperwork of transportation, and supplemental carriers that serve the needs of certain specialized markets.

Warehousing has vastly increased its technological level. Automated warehouses have become common, and the study of warehouse location has changed the ways in which warehouses handle goods The advent of practical, inexpensive computers and software packages for them has allowed two of the remaining elements of logistics – inventory control and order processing – to achieve a level of sophistication undreamt of just a few years ago. Finally, the development of new, composite packaging materials and more sophisticated and gentler materials handling processes have reduced damage in the logistics stream.

Harcourt, Inc.

Wholesaling intermediaries create utility, provide services, and lower costs by limiting contacts between buyers and sellers. They include manufacturer-owned facilities, independent wholesaling intermediaries who may or may not take title to the goods they sell, and retailer-owned cooperatives and buying offices. Manufacturer-owned facilities include sales branches, sales offices, trade fairs, and merchandise marts. Among the independents, merchant wholesalers actually take title to the goods they intend to sell. They thus engage in speculative buying in the hope that purchasers will be found. Merchant wholesalers develop long-term relationships with manufacturers and retailers or industrial users. Agents and brokers are independent wholesaling middlemen who perform primarily a selling function. There are five types: commission merchants, auction houses, brokers, selling agents, and manufacturers' agents.

Retailers sell goods and services to the ultimate consumer. Numerous types of retailers exist. Retailers may be classified on the basis of the form of their ownership, by the effort expended to shop at them, by the services they provide, and by the product lines they handle. Non-store retailing is a growing nontraditional form of retailing that includes direct marketing, telemarketing, Internet marketing, and automatics merchandising.

Retailing often changes in an evolutionary process called the wheel of retailing as products, institutional structures, and consumer buying habits change. After selecting a target market, a retailer must develop a merchandising strategy, customer service strategy, location-distribution strategy, promotional strategy, and pricing strategy. Many recent trends in retailing, such as scrambled merchandising, hypermarkets, planned shopping centers, teleshopping, and Internet retailing are evidence that retailers are attempting to provide consumers with increased shopping convenience.

Part 6 Distribution Strategy

Chapter 13

Marketing Channels and Logistics Management

Chapter Outline

Use the following as a guide in taking notes.

I. Chapter Overview – Critical components of distribution strategy, marketing channels and logistics, get products from manufacturer to ultimate user

II. Strategic Implications: The Role of Marketing Channels in Marketing Strategy

III. Types of Marketing Channels

    A. Direct Selling

    B. Channels using marketing intermediaries

        1. Producer to wholesaler to retailer to consumer

        2. Producer to wholesaler to business user

        3. Producer to agent to wholesaler to retailer to consumer

        4. Producer to agent to wholesaler to business user

        5. Producer to agent to business user

IV. Dual Distribution

V. Reverse Channels

VI. Channel Strategy Decisions

    A. Selection of a marketing channel

        1. Market factors

        2. Product factors

        3. Organizational factors

        4. Competitive factors

    B. Determining distribution intensity

        Intensive distribution

Harcourt, Inc.

Selective distribution

Exclusive distribution

    C. Who should perform channel functions?

VII. Channel Management and Leadership

    A. Channel conflict

Horizontal conflict

Vertical conflict

The grey market

    B. Achieving channel cooperation

VIII. Vertical Marketing Systems

    A. Corporate systems

    B. Administered systems

    C. Contractual systems

        1. Wholesaler-sponsored voluntary chain

        2. Retail cooperative

        3. Franchise

IX. The Role of Logistics in Distribution Strategy

    A. Enterprise Resource Planning (ERP)

    B. Logistical cost control

X. Physical Distribution

    A. The problem of suboptimization

    B. Customer service standards

    C. Transportation

        1. Transportation deregulation

        2. Classes of carriers

3. Major transportation modes

4. Freight forwarders and supplemental carriers

5. Intermodal coordination

D. Warehousing

1. Automated warehouse technology

2. Warehouse locations

E. Inventory control systems

F. Order processing

G. Protective packaging and materials handling

Contemporary Marketing

Name_____   Instructor_____

Section_____   Date_____

Key Concepts

The purpose of this section is to allow you to determine if you can match key concepts with their definitions. It is essential that you know the definitions of the concepts prior to applying the concepts in later exercises in this chapter.

From the list of lettered terms, select the one that best fits each of the numbered statements below. Write the letter of that choice in the space provided.

Key Terms

a. marketing channel
b. marketing intermediary
c. wholesaler
d. direct channel
e. direct selling
f. enterprise resource planning
g. dual distribution
h. distribution intensity
i. intensive distribution
j. selective distribution
k. exclusive distribution
l. exclusive-dealing agreement
m. closed sales territory
n. tying agreement
o. channel captain
p. grey good
q. vertical marketing system (VMS)
r. corporate marketing system

s. administered marketing system
t. contractual marketing system
u. logistics
v. physical distribution
w. supply (value) chain
x. value-added service
y. third-party (contract) logistics firm
z. system
aa. suboptimization
ab. customer service standard
ac. class rate
ad. commodity rate
ae. storage warehouse
af. distribution warehouse
ag. stockout
ah. materials handling
ai. unitizing
aj. containerization
ak. reverse channel

____ 1. An order for a product that is unavailable for shipment or sale.

____ 2. A marketing channel that moves goods directly from a producer to an ultimate user.

____ 3. Network that moves products to a firm's target market through more than one channel.

____ 4. Strategy designed to make direct sales contact between producer and final user.

____ 5. The process of combining individual materials into large loads for ease of handling.

____ 6. Vertical marketing system that achieves channel coordination when a dominant channel member exercises its power.

_____ 7. Organized system of marketing institutions responsible for the physical flow of goods and services, as well as titles of ownership, from producer to consumer or business user.

_____ 8. A statement of goals and acceptable performance for the quality of service that a firm expects to deliver to its customers.

_____ 9. A standard transportation rate established for shipments of a specific commodity between any source-destination pair.

_____ 10. A company that specializes in handling logistics activities for other firms.

_____ 11. Process which coordinates the flow of information, goods, and services among members of the distribution channel.

_____ 12. Vertical marketing system in which a single owner operates at each level in its marketing channel.

_____ 13. Vertical marketing system that coordinates channel activities through formal agreements among channel members.

_____ 14. Software system that moves data among a firm's units.

_____ 15. Marketing intermediary that takes title to goods and then distributes them further.

_____ 16. Product manufactured abroad under license from a U.S. firm and then sold in the U.S. market in competition with that firm's own domestic output.

_____ 17. A channel policy in which a manufacturer of a convenience product attempts to saturate the market.

_____ 18. A dominant and controlling member of a marketing channel.

_____ 19. The number of intermediaries through which a manufacturer distributes its goods.

_____ 20. Organized group of components linked according to a plan for achieving specific objectives.

_____ 21. Channel policy in which a firm grants exclusive rights to a single wholesaler or retailer to sell its products in a particular geographic area.

_____ 22. Set of activities that move production inputs and other goods within plants, warehouses, and transportation terminals.

_____ 23. Facility designed to assemble and then redistribute goods in a way that facilitates rapid movement to purchasers.

_____ 24. An improved or supplemental service that customers do not normally receive or expect.

_____ 25. Arrangement between a manufacturer and a marketing intermediary that prohibits the intermediary from handling competing product lines.

_____ 26. The sequence of suppliers that contributes to the creation and delivery of a good or service.

_____ 27. Activities to achieve efficient movement of finished goods from the end of the production line to the consumer.

_____ 28. Arrangement that requires a marketing intermediary to carry items other than those they want to sell.

_____ 29. The process of combining several unitized loads into a single, well-protected load.

_____ 30. The exclusive geographic selling region of a distributor.

_____ 31. Warehouse that inventories goods for moderate to long periods prior to shipment, usually to buffer seasonal demand.

_____ 32. Special favorable transportation rate granted by a carrier to a selected shipper as a reward either for regular business or a large-size shipment.

_____ 33. Business firm, either wholesaler or retailer, which operates between producers and consumers or business users, sometimes called a middleman.

_____ 34. Condition that results when individual operations achieve their objectives but interfere with progress toward broader organizational goals.

_____ 35. Channel policy in which a firm chooses only a limited number of retailers to handle its product line.

_____ 36. Planned channel system designed to improve distribution efficiency and cost effectiveness by integrating various functions throughout the distribution chain.

_____ 37. Backward movement of goods from users to producers.

Name_____ Instructor_____

Section_____ Date_____

Self-Quiz

You should use these questions to test your understanding of the chapter material. You can check your answers with those provided at the end of the chapter.

While these questions cover most of the chapter topics, they are not intended to be the same as the test questions your instructor may use in an examination. A good understanding of all aspects of the course material is essential to good performance on any examination.

True/False

Write "T" for True and "F" for False for each of the following statements.

_____ 1. Sorting alleviates discrepancies in assortment by channeling products to suit both the buyer's and the producer's needs.

_____ 2. In general, business purchasers tend to prefer to buy from middlemen rather than directly with manufacturers.

_____ 3. The producer to agent to business user channel is typically used when the product is sold in small quantities to each purchaser and the cost of product transportation is relatively high.

_____ 4. Dual distribution occurs when a manufacturer uses more than one wholesaler or retailer in any given geographical market to reach the selected target market segment.

_____ 5. If a state or the federal government were to pass a law that paid consumers for returning beer and soft drink bottles to their place of purchase, it would be forcing the creation of a reverse channel of distribution.

_____ 6. Horizontal conflict within a distribution channel occurs when members of the channel at the same level, such as wholesaling, disagree.

_____ 7. A tying agreement is a contract between a manufacturer and a wholesaler or retailer that grants an exclusive territory but requires the retailer or wholesaler to carry products other than those they want to sell.

_____ 8. Retailers are prohibited from buying grey market goods from distributors because foreign licensees have no right to sell them outside the countries for which the license was granted.

_____ 9. A wholesaler is a marketing intermediary, but not all marketing intermediaries are wholesalers.

_____ 10. Large retailers that bypass wholesalers and deal directly with manufacturers make the functions previously performed by the wholesalers unnecessary.

____11. To grow profitably in a competitive environment, a wholesaler must provide better service at lower cost than manufacturers or retailers can provide for themselves.

____12. Not all channel members wield equal power in the distribution chain. The dominant and controlling power in a marketing channel is called the channel commodore.

____13. Historically, managers have attempted to cut costs by improving the economies of goods production.

____14. An important component of the supply chain can be a value-added service, an improved or supplemental service that customers do not normally expect or receive.

____15. Each component of a system operates independently of every other component in the system.

____16. Suboptimization occurs when a specified level of customer service is achieved while the total cost of physically moving and storing products as they move from point of production to point of ultimate purchase is minimized.

____17. Reductions in any physical distribution cost should be made only if the required level of customer service is maintained.

____18. The largest category of logistics-related expenses for most firms is the cost of inventory control systems.

____19. In transportation, negotiated rates are sometimes called special rates and are the standard rate for every commodity moving between any two places.

____20. Common carriers are for-hire carriers that serve the general public and whose rates and services are still regulated by government.

____21. Motor carriage suffers from the drawbacks of being only able to accommodate a small number of products and operating at low speed – only three to four miles per hour.

____22. Though many people are scarcely aware of its existence, the network of 214,000 miles of pipelines that crisscrosses the United States ranks third in number of ton-miles of cargo transported per year.

____23. United Parcel Service, Federal Express, and the U.S. Postal Service are examples of supplemental carriers.

____24. Two categories of costs influence the number and locations of storage facilities used by a firm; warehousing and materials-handling costs and delivery costs from suppliers to the firm.

____25. Order processing typically consists of four major activities: (1) check writing; (2) credit issuance; (3) correcting the order; and (4) locating the customer.

Multiple Choice

Circle the letter of the word or phrase that best completes the sentence or answers the question.

26. In the business market, most major installations and accessory equipment are sold
    a. directly from producer to ultimate user.
    b. to the ultimate user through wholesalers.
    c. through agents who sell to wholesalers who then sell to the ultimate user.
    d. directly through agents to the ultimate user.
    e. by retailers direct to the ultimate user.

27. The so-called "traditional" channel of distribution for consumer products involves
    a. distribution by a producer through wholesalers and retailers to the consumer.
    b. distribution by a producer through retailers to the consumer.
    c. a producer selling directly to the ultimate user of the product.
    d. manufacturers, agents, insurors, wholesalers, and retailers.
    e. distribution by producers to the user through wholesalers and agents.

28. Which of the following would be a reverse channel of distribution?
    a. A manufacturer ships high-fashion clothing direct to a retailer.
    b. A supermarket receives returnable bottles from consumers and ships them back to the bottling plant to be sterilized and refilled.
    c. A manufacturer of industrial installations custom-designs a metal stamping plant for Kaiser Industries.
    d. The Electromatic Corporation supplies the state of Delaware with a complete traffic control system for the city of Wilmington.
    e. Your little brother sets up a stand in front of the house and, using lemons and sugar he's filched from the pantry, becomes a small businessman selling lemonade to passers by.

29. A dual distribution system is best exemplified by
    a. the use of insurance companies to absorb some of the risks of doing business.
    b. creation of a channel of distribution to handle the return of recyclable materials to factories for reprocessing.
    c. the practice by some social welfare agencies of opening neighborhood offices to be more convenient to their clients.
    d. the use of its own sales force and a parallel system of outside jobbers by a manufacturer of mechanics' tools.
    e. the action of an agent who brings together orange growers and wholesale grocers to create a market for fresh fruit.

30. In addition to their use as a device to facilitate recycling, reverse channels of distribution are often used
    a. for the distribution of services; intangible goods call for unique relationship between producer and ultimate user.
    b. in the industrial market for the distribution of high-tech products where a substantial degree of customization is required.
    c. for the handling of products which have been recalled by their maker or which must be returned to the factory for repairs.
    d. when a very short channel of distribution is called for by some characteristic of the product or the market.
    e. by facilitating agencies to facilitate the performance of the services they render.

Harcourt, Inc.

Contemporary Marketing

31. Which of the following is an example of vertical channel conflict?
    a. conflict between two or more sporting-goods wholesalers
    b. conflict among a group of retail florists
    c. conflict among drug, variety, and discount retailers all of which sell the same branded products
    d. conflict between company-owned and independently-owned retail outlets in the same chain
    e. conflict between manufacturers and retailers that develops when the retailers develop private brands

32. The basic antidote to channel conflict is
    a. strict enforcement of all contractual provisions of the relationships among members of the channel.
    b. effective cooperation among channel members in well-organized efforts to achieve maximum operating efficiency.
    c. for members of the channel who don't agree with the way things are going to abandon that channel and start their own.
    d. creation of an integrated, single-company controlled channel from production to retail sale to prevent any conflict.
    e. dissolution of the channel by the channel captain; conflict can never be overcome, only contained.

33. Among the market factors that determine the structure of a distribution channel is
    a. the perishability of the product.
    b. the product's requirement for regular maintenance service.
    c. whether the product is designed for the consumer or the business market.
    d. the fact that a producer who is financially strong can hire its own sales force.
    e. that the single-product firm often discovers that direct selling is an unaffordable luxury.

34. Some firms feel compelled to develop new distribution channels because
    a. independent marketing intermediaries do not adequately promote their offerings.
    b. there is such a small market for their offerings that intermediaries refuse to handle them.
    c. they wish to hold onto the lion's share of the profits from sales of their products.
    d. their products are so unique that no one exists to deal in them.
    e. they have such a bad reputation as suppliers that intermediaries will not handle their products.

35. Which of the following is most true of exclusive distribution?
    a. Some market coverage may be sacrificed by choosing this policy, but the loss is often offset by the image of quality and prestige that is created.
    b. Mass coverage and low unit prices make the use of wholesalers almost mandatory with this policy.
    c. The firm reduces total marketing costs and establishes better working relationships within the channel by choosing this policy.
    d. Adoption of this policy allows the consumer to buy the product with a minimum of effort.
    e. Cooperative advertising can be used for mutual benefit and marginal retailers can be avoided.

36. An exclusive-dealing agreement
    a. restricts the geographical territory of each of a producer's distributors.
    b. requires that a dealer who wishes to become the exclusive dealer for a producer's products also carry other products of that producer.
    c. is legal if the producer's or dealer's sales volume represents a substantial percentage of total sales in the market area.
    d. prohibits the distributors from opening new facilities or marketing the manufacturer's products outside their assigned territories.

Harcourt, Inc.

e. prohibits a marketing intermediary from handling competing products.

37. If a group of retailers were to start their own wholesaling operation, purchasing ownership shares in it and agreeing to buy a minimum percentage of their inventory from it, they would have created
    a. a corporate marketing system.
    b. a retail cooperative.
    c. a wholesaler-sponsored voluntary chain.
    d. an administered marketing system.
    e. a franchise system.

38. Which of the following states the fundamental principle that applies to channel decisions?
    a. Channels of distribution operate in such a way that it is virtually impossible to change the structure of an existing channel.
    b. When a particular member of a marketing channel is eliminated, the cost of channel operation is always reduced.
    c. You can eliminate some of the members of a marketing channel, but you can't eliminate the marketing functions that must be performed.
    d. Eliminating independent wholesalers from a marketing channel should increase profit margins of other channel members by at least 10 percent.
    e. The structure of a marketing channel is such that changes in the structure often result in changes in the functions that must be performed.

39. Containerization involves
    a. combining as many packages as possible into one load, preferably on a pallet.
    b. properly packing each item of a shipment into its own carton or container.
    c. recording the exact contents of each package which becomes part of a shipment.
    d. combining several unitized loads; a shipping container with standard dimensions is typically used.
    e. moving products within a manufacturer's plant and warehouses; special "tote boxes" are used.

40. The objective of an organization's physical distribution system is to
    a. deliver more goods faster and better than the competition.
    b. satisfy all the firm's customers all the time with the best quality products delivered fastest from a storage facility operated at the highest level of efficiency.
    c. develop the most modern, high-tech transportation network in the firm's marketplace so as to reduce competition and improve customer service.
    d. serve each manager with the minimum cost-profile of the distribution function under his supervision.
    e. achieve a specified level of customer service while minimizing the costs involved in physically moving and storing goods as they move from production point to ultimate users.

41. Suboptimization occurs in physical distribution when
    a. inventory management fails, causing the system to run out of stock of important goods just when they're needed most.
    b. there is too much emphasis on customer service and not enough emphasis on reducing the cost of each physical distribution function.
    c. too ambitious a level of customer service is chosen as a standard, thereby driving up operations costs.
    d. each logistics activity is judged by its ability to minimize its own costs, but the impact of one task on the others leads to less than optimal results.
    e. firms find themselves operating out-dated, old-fashioned warehouses and can't afford to develop better, more efficient facilities.

Harcourt, Inc.

Contemporary Marketing

42. Which of the following would be a valid and realistic customer service standard?
    a. All shipments will be sent motor freight unless the customer specifies another mode.
    b. Shipment will be made open-account to firms credit-rated BAA or better by Dun and Bradstreet; all others must pay cash with their order.
    c. Ninety percent of all orders are filled within twenty-four hours after receipt; all orders will be filled within forty-eight hours after receipt.
    d. Returns will be accepted only with prior approval by management and then only if it can be proven that they were bought from us within the last fifteen days.
    e. We dry-store merchandise ordered from us for seventy-two hours after we receive the order; after that, it is returned to stock and the customer is charged 15 percent for restocking.

43. The largest single expense item in physical distribution for most firms is
    a. warehousing.
    b. materials handling.
    c. order processing.
    d. transportation.
    e. inventory maintenance.

44. The name of the transportation rate that is set when the shipper and the carrier decide on the terms under which they will do business and set them out in a contract is a
    a. class rate
    b. negotiated rate.
    c. special rate.
    d. commodity rate.
    e. parametric rate.

45. Automated warehouses are capable of
    a. providing major savings for high-volume distributors such as grocery chains.
    b. reducing labor costs and worker injuries.
    c. lowering the amount of pilferage, fires, and breakage.
    d. all of the effects mentioned above.
    e. none of the things mentioned above.

46. If a freight carrier does not offer its services to the public but is for-hire by members of some specific industry, it is typically a
    a. contract carrier.
    b. designated carrier.
    c. private carrier.
    d. common carrier.
    e. bulk carrier.

47. Railroads continue to control the largest share of the freight business because they are
    a. hauling about 47 percent of all shipments sent.
    b. forcing other media to follow their rate schedules.
    c. moving freight faster and better than any other medium.
    d. the most efficient way to move bulky commodities over long distances.
    e. commanding over 90 percent of the long-haul volume.

48. For which of the following cargo lists would motor carriage be the most likely choice?
    a. finished lumber, automobiles, production machinery, industrial chemicals

Harcourt, Inc.

b. clothing, food products, furniture and fixtures, machinery
   c. grain, gravel, sand, and steel
   d. natural gas, coal slurries, crude oil, jet fuel
   e. cut flowers, microchips, medical instruments, precision tools

49. If you sought to ship a product domestically by the cheapest method, the obvious choice would be
    a. railroad.
    b. motor freight.
    c. pipeline.
    d. air freight.
    e. inland water carrier.

50. The warehouse most often used by firms facing seasonal fluctuations in the supply of or demand for their products is
    a. a storage warehouse.
    b. a make-bulk center.
    c. an automated warehouse.
    d. a distribution warehouse.
    e. a break-bulk facility.

Contemporary Marketing

Name_____   Instructor_____

Section_____   Date_____

Applying Marketing Concepts

The Panhandle Mercantile Company, a retailer located in Enid, Oklahoma, is in the process of analyzing its relationships with its various suppliers and customers. Company management has discovered, as it expected, that most purchasing of soft goods (clothing, piece goods, furs) by the company is directly from the manufacturer of the item. Some of Panhandle Mercantile's other lines, however, are bought in a very different manner. Household electrics, if the quantity to be bought is large enough, can often be bought directly from the producer. If the order is small or if repair parts are needed, however, a local industrial distributor is often the source of products from the same manufacturers.

Panhandle Mercantile people also seem to be spending an inordinate amount of time handling goods that have been returned to the store for shipment back to manufacturers for repair under warranty or because a recall order was issued. The company also found that, in recent years, the furniture department, which has its own separate building and has always been somewhat autonomous in its operations, has gone heavily into office furniture and supplies, and sells more furniture, fixtures, and supplies to local businesses than it does household furnishings to the company's traditional customers.

Executives realize that times have changed, but are somewhat puzzled by all these relationships, and to top it all off, they have been approached by several other medium-sized retailers with the proposal that they all get together and set up their own captive wholesaling operation to sell to themselves so they can buy in larger overall quantities and save some money.

1. Panhandle Mercantile typically purchases soft goods
   a. through a "traditional" consumer goods channel.
   b. through a channel direct from producer to retailer.
   c. wherever they can be gotten at the best price.
   d. only during peak seasons.
   e. from wholesalers specializing in soft goods.

2. Panhandle Mercantile purchases of household electrics indicate the presence of
   a. collusion which probably violates the Sherman Act.
   b. much confusion in Panhandle Mercantile's buying department.
   c. a dual distribution system for this class of product.
   d. the inadequacy of Panhandle Mercantile's inventory control system.
   e. a high level of demand for this merchandise in Enid.

3. The time which Panhandle Mercantile personnel are spending handling merchandise that is to be sent off for repair or other manufacturer adjustment should tell you that
   a. Panhandle Mercantile must handle very inferior goods; quality merchandise simply shouldn't be giving that much trouble.
   b. the channel of distribution from those manufacturers to Panhandle Mercantile must be somehow in disarray.
   c. times have changed a lot; in years past it would have been the retailer's responsibility to make good on these items.

Part 6 Distribution Strategy

    d. Panhandle Mercantile has become involved in reverse channels of distribution; these typically appear under these conditions.
    e. Panhandle Mercantile's New York buying group needs to be made aware of the deficiencies in the goods they are shipping.

4. Panhandle Mercantile's furniture department
    a. seems to have become a wholesale operation in office furnishings and supplies; it probably should be set up that way and the retail furniture and home furnishings department separated from it.
    b. seems to be one of the most efficient parts of the Panhandle Mercantile operation.
    c. is acting as a producer rather than as a marketing intermediary.
    d. is engaging in direct distribution, acting as agent for a broad range of manufacturers.
    e. serves primarily as the base for a reverse channel of business equipment and supplies.

5. If Panhandle Mercantile joins with the other retailers to create the wholesale operation they will have created a
    a. wholesaler-sponsored voluntary chain.
    b. franchise.
    c. corporate marketing system.
    d. administered marketing system.
    e. retail cooperative.

Peramendica Specialties is a chain of retail stores catering to gourmet cooks. The company stocks everything the avid kitchen craftsman or craftswoman might need. Pots, pans, spoons, measuring devices, all the bells and whistles – you name it, they've got it. Peramendica's history has been short but exciting. Founded only eight years ago as a small store in Chickasaw, Alabama, the company now has over 250 stores nationwide. This rapid growth has brought not only profits but also problems. The main problem facing Peramendica's founder and chief executive, Helmut Oberraeder, is the challenge of physical distribution.

The company has over 300 suppliers scattered all over the country. At present, each supplier receives orders from and ships directly to each Peramendica store. Store managers are responsible for all shipping and materials-handling related to their stores. Mr. Oberraeder realizes that the system is causing problems. Suppliers charge more for small shipments to the stores than they would for large shipments to a company warehouse. Moreover, if Peramendica buys in larger quantities, it can get the benefit of quantity discounts it is not now receiving.

There is also a problem with delivery; shipments are often late or simply don't arrive at the company's stores. Recently, store managers have begun to complain about having to inspect incoming shipments for defective merchandise, do paperwork on returns to suppliers, and handle special orders, all of which are very time-consuming. Personnel at company headquarters, meanwhile, are up in arms over their lack of control of buying activities at the local stores and their lack of information about inventory. To top it all off, sales are being lost because of too many stockouts in the retail stores.

Something must be done! Mr. Oberraeder has received several suggestions from other members of management, from lower-level employees who work in the affected areas of the company, and even from a certain number of irate customers. He has disregarded those suggestions that would have been too personally painful or physically impossible. Others he has given substantial thought. One of the more interesting suggestions involves setting up a central, automated warehouse to receive all supplier shipments. From that location, goods could be shipped to the stores by common carrier. A second suggestion is to set up several automated warehouses rather than one to cut down on delivery time.

Contemporary Marketing

Before a meaningful decision can be made, a number of questions must be answered and problems addressed.

Write "T" for True and "F" for False for each of the following statements.

_____ 6. Paramendica's should consider becoming a producer of some of the products they sell, thereby shortening the distribution chain and making more money.

_____ 7. Because avoiding stockouts is so important to a firm like Peramendica's, the just-in-time system of inventory control would probably not be a very good choice for them.

_____ 8. Automated warehouses are probably quite feasible for the needs of a firm like Peramendica's.

_____ 9. Freight forwarders should be used by Peramendica's, especially if the company does buy a fleet of trucks.

_____ 10. The Motor Carrier Act of 1980 could be of benefit to the company if they decide to use common carriers.

Circle the letter of the word or phrase that best completes the sentence or answers the question.

11. What type of warehouse is the company thinking of installing?
    a. a storage warehouse
    b. a distribution warehouse
    c. a make-bulk facility
    d. a manufacturing warehouse
    e. a bonded warehouse

12. A key function of the warehouse the company is thinking of building is
    a. unitizing.
    b. containerizing.
    c. assembling and redistributing goods.
    d. long-term storage.
    e. making bulk.

13. If the company uses a common carrier to deliver orders to the individual stores, what type of rate would do you expect it to be charged?
    a. a class rate
    b. a commodity rate
    c. a special rate
    d. a negotiated rate
    e. a flat rate

14. If Paramendica's were to install a physical distribution system, a basic systems orientation would require the inclusion of certain features. Others would remain optional. Which of the following would constitute an optional feature in such a system?
    a. order processing
    b. inventory control
    c. intermodal coordination
    d. customer service
    e. materials handling

15. If the company is losing sales due to stockouts in stores, then
    a. customer service standards are not being met.
    b. the stores are too far from the suppliers.
    c. the company needs to hire better store managers.
    d. customers are demanding too much; the company should take a "if we don't have it, you probably don't need it" posture.
    e. a careful analysis of the salesmen's activity sheets is in order; they're probably overselling some lines.

Contemporary Marketing

Name_____ Instructor_____

Section_____ Date_____

Surfing the Net

Keeping in mind that addresses change and what's on the Web now may have changed by the time you read this, let's take a look at some of the places on the Net that reflect aspects of distribution. We are not endorsing or recommending any of these sources, merely making note of the information and services that people have elected to offer through the Internet.

Services distributed over the Net? So it would seem, or at least they call themselves an index of services. This Web site lists links to web services, health, travel ideas, business opportunities, investments, and entertainment services. Try accessing them at **http://www.infiniteHorizon.com**

Does the Net really cover the globe? Domestically, try **http://www.bestofnewengland.com** To see a selection of Italian products, access **http://made-in-italy.com**. Some other Online malls are the Swiss site at **http://www.marktplatz.ch** and the English one at **http://www.edirectory.co.uk**. At the Swiss mall you can take your pick from listings in English, French, Italian, and German.

Got a hobby? You can probably find something to keep you happy on the Web. One general site is **http://www.ehobbies.com**. Antiques can be investigated at **http://www.theantiquecollection.com** Collect baseball, comic, science fiction, basketball cards? Try **http://www.baseball-cards.com** Fishing more your style? This site offers gear for all kinds of fishing aficionados. It's at **http://www.iwol.com/640**.

Aw, go ahead, buy a car! They're on the Web at **http://www.autotrader.aol.com** and **http://www.cars.com**. Any make, model, or year is supposedly available from them at the above addresses. Alternatives include Dealernet at **http://www.dealernet.com**.

Sites verified January 9, 2000.

Harcourt, Inc.

Part 6 Distribution Strategy

Chapter 14

Retailing, Wholesaling, and Direct Marketing

Chapter Outline

Use the following as a guide for taking notes.

I. Chapter Overview: Wholesaling, retailing, and direct marketing are integral components of the marketing channel

II. Wholesaling Intermediaries

    A. Functions of wholesaling intermediaries

        1. Creating utility

        1 Providing services

        2 Lowering costs by limiting contacts

    B. Types of wholesaling intermediaries

        1. Manufacturer-owned facilities

        2. Independent wholesaling intermediaries

            a. Merchant wholesalers

            b. Agents and brokers

        3. Retailer-owned cooperatives and buying offices

III. Retailing

    A. Evolution of retailing

    B. Wheel of retailing

IV. Strategic Implications: Retailing Strategy

    A. Picking a target market

    B. Merchandising strategy

        1. The battle for shelf space

    C. Customer service strategy

Harcourt, Inc.

D. Pricing strategy

  1. Markups

  2. Markdowns

E. Location-Distribution strategy

  1. Locations in planned shopping centers

F. Promotional strategy

G. Store atmospherics

V. Types of Retailers

VI. Classification of Retailers by Forms of Ownership

  A. Chain stores

  B. Independent retailers

  C. Scrambled Merchandising

VII. Classification by Shopping Effort

VIII. Classification by Services Provided

IX. Classification by Product Lines

  A. Specialty stores

  B. General merchandise retailers

   1. Variety stores

   2. Department stores

   3. Mass merchandisers

    a. Discount houses

    b. Off-price retailers

    c. Hypermarkets and supercenters

    d. Showroom and warehouse retailers

X. Direct Marketing and Other Non-Store Retailing

Harcourt, Inc.

A. Direct mail

B. Direct selling

C. Direct-response retailing

D. Telemarketing

E. Internet retailing

F. Automatic merchandising

Contemporary Marketing

Name_____ Instructor_____

Section_____ Date_____

Key Concepts

The purpose of this section is to allow you to determine if you can match key concepts with their definitions. It is essential that you know the definitions of the concepts prior to applying the concepts in later exercises in this chapter. In this chapter, many terms appear similar at first glance. Be careful in making your matching choices.

From the list of lettered terms, select the one that best fits in the blank of the numbered statement below. Write the letter of that choice in the space provided.

Key Terms

a. retailing
b. direct marketing
c. wholesaling intermediary
d. sales branch
e. sales office
f. trade fair
g. merchandise mart
h. merchant wholesaler
i. rack jobber
j. cash-and-carry wholesaler
k. truck wholesaler
l. drop shipper
m. mail-order wholesaler
n. agents and brokers
o. commission merchant
p. auction house
q. broker
r. selling agent
s. manufacturer's agent
t. wheel of retailing
u. retail image
v. markup
w. markdown

x. planned shopping center
y. selling up
z. suggestion selling
aa. atmospherics
ab. specialty store
ac. limited-line store
ad. category killer
ae. general merchandise retailer
af. variety store
ag. department store
ah. mass merchandiser
ai. discount house
aj. off-price retailer
ak. outlet mall
al. hypermarket
am. supercenter
an. home shopping
ao. chain store
ap. scrambled merchandising
aq. Slotting allowance
ar. stockkeeping unit
as. category management
at. planogram
av. wholesaler

____ 1. Agent wholesaling intermediary responsible for the entire marketing program of a firm's product line.

____ 2. Establishment that gathers buyers and sellers in one place where buyers can examine merchandise before submitting competing offers to buy.

____ 3. Agent wholesaling intermediary who takes possession of goods shipped to a central market for sale, acts as the producer's agent, and collects an agreed-upon fee at the time of sale.

Part 6 Distribution Strategy

____ 4. Permanent exhibition facility in which manufacturers display products for visiting retail and wholesale buyers.

____ 5. A large store, smaller than a hypermarket, that combines groceries with discount store merchandise.

____ 6. Store that carries a wide variety of product lines, stocking all of them in some depth.

____ 7. Independent wholesaling intermediaries who may or may not take possession of goods, but who never take title to them.

____ 8. An independently owned wholesaling intermediary that takes title to the goods that it handles.

____ 9. Shopping center that houses only off-price retailers.

____ 10. Method of retail selling that uses television to sell merchandise through telephone orders for home delivery.

____ 11. A specific product offering within a product line used to identify the varying items within the line.

____ 12. Consumers' perception of a store and the shopping experience it provides.

____ 13. Retailing strategy in which each product category is viewed as an individual profit center and the retailer manages the performance and growth of the entire category.

____ 14. A comprehensive term that describes wholesalers as well as agents and brokers

____ 15. Stores that operate under central ownership and management to sell essentially the same product lines.

____ 16. A store that stocks a wider line of goods than a department store, usually without the same depth of assortment within each line.

____ 17. Retailer that offers an extensive range and assortment of low-priced merchandise.

____ 18. Fee that retailers receive from manufacturers to secure shelf space for new products.

____ 19. A retailer that handles only part of a single product line.

____ 20. Retail sales technique that attempts to broaden a customer's original purchase to add related items, special promotional products, or holiday or seasonal merchandise.

____ 21. Manufacturer-owned facility that carries inventory and processes orders for customers from available stock.

____ 22. Periodic show at which manufacturers in a particular industry display their products for visiting retail and wholesale buyers.

Contemporary Marketing

_____ 23. A large store that handles a variety of merchandise, including clothing, household goods, appliances, and furniture.

_____ 24. A store that finds exceptional deals on well-known, brand-name clothing and resells it at unusually low prices.

_____ 25. All activities involved in selling goods and services to ultimate consumers.

_____ 26. Retail sales technique that tries to convince a customer to buy a higher-priced item that he or she had originally intended.

_____ 27. Full-function merchant wholesaler who markets specialized lines of merchandise to retail stores.

_____ 28. Giant mass merchandiser of soft goods and groceries that operates on a low-price, self-service strategy.

_____ 29. Diagram of how to exhibit selections of merchandise within a store.

_____ 30. Group of retail stores planned, coordinated, and marketed as a unit.

_____ 31. A store that charges low prices but may not offer services such as credit.

_____ 32. A manufacturer's facility that serves as a regional office for salespeople but carries no inventory.

_____ 33. Agent wholesaling intermediary who represents a number of manufacturers of related but noncompeting products, receiving a commission on each sale.

_____ 34. Retailer that offers a large assortment within a single product line or a few related product lines.

_____ 35. Limited-function merchant wholesaler who markets perishable food items.

_____ 36. Distribution channel consisting of direct communication to a consumer or business recipient.

_____ 37. Amount by which a retailer reduces the original selling price of a product.

_____ 38. Limited-function merchant wholesaler who distributes catalogs instead of sending sales representatives to contact customers.

_____ 39. A limited-function merchant wholesaler who performs most wholesaling functions except financing and delivery.

_____ 40. Retailing practice of combining dissimilar products to boost sales volume.

_____ 41. The combination of physical characteristics and amenities that contribute to a store's image.

_____ 42. Hypothesis that each new type of retailer gains a competitive foothold by offerings lower prices than current suppliers charge, maintaining profits by reducing or eliminating services.

____ 43. Limited-function merchant wholesaler who accepts orders from customers and forwards them to producers who ship directly to the customers that place the orders.

____ 44. A retailer that combines huge selection and low prices within a single product line.

____ 45. An amount that a retailer adds to the retailer's cost of the product to determine its selling price.

____ 46. Agent wholesaling intermediary that does not take title to or possession of goods in the course of its primary function – to bring together buyers and sellers.

____ 47. Intermediary that takes title to goods it handles and then distributes these goods to retailers, other distributors, or sometimes other end users.

Contemporary Marketing

Name_____Instructor_____

Section_____Date_____

Self-Quiz

You should use these questions to test your understanding of the material in this chapter. You can check your answers with those provided at the end of the chapter.

While these questions cover most of the chapter topics, they are not intended to be the same as the test questions your instructor may use in an examination. A good understanding of all aspects of the course material is essential to good performance on any examination.

True/False

Write "T" for True or "F" for False for each of the following statements.

_____ 1. Wholesaling intermediaries are involved in the production of three types of utility: time utility, place utility, and ownership (or possession) utility.

_____ 2. The basic distinction between a manufacturer's sales office and a sales branch is that the sales office carries inventory and the sales branch does not.

_____ 3. When they serve the business-goods market, full-function merchant wholesalers usually market machinery, inexpensive accessory equipment, and supplies.

_____ 4. Rack jobbers are limited-function merchant wholesalers because they have restricted their activities to certain specialized types of merchandise.

_____ 5. Auction houses bring buyers and sellers together, operating in businesses such as frozen foods, real estate, and used machinery, where there are a large number of small suppliers and purchasers.

_____ 6. Drop shippers operate in industries such as coal and lumber where goods are bulky and customers make purchases in carload lots.

_____ 7. Brokers can serve as a reliable channel for manufacturers seeking regular, continuing service because their ability to "make a market" places them in a unique position in the wholesale marketplace.

_____ 8. If a manufacturer decides to use a selling agent to handle its merchandise, it should realize that the selling agent will typically assume full control of its marketing program.

_____ 9. Manufacturers' agents differ from selling agents in that a manufacturer's agent takes the entire output of its principal, while the selling agent usually is only one of a number of such intermediaries being used by that manufacturer.

Part 6 Distribution Strategy

____ 10. Cash-and-carry wholesalers typically market perishable food items such as bread, tobacco, potato chips, and dairy products, making regular deliveries to retailers, performing sales and collection functions, and promoting product lines.

____ 11. Retailers often perform an important feedback role by obtaining information from customers and transmitting it to manufacturers and other channel members.

____ 12. The development of retailing illustrates the marketing concept in action because retailing changes to satisfy changing consumer wants and needs.

____ 13. Suburban shopping centers, convenience food stores, and vending machines are excellent examples of the "wheel of retailing" in action.

____ 14. Slotting allowances are fees that wholesalers receive from retailers to secure shelf space for new products.

____ 15. In an attempt to counter competition from discount stores and category killers, some department stores have eliminated high-cost, low-profit lines such as electronics.

____ 16. The basic retailing objective of providing services such as gift wrapping, alterations, bridal registries, and interior designers is to attract and retain target customers.

____ 17. A retailer's customer service strategy cannot support efforts to build demand for a specific line of merchandise.

____ 18. The amount of markup used by a retailer is typically determined by the number and types of services it provides and the rate of inventory turnover.

____ 19. The markup on selling price for a product that a retailer purchases for $.60 and sells for $1.20 is 100%.

____ 20. If you know the selling price and cost of a good, you can compute the markup based both on selling price and cost.

____ 21. Among the nontraditional retailing locations that have become attractive in recent years are airports.

____ 22. Location is seldom a determining factor in the success or failure of a retail business.

____ 23. If a good has been marked down, the markdown percentage may be determined by dividing the dollar amount of the markdown by the original price and multiplying by 100.

____ 24. The smallest of the types of planned shopping centers is the community shopping center, which usually contains only 10-30 stores.

____ 25. Atmospherics include physical characteristics and amenities both interior and exterior to the store that are designed to attract customers and satisfy their shopping needs.

____ 26. If "selling up" is used with due consideration for customers' needs and they are sold something they really need, the potential for repeat sales dramatically diminishes.

Harcourt, Inc.

_____ 27. Category killers, which include stores like Borders Books and Home Depot, combine huge selections and low prices in a single product line.

_____ 28. Off-price retailers take advantage of special price offers from manufacturers selling excess merchandise.

_____ 29. Scrambled merchandising refers to the practice of locating goods randomly in the store to force consumers to search for what they need.

_____ 30. Combining dissimilar product lines in an attempt to boost retail sales volume is called "mixing SKUs."

Multiple Choice

Circle the letter of the word or phrase that best completes the sentence or best answers the question.

31. Slotting allowances are most often paid
    a. by manufacturers to retailers to induce them to carry new, relatively unknown products.
    b. by retailers to manufacturers to prevent them from selling high-demand products to competitors.
    c. by retailers to manufacturers because they are so dependent on sales of a particular product that they'll pay a substantial premium to stock it.
    d. by manufacturers to wholesalers when the manufacturers are concerned that their permission to use a customer's warehouse space to store excess inventory will be revoked.
    e. when shelf space is shifted from one brand to another even though they both sell at the same price.

32. In the most technical sense, the term "wholesaler"
    a. should be applied only to merchant wholesaling intermediaries.
    b. applies across the board to all those institutions that are intermediaries in the channel of distribution.
    c. can be applied only to full-service marketing intermediaries.
    d. should be used only to describe a firm that deals in business goods.
    e. cannot be used to describe a firm that does not offer credit to its customers.

33. The marketing intermediary that predominates in markets for agricultural products, takes possession of such products when they are shipped to central markets for sale, acts as a producers' agent, and receives agreed-upon fees when it makes sales is the
    a. auction house.
    b. commission merchant.
    c. selling agent.
    d. drop shipper.
    e. khalish basrahmi.

34. The marketing function being performed by wholesalers when they provide their customers with information about new products and report on competitors' activities and industry trends is
    a. buying.
    b. financing.
    c. risk taking.
    d. providing market information.

e. reducing market contacts between manufacturers and end users.

35. A limited function merchant wholesaler that accepts orders from customers and forwards them to producers, who ship directly to the customers, is a
   a. mail-order wholesaler.
   b. commission merchant.
   c. retailer-owned cooperative.
   d. industrial broker.
   e. drop shipper.

36. A manufacturer-owned facility that serves as a regional office for salespeople and processes customer orders from inventory on hand is a
   a. merchandise mart.
   b. sales branch.
   c. manufacturer's representative.
   d. brokerage house.
   e. sales office.

37. A permanent facility that provides space in which manufacturers rent space for showrooms and exhibits to market their goods is an example of a
   a. sales branch.
   b. trade fair.
   c. public warehouse.
   d. brokerage house.
   e. merchandise mart.

38. The gathering that takes place once a year at High Point, North Carolina, during which furniture manufacturers display their wares for visiting retail and wholesale buyers is an example of a
   a. manufacturer's agency.
   b. retail buying office.
   c. public market.
   d. merchandise mart.
   e. trade fair.

39. Which of the following is a full-function merchant wholesaler?
   a. a commission merchant
   b. a rack jobber
   c. an auction company
   d. a truck wholesaler
   e. a drop shipper

40. Which of the following product assortments would you expect to find being handled by an auction company?
   a. bread, tobacco products, potato chips, candy
   b. hardware, cosmetics, jewelry, sporting goods
   c. tobacco, used cars, art works, livestock, furs
   d. health and beauty aids, housewares, paperback books, compact discs
   e. industrial chemicals, building materials

Contemporary Marketing

41. The "wheel of retailing" concept
    a. postulates that new types of retailers succeed by entering the market at a fairly high price level and offering a complete service package.
    b. seems to describe well the development of such outlets as chain stores, discount stores, and supermarkets.
    c. applies most appropriately to the development of suburban shopping centers, convenience stores, and vending machines.
    d. theorizes that, after a new type of marketing institution has established itself in the market, it changes its ways of operating by reducing prices and services.
    e. relates best to the demise of the general store in the U.S.

42. A store or other retail outlet's "retail image" is
    a. the owner's perception of the store and the shopping experience it provides.
    b. its suppliers' perceptions of the store's operating philosophy, place in the market, and profitability.
    c. consumers' perceptions of the store and the shopping experience it provides.
    d. competitors' perceptions of the store and the market niche it occupies.
    e. always consistent with the expectations of the owner, competitors, and the shopping consumer.

43. One of the more interesting trends of target market selection in modern retailing is
    a. the tendency for retailers to concentrate their efforts in one or another part of the country and to avoid the national market.
    b. a strong pull toward combining market segments into larger, less homogeneous targets for marketing effort.
    c. for firms to abandon the markets in which they have been most strongly entrenched for the longest periods of time and to strike out into new fields of endeavor.
    d. for firms that used to serve the mass market to shift their strategy to target more narrowly defined segments.
    e. the thrust toward segmentation on highly ethnic grounds.

44. The use of cable television networks to sell merchandise through telephone orders is
    a. the form of direct-response retailing known as home shopping.
    b. proving to be much less successful than was formerly hoped.
    c. a type of direct selling known as party selling.
    d. selling through an electronic catalog.
    e. catalog retailing.

45. If a retailer purchases a refrigerator from its supplier for $350 and offers it for sale for $650, the markup as a percent of the selling price, rounded to the nearest whole percent, is
    a. 24 percent.
    b. 30 percent.
    c. 35 percent.
    d. 46 percent.
    e. 54 percent.

46. Vending machines
    a. have experienced strong resistance in many parts of the world such as Japan.
    b. are among the most profitable of all retailing institutions, averaging 8 percent profit on sales.
    c. are limited in growth potential by their inability to accept credit or debit cards.
    d. have now become a $25 billion a year industry in the United States.

e. really got their start right after the First World War, selling books and magazines on the streets of Detroit.

47. The Sooper Market has overbought fresh cauliflower and is going to take a markdown on it to get it out the door before it goes bad. If the original price was $1.29 per head and a markdown to $0.89 per head is taken, what is the percent markdown? (Round to the nearest percent.)
    a. 25 percent
    b. 28 percent
    c. 31 percent
    d. 45 percent
    e. 69 percent

48. A neighborhood shopping center is usually characterized by
    a. a market size of from 20,000 to 100,000 persons; the facility is usually anchored by a branch of a local department store or a large variety store.
    b. a size of from 5 to 15 stores serving 5,000 to 50,000 persons living nearby with convenience goods and some shopping goods.
    c. the presence of some professional offices such as those of physicians, dentists, and attorneys.
    d. a theme park on site somewhat like a mini Disney World.
    e. at least 400,000 square feet of shopping area.

49. When a salesperson in a store suggests that a new tie certainly would go well with that new shirt you just bought, he or she is practicing
    a. suggestion selling.
    b. selling up.
    c. use of atmospherics.
    d. franchising.
    e. simple selling.

50. When a store focuses its marketing efforts on accessible locations, long store hours, rapid checkout service, and ample parking, it would be reasonable to assume, considering classification by shopping effort, that it is
    a. a shopping store.
    b. a variety store or specialty store.
    c. a mass merchandiser like an off-price retailer.
    d. a department store.
    e. a convenience retailer.

51. Using classification by services provided as a base, a store that focuses on fashion-oriented shopping goods and specialty products would most likely be a
    a. full-service retailer.
    b. a self-service store.
    c. a specialty store.
    d. a limited-service store.
    e. a convenience store.

52. Using product lines carried as the basis for classification, "category killers" are
    a. hardware stores.
    b. single-line stores.
    c. mixed merchandise marketers.
    d. limited-line stores.

e. specialty stores.

53. A general merchandise retailer that offers an extensive range and assortment of low-priced merchandise is called a
   a. variety store.
   b. department store.
   c. discount house.
   d. hypermarket.
   e. catalog retailer.

54. The newest kind of store in the discount house "true discounter" category is the
   a. factory-direct retail outlet.
   b. variety store.
   c. micromarket.
   d. mass merchandiser.
   e. warehouse club.

55. Discount houses, off-price retailers, and hypermarkets are all examples of
   a. catalog retailers.
   b. department stores.
   c. mass merchandisers.
   d. specialty stores.
   e. small-scale independent retail merchants.

56. Mass merchandisers have made a place for themselves in the retail marketplace by emphasizing
   a. relatively low prices for not-so-well-known products, high turnover of goods, and limited services.
   b. high prices for well-known brand name products, low turnover of goods, and a high level of quality service.
   c. relatively low prices for well-known brand name products, high turnover of goods, and limited services.
   d. relatively low prices for well-known brand name goods, high turnover of goods, and a high level of quality service.
   e. really low prices for well-known brand name goods, low inventory turnover, and a high level of quality service.

57. Department stores have been vulnerable to competition from mass merchandisers because
   a. of their refusal to modernize their central city locations to provide the convenience factors people are looking for.
   b. they have been slow to adapt to conditions in the marketplace, often refusing to serve the need of urban residents from motives of tradition.
   c. their suburban locations isolated them from the real bases of their markets.
   d. their bare-bones approach to merchandising has turned a lot of people off to the way they do business.
   e. they have relatively high operating costs, averaging from 45 to 60 percent of sales.

58. The hypermarket
   a. originated in Germany and has spread throughout Europe and the Middle East.
   b. differs from a supermarket primarily in the merchandise carried and not so much in size and operating philosophy.

c. usually features over 200,000 square feet of selling space stocked with a wide selection of grocery items and general merchandise at discount prices.
d. has not as yet had marked success in any market in which it has thus far been introduced. It may be a blind alley in retail evolution.
e. is just another name for the warehouse club type of retail store.

59. Maximiano Fanducci Tile Company just bought an odd lot of some really nice Italian ceramic tile. The tile cost 65 cents per square foot and Fanducci usually marks up its merchandise 35 percent on selling price. What should be the asking price on this tile? (Rounded to the nearest cent.)
   a. $0.88 per square foot.
   b. $1.00 per square foot.
   c. $1.22 per square foot.
   d. $1.64 per square foot.
   e. $2.00 per square foot.

60. Scrambled merchandising refers to
   a. the fact that most retailers are so disorganized that they do not know what their merchandise inventory includes, much less how much of each item is on hand.
   b. the practice of allowing merchandise normally housed in one department to be shifted to another department for a special sales event, thus "scrambling" the inventory.
   c. the practice of buying up stock from failed stores and mixing it in with fresh stock purchased for normal inventory, a questionable practice at best.
   d. the practice of carrying dissimilar lines in an attempt to generate additional sales volume.
   e. the habit which many consumers have gotten into of failing to replace merchandise that they have decided not to buy back on the proper shelves, dumping it instead any old place in the store, thus scrambling the merchandise.

Contemporary Marketing

Name_____Instructor_____

Section_____Date_____

Applying Marketing Concepts

Golflink, Inc., is an independently owned retail store that sells golf clubs, balls and accessories, and golf clothing for men, women, and children. In addition, it offers a complete repair department and its specialists can repair any club – even old, wood-shaft ones. Through an arrangement with a group of local professionals, golf lessons are available for interested players.

Write "T" for True or "F" for False for each of the following statements.

_____ 1. Because of its combination of merchandise and services, Golflink, Inc. can be said to practice scrambled merchandising.

_____ 2. Golflinks, Inc., is a not a good candidate to engage in direct selling.

_____ 3. Golflink, Inc.'s product lines would be easy to market via teleshopping.

_____ 4. If the store added a line of water skis, it would be engaging in scrambled merchandising.

_____ 5. In order to compete with the large chain stores, Golflinks, Inc., should carry exclusive lines, provide superior service, and stress their knowledge of local market conditions.

Circle the letter of the word or phrase that best completes the sentence or best answers the question.

6. This store would be classified as a
    a. specialty store.
    b. general merchandise store.
    c. department store.
    d. limited-line store.
    e. discount house.

7. If a store like Golflinks, Inc., requires convenient access by at least 150,000 people to survive, which of the following locations would be most advantageous for it?
    a. neighborhood shopping center
    b. community shopping center
    c. suburban shopping center
    d. regional shopping center
    e. central business district

8. If this store sold only golf clubs, it would be an example of a
    a. specialty store.
    b. general merchandise store.
    c. department store.
    d. limited-line store.
    e. mass merchandiser.

Harcourt, Inc.

Part 6 Distribution Strategy

9. If Golflinks, Inc., hired an interior designer to make the interior of the store resemble a tennis club, it would be attempting to use
   a. distribution to attract a target market.
   b. product/service strategy to attract buyers.
   c. retail image to attract a target market.
   d. location to attract customers.
   e. product/service strategy to attract new customers.

10. Golflinks, Inc., is thinking about publishing a catalog and taking orders by phone and mail. They would send the ordered merchandise to the customer by mail or private carrier. What type of nonstore retailing would this be?
    a. personal retailing
    b. direct-response retailing
    c. automatic merchandising
    d. off-price retailing
    e. direct selling

Jerry and Rebecca Fein have operated Fein's Kosher Corner Market for over thirty years. During all that time, they have run their store the way they thought their customers would want them to. They open the doors at seven in the morning and close at ten at night, seven days a week. Their parking lot is large and well lighted, and they make sure there are never more than three people in line at the cash register.

They have always been very proud of the fact that their store kept away from what they referred to as "faddish merchandise" and stuck to the basics. Good quality meats, breads, dairy products, and standard fruits and vegetables. And everything in the store, without exception, was strictly Kosher for all Jews – Orthodox, Conservative, and Reformed. Of course, not all their clientele was Jewish, hence they could stay open on the Sabbath with the help of their non-Jewish employees.

11. In terms of the shopping effort required to shop at Fein's, the store is a
    a. shopping store.
    b. convenience store.
    c. specialty store.
    d. self-selection store.
    e. full-service retailer.

12. Looking at the product lines carried by Fein's we would have to come to the conclusion that the store was
    a. a specialty store.
    b. a limited-line store.
    c. a general merchandise store.
    d. a general store.
    e. a variety store.

13. Considering their pride in their resistance to carrying dissimilar lines of merchandise from the basics of grocerydom, it should be concluded that the Feins
    a. have resisted the temptation to go into scrambled merchandising.
    b. should move with the times and broaden their merchandise assortment.
    c. have accommodated themselves to the inevitable pressures of the need to make a profit by adding lines which scrambled their merchandise assortment.
    d. have successfully practiced selling up on their customers.
    e. know how to apply suggestion selling.

Harcourt, Inc.

Alta Vista Supply Company of Cascade Heights sells hand and electric tools and supplies in several different ways. The company publishes a quarterly catalog it mails to any retailer with which it has done more than $500 in business during the three months before the mailing. It also operates a fleet of trucks that run weekly routes to regular customers (over $1,500 in business during the last three months) in its operating area. These trucks carry a selection of the most popular items in the company's line for immediate delivery, and the drivers take orders for any other items that are needed and deliver them on the next trip.

If an account is sufficiently large ($10,000 in volume during the last three months), Alta Vista Supply will even dispatch a truck to make immediate delivery of any order and will carry the balance owed on an open account for thirty days. Certain items in the Alta Vista line are now handled by a special division of the company whose representatives visit all customers at least once a month and replenish their stock of "expendable items" – packaged screws, nuts, and washers; wiring devices, and very small tools like screwdrivers. They even put the merchandise on display for the customers and keep track of inventory as well. The company calls this division the "small stuff" department.

Write "T" for True or "F" for False for each of the following statements.

_____ 14.   Even though it operates in several ways, Alta Vista Supply remains a merchant wholesaler.

Circle the letter of the word or phrase that best completes the sentence or best answers the question.

15. In serving its smaller customers (more that $500 but less than $1,500 in sales), the company acts like a
   a. drop shipper.
   b. cash-and-carry wholesaler.
   c. mail-order wholesaler.
   d. broker.
   e. rack jobber.

16. Alta Vista handles its middle-sized accounts ($1,500-$10,000) like a
   a. truck wholesaler.
   b. manufacturers' agent.
   c. drop shipper.
   d. commission merchant.
   e. selling agent.

17. Alta Vista's large accounts are handled as if the company was a
   a. manufacturers' sales branch.
   b. full-function wholesaler.
   c. limited-function wholesaler.
   d. drop shipper.
   e. commission merchant.

18. In terms of the way it operates, the "small stuff" division of Alta Vista Supply is a
   a. trade fair.
   b. merchandise mart.
   c. drop shipper.
   d. rack jobber.
   e. public warehouse company.

Part 6 Distribution Strategy

Name_____ Instructor_____

Section_____ Date_____

Surfing the Net

Keeping in mind that addresses change and what's on the Web now may have changed by the time you read this, let's take a look at some of the places on the Net that reflect aspects of retailing. We are not endorsing or recommending any of these sources, merely making note of the information and services that people have elected to offer through the Internet.

What do you want to buy? The Internet is replete with retailing sites. Let's start with the biggies. WalMart is on the Net at **http://www.wal-mart.com.** Something a little more upscale? Nordstrom, the very customer service-oriented department store, can be reached at **http://www2.nordstrom.com** The claim is that as they get to know a customer at this site, they e-mail you information about new items or special promotions that suit your tastes.

Any other major retailers on the Net? I guess we shouldn't leave out K-Mart. They're at **http://www.bluelight.com** of course.

Need copies? Kinko's can be reached at **http://www.kinkos.com.** For other writing and study supplies, try the Office Max site at **http://www.officemax.com.** If there's no Office Max in your neighborhood, how about Office Depot at **http://www.officedepot.com**?

My kids have always said I had no intention of ever growing up. And they were right. The toy stores are on the Net and there's no harm in visiting. FAO Schwarz, one of my favorites (remember the giant piano keyboard in the movie *BIG)* is at **http://www.faoschwarz.com.** Not ready to order from New York? There's always Toys "R" Us. They're at **http://www.toysrus.com.**

Hungry? Just today I heard of a restaurant called the Red Ochre Grill with a really neat menu. It features Moreton Bay bug tails and Kangaroo sirloin, emu paté and wattleseed lavosh – native Australian cuisine, I'm informed. For a menu or reservations, try **http://www.redochregrill.com.au.**

Sites verified January 12, 2000.

Contemporary Marketing

Name_____   Instructor_____

Section_____   Date_____

Cases for Part 6

1. *Tachikawa Lettuce Farms, LLC**

Roy Tachikawa, owner and chief executive of Tachikawa Lettuce Farms, a large head-vegetable operation near Fresno, California, is considering a suggestion made to him by his son, Roy, Jr., a recent graduate of Cal State Fullerton. Junior has suggested that the family corporation, now one of the largest independent growers of lettuce and specialty cabbage on the West Coast, abandon its long-standing relationship with Greengrocer Wholesale Food Brokerage Company and handle its own distribution. Junior contends that Tachikawa's own railroad sidings and truck fleet are adequate to handle outbound shipments and that the special services available from the railroads, like diversion in transit, will make it possible for Tachikawa to process orders that come in during the picking season even after the lettuce and cabbage have been shipped. Diversion in transit allows goods to be shipped before a destination for them is known and diverted to it when one is determined.

Dad is not so eager to abandon the relationship between the farm and Greengrocer. Greengrocer has always been very efficient in preselling Tachikawa's output before it was harvested, and paid promptly. Roy never had to bother with worrying about the mechanics of getting the goods where they were needed. He simply shipped in carload lots where Greengrocer told him. Now he was concerned. Junior seemed so confident in their ability to handle this new state of affairs.

Question

Before making a decision, what are some additional factors that Mr. Tachikawa had better consider before implementing Junior's plan?

* Limited Liability Company – usually means a family corporation.

Harcourt, Inc.

2. Airpark Industries, Incorporated

Airpark Industries, a well-established travel trailer builder with plants in Red Level and Cullman, Alabama, and Denton, Texas, builds and sells twenty- to thirty-foot trailers designed specifically for use as short-term lodgings for people who enjoy traveling. Since the company's beginning in 1956, sales have grown steadily during periods of economic growth and have been stable during downturns of the economy. Recently, however, Mike Aldrich, sales manager for Airpark, has been under pressure from Harbie Mellner, the company president, to increase sales and profits. John believes this can best be done through the company's existing marketing channels. After analyzing his firm's distribution pattern, Aldrich has come to the conclusion that increased sales through selected high-quality trailer dealers, the company's only distributors, are unlikely.

An additional marketing channel for Airpark has been suggested by Rick Mingus, a volume used-car dealer in a major Arkansas city. Mingus wants to sell Airpark trailers on his used-car lots, because "for many middle-class customers the choice is between a second car and a travel trailer." Mingus has pledged to promote Airpark trailers aggressively and, in return for an exclusive dealership, to carry no competing lines.

John realizes that marketing channels do change over time, and he is interested in experimenting with new channel arrangements. Perhaps this new channel would increase sales and profits for Airpark.

Questions

a. What factors constitute important considerations for Airpark's decision?

b. What steps should be included in the selection of a new marketing channel?

c. Should Aldrich accept Mingus' offer?

3. Mimi's Mart

Mimi Delachaise, owner of Mimi's Mart, a medium-sized supermarket located in Plaisance, a growing midwestern city of 15,000, has enjoyed ten years of successful operation. Recently, however, her dreams of an uncomplicated existence were rudely disrupted when Market Giant Stores, a national discount supermarket chain, announced plans to build a store in a new shopping center located at the southern edge of Plaisance.

Market Giant is an efficient chain that sells on a high-volume, low-price basis. Not only does Market Giant sell national brand merchandise at low prices, it also has an excellent house brand, Market Gold. Market Gold is a fast-selling line of food products that is always priced a few cents less than national brands. Market Giant also stocks an economy brand called Mighty Good that attracts some buyers.

Ms. Delachaise realizes that Mimi's Mart can't compete on a price basis. She is hoping, however, that the fine, friendly service and excellent reputation of her store will keep her customers from leaving to shop at Market Giant.

Garrison Alidont, general manager of Alidont Grocery Supply Company, has proposed that Ms. Delachaise join his organization. Alidont pointed out that this organization, a voluntary chain of 35 independent supermarkets, buys in quantity and obtains discounts similar to those enjoyed by Market Giant. In addition, his organization has its own line of branded merchandise, Gourmet Delight, which is comparable in quality and price to Market Gold. Alidont alleged to Ms. Delachaise that if she joined his chain she could "compete with Market Giant in every way."

Questions

a. What benefits can a voluntary chain provide a retailer?

b. Should Ms. Delachaise accept Mr. Alidont's invitation to join his voluntary chain?

4. Sandoval

Sandoval, a Monterrey, Mexico-based medium-priced department store, is considering opening an outlet in Seguin City, a town of some 300,000 located in a southwestern state of the U.S. Two locations are under serious consideration by Sandoval. The first would be in a new, medium-sized shopping center located at the opposite end of town from a five-year-old, existing center which contains the flagship location of Seguin City's only home-owned department store chain.

The new shopping center will contain a department store (which could be Sandoval), a grocery store, a hardware store, a variety store, a a drug store, a discount department store, a bank, and about 30 specialty shops. The developer of the new shopping center has asked Sandoval to be the department store. It is understood that if Sandoval does not accept, the home-owned chain will probably take that location.

Some of Sandoval's people are in favor of the new shopping center location. Their enthusiasm is tempered, however, by the belief that if the branch is not profitable in four years, there could be financial problems. The other location that is being examined by Sandoval is in the central business district of Seguin City. Even though the home-owned department store closed its downtown location five years ago to move to the shopping center, there is another department store in the CBD that is doing well. In addition, the federal government is planning a major office complex downtown, and there are strong rumors that a major New York corporation might be shifting its corporate headquarters to a location in downtown Seguin City.

Sandoval officials are somewhat turned off to the new shopping center because there will be a discount department store located there. They feel the discounter will provide serious competition. Sandoval, because it offers higher levels of service and a repair facility for appliances, can't match the prices of the discount operation. The shopping-center developer can't be talked out of that feature of the center.

Question

What action do you think Sandoval should take?

5. Milkmaid Manufacturing Company

Milkmaid Manufacturing Company makes mechanical milking machines sold through dealers. They are thinking of changing their distribution system. Currently, each dealer maintains a small inventory of one or possibly two of the bulky milkers and storage units in an assembled condition. Final assembly of milker/storage units takes place at one of four strategically located Milkmaid warehouses before shipment to dealers takes place. Common carriers are used to ship the units from the main plant to the regional warehouses and from the regional warehouses to the dealers.

There have been problems with this system of late. Carrier service has at times been poor. Some deliveries have been late and others have arrived in damaged condition. Melrose Mescaline, marketing manager for Milkmaid, has been searching for alternatives that will reduce dealer complaints and, if at all possible, reduce physical distribution expenses. You have been called in to render your expert opinion.

Questions

a. What alternative transportation arrangement would you suggest Milkmaid consider? Should it buy or lease its own trucks, use a contract carrier, or possibly resort to some sort of intermodal transportation?

b. What do you think of Milkmaid's assembly/storage warehouses? Is there a better way to provide for storage and assembly?

6. Wilson Textbook Company

Wilson Textbook Company publishes college textbooks that are used throughout the United States and Canada. Textbooks are ordered by college bookstores as soon as professors place orders for their courses. All orders are filled from the company plant located at Ridiculous Falls, Ohio.

Every term a number of professors are late ordering books. This creates a flurry of activity at the beginning of every semester. Recently, the number of late orders has been growing, and delivery of some texts has been as late as two weeks after the beginning of classes. Needless to say, complaints from professors and students have increased in number and vehemence. The management of Wilson, however, sees no way to solve the problem as long as professors continue to place late orders.

Questions

a. What changes would you suggest be made in Wilson's distribution system?

b. Should Wilson attempt to advise professors to order early? Can company salespeople obtain accurate order estimates? In other words, can the order-processing system be improved?

Creating a Marketing Plan

The information that you will receive in this episode should allow you to complete Part III.C. of your marketing plan.

Episode Five: Let's Find a Place to Hang Our Hats

"If I ever have to look at another dump like that last one, I'll quit!" was Laura's vehement comment after she and Brian drove away from the address the commercial real estate agent had given them. She and the guys knew what they needed: a place of about 2,000 square feet, part warehouse/service area, part office, located near the center of concentration of the businesses in New Essex. The problem seemed to be that the places they felt they could afford suffered from one or more fatal flaws, like inadequate wiring or lack of securability – after all, the place was going to be full of computers, equipment, and sensitive software as Web sites were written.

"Let's try one more place, L," said Brian the ever optimistic. Now that we've established our credit with Microscene for domain registry services, we can get going as soon as we get a place. It was rare luck that we were able to buy those two cars the police force ordered but never had delivered. I doubt that we could have found such nice machines anywhere else for the price. It's a good thing your uncle is in the automobile business and knew about them."

"That's true. I guess I can't expect everything to go smoothly all the time. Didn't you say you had seen an ad in today's paper for a place that sounded like we could use?" asked Laura.

"Yes," replied Brian, "it's right around the next corner. Let's take a look." And so saying, they turned the corner and parked next to nicely maintained concrete block building. "I see there's someone here," said Laura, pointing to a small van parked next to the open side door of the structure.

"Maybe we can get in and take a look," was Brian's reply, "or maybe whoever's there can tell us something about the place." They approached the open door.

Thirty minutes later they emerged in the company of an older man. "The place is just perfect, Mr. Cressy. We'll have our attorney call yours tomorrow to iron out the details, but I think we've got a deal," said Laura, shaking hands with the older man. "Very good, Ms. Claire," was his response, "I think you'll find the building and the location are perfect for your plans." Later, back at Laura's house, where Terry was waiting, the threesome sat down to organize their thoughts. Terry passed out sheets of paper to the other two and said, "Well, I've talked to three people that we all know either from school or the Institute, and they've all agreed to come work with us. I guess in the beginning we'd all better hit the road and start making contact with the businesses that most need our services. We'll leave one person in the office to man the phones, while the rest of us go out and make ourselves known. The signmakers said they could have the sign hung by Monday afternoon and the stationery and business cards will be ready tomorrow afternoon. Since this is only Tuesday, we may be able to plead our case with a lot of people by the time the weekend rolls around."

"You know, I wonder if we really need that building," said Brian, thinking out loud. "I mean, it'll be great to have a real office to work in, but it's not like we have to have a place to store products or anything."

Harcourt, Inc.

"I go with having the building," said Laura. "We need a place to work, and we need a place where people can come to us. At some point in site development, we're going to have to fine-tune what we're doing, and if they can come to us and see their sites on our 25-inch monitors driven by high speed CPUs with lots of working RAM, they'll know how good those sites will ultimately look. They can't see that if we make our presentations on laptops or their in-office machines."

"Too true," said Terry. "If we become well-known, and I hope we do, people are going to come looking for us and are going to need a place to find us. It's like the 24-hour a day availability. We may discover we don't actually have to man the office on a 24/7 basis, but there's a lot of comfort to knowing your Web site can be modified at a moment's notice, or fixed by somebody who knows how if something happens to it in the middle of the night. You know, since February of 2000 when all those major sites were hacked by that computer terrorist group, Web businesses have been very scared about site security."

"I guess you're right" was Brian's reply.

"You guys get on home now," said Laura, "and we'll meet again tomorrow morning to get the lease finalized with the lawyer."

Guidelines:

Review the requirements of Part III.C. of your Marketing Plan, and, using the information in this episode, complete that Part of the plan. Some materials in this episode will also be relevant to completion of Part III.D. of the Plan as well.

Part 7

Promotional Strategy

Promotion is one of the most dynamic and severely criticized aspects of marketing. It is the marketing activity charged with informing, persuading, and influencing the consumer's purchase decision. Integrated marketing communications coordinate all promotion activities to produce a unified promotional message, often using extensive databases to identify potential customers. Promotion objectives often include increasing demand, differentiating a product, accentuating a product's value, stabilizing sales, and providing information to consumers and others. The promotional mix includes personal selling and nonpersonal selling activities.

Recent years have seen tremendous growth in the promotional use of sponsorships, especially of various events in the sporting world. Sponsorships serve to integrate a promotional effort. Direct marketing has also grown markedly in the last twenty years as well, now including, in additional to the traditional direct mail, telemarketing, direct mail via TV, and use of the Internet.

An optimal promotional mix considers the nature of the product, the nature of the market, the product's stage in its product life cycle, its price, and the funds available for promotional activities. Some promotional programs favor pushing strategies that promote to intermediaries to bring the product to market, while others promote to ultimate users in a pulling strategy. The objects of promotion determine the setting of a promotional budget. Traditional methods of allocating a promotional budget are percentage of sales, a fixed sum per unit, meeting the competition, and task-objective. Measurement of the effectiveness of promotion is difficult, pretesting and posttesting of advertising being the most common methods, but it is certain that promotion has social, business, and economic importance.

Nonpersonal selling includes advertising, sales promotion, direct marketing, and public relations. Advertising, any paid nonpersonal sales presentation carried by a medium and usually directed to a large number of potential customers, is an important part of modern business. Advertising strategies include comparative, retail, and interactive advertising and celebrity testimonials. Creating ads is a multi-billion dollar industry, as is delivering them through TV, radio, newspapers, magazines, direct mail and interactive and outdoor media.

Sales promotion is designed to stimulate consumer purchasing and dealer effectiveness. The basic types of sales promotion to consumers include coupons and refunds, contests, sweepstakes, samples, premiums, bonus packs, and specialty advertising. Trade-oriented promotions include trade allowances, point-of-purchase advertising, trade shows, dealer incentives, contests, and training programs. Both may also include other nonrecurrent, irregular selling efforts.

Public relations, a firm's communications and relationships with its publics, often supplements other promotional efforts in the marketing mix. Publicity, part of public relations, obtains favorable media coverage for a firm without payment to the media.

Harcourt, Inc.

Personal selling, a vital part of the promotional mix, has evolved from the role of the old-time peddler to today's professional sales practitioner who may use relationship, consultative, or team selling techniques. Sales channels include over-the-counter selling, field selling, telemarketing, and inside selling. Sales representatives may be called upon to process orders, sell creatively, or do missionary work.

The sales process usually follows seven steps beginning with prospecting and qualifying. Then follow the approach and sales presentation. The content and emphasis of the sales presentation depend on whether the sales practitioner is responsible for order processing, creative selling, or missionary sales. Then follow the demonstration and handling of objections. The sales rep then closes the sale and the whole process and ends with follow-up after the sale has been made.

A personal sales force means there must be sales management. Someone must recruit, select, train, organize, supervise, motivate, pay, control, and evaluate sales practitioners and act in a boundary-spanning role between them and upper-level management.

Ethical issues certainly form a part of the scope of the promotional responsibility and are probably best summed up simply be restating the marketing concept – find out what people want, offer it to them at a reasonable price, and make sure they are happy with it if they buy it.

Chapter 15

Integrated Marketing Communications

Chapter Outline

Use the following as a guide in taking notes.

I. Chapter Overview – Ideas on the elements of the promotional process

II. Integrated Marketing Communications

    A. Importance of teamwork

    B. Role of databases in effective IMC programs

III. The Communications Process

IV. Objectives of Promotion

    A. Provide information

    B. Increase demand

    C. Differentiate the product

    D. Accentuate the product's value

    E. Stabilize sales

V. The Promotional Mix

    A. Personal selling

    B. Nonpersonal selling

VI. Sponsorships

    A. Sponsorship spending

    B. Growth of sponsorships

    C. How sponsorship differs from advertising

    D. Assessing sponsorship results

    E. Using sponsorships in a promotional strategy

VII. Direct Marketing

A. Direct marketing communications channels

B. Direct mail

C. Telemarketing

D. Direct marketing via broadcast channels

E. Electronic direct marketing channels

F. Other direct marketing channels

VIII. Developing an Optimal Promotional Mix

A. Nature of the market

B. Nature of the product

C. Stage in the product life cycle

D. Price

E. Funds available for promotion

IX. Pulling and Pushing Promotional Strategies

X. Budgets for Promotional Strategy

XI. Measuring the Effectiveness of Promotion

A. Measuring Online Promotion

XII. The Value of Marketing Communications

A. Social importance

B. Business importance

C. Economic importance

XIII. Strategic Implications

Name_____Instructor_____

Section_____Date_____

Key Concepts

The purpose of this section is to allow you to determine if you can match key concepts with their definitions. It is essential that you know the definitions of the concepts prior to applying the concepts in later exercises in this chapter.

From the list of lettered terms, select the one that best fits in the blank of the numbered statement below. Write the letter of that choice in the space provided.

Key Terms

a. promotion
b. marketing communication
c. integrated marketing
    communications (IMC)
d. AIDA concept
e. promotional mix
f. personal selling
g. advertising
h. sales promotion
i. trade promotion
j. direct marketing
k. public relations
l. publicity
m. sponsorship
n. telemarketing
o. infomercial
p. pulling strategy
q. pushing strategy
r. percentage-of-sales method
s. fixed-sum-per-unit method
t. meeting competition
u. task-objective method

_____ 1. Marketing activities other than personal selling, advertising, and publicity that stimulate consumer purchasing and dealer effectiveness.

_____ 2. Interpersonal promotional process involving a seller's presentation conducted on a person-to-person basis with a prospective buyer.

_____ 3. Paid, nonpersonal communication through various media by an entity that is identified in the message and that hopes to inform or persuade members of a particular audience.

_____ 4. Transmission from a sender to a receiver of a message dealing with the buyer-seller relationship.

_____ 5. Sales promotions aimed at marketing intermediaries rather than ultimate consumers.

_____ 6. Firm's communications and relationships with its various publics.

_____ 7. Promotional effort by a seller to stimulate demand among final users who will exert pressure on the distribution channel to provide the good or service.

_____ 8. Allocation method in which budgeted promotional expenditures are set at a predetermined dollar amount for each sales or production unit.

_____ 9. Blend of personal selling and nonpersonal selling created by marketers to achieve promotional objectives.

_____ 10. Stimulation of demand by unpaid placement of commercially significant news or favorable media presentations by an identifiable entity.

_____ 11. Promotional presentation of a single product running 30 minutes or longer in a format that resembles a regular television program.

_____ 12. Use of the telephone for outbound contacts by salespeople or inbound contacts initiated by customers who want to obtain information or place orders.

_____ 13. Provision of funds for a sporting or cultural event in exchange for a direct association with the event.

_____ 14. Acronym for the traditional explanation of the steps an individual must take to complete a purchase decision.

_____ 15. Promotional budgeting method in which a firm defines its goals and then determines the amount of promotional spending needed to achieve them.

_____ 16. Budget allocation method that matches competitors' promotional outlays on either an absolute or relative basis.

_____ 17. Method in which the funds allocated for promotion during a given time are based on a specified percentage of either past or forecast sales.

_____ 18. Function of informing, persuading, and influencing the consumer's purchase decision

_____ 19. Direct communications other than personal sales contacts between buyer and seller.

_____ 20. Effort by a seller to members of the marketing channel to stimulate personal selling of the good or service.

_____ 21. Coordination of all promotional activities to produce a unified promotional message that is customer-focused.

Part 7 Promotional Strategy

Name_____ Instructor_____

Section_____Date_____

Self-Quiz

You should use these questions to test your understanding of the material in this chapter. You can check your answers with those provided at the end of the chapter.

While these questions cover most of the chapter topics, they are not intended to be the same as the test questions your instructor may use in an examination. A good understanding of all aspects of the course material is necessary to good performance on any examination.

True/False

Write "T" for True and "F" for False for each of the following statements.

____ 1. Integrated marketing communication broadens promotion to include all the ways a customer has contact with the organization to present a unified, consistent message.

____ 2. Mass media such as TV ads are the mainstays of marketing campaigns.

____ 3. Indirect sampling is a method that can be used to quickly obtain customer opinions about a firm's goods and services.

____ 4. In communications, for a message to be effective, it must only gain the receiver's attention and be understood by both receiver and sender.

____ 5. E. K. Strong's "AIDA concept" pointed out that promotional messages had as their ultimate objective producing action in the form of a purchase or a more favorable attitude that might lead to future purchases.

____ 6. A classic example of noise in the communications process is the statement in the Japanese information booklet about using a hotel air conditioner that read "Cooles and Heates: If you want just condition of warm in your room, please control yourself."

____ 7. Videocassettes containing promotional messages have proven to be relatively unsuccessful, research showing that only about 10 percent of recipients view them and response rates average only 4 percent.

____ 8. While some promotions are aimed at increasing selective demand, most seek to increase primary demand.

____ 9. Under conditions of homogeneous demand, the firm has almost no control over marketing variables such as the price of its products.

____ 10. While many people equate direct marketing with direct mail, it also includes telemarketing, direct response advertising, infomercials on TV and radio, direct-response print ads, and interactive electronic media.

Harcourt, Inc.

Contemporary Marketing

_____ 11. Advertising, direct marketing, and sales promotion typically account for the bulk of a firm's promotional expenditures.

_____ 12. Sales promotion includes displays, trade shows, coupons, contests, samples, premiums, product demonstrations, and various nonrecurring, irregular selling efforts.

_____ 13. Sponsorship as a promotional alternative is a new phenomenon, never having existed until the beginning of commercial radio in the United States.

_____ 14. A pulling promotional strategy relies heavily on personal selling to convince members of the channel of distribution to spend extra time and effort promoting the vendor's product.

_____ 15. Stabilizing fluctuations in sales that result from cyclical, seasonal, or irregular demand is often an objective of promotional strategy.

_____ 16. In the communications process, the message must be decoded before it can be transmitted through a communications channel.

_____ 17. The ideal method of allocating a promotional budget is to increase the budget until no further money is available to be spent for promotion; in other words, to use every penny you can lay your hands on for promotion.

_____ 18. Companies actually spend about as much on trade promotion as on advertising and consumer-oriented sales promotion combined.

_____ 19. Criticisms of advertising which accuse it of being "tasteless" and "without contribution to society" sometimes ignore the fact that no commonly accepted set of priorities for such judgments exists within our social framework. In other words, there's no such thing as "bad taste" or "good taste," only your taste and my taste.

_____ 20. Probably the most common way to set promotional budgets, the "fixed-sum-per-unit method" applies a predetermined money allocation to each unit of sale or production.

_____ 21. Direct mail offers advantages such as the fact that response rates are measurable and higher than other types of advertising.

_____ 22. Marketers have overcome the difficulty of isolating the effects of promotion from those of other marketing elements and outside environmental variables.

_____ 23. Among the indirect methods of evaluating the effectiveness of advertising are recall and readership measurements.

_____ 24. Integrated marketing communications looks at the parts of the promotional mix from the point of view of the consumer.

_____ 25. A customer-specific marketing strategy such as is used in online marketing requires not only a means of identifying and communicating with the firm's target market but also information regarding important characteristics of each prospective customer.

Harcourt, Inc.

Multiple Choice

Circle the letter of the phrase or sentence that best completes the sentence or best answers the question.

26. An effective message must
    a. be understood by the receiver.
    b. stimulate the receiver's needs and suggest an appropriate method of satisfying them.
    c. be understood by the sender.
    d. gain the receiver's attention.
    e. achieve all of the above objectives.

27. The AIDA concept proposed by E. K. Strong over sixty years ago explains
    a. why Giuseppe Verdi named his opera in this peculiar fashion.
    b. the steps through which an individual reaches a purchase decision.
    c. the relationship among ability, intelligence, dedication, and activity in the marketing process.
    d. the structural relationships among variables in the promotional mix.
    e. the components of the promotion process: advertising, indoctrination, description, and acceptance.

28. In the communications process, attitude change, purchase, or nonpurchase are forms of
    a. feedback, and complete the communication system.
    b. transmission, the use of the communications channel.
    c. encoding, reduction of the message to understandable terms.
    d. decoding, interpretation of the message.
    e. noise, a continuous hazard to effective communication.

29. This promotional tool provides a short-term incentive, usually in combination with other forms of promotion, to emphasize, assist, supplement, or otherwise support the objectives of the promotional program:
    a. advertising.
    b. personal selling.
    c. sales promotion.
    d. public relations.
    e. publicity.

30. Of the following, which most correctly exemplifies noise in the marketing communications process?
    a. A viewer of a television commercial for a lemon-scented dishwashing detergent becomes confused and believes he/she is watching a commercial for a lemonade mix.
    b. A viewer of the President's State of the Union message refuses to believe a word of it because he/she is a member of a different political party.
    c. An individual isn't there when a promotional message appears on television.
    d. Visitors to a city in "tornado alley" laugh off a tornado alert because they've never been through a twister and don't believe in the danger.
    e. A commercial is presented at the right time to the right audience using an appropriate advertising medium.

31. A newspaper advertisement that emphasizes information about a retail store's location, its hours of opening, and the lines of merchandise it carries is designed primarily to
    a. differentiate the store's offerings from competitive merchandise in the same marketplace.
    b. increase primary demand for the store's product lines.
    c. provide information to consumers and others.

Harcourt, Inc.

d. stabilize sales of the products over a period of time.
   e. promote the business rather than the merchandise itself.

32. A hotel which offers "weekend retreat" packages at lower rates than it rents those same rooms during the week is attempting to
   a. build brand image and equity for the hotel and stimulate selective demand.
   b. focus interest on their offering's novelty and demonstrate its superiority.
   c. provide product information for potential customers.
   d. supplement high occupancy during the week from business travelers and stabilize sales.
   e. differentiate their product and take control over its price.

33. The major advantages of direct marketing as a promotional mix element are
   a. accuracy in monitoring and measurement, production of immediate consumer response, and provision of short-term sales increases.
   b. substantially higher credibility than other promotional techniques and extremely low media cost.
   c. ability to create instant awareness of a product and build brand equity.
   d. provision of an action-oriented choice, permitting narrow audience segmentation and customization of communications, and production of measurable results.
   e. difficulty in measurement of effectiveness and high media costs.

34. A firm's communications and relationships with its various publics defines its
   a. publicity efforts.
   b. public relations activities.
   c. advertising expenditures.
   d. sales promotional program.
   e. personal selling commitments.

35. Advertising, sales promotion, direct marketing, and public relations are all
   a. paid communications through various media that include identification of the sponsor and hope to inform or persuade members of a particular audience.
   b. examples of promotion through mass media such as newspapers, television, radio, magazines, and billboards.
   c. particularly appropriate methods of promoting products that rely on sending the same promotional message to large audiences.
   d. nonrecurrent personal promotional methods used on an irregular basis.
   e. forms of nonpersonal selling; advertising and sales promotion are usually regarded as the most important.

36. The original form of promotion, the one with the longest history, is
   a. advertising; advertising messages have even been found on the walls of the ruins of Pompeii.
   b. personal selling; presumably, the very first exchanges in trade were made by two individuals acting face to face.
   c. sponsorship; in Rome, competing businesses supported teams of gladiators who wore their sponsors' logos.
   d. public relations; the Phoenicians were careful to keep on good terms with their customers and competitors.
   e. publicity; Pepsi bottles at least three thousand years old have been found at stage level in the ruins of the Greek theater at Catharsis in the Peridontium.

37. If the sponsorship of an event purchased by a particular sponsor included display of the sponsor's name in the hospitality tent, on on-site signs, on merchandise associated with the event, and even on the tickets, but not in the title of the event itself, the level of sponsorship would be called
    a. title sponsorship.
    b. presenting sponsorship.
    c. associate sponsorship.
    d. interim sponsorship.
    e. continuing sponsorship.

38. The fact that highly standardized products with minimal servicing requirements are less likely to depend on personal selling than are custom products that are technically complex is an example of the way the promotional mix can be influenced by
    a. the nature of the market.
    b. the product's stage of the product life cycle.
    c. the nature of the product itself.
    d. the product's price in the marketplace.
    e. the funds available for promotion.

39. The stage of the product life cycle during which creative promotions often become necessary to keep the product in the minds of consumers is
    a. maturity.
    b. mid-growth.
    c. decline.
    d. early growth.
    e. introduction.

40. If a manufacturer begins advertising a new product to consumers before that good has become available to marketing intermediaries in the channel of distribution, it is probably using a
    a. pushing strategy to secure distribution at the wholesale level of the channel.
    b. thrust-off promotion to get the product adopted by the members of the channel before the public becomes aware of it.
    c. mixed-bag strategy designed to create the proper atmosphere for product introduction to the consumer market.
    d. pulling strategy to develop end-user demand so that final consumers will put pressure on intermediaries to stock the product.
    e. forced-choice program to make channel members decide which of two competing products they're going to stock.

41. Which of the following statements is most true of direct marketing?
    a. The direct marketer has little control of events beyond matching audiences to profiles of its own target markets.
    b. It can deliver the marketer's message to mass audiences for a relatively low cost per contact.
    c. Its use does not necessarily lead directly to orders, sales leads, store traffic, or increased sales.
    d. It now accounts for over half of total U.S. advertising expenditures – $285 million in 1998.
    e. It suffers from a rate of growth slower than that of most other promotional alternatives.

42. The two major techniques for setting Internet advertising rates are
    a. number of hits per day and recall measurements of how much members of the target market remember of their use of the site.
    b. number of visits to the site and readership of site content.
    c. cost per impression (CPM) and cost-per-response (click-throughs).

d. indirect measurement of scanner data.
e. store audits and customer counts.

43. The method of allocating a promotional budget based on a sound evaluation of the firm's promotional objectives is the
    a. percentage of sales method.
    b. fixed-sum-per-unit method
    c. the task-objective method.
    d. method of meeting competition.
    e. method of allocating a fixed sum for advertising: when it's gone, it's gone.

44. The most common way of establishing promotional budgets is most likely the
    a. marginal analysis method of Paul Samuelson.
    b. percentage-of-sales method.
    c. fixed amount available method.
    d. fixed-sum-per-unit method.
    e. method described by Alois Svoboda in *Alligators and Advertising*.

45. Effective use of marginal analysis for promotional budgeting requires
    a. carefully hoarding money from one year to the next until it can be most effectively spent.
    b. having available a very large sum of uncommitted funds to support the promotional program.
    c. understanding the necessity for a concentration of funds on advertising and the lesser importance of personal selling.
    d. retarding the promotional expenditure flow until results are apparent.
    e. identifying the optimal point, which requires a precise balance between marginal expenses for promotion and resulting marginal receipts.

46. Personal selling is usually considered to work better than advertising under which set of conditions?
    a. when the target market is made up of industrial purchasers or retail or wholesale intermediaries
    b. when the product being promoted to the ultimate consumer is an over-the-counter drug
    c. when the market is composed of a large number of buyers scattered over a large geographic area
    d. when the product is a highly standardized, non-technical item available almost everywhere
    e. when the product is of low unit value

47. Given the capacity to control for other variables operating in the marketplace, most marketers would prefer to measure promotional effectiveness using
    a. standard statistical tools such as mean difference testing.
    b. sales inquiries and studies of attitude change caused by promotion.
    c. indirect evaluation of effectiveness using such devices as recall and readership analysis.
    d. direct-sales-results tests which would reveal the impact on sales of every dollar spent on advertising.
    e. traditional methods based on the expertise of company executives.

48. Promotion has assumed a degree of economic importance if for no other reason than that
    a. government decisions eventually determine what is acceptable practice in the marketplace.
    b. most modern business institutions cannot survive in the long run without promotion.
    c. business enterprises recognize the importance of promotional efforts.
    d. many television commercials contribute to cultural pollution.
    e. it provides employment for thousands of people.

49. Comments such as "Most advertisements assume I'm an idiot" and "Advertising is almost always in bad taste" relate to
    a. the importance of advertising to the economic well-being of the country.
    b. advertising's role in perpetuating undesirable stereotypes.
    c. advertising's importance as a business phenomenon.
    d. relationships we've all noticed between advertising and mental capacity.
    e. perceptions of advertising relating to its social importance.

50. Promotion can be said to have business importance because
    a. most modern institutions simply cannot survive in the long run without promotion.
    b. it reduces sales volume, thus increasing per-unit cost.
    c. it subsidizes the communications media.
    d. it performs all of the functions outlined above.
    e. None of the above constitutes a valid reason to call promotion "important."

Contemporary Marketing

Name_____   Instructor_____

Section_____   Date_____

Applying Marketing Concepts

It's always a little rough to report for work at a new place for the first time, and Malcolm Carmichael admitted to himself that he felt uneasy about his new job at Heindorf Chemie, one of Schwabisch-Gmund's best known makers of essential chemicals. Replacing a promotions manager who had been there for twenty-five years was not an enviable task. It didn't take Malcolm long to get into the swing of things and settle down to a long, close look at the company's promotional program.

Some things were pretty much as he expected them to be. As an industrial supplier, Heindorf followed fairly conventional advertising and personal selling practices. John was disturbed, however, when he discovered that there was no mechanism by which the comments and actions of customers were reported back to his department. He also observed that many of the company's promotional pieces – advertisements, catalogs, and mailers – were poorly written and hard to understand. He also noticed that a large number of items that had been mailed to customers and prospective customers were returned by the post office as undeliverable.

He also felt he had cause to worry about the company's relationship with the local community. Fences surrounding the plant bore signs saying "No Trespassing–Keep Out" and the main gate, which was guarded by armed security personnel, was even more intimidating with its "Stop–Show Identification–Authorized Personnel Only" sign. Such isolation seemed a bit much to John, as did the fact that Heindorf had no athletic teams playing in the local junior or adult leagues.

Circle the letter of the phrase or sentence that best completes the sentence or best answers the question.

1. Heindorf's promotional program probably
   a. puts more emphasis on personal selling than on advertising.
   b. puts more emphasis on advertising than on personal selling.
   c. emphasizes personal selling and advertising about equally.
   d. uses neither personal selling nor advertising.
   e. relies on publicity to carry the burden of promotion.

2. Malcolm's concern about the lack of a way for him to get to know customers' comments and actions indicates he was distressed
   a. with the effectiveness of his sales promotion program.
   b. with the degree to which his advertising money was being wasted on fancy artwork by the layout department.
   c. that feedback from the marketplace was not being used to make adjustments to the company's programs and practices.
   d. that his position in the company was isolated from the decision makers at headquarters.
   e. that salespeople weren't doing their jobs in the field properly.

3. The large number of returns of mailed material, if they are not the post office's fault, probably resulted from
   a. errors or missed classifications in the database from which the mailings are compiled.
   b. refusals by recipients because they don't like Heindorf.

c. a problem with noise in the communications process.
   d. difficulties with decoding by recipients of the mailings.
   e. interference with the mail by the vampires who are rampant in Schwabisch-Gmund.

4. Difficulty in understanding an advertising message, a catalog entry, or the vocabulary of a mailer means
   a. that Heindorf Chemie must be on the verge of failure.
   b. very little; these sorts of things are used merely to get the customer's attention.
   c. that someone in the production department probably wrote the catalogs.
   d. that there is a danger that enough noise will be created in the communications channel to defeat the intent of the communication.
   e. that someone has probably been trying to do two jobs at once: write advertising and learn to read.

5. Heindorf Chemie's seeming isolation from the local community is probably evidence
   a. of good legal thinking; the company doesn't want to have to worry about paying for injuries to unauthorized persons on its grounds. It's better to shoot them for trespassing before they can hurt themselves.
   b. of the fact that they've got something evil to hide at their plant location.
   c. that the president of the company really did say "Bah, humbug!" last Christmas when approached by the local Church Fund.
   d. of the low level of competitiveness in the chemical market these days.
   e. of a serious weakness in their public relations program.

Movable Magnetic Memory Corporation (M3), a manufacturer of removable hard drive disks for computers, sells M3's 10 gigabyte removable disks to wholesalers in units of twelve to a case, which is the standard unit for sales and cost analysis purposes. Winnie Do Illepu, the promotions manager for M3, is concerned that intermediaries are not making a strong effort to tell ultimate users about the benefits of the removable disks. She is considering mounting a promotion campaign aimed directly at her ultimate target market rather than promoting to the intermediaries and leaving promotion to ultimate users primarily in their hands, as is presently the case.

Winnie is also concerned about how money for promotional activities is budgeted. At present, she is allotted $18 per case of disks shipped to use for promotional purposes. Corporate goals are to increase M3's market share from the present 8 percent to 15 percent in three years. Winnie doesn't see how she can do that with the money that's been budgeted.

6. Winnie's concern with the efforts of the intermediaries reflects her doubt about the effectiveness of the present
   a. waffling strategy being used by M3.
   b. pushing strategy used by the company.
   c. running strategy in place.
   d. "smoking gun" approach to promotion.
   e. pulling strategy favored by management.

7. Conversion to a promotion strategy that would call for M3 to promote directly to ultimate users would result in a
   a. timing approach to promotion.
   b. strong pushing effect by intermediaries.
   c. great deal of confusion about where to buy M3 disks.
   d. pulling strategy for the M3 disks.

Harcourt, Inc.

e. lawsuit by competitors; you can't do it that way.

8. Which of the following promotional budgeting techniques is M3 using now?
   a. percentage of sales
   b. task-objective method
   c. fixed sum per unit
   d. meeting competition
   e. spend what you have

9. If 10 percent of total sales had been the promotional allocating rule, the method would have then been
   a. percentage of sales.
   b. fixed sum per unit.
   c. meeting competition.
   d. task-objective method.
   e. marginal analysis method.

10. If Winnie can convince management that she needs to spend $15 million over the next three years to achieve the desired market share, regardless of how many units are shipped during the period, she will have converted them to which of the following budgeting approaches?
    a. meeting competition
    b. arbitrary allocation
    c. task-objective method
    d. marginal revenue approach
    e. perfect world method

Name_____ Instructor_____

Section_____ Date_____

Surfing the Net

Keeping in mind that addresses change and what's on the Web now may have changed by the time you read this, let's take a look at some of the places on the Net that reflect aspects of integrated promotion. We are not endorsing or recommending any of these sources, merely making note of the information and services that people have elected to offer through the Internet.

Looking to sell your home? There are several sites that feature *Sale by Owner* areas, places that list and describe homes offered by their owners. Two of these advertising vehicles may be found at: **http://www.AbetterFSBO.com** and **http://www.virtualfsbo.com**

Direct Marketing Online? Try the *a2z Online Mall* at **http://a2zshopping.net/cgi-bin** or *Downtown Anywhere*, "conveniently located in central cyberspace" at **http://awa.com**. These sites feature retail merchandise.

Need a bear? Teddy, that is. The Vermont Teddy Bear Company at **http://www.vtbear.com** manufactures Teddy Bears and sells them on the Net. Even this small firm has found the Internet an appropriate vehicle for its message.

Need photographs for your ads, brochures, and other promotional materials? Online at **http://www.ppa-world.org**, the Professional Photographers' Association or **http://metalab.unc.edu/nppa**, the National Press Photographers' Association, can put you in touch with a photographer or a photo library that should be able to help you out.

How about some people to do the work? Well, we've got public relations firms at **http://www.prfirms.org**, their trade organization Web site, and advertising agencies (for the UK, anyway) at **http://www.adassoc.org.uk**. I was somewhat surprised not to find a Web site for the American Association of Advertising Agencies, but I could have missed it. Perhaps one might look in the listings at **http://www.mediapost.com**, which claims to publish a comprehensive list of all media professionals, and find something on a local basis. Finally, there's a firm that looks quite interesting at **http://www.commando.com**, that claims to be an "alternative marketing communications firm," whatever that means.

Sites verified January 15, 2000.

Part 7 Promotional Strategy

Chapter 16

Advertising, Sales Promotion, and Public Relations

Chapter Outline

Use the following as a guide in taking notes.

I. Chapter Overview: The Nonpersonal Elements of Promotion

II. Advertising

    A. Types of advertising

    B. Objectives of advertising

III. Advertising Strategies

    A. Comparative advertising

    B. Celebrity testimonials

    C. Retail advertising

    D. Interactive advertising

IV. Creating an Advertisement

    A. Translating advertising objectives into advertising plans

    B. Advertising Messages

    C. Developing and preparing ads

    C. Creating interactive ads

V. Media Selection

    A. Television

    B. Radio

    C. Newspapers

    D. Magazines

    E. Direct mail

    F. Outdoor advertising

Harcourt, Inc.

G. Interactive media

H. Other advertising media

VI. Media Scheduling

A. Hypothetical media schedule

VII. Organization of the Advertising Function

A. Advertising agencies

VIII. Sales Promotion

A. Consumer-oriented sales promotion

1. Coupons and refunds

2. Samples, bonus packs, and premiums

3. Contests and sweepstakes

4. Specialty advertising

B. Trade-oriented promotions

1. Trade allowances

2. Point-of-purchase advertising

3. Trade shows

4. Dealer incentives, contests, and training programs

IX. Public Relations

A. Marketing and nonmarketing public relations

B. Publicity

X. Cross Promotion

XI. Measuring Promotional Effectiveness

A. Measuring advertising effectiveness

1. Pretesting

2. Posttesting

    B. Measuring sales promotion effectiveness

    C. Measuring public relations effectiveness

    D. Evaluating interactive media

XII. Ethics in Nonpersonal Selling

    A. Advertising ethics

        1. Puffery and deception

    B. Ethics in sales promotion and public relations

XIII. Strategic Implications of Advertising and Sales Promotion

Contemporary Marketing

Name_____ Instructor_____

Section_____ Date_____

Key Concepts

The purpose of this section is to allow you to determine if you can match key concepts with their definitions. It is essential that you know the definitions of the concepts before applying the concepts in later exercises in this chapter.

From the list of lettered terms, select the one that best fits in the blank of the numbered statement below. Write the letter of that choice in the space provided.

Key Terms

a. advertising
b. product advertising
c. institutional advertising
d. informative advertising
e. persuasive advertising
f. reminder advertising
g. comparative advertising
h. retail advertising
i. cooperative advertising
j. interactive media
k. banner
l. keyword ad
m. interstitials
n. media scheduling

o. advertising agency
p. sales promotion
q. specialty advertising
r. trade promotion
s. trade allowances
t. point-of-purchase advertising
u. public relations
v. publicity
w. cross promotion
x. pretesting
y. posttesting
z. cookie
aa. puffery
ab. bandwidth

_____ 1. Timing and sequencing of advertisements.

_____ 2. Marketing activities other than personal selling, advertising, and publicity that stimulate consumer purchasing and dealer effectiveness.

_____ 3. Displays and other promotions located near the site of the actual buying decision.

_____ 4. Assessment of an advertisement's effectiveness after it has been used.

_____ 5. Deals offered to wholesalers and retailers for purchasing or promoting specific products.

_____ 6. Web advertisements that pop up between Web pages of related content.

_____ 7. Sales promotion technique that involves the distribution of articles such as key rings and ball-point pens that bear the advertiser's name, address, and advertising message.

_____ 8. Small text file that is automatically downloaded to a user's computer whenever a site is visited and is capable of gathering information on the user.

Part 7 Promotional Strategy

____ 9. Sales promotion geared to marketing intermediaries rather than consumers.

____ 10. Nonpersonal selling effort that makes direct or indirect promotional comparisons with competing brands.

____ 11. Firm's communications and relationships with its various publics.

____ 12. A technique in which marketing partners share the cost of a promotional campaign that meets their mutual needs.

____ 13. Promotion seeking to reinforce previous promotional activity by keeping the name of the good, service, organization, person, place, idea, or cause in front of the public.

____ 14. Nonpersonal selling of a good or service.

____ 15. Nonpersonal selling by stores that offer goods or services directly to the consuming public.

____ 16. Exaggerated claims of a product's superiority or the use of subjective or vague statements that may not be literally true.

____ 17. Web advertisement that links to an advertiser's site.

____ 18. Assessment of an advertisement's effectiveness before it is actually used.

____ 19. Web advertisement that appears on the results page of a search function, specific to the searched item.

____ 20. Promoting a concept, an idea, a philosophy, or the goodwill of an industry, company, organization, place, person, or government agency.

____ 21. Paid, nonpersonal communication through various media by business firms, nonprofit organizations, and individuals who are identified in their messages and who hope to inform or persuade members of particular audiences.

____ 22. Sharing of advertising costs between the manufacturer and the retailer of a good or service.

____ 23. Marketing specialist firm that assists advertisers in planning and implementing advertising programs.

____ 24. Communication channels in which message recipients actively participate in promotional efforts.

____ 25. Number of bytes that can be transmitted over the Internet at one time, enabling use of elaborate interactive programs.

____ 26. Promotion that seeks to announce the availability of and develop initial demand for a good, service, organization, person, place, idea, or cause.

____ 27. Stimulation of demand for a good, service, place, idea, person, or organization by disseminating commercially significant news or obtaining favorable media presentation not paid for by the sponsor.

_____ 28. Competitive promotion that seeks to develop demand for a good, service, organization, person, place, idea, or cause.

Part 7 Promotional Strategy

Name_____ Instructor_____

Section_____ Date_____

Self Quiz

You should use these questions to test your understanding of the chapter material. You can check your answers with those provided at the end of the chapter.

While these questions cover most of the chapter topics, they are not intended to be the same as the test questions your instructor may use in an examination. A good understanding of all aspects of the course material is essential to good performance on any examination.

True/False

Write "T" for True and "F" for False for each of the following statements.

_____ 1. The term institutional advertising is broader in meaning than the term corporate advertising, though they both refer to nonproduct promotion.

_____ 2. The nation's two leading advertisers – Philip Morris Companies and Procter & Gamble – spend more than $4.5 billion each per year on advertising.

_____ 3. One would expect to find persuasive advertising being used in the introductory stage of the product life cycle.

_____ 4. Ultimately, the three primary objectives of advertising are to inform, to persuade, and to remind – either individually or together – the target of the advertisement of something.

_____ 5. The Web is now capable of matching television's ability to provide high-quality moving pictures, sound, and entertainment to the viewer.

_____ 6. Advertising attempts to condition consumers to adopt favorable viewpoints toward the promotional message.

_____ 7. Interactive media differ from traditional advertising by providing brief, entertaining, attention-getting messages rather than helping the consumer through the purchase and consumption processes.

_____ 8. Product advertising is the type of promotion that comes to the average person's mind when advertising is the topic of conversation.

_____ 9. Cartoon characters delivering celebrity testimonials are seldom used by advertisers because they lack credibility – after all, who's really going to believe a cartoon character uses a product?

_____ 10. Cooperative advertising is another name for institutional advertising sponsored by a specific firm.

Harcourt, Inc.

_____ 11. The objective of media selection is to obtain adequate media coverage without advertising beyond the identifiable limits of the potential market.

_____ 12. Most newspaper advertising revenues come from national advertisers, while television derives the bulk of its revenues from local sources.

_____ 13. In the past decade, cable television's share of advertising revenues has grown by more than 30 percent, while the networks' share is declining.

_____ 14. Among the disadvantages of television advertising are its lack of impact, inflexibility, and low prestige rating.

_____ 15. Radio – thanks to the Internet – has become a means of staying in touch with home, wherever home may be.

_____ 16. Magazines are divided into three basic categories – consumer, farm, and business publications.

_____ 17. Outdoor advertising as a medium is growing faster than newspapers, magazines, and network TV and lagging behind only the Internet and cable television in rate of growth.

_____ 18. Interactive media like the Web and e-mail are being used by companies to replace their messages over traditional media.

_____ 19. Advertising agencies are often used by large advertisers because they employ highly qualified specialists who provide a degree of creativity and objectivity that is difficult to sustain in a corporate advertising department.

_____ 20. Posttesting is generally more desirable than pretesting of advertising because of the potential cost savings.

_____ 21. Sales promotion, on a dollars-and-cents basis, is actually more important than advertising, commanding double the promotional dollar outlays of advertising.

_____ 22. Specialty advertising began when early automobile vendors began giving their customers free key chains as a souvenir of their visit to the showroom.

_____ 23. Sales promotion premiums are items given free or at reduced cost when another product is purchased, the objective often being to motivate consumers to try new products or different brands.

_____ 24. Public relations is an efficient indirect communications channel for promoting products, although its objectives are broader than those of other components of promotional strategy.

_____ 25. Relationship marketing programs like co-branding and co-marketing are forms of cross promotion.

Part 7 Promotional Strategy

Multiple Choice

Circle the letter of the word or phrase that best completes the sentence or best answers the question.

26. An advertisement that emphasizes the superiority of one product over another – and names the products – is a(n)
    a. reminder advertisement.
    b. comparative advertisement.
    c. institutional advertisement.
    d. creative advertisement.
    e. illegal advertisement.

27. About 20 percent of U.S. ads and 80 percent of Japanese ads include
    a. celebrities.
    b. price comparisons.
    c. puffery.
    d. appeals to patriotism.
    e. musical references.

28. The dominant advertising medium in the United States is
    a. television, though it is being challenged by direct mail.
    b. radio, because of the tremendous flexibility it offers.
    c. the newspaper, though television has come to rival this choice.
    d. magazines, because everybody reads them.
    e. direct mail because no one has time to shop anymore.

29. Advertising that seeks to develop initial demand for a good, service, organization, person, place, idea, or cause is called
    a. product advertising.
    b. persuasive advertising.
    c. informative advertising.
    d. reminder advertising.
    e. comparative advertising.

30. Advertising that strives to reinforce previous promotional activity by keeping the name of the advertised thing or concept before the public is called
    a. selective advertising.
    b. reminder advertising.
    c. informative advertising.
    d. selective advertising.
    e. persuasive information.

31. If an advertisement by the National Fisheries Council were to appear that featured the idea that it is a good thing to eat lots and lots of any kind of fish – because fish is a good source of vitamins and minerals not found elsewhere – we could categorize that ad as
    a. product advertising.
    b. persuasive advertising.
    c. reminder advertising.
    d. political advertising.
    e. institutional advertising.

Harcourt, Inc.

Contemporary Marketing

32. Radio advertising has become "the fastest growing media alternative" in recent years because
    a. of its quality reproduction, long life, ease of carriage, and prestige.
    b. it possesses formal flexibility, completeness of information, and personalization.
    c. it is quite popular in rural areas where other media are not available.
    d. in additional to its traditional virtues, it has become a force on the Internet as well.
    e. it has powerful multisensory impact, mass coverage, flexibility, and repetition of message.

33. Which advertising medium offers the advantages of selectivity, intensive coverage, speed, completeness of information, and personalization, among others?
    a. radio
    b. television
    c. newspapers
    d. magazines
    e. direct mail

34. Some of the disadvantages of using the newspaper medium as an advertising vehicle are
    a. lack of flexibility found in other media, long lead time between ad placement and appearance.
    b. short life span, relatively poor reproduction quality, and haste in reading.
    c. high cost, loss of control of the promotional message, and public distrust of the medium.
    d. consumer resistance to the medium and high per-person acquisition cost.
    e. the necessity for an extremely brief message and lack of aesthetics in the eyes of the public.

35. Interactive media
    a. enhances two-way communication but discourages audience participation.
    b. supplements messages delivered traditionally, causing confusion among its viewers.
    c. contains characteristics of both print and broadcast media.
    d. suffers from a low-level of consumer involvement, with e-mail responses around 1 percent.
    e. is too expensive right now to be considered a viable medium.

36. Outdoor advertising is particularly effective
    a. in rural locations where the message can be seen at a great distance.
    b. when placed along lightly traveled streets so that people can pay more attention to the advertising and less to driving.
    c. when fairly large blocks of print are used to communicate the desired information.
    d. when placed along metropolitan streets and in other high-traffic areas.
    e. when placed so that foot traffic is forced to detour around the billboards to get where it's going.

37. Within most businesses, the advertising function is usually set up as
    a. a staff department reporting to the vice-president or director of marketing.
    b. a line department reporting directly to the chief executive officer of the company.
    c. a home-office department housed in the engineering division.
    d. a staff department responsible directly to the president of the firm.
    e. a functional division of the company with its own vice-president and an equal voice in company policymaking with all other divisions.

38. The world's largest advertising agency
    a. is the Japanese government agency, All-Nippon Advertising.
    b. has become Moscow-based NovoRuss Information.
    c. is the London-based WPP Group.
    d. is the international McCann-Erickson Worldwide.

e. is Madrid-based Publicidad Generale de Espana.

39. The final step in the advertising process is
a. choice of a medium to carry the message.
b. definition of a target market to which to appeal.
c. retention of an advertising agency to develop the program.
d. development and production of an actual advertisement.
e. measurement of the effect of the advertisement.

40. This type of consumer-oriented sales promotion is typically distributed as mail, magazine, newspaper, and package insertions, and is the most widely used form of sales promotion. It is
a. refunds.
b. samples of products.
c. contests.
d. bonus packs.
e. coupons.

41. When a manufacturer agrees to pay a reseller a certain amount to pay the costs of special promotional displays or extensive advertising that features the manufacturer's product, you have an example of
a. a buying allowance.
b. an off-invoice allowance.
c. a promotional allowance.
d. a slotting allowance.
e. a point-of-purchase allowance.

42. Every year, in the United States and Canada, over 4,300 of these sales promotions draw over 1.3 million exhibitors and 85 million visitors. They are
a. professional conventions.
b. advertising councils.
c. county fairs.
d. trade shows.
e. rock concerts.

43. The form of consumer-oriented sales promotion that requires the entrant to solve a problem or write an essay and perhaps also submit a proof of purchase to participate, is
a. the sweepstakes.
b. a contest.
c. point-of-purchase promotion.
d. consumer sampling.
e. couponing.

44. A company's communication with its various publics about general management issues are
a. public relations activities that support marketing goals.
b. nonmarketing public relations.
c. proactive MPR.
d. reactive MPR.
e. publicity.

45. When a manufacturer shares the cost of a retailer's advertising its products, it is practicing
a. demonstrative advertising.

b. comparative advertising.
c. retailer-sponsored advertising.
d. testimonial advertising.
e. cooperative advertising.

46. When interviewers from McCann-Erickson ask heavy users of a product which of two alternative advertisements would convince them to purchase it, they are conducting a
    a. sales conviction test.
    b. blind product test.
    c. dummy ad test.
    d. recognition pretest.
    e. aided recall test.

47. The posttest of advertising effectiveness in which interviewers ask people who have read selected magazines whether they observed various ads in them is
    a. the *Starch Readership Report*.
    b. the Gallup and Robinson *Unaided Recall Test*.
    c. Burke's *Day-After Interview System*.
    d. *AdWatch*, a joint venture of the Gallup Organization and *Advertising Age*.
    e. Inquiry Corporation's *Split Runs*.

48. Looked at from the point of view of dollars spent on the activity,
    a. advertising and sales promotion are virtually tied on a year-to-year basis on the amount spent on each.
    b. advertising accounts for roughly twice as much promotional spending each year as does sales promotion.
    c. sales promotion leads advertising by two-to-one in terms of the dollars spent on each.
    d. public relations and sales promotion together still don't approach the dollar value of advertising each year.
    e. Sales promotion lags both advertising and public relations in yearly expenditures.

49. Created by creating special events, holding press conferences, and preparing news releases and media kits, this aspect of promotion is
    a. point-of-purchase promotion.
    b. sampling.
    c. trade show promotion.
    d. publicity.
    e. specialty advertising.

50. Every year, marketers spend about $8 billion distributing
    a. point-of-purchase displays to retailers all over the United States.
    b. trading stamps through more than 1.5 million supermarkets and small businesses.
    c. samples of product to consumers in stores, by mail, and by hand.
    d. specialty advertising pieces to potential customers in the industrial and consumer markets.
    e. coupons at a rate of about 3,000 per average household.

Part 7 Promotional Strategy

Name_____ Instructor_____

Section_____ Date_____

Applying Marketing Concepts

Your job as national advertising manager for Gherkin-Milk Soap has become a source of great frustration to you. You know that your product is superior to any other cleansing and beauty soap on the market and that the addition of genuine Gherkin juice (Gherkins are small, flavorful cucumbers with a highly concentrated natural drying agent in their juice) makes your product an excellent deodorant and antiperspirant. It is also a totally natural product, containing only organically produced ingredients. But your firm is so small (less than 1 percent of the market) that you can't afford to buy advertising like Procter & Gamble, Lever Brothers, Colgate, or any of the "big boys" of the industry. Faced with this problem, you are considering how best to use your rather modest advertising budget.

Circle the letter of the word or phrase that best completes the sentence or best answers the question.

1. Convinced that your very modest share of the market is due to the fact that the majority of the population doesn't know about your product, you feel that you must use your advertising to tell them who and what you are. The type of advertising to use in this instance would be
   a. product advertising.
   b. persuasive advertising.
   c. outdoor advertising.
   d. reminder advertising.
   e. informative advertising.

2. Very aware that your unique selling proposition requires the use of an advertising medium that will be highly selective, speedy in effect, highly personalized, and capable of delivering a complete message, you choose as your major medium
   a. local newspapers.
   b. direct mail.
   c. specialty magazines.
   d. outdoor advertising.
   e. radio.

3. Convinced that part of the reason your market share is so small is because very few people have ever tried your product, you authorize your local sales representatives to stand near the display of your product in local stores and give away special miniature bars of Gherkin-Milk Soap you've had made up. This promotional technique is
   a. the form of sales promotion known as sampling.
   b. point-of-purchase advertising.
   c. pretesting: recipients of the free bars get to pretest them before buying your soap.
   d. sales promotion by means of specialty advertising.
   e. sales promotion through the use of a premium.

4. Upon reflection, you decide that one way to improve your competitive position would be by advertising your product in such a way as to point out its obvious superiority to Zest, Dial, Irish Spring, and other well-known bath soaps, each of which would be mentioned by name. This type of advertising is called

Harcourt, Inc.

a. competitive advertising.
b. compulsive advertising.
c. comparative advertising.
d. "cause" advertising.
e. corporate advertising.

5. Further thought – you think a lot – convinces you that making a frontal attack on all the major soap companies might not be the best way to develop Gherkin-Milk's market. You consider, however, creating for Gherkin-Milk an advertising program that will stress its extreme gentleness to the skin. Such a program would position your product against the competition by its
   a. applications – it's used differently than all those other soaps.
   b. price – it's bound to be cheaper than the competition.
   c. user characteristics – Gherkin-Milk is not for just anybody.
   d. performance attributes – it's milder and gentler than they are.
   e. product class – there is simply nothing like it anywhere.

6. Finally, you decide to print a little document on the inside of the wrapper of each of those miniature bars of Gherkin-Milk that you are giving away in stores. When presented to the vendor for redemption, it entitles the bearer to a 25-cent reduction on their purchase of another, full-size bar of Gherkin-Milk. The document is
   a. a fraud. You'll just raise the price of the soap to make up the difference.
   b. useless. No merchant will honor your pledge to ante up a quarter a bar against that pledge.
   c. a coupon. Millions of these are distributed daily as incentives to try a new or unfamiliar product.
   d. a rebate. Sort of like when you buy a new car and they send you money for doing it.
   e. a sweepstakes entry. If you're lucky, you'll get a lot more than a quarter for redeeming it.

Mindy Hazelnut has the task of creating her firm's advertising plan for the next fiscal year. She has reviewed all the information she was able to gather very carefully. Her Firm, Foo Fan Fungus Importers, a major international trader in mushrooms, truffles, and related products from Europe and the Far East, spent over $1 million on advertising last year, but Mindy isn't sure what happened to the money. Top management at FFFI set no specific promotional objectives, though they did spend a lot on audience analysis reports and research aimed at identifying the characteristics of the readers of the ads for the company's products. Invoices from research suppliers also note that a substantial sum was paid to McCann-Erickson for some pretesting of ads, and a firm called, Pens, Calendars, and Mugs, Inc., was paid several thousand dollars from the promotional budget. Another large sum was paid to the European Fungus Foundation, Inc., for "Exhibit at Commercial FungusFest 2000."

7. Ms. Hazelnut will probably be unable to come to any conclusions concerning the success of last year's advertising program because
   a. no audience analysis was undertaken.
   b. no objectives were set.
   c. pretesting was done incorrectly.
   d. media choices were improperly made.
   e. the budget was too small for analysis.

8. The research that was done to identify the characteristics of the firm's audience was
   a. a pretest of the company's advertising.
   b. a wise use of a portion of the advertising budget.
   c. budgeted as a test of the achievement of advertising objectives.
   d. a posttest of advertising effectiveness.
   e. the perfect test of the validity of promotional objectives.

9. The money paid to McCann-Erickson for ad pretesting probably went for
   a. galvanic skin response measurements.
   b. the use of a hidden camera to photograph eye movement of ad readers.
   c. studio screening of ads for selected consumers.
   d. blind product tests.
   e. sales conviction tests.

10. The money paid to Pens, Calendars, and Mugs, Inc., was probably for
    a. specialty advertising items like mushroom desk sets and "Fungus-of-the-Month" calendars.
    b. participation in industrial and consumer trade shows.
    c. production of materials to be used in company sales contests.
    d. manufacture of miniature samples of company products to be given as inducements to buyers.
    e. bribes paid to obscure European officials to sign permits allowing the exportation of truffles, tribbles, and other trifles.

11. The check to FungusFest 2000 was probably for
    a. participation in the yearly fungus growers and distributors trade show in Pilsen, Czech Republic.
    b. medical treatment for FFFI employees who, in the course of their labors, picked up a fungus infection.
    c. advertisement in a technical publication celebrating the glory of edible fungi.
    d. breeding fees to a famous agronomist for crossbreeding to upgrade the quality of FFFI's fungi.
    e. rental for outdoor ads all over Europe showing fungi in attractive, tasty-appearing poses.

Name_____ Instructor_____

Section_____ Date_____

Surfing the Net

Keeping in mind that addresses change and what's on the Web now may have changed by the time you read this, let's take a look at some of the places on the Net that offer insights into advertising, sales promotion, and public relations. We are not endorsing or recommending any of these sources, merely making note of the information and services that people have elected to offer through the Internet.

Want to get the scoop on your favorite packaged food maker's offerings? First, check the pantry and see what YOUR cans and boxes say. That's the stuff YOU like. I checked mine and discovered that I could communicate with Tony the Tiger at **http://www.kelloggs.com** or drop an e-mail line to another major cereal maker at a product-specific site: **http://www.cheerios.com**. I also discovered that Quaker Oats was there – we can't leave the hot cereal people out, can we – at **http://www.quakeroats.com** It took a bit more work to find, but for us deep Southerners Falls Mills, out of Belvidere, Tennessee, maintains the site du jour of hot cereal. Give it a look at **http://www.grits.com**. Having discovered this rather interesting nom de site, I wondered what would happen if I tried **http://www.mayonnaise.com** Why don't you have a go at it and see who's there?

Curious about the way public relations works? Check some of the press release databases on the net, like PR Newswire's "Company News on Call" feature at **http://www.prnewswire.com**. That's just one of several services offered at this web site. An alternative source for company news is Business Wire at **http://www.businesswire.com**.

Into trade shows and conferences? Welcome to Trade Show Central at **http://www.tscentral.com**. Can't f what you're looking for there. Go on to **http://expoguide.com** for information on more than 6,000 shows and exhibitions.

As you might expect, the big boys of advertising all have sites. It shouldn't be too hard for you to figure out who's located at **http://www.mccann.com, http://www.ddb.com,** or **http://www.grey.com/frontpage** if you read this chapter.

Sites verified January 19, 2000.

Harcourt, Inc.

Chapter 17

Personal Selling and Sales Force Management

Chapter Outline

Use the following as a guide in taking notes.

I. Chapter Overview – Interpersonal influence processes

II. The Evolution of Personal Selling

III. The Four Sales Channels

    A. Over-the-counter selling

    B. Field selling

    C. Telemarketing

    D. Inside selling

    E. Integrating the various selling channels

IV. Recent Trends in Personal Selling

    A. Relationship selling

    B. Consultative selling

    C. Team selling

    D. Sales force automation

V. Sales Tasks

    A. Order processing

    B. Creative selling

    C. Missionary sales

VI. The Sales Process

    A. Prospecting and qualifying

    B. Approach

        C.   Presentation

        D.   Demonstration

        E.   Handling Objections

        F.   Closing

        G.   Follow-up

VII.   Managing the Sales Effort

        A.   Recruitment and Selection

        B.   Training

        C.   Organization

        D.   Supervision

        E.   Motivation

        F.   Compensation

        G.   Evaluation and control

VIII.   Ethical Issues in Sales

IX.   Strategic Implications of Personal Selling

Part 7 Promotional Strategy

Name_____ Instructor_____

Section_____ Date_____

Key Concepts

The purpose of this section is to allow you to determine if you can match key concepts in the chapter with their definitions. It is essential that you know the definitions of the concepts before using the concepts in later exercises in this chapter.

From the list of lettered terms, select the one that best fits the numbered statement below. Write the letter of that choice in the space provided.

Key Terms

a. personal selling
b. over-the-counter selling
c. field selling
d. telemarketing
e. canned approach
f. inside selling
g. relationship selling
h. consultative selling
I. team selling
j. sales force automation (SFA)
k. order processing
l. creative selling
m. missionary sales
n. prospecting
o. qualifying
p. approach
q. precall planning
r. presentation
s. closing
t. follow-up
u. sales management
v. boundary-spanning role
w. national accounts organization
x. expectancy theory
y. commission
z. salary
aa. sales quota

_____ 1. Determining that a prospect has the needs, income, and purchase authority necessary to become a potential customer.

_____ 2. Promotional presentation involving outbound telephone contacts by salespeople or inbound contacts by customers who want to obtain information and place orders.

_____ 3. Sales manager's activities to link the sales force to other elements of an organization's internal and external environments.

_____ 4. Indirect selling in which specialized salespeople promote the firm's goodwill among indirect customers, often by assisting customers in product use.

_____ 5. Personal selling conducted in retail and in some wholesale locations in which customers come to the seller's place of business.

_____ 6. Theory that motivation depends on an individual's expectations of his or her ability to perform a job and how that performance relates to attaining a desired reward.

Harcourt, Inc.

_____ 7. Meeting customer needs by listening to them, understanding – and caring about – their problems, paying attention to details, and following through after the sale.

_____ 8. Personal selling function of identifying potential customers.

_____ 9. Personal selling situations in which buyers must undertake considerable analytical decision making, creating a need for skillful vendor proposals of solutions for customer needs.

_____ 10. Postsales activities that often determine whether a one-time purchase will lead a buyer to become a repeat customer.

_____ 11. Stage of the personal selling process at which the salesperson asks the customer to make a purchase decision.

_____ 12. Incentive compensation directly related to the sales or profits achieved by a salesperson.

_____ 13. Interpersonal promotional process involving a seller's promotional presentation conducted face-to-face with a buyer.

_____ 14. Memorized sales talk used to ensure uniform coverage of the selling points that management deems important.

_____ 15. Performing field selling functions but avoiding travel expenses by relying on phone, mail, and electronic commerce to provide sales and product service for customers on a continuing basis.

_____ 16. Level of expected sales for a territory, product, customer, or salesperson against which actual results are compared.

_____ 17. Organizational scheme that assigns sales teams to a firm's largest accounts.

_____ 18. Selling, mostly at wholesale and retail levels, that involves identifying customer needs, pointing them out to customers, and completing orders.

_____ 19. Describing a product's major features and relating them to a customer's problems or needs.

_____ 20. Salesperson's initial contact with a prospective customer.

_____ 21. Applications of computer and other technologies to improve the efficiency and competitiveness of the sales function.

_____ 22. Use of information collected during prospecting and qualifying and during previous contacts with the prospect to tailor the approach and presentation to match the customer's needs.

_____ 23. Regular contacts over an extended period to establish a sustained buyer-seller relationship.

_____ 24. Planning, organizing, staffing, motivating, compensating, evaluating, and controlling a sales force to ensure its effectiveness.

_____ 25. Combination of salespeople with specialists from other functional areas to promote a product.

_____ 26. Face-to-face sales presentations made at prospective customers' homes or places of business.

_____ 27. Fixed compensation payments made periodically to an employee.

Contemporary Marketing

Name_____ Instructor_____

Section_____ Date_____

Self-Quiz

You should use these questions to test your understanding of the material in this chapter. You can check your answers with those provided at the end of the chapter.

While these questions cover most of the chapter topics, they are nor intended to be the same as the test questions your instructor may use in an examination. A good understanding of all aspects of the source material is essential to good performance on any examination.

True/False

Write "T" for True and "F" for False for each of the following statements.

_____ 1. Expenditures for advertising almost always exceed expenditures for personal selling in the average American firm.

_____ 2. Although the traditional method of selling one-on-one is gaining in popularity, salespeople may need to sell to teams of corporate representatives called decision-making units.

_____ 3. In team selling, a single sales practitioner seeks to build a mutually beneficial relationship with a large customer on a regular basis over an extended period.

_____ 4. Approximately 60 percent of college marketing graduates choose sales as their first marketing position, in part because of the attractive salaries and career potentials.

_____ 5. Direct-to-customer sales involve sales personnel calling on wholesalers and retailers and selling to purchasing agents and committees in businesses and institutions.

_____ 6. A salesman whose job is to answer the phone and take orders or answer customers' questions is involved in outbound telemarketing.

_____ 7. Consultative selling works hand-in-hand with relationship selling to build customer loyalty.

_____ 8. A key fixture of the virtual office is voice mail, a computer-based call processing system that can handle both incoming and outgoing calls.

_____ 9. Order processing is part of most sales positions, but assumes primary importance in situations where it is difficult for the customer to readily identify and acknowledge needs.

_____ 10. New products often require a high degree of creative selling, which may involve reorganizing a firm's entire approach to sales.

_____ 11. Many aspects of team selling can also be described as missionary sales, such as when technical support sales personnel train customers' employees.

Harcourt, Inc.

_____ 12. The first step in the selling process is making the approach to the prospective customer.

_____ 13. One of the most frustrating things about prospecting is the likelihood that it will yield no immediate payback.

_____ 14. Effective pre-call planning gives the salesperson relevant information about the prospect's purchasing habits, attitudes, activities, and opinions.

_____ 15. The seller's objective in a features-benefits presentation is to talk about the technical features of a good or service, rather than explaining benefits the buyer might receive from their use.

_____ 16. Objections raised by sales prospects should be treated as opportunities to provide additional information to the potential customer.

_____ 17. The moment of truth in selling is the closing – the point at which the sales representative asks the prospect for an order.

_____ 18. The "If-I-can-show-you…" closing technique warns the prospect that a sales agreement should be concluded now because some important feature of the deal being offered, such as price or availability, will soon be changed.

_____ 19. One of the problems with successfully recruiting people to become sales practitioners is the low degree of job security offered by this kind of employment.

_____ 20. In a typical geographical sales structure, zone managers typically report to a district or division sales manager who might report to a regional sales manager or vice-president.

_____ 21. Much ongoing sales training, an important feature of the job even for veteran sales personnel, is conducted by sales managers in an informal manner.

_____ 22. Canned sales presentations still represent the best way of assuring that all significant selling points are covered and are widely used by most sales organizations.

_____ 23. A straight salary compensation plan gives management more control over how sales personnel allocate their efforts, but it reduces the incentive to expand sales.

_____ 24. Compensating sales representatives by commission combines maximum selling incentive with ample reason to perform nonselling activities such as completing sales reports, delivering sales promotional materials, and normal account servicing.

_____ 25. The process area of the work environment refers to the sales practitioner's technical ability – knowledge of the products, customers, and company, as well as selling skills.

Contemporary Marketing

Multiple Choice

Circle the letter of the word or phrase that best completes the sentence or best answers the question.

26. The percentage of sales the average firm spends on personal selling activities are likely to fall into which of the following ranges?
    a. 1 to 3 percent
    b. 3 to 5 percent
    c. 5 to 10 percent
    d. 10 to 15 percent
    e. 15 percent or more

27. If, in a field selling situation, the sales practitioner is joined by specialists from other functional areas of the firm to assist with the sales process,
    a. relationship selling is taking place.
    b. team selling is probably taking place.
    c. confusion can result because of all the points of view that have to be reconciled.
    d. expectancy theory is being applied to the selling process.
    e. a major accounts organization is probably in place.

28. A sales practitioner whose job involves selling in a retail or wholesale situation where customers typically visit the seller's location on their own initiative is engaged in
    a. creative sales.
    b. over-the-counter sales.
    c. field selling.
    d. missionary work.
    e. demand selling.

29. A selling approach in which the sales force relies on use of the telephone to contact customers is best known as
    a. inbound telemarketing.
    b. under-the-counter selling.
    c. creative selling.
    d. rule-bound order processing.
    e. outbound telemarketing.

30. Sales practitioners engaged in inside selling
    a. turn opportunities into sales and support technicians and purchasers with current solutions.
    b. provide maximum convenience for customers who initiate the sales process.
    c. regularly visit local stores and businesses calling on established customers.
    d. typically work in teams of ten or twelve to give the impression of competence.
    e. go for the "good old boy" sales style in a big way.

31. When a sales practitioner meets customer needs by listening to customers, understanding and caring about their problems, paying attention to details, and following through after the sale, the sales practitioner is
    a. practicing consultative selling.
    b. completing a creative selling assignment.
    c. engaged in sales engineering.
    d. acting as a missionary to that customer.
    e. functioning as a "drummer" in the classic sense of the word.

Part 7 Promotional Strategy

32. Which of the following statements is true concerning the sales activity of prospecting?
    a. Leads about prospects seldom come from previous customers of the company.
    b. Prospecting is difficult work involving many hours of diligent effort.
    c. Prospecting is exciting to new sales personnel because of the immediate payback from doing it.
    d. Once a good client base has been established, the sales practitioner can stop prospecting; sales will come from the referrals existing clients will provide.
    e. Direct mail and advertising almost never serve as a useful vehicle for new customer prospecting.

33. The process of qualifying a sales prospect
    a. involves gathering relevant information about the prospect to make initial contact go more smoothly.
    b. is the task of making sure that the prospect has the authority and resources to make purchase decisions and securing agreement from the prospect that he/she is a candidate for the goods or services being offered.
    c. is used less frequently by retail sales practitioners than it is by wholesalers' and manufacturers' sales representatives.
    d. involves making the initial personal contact with the prospect.
    e. is considered by many sales management experts to be the very essence of the sales process.

34. One important advantage of personal selling over most advertising is its ability to
    a. represent accurately the appearance of the product.
    b. describe and itemize the product's significant features.
    c. gain the customer's attention and develop interest.
    d. present a standardized treatment of the product to all prospects.
    e. actually demonstrate the product to the potential buyer.

35. The traditional approach to sales presentations pioneered by the National Cash Register Company during the late 1800s is
    a. the semi-prepared approach; the sales representative acquires only basic product knowledge and expects natural selling talent to carry the presentation.
    b. the "never-take-no-for-an-answer" approach; the name of this approach says it all.
    c. the professional approach; the sales practitioner approaches the prospect in a professional manner to deal with any questions that individual has.
    d. the canned approach; a memorized, standard sales talk delivered to the prospect covering management's view of the important points about the product.
    e. the basic approach; the sales professional deals with basics first, getting technical only when the prospect asks for technical information.

36. The key to a successful product demonstration is
    a. impact; the demonstration must be really impressive.
    b. planning; the salesperson should check and recheck every aspect of the demonstration before is or her delivery.
    c. novelty; the prospect should be shown the product in a new and different way.
    d. effect; some practitioners say that the demonstration should sell the product all by itself.
    e. detail; the demonstration should show the product in every possible use or application.

37. In the sales process, the closing technique that poses choices for the prospect in which either alternative is favorable to the sales person is the
    a. "If I can show you…" procedure.
    b. the standing-room-only ploy.

c. silent close.
d. extra-inducement close.
e. alternative-decision technique.

38. Broadly used, this term refers to the use of everything from pagers and cellular phones, to voice and electronic mail, to laptop and notebook computers in personal selling. It is
    a. the technology revolution.
    b. the electronic evolution.
    c. sales force automation.
    d. the era of technical wonder.
    e. the nerd phenomenon.

39. The most-often cited benefit of the move to sales force automation is
    a. gains in employee productivity.
    b. reduction in overall cost of sales.
    c. ease of maintaining contact with sales personnel.
    d. the possibility of avoiding technical mixups by better product description.
    e. better customer service and satisfaction.

40. The successful sales practitioner seeks to ensure that today's customers will be future customers through effective
    a. handling of prospect objections; a convinced customer is a repeat customer.
    b. sales presentations; a customer well-sold is a repeat customer.
    c. closing techniques; a customer who believes it was all his or her own idea will come back again.
    d. follow-up; this post-sales activity often determines whether a person will become a repeat customer.
    e. prospecting; a customer from the beginning is a customer for life.

41. Linking by sales managers of the sales force with other elements of the internal and external environments of the firm is a
    a. boundary-spanning role that they normally occupy.
    b. task that many sales managers avoid.
    c. new development in the field of organization theory.
    d. most unusual occurrence, not normally found in American business.
    e. unique phenomenon that occurs only in retail environments.

42. The first step and one of the sales manager's greatest challenges in building an effective sales force is
    a. organizing the sales practitioners in a format consistent with the firm's needs.
    b. training sales personnel in correct selling techniques.
    c. motivating sales personnel to persist in their selling efforts.
    d. compensating sales personnel fairly and equitably.
    e. recruiting and selecting a group of qualified personnel.

43. Which of the following statements concerning selling as a profession is true?
    a. Advancement laterally to a more responsible position in some other functional area of the firm seldom happens to sales personnel.
    b. Economic downturns affect personnel in sales more than they do people in most other employment areas.
    c. The earnings of successful sales practitioners compare favorably with those of successful people in other professions.

Part 7 Promotional Strategy

d. Sales practitioners seldom operate as "independent" businesspeople but usually as part of a selling team.
e. Sales practitioners derive satisfaction in their profession largely from their incomes and seldom from helping customers satisfy their wants and needs.

44. In the selection of sales personnel, which of the following is often the step before the applicant is sent to the assessment center for testing?
    a. an in-depth interview
    b. a physical examination
    c. a screening interview
    d. reference checks
    e. filling out the application

45. A firm whose sales organization markets large numbers of similar but separate products of a very technical or complex nature sold through an array of marketing channels should probably be organized
    a. geographically.
    b. along customer lines.
    c. using engineering specialties as a base.
    d. by product category.
    e. according to the sizes of the various customers of the firm.

46. The most common method of compensating sales practitioners is
    a. straight commission, no salary.
    b. straight salary, no commission.
    c. a salary-plus-bonus plan.
    d. a salary-plus-commission program.
    e. a plan involving salary, bonuses, commissions, and other incentives.

47. Simulations are often elements of
    a. the training program for new sales personnel.
    b. a cover-up when sales managers make mistakes and have to be transferred.
    c. the testing program for potential recruits for sales positions.
    d. the motivational structure to impel sales personnel to higher achievement.
    e. the compensation program for sales personnel..

48. Each aspect of sales performance for which a standard exists should be measured separately. This helps prevent
    a. evaluation of the process of selling rather than the achievements of the sales operative
    b. confusion on the part of the evaluated individual as to how the evaluation was conducted.
    c. the halo effect in which the rating on one factor is carried over to other performance variables.
    d. personalities becoming the basis for evaluation, rather than performance.
    e. the bad news being transmitted back to the sales employee through unauthorized channels.

49. Motivation of sales personnel
    a. is not a complex process because of the simplicity of the work.
    b. seldom appeals to ego needs, peer acceptance, or recognition.
    c. usually takes the form of debriefings, information sharing, and financial and psychological encouragement.
    d. requires tight supervision and constant monitoring of the work of the sales force.
    e. seldom involves monetary awards or fringe benefits such as club memberships.

Harcourt, Inc.

50. The compensation plan giving management the greatest control over how sales personnel allocate their efforts but least incentive to expand sales volume is
    a. straight commission.
    b. salary plus bonus.
    c. commission with bonus.
    d. straight salary.
    e. salary with commission.

Name_____ Instructor_____

Section_____ Date_____

Applying Marketing Concepts

Whew! Vendamille Tourascent finally realized she was going to make it. She really was going to graduate from college! Armed with the happy knowledge that she had made it to her last semester, she went to East North Central State's placement office to sign up for interviews with firms seeking people with her qualifications. She was surprised to discover that there were quite a few positions available with local companies that called for sales skills involving strong interest in problem solving and customer service but indicated that no outside work or travel would be required. A number of other positions called for degrees in finance or marketing, and showed that "business development" was the area for which personnel were being sought. A little investigation revealed that the accounting firms and financial institutions listing these positions were among the most aggressive in the area, seeking new commercial accounts in an active fashion. She signed up for several of these interviews, and was somewhat surprised when she was told that a number of the companies specified that potential applicants must have had certain courses before they could even be interviewed.

Either because of good planning or dumb luck, Vendamille had taken and done well in all the required courses, and was able to interview with a number of these firms. They all required a seemingly endless stream of paperwork. First, there was the placement office form to fill out, then each company seemed to want her to fill out a "personal data sheet," and finally there was the interview. She wondered who the people who were interviewing her were. They seemed to know the company and its products quite well, and indicated that if she were to be chosen to fill an open position, she would be working for them. After her third interview in two days, she decided to go somewhere quiet and think about this whole process. It seemed very detailed and confusing.

Circle the letter of the word or phrase that best completes the sentence or best answers the question.

1. The positions with local wholesalers calling for selling and problem-solving skills and but no outside work were probably
   a. missionary sales positions.
   b. positions as sales trainers.
   c. inside selling positions.
   d. creative selling positions.
   e. field sales positions.

2. The positions with the accounting firms and financial institutions were most likely
   a. portfolio analysts' positions.
   b. openings for staff accountants in the auditing division.
   c. related to sector analysis or loan profitability.
   d. field sales positions in the commercial accounts area.
   e. missionary sales positions designed to build public image.

3. If the interviewing process is looked at as a sales opportunity for the companies interviewing (selling the idea of working for them), then their requirement that Vendamille have a degree in a particular major and/or have taken particular courses would be part of the
    a. prospecting and qualifying process.
    b. approach to the prospect.
    c. presentation of company advantages.
    d. preapproach planning.
    e. follow-up step in sales.

4. If one of the firms with whom Vendamille interviewed was interested in her, what do you suppose would happen next?
    a. She would be asked to report to a doctor's office for a physical examination.
    b. She would be called in for a second interview.
    c. The company would make her take a battery of placement tests.
    d. She would be hired immediately.
    e. They would keep her on the hook for a while, then make her an offer.

5. The people with whom Vendamille had her first interview were probably
    a. professional interviewers who do this sort of thing all the time.
    b. people who occupied the same position she would and had been told to find a successor so they could be transferred.
    c. sales managers for the companies in the local area, doing part of their job.
    d. representatives of her college filling in for people who worked for the interviewing companies.
    e. staff people from the interviewing companies who had nothing better to do.

Craig Lerner recently went to a nearby music store to buy a new CD by his favorite musical group, the Shrieking Blue Herons. Brenda, a helpful salesperson, assisted him to find the CD he wanted and he was in the process of walking with her to the cash register to pay for it when she stopped at a display of CD storage boxes and asked if he had the same problem she did storing her tunes neatly and conveniently. Though Craig said he'd never had such a problem – his old shoe box worked just fine – Brenda showed him how a particular storage container had little partitions in it that separated the CDs and that it could even be locked to keep out the curious and light-fingered. Craig was impressed – the container was functional and Brenda was cute and well informed – so he added a storage container to his purchase.

6. Brenda's demonstration of the storage container is an example of
    a. order processing.
    b. creative selling.
    c. telemarketing.
    d. closing.
    e. prospecting.

7. Brenda's assistance of Craig in finding the CD that met his needs and ringing up the sale is an example of retail
    a. order processing.
    b. creative selling.
    c. missionary selling.
    d. passive selling.
    e. qualifying.

8. Brenda's job category would be stated in terms of
    a. field selling.

b. missionary selling.
   c. telemarketing.
   d. over-the-counter sales.
   e. merchandising.

The sales force at Devosil, S.A., a major French maker and distributor of high-tech adhesives, is divided into three groups: the consumer products group, the major accounts group, and the industrial products group. Sales people in the consumer products group are paid a base salary plus 10 percent of their gross sales after they have met a minimum sales volume requirement for the month. The requirement is set on a month-by-month basis.

The industrial sales force is also salaried, but they receive an additional payment each month based on the new account activity they generate. The amount is based on the number of new accounts each sales representative opens weighted by management's estimate of the ultimate volume each account will generate. The amount the sales representative sold the account on opening does not matter.

The members of the major accounts group are not thought of as sales representatives. They number among themselves work-design specialists, process engineers, materials specialists, and even a group of adhesive chemists. A delegation from Devosil will often visit one of the major accounts as a group, each member prepared to deal with customer interaction in his or her own specialty. They try to develop the customers' confidence in their ability to solve his or her firm's problems better than anyone else.

9. The sales force at Devosil is organized along
   a. product lines.
   b. customer lines.
   c. geographical lines.
   d. a combination of geographical and customer lines.
   e. a combination of product and geographical lines.

10. Sales representatives in the consumer products group are compensated on a
    a. straight salary basis.
    b. salary plus commission basis.
    c. salary plus bonus basis.
    d. straight commission basis.
    e. basis no one understands.

11. Sales representatives in the industrial products group are paid
    a. a straight commission.
    b. salary plus commission.
    c. straight salary.
    d. salary plus bonus based on new business.
    e. commission plus bonus.

12. If we identify the members of the major accounts group as members of the sales force, how might we best characterize their working together in groups to fill customer needs?
    a. telemarketing
    b. consultative selling
    c. team selling
    d. sales force automation
    e. field selling

13. Whether the members of the major accounts group are classed individually as sales representatives or not, their efforts to develop customer confidence in their ability to solve the customer's problems (a long-term outlook) is an example of
    a. a "take the money and run" approach.
    b. follow-up as part of the selling process.
    c. boundary-spanning.
    d. relationship marketing.
    e. an ethical issue in sales organization.

Name_____ Instructor_____

Section_____ Date_____

Surfing the Net

Keeping in mind that addresses change and what's on the Web now may have changed by the time you read this, let's take a look at some of the places on the Net that reflect aspects of personal selling and sales management. We are not endorsing or recommending any of these sources, merely making note of the information and services that people have elected to offer through the Internet.

What a wreck! No, this really doesn't have much to do with anything, but selling and sales management sites are sort of thin on the Web, so I thought I'd just plug my old alma mater and let you know that the Georgia Tech student radio station has a Web site at **http://cyberbuzz.gatech.edu/wrek/**

But seriously, folks, there are some interesting Web sites that have a bearing on the field of sales. One that, at this writing, looks promising, is CommerceNet. This service is designed to provide an interactive forum for business. At this site you can get detailed product information, make product comparisons, and make purchases. Take a look at **http://www.commerce.net** and its associated links.

J. P. Morgan and Company, a name that should be familiar to many of you, has a Web site that provides a daily list of risk rates in the financial market. But this investment-banking firm also has digital recruiting brochures to attract new talent to the investments field. Check it out at **http://www.jpmorgan.com.**

Employment opportunities and Resumé Postings server may be the place to find that sales job. This location on the Net links with a number of sites where job opportunities are listed. Try them at **http://www.careermosaic.com/cm/home.html.**

Really looking for a job? There are several employment agencies on the Web that claim to offer sales opportunities. You might try **http://www.peoplesource.com** or **http://www.scientificresources.com**, or this last one which I was surprised to discover is located in tiny (but rather pretty) Daphne, Alabama, just across Mobile Bay from the city of the same name. This certainly illustrates how the Internet frees business from having to locate in major cities. The site is **http://www.industrial-sales.com**. They apparently place sale personnel in the bearing and transmission parts industries.

Sites verified January 21, 2000.

Contemporary Marketing

Name_____Instructor_____

Section_____Date_____

Cases for Part 7

1. *Servicios Tecnicos y Comercial por Empresas Pequeñas de Cataluña, S.A.*

Servicios Tecnicos y Comercial por Empresas Pequeñas de Cataluña (STECEPCA, for short), is a well-known financial planning firm headquartered in Barcelona. For the last 25 years, it has provided investment and portfolio planning services to small and medium-size businesses all over Spain. Its promotional program has consisted of advertisements in the financial sections of the major regional newspapers, outlining the benefits of investment and portfolio planning for the smaller business and the advantages of working with a firm like STECEPCA.

Recently, responses to STECEPCA's advertising have been on a decline, and the sales staff is wondering how they might better prospect for new clients. The newspaper ads had been quite successful in generating qualified leads. Part of this success was attributable to their placement in the financial section, but part also must be credited to the style of the ads, which made a direct appeal to senior executives of companies with funds to invest.

STECEPCA doesn't believe that the number of firms in need of its services has decreased, but the number of companies offering similar services has increased markedly. Some are national, like STECEPCA. Others, like Servicios Financieros de Madrid (SEFIM), serve only their province. None of the new firms have the expertise or experience of STECEPCA.

Question

Suggest several ways in which STECEPCA can generate more qualified prospects for its sales force to call on.

2. *O. Lee O'Leahy*, Inc.*

O. Lee O'Leahy, Inc., whose corporate offices are located in Geneva, Indiana, is one of America's premier producers of mountain-climbing boots. The firm makes not less than 27 different kinds of mountaineering footwear. Over the last five years, sales have leveled off but expenses have continued to increase. The president of the firm, Natalie Ahtired, has asked the promotions manager for some suggestions.

Wally Ballou, promotions manager for the firm, is in a quandary. He feels that the way promotions are budgeted may affect sales. Until now, the amount available for promotion was a percentage of the prior quarter's sales.

*With fond apologies to the late Bob Elliott and not-so-late Ray Goulding – network radio's Bob and Ray.

Question

From Wally's point of view, what could O'Leahy do to help remedy this situation? What changes would your solution involve? Use numbers, if necessary, to illustrate your answer.

3. Large Major Appliance Corporation

As the name implies, the Large Major Appliance Corporation is a large producer of major home appliances. The company's sales staff sells to wholesalers and distributors throughout the United States and Canada. Because of the nature of their selling job, they have traditionally been paid a straight salary. Larry Large, president and CEO, is thinking about adding a new division that will sell direct to property developers – builders specializing in construction of condominiums, tract homes, and apartment complexes. This would be "package selling" in which Large would furnish all the electrical appliances for the development: stoves, refrigerators, water heaters, dishwashers, garbage disposers, washing machines, clothes dryers, and heating and cooling systems. Some of these items would not be made by Large but would be part of the package through arrangements with other manufacturers and would bear the Large name. One consideration in establishing the new division is the sales force. Large believes the creative type of sales practitioner is appropriate in this case.

Question

What type of compensation plan might be most effective for the new division? Why?

4. Industrial Drive Belt Company

Industrial Drive Belt is a large manufacturer of drive belts for manufacturing equipment and is known as a leader in its industry. The firm's research and development department is particularly effective. Just over a year ago, Industrial placed on the market a revolutionary type of belt called the Nowear belt. Made of a synthetic leather and finished with a special treatment that made it scuff, scratch, and crack proof – not just resistant – it lasted four times as long as standard drive belts. For six months after the introduction, Industrial had the high-wear segment of the market to itself – except for the older types of belt, of course, to which many users stubbornly clung – but within the most recent six months, several other firms have begun to market drive belts with what they claim are all the advantages of the Industrial belt. Industrial's advertising program for the last year has centered on informing their market of the availability of the new belt. Management now feels that the basic objective of its advertising should change.

Question

What new objective for advertising should be established? Give some examples of ads that might be used to accomplish the new objective.

Part 7 Promotional Strategy

Creating a Marketing Plan

Episode Six is designed to provide you with information that will let you complete Part III.D. of your marketing plan.

Episode Six: Now Let's Get the Message Out — We're Here!

When we left our intrepid entrepreneurs, they were in the process of arranging for quarters into which to move their new business. It is now several weeks later, and most of the mechanics of set-up have been accomplished. The firm now has a business address, all of the appropriate licenses and permits, a work space equipped with excellent graphics-capable computers, and two rather nice cars – Ford Crown Vics with Police Interceptor Packages – for business use.

The problem now is to let people know that the firm exists, and that it is eager to provide the high-quality service its owners have made as their objective. The three partners have met to discuss the promotional means they're going to use to get their message across.

"Well, I think it's obvious that we need a display ad in the Yellow Pages," said Terry. "As I said before, there are all these other firms which have listings, but only a very few ads. I think we need something to tell our target market we're out there to serve them."

"Good thought," replied Brian, "but the next edition of the Yellow Pages doesn't come out for four months. What are we going to do in the meantime? I propose we advertise in the business section of the newspaper; just a small ad once a week, and we can offer a free "Web analysis" as a get-acquainted deal."

"Now I know why you wanted those stickers with our name, address, phone number and "Web site development and maintenance" printed on them," commented Laura, "you plan on sticking those on any piece of machinery we get our hands on!"

"And on any other logical surface that would give us a shot at being the first firm they think of when the idea of a Web site occurs to those that don't have them or something happens to the site of those that do," laughed Brian. "Better than that. I propose that, for the time being, we all keep acting as a sales force and get out there dropping off business cards and stickers at every business whose door we can get through. How about it?"

"Real good," remarked Laura, "but I've been thinking; why just try to let these people know who we are? Why not generate cash flow as soon as possible by selling them Web maintenance service right off the bat? I've written up a little promotional piece that we can drop off along with our business cards when we call on people. See, it tells them a little about the three of us – let's face it, we've got pretty good credentials and if we don't toot our own horn who's going to toot it for us – along with some information on the cost of lost business that can crop up when you don't update your Web site regularly. Having access to people who know how to do the job right – and fast – is very important and having a maintenance contract for your Web site is very important to these businesses. I think we can generate some business that way. I've even had the back page of the flier printed with some important Internet facts that will let them spot problems they can correct without calling us. That may keep them from throwing the brochure away."

Harcourt, Inc.

Contemporary Marketing

"Super job!" was Terry's comment, "and though it may be a little bit off the track, let me volunteer to do something that may seem a little strange but I think will do us a world of good. I'm going to hire my niece –she's your cousin Erin, Brian (aren't big families wonderful) – to come over on Saturday mornings and work on the grass and shrubs around this building. Have you noticed what dumps most of our competitors' facilities are? I don't see any reason why we shouldn't have a good looking place. And I think we should spend time keeping the inside neat, too."

"Not off the track at all, Ter," said Laura, "people do react to the appearance of a place, and we have to expect our customers to come by here to talk with us and see what we're doing for them. They might as well get a good impression of us from our store as well as from our work. Besides, this isn't a bad neighborhood for a commercial street. We might as well get along with our neighbors, too. I know Erin loves to work in the yard. Maybe we can get her to plant some of those flowering shrubs she put in around your aunt's house."

Guidelines:

Examine the suggestions the partners have made and use them and your own ideas to complete Part. III. D. of the marketing plan.

Part 8

Pricing Strategy

Price is the component of the marketing mix most universally affected by the legal environment. Antitrust legislation provides the basic foundation for regulation of price, amplified by the Robinson-Patman Act that prohibits a broad range of price-discriminatory actions. At the state level, unfair-trade laws (also called Unfair Trade Practices Acts) also have an effect on price-setting.

Pricing objectives can be related to profitability, sales volume, meeting competition, and creating a prestige image for one's product or firm. The PIMS studies determined that product quality and market share are major contributors to firm profitability. Pricing objectives for not-for-profit organizations differ somewhat from those of for-profits. Elasticity of demand with respect to price is another factor that must be considered in the pricing of a product.

Price theory and cost provide the rational framework for pricing. Price theory is seldom used in the setting of actual prices. Cost, on the other hand, is the most commonly used basis for setting prices today. The typical cost-plus approach to pricing attempts to set a price for the product that will recover the cost of producing and distributing it and allow for some margin of profit. Two methods of applying cost-plus pricing exist, the full-cost method and the incremental cost method.

Breakeven analysis is a technique that is often used to help marketing executives decide whether required sales levels to achieve profitability is a realistic goal. A modified breakeven model that superimposes an estimated demand curve over the cost and revenue curves of the breakeven chart helps identify the range of feasible prices and provide a more realistic base for deciding on the price to actually ask in the marketplace. In the global market, prices may be subject to factors that change somewhat the way in which they are formulated.

The making of pricing decisions is a two-step process that involves (1) setting prices and (2) administering the pricing structure. Alternative pricing strategies include a skimming strategy, a penetration pricing strategy, and competitive pricing. Competitive conditions have a significant effect on which of these strategies is chosen by a particular firm.

There are numerous influences on price quotes, among them being a firm's costs and policies and discounts and allowances, which may prevail, in a particular industry. Shipping costs often represent a part of price, and it is important to know whether they will be paid by purchaser or vendor.

Pricing policies include psychological pricing, product line pricing, promotional pricing, and flexible pricing. Price limits often relate the price/quality relationship in the consumer's mind.

Prices in the industrial market are often subject to negotiation or may be based on competitive bids. In large corporations, the necessity to set transfer prices when goods are transferred among profit centers of the same firm is a major decision problem. The market globalization that expresses itself in part in the online market has resulted in changes in traditional global pricing policies.

Harcourt, Inc.

Part 8 Pricing Strategy

Chapter 18

Price Determination

Chapter Outline

Use the following as a guide in taking notes.

I. Chapter Overview – How much is a product worth?

II. Legal Constraints on Pricing

    A. Robinson-Patman Act

    B. Unfair-trade laws

    C. Fair-trade laws

III. The Role of Price in the Marketing Mix

IV. Pricing Objectives

    A. Profitability Objectives

    B. Volume Objectives

        1. The PIMS Studies

    C. Meeting Competition Objectives

    D. Prestige Objectives

    E. Pricing Objectives of not-for-profit organizations

V. Methods for Determining Prices

VI. Price Determination in Economic Theory

    A. Cost and revenue curves

    B. The concept of elasticity in pricing strategy

        1. Determinants of Elasticity

        2. Elasticity and Revenue

    C. Practical problems of price theory

Harcourt, Inc.

VII. Price Determination in Practice

    A. Alternative pricing procedures

    B. Breakeven analysis

        1. Target Returns

        2. Evaluation of Breakeven Analysis

VIII. Toward Realistic Pricing

    A. The Modified Breakeven Concept

    B. Yield Management

IX. Global Issues in Price Determination

X. Strategic Implications of Pricing in the 21st Century

Key Concepts

The purpose of this section is to let you determine if you can match key concepts with their definitions. It is essential that you know the definitions of the concepts prior to applying the concepts in later exercises in this chapter.

From the list of lettered terms, select the one that best fits each of the numbered statements below. Write the letter of that choice in the space provided.

Key Terms

a. price
b. Robinson-Patman Act
c. unfair-trade laws
d. fair-trade laws
e. profit maximization
f. target-return objectives
g. Profit Impact of Market Strategies (PIMS) project
h. value pricing
i. customary prices
j. demand
k. supply
l. pure competition
m. monopolistic competition
n. oligopoly
o. monopoly
p. elasticity
q. cost-plus pricing
r. breakeven analysis
s. modified breakeven analysis
t. yield management

_____ 1. Point at which the additional revenue gained by increasing the price of a product equals the increase in total costs.

_____ 2. Pricing strategy emphasizing benefits a product provides in comparison to the price and quality levels of competing offerings.

_____ 3. Pricing technique that evaluates consumer demand by comparing the quantities that a firm must sell at a variety of prices in order to cover total cost with estimates of expected sales at those prices.

_____ 4. In pricing strategy, the traditional amounts that customers expect to pay for certain goods or services.

_____ 5. Pricing technique that determines the number of products that must be sold at a specified price in order to generate sufficient revenue to cover total cost.

_____ 6. Federal legislation prohibiting price discrimination that is not based on a cost differential; this law also prohibits selling at an unreasonably low price to eliminate competition

_____ 7. Market structure in which relatively few sellers compete, while high start-up costs form barriers to keep out new competitors.

_____ 8. Short-run or long-run pricing practice intended to achieve a specified return on either sales or investment.

_____ 9. Pricing strategies designed to maximize revenues in situations such as airfares, lodging, auto rentals, and theater tickets where costs are fixed.

_____ 10. Exchange value of a good or service.

_____ 11. Statutes enacted in most states that permit manufacturers to stipulate minimum retail prices for their products.

_____ 12. Practice of adding a percentage of specified dollar amount (markup) to the base cost of a product to cover unassigned costs and provide a profit.

_____ 13. Schedule of the amounts of a product or service that a firm will offer for sale at different prices during a specified time period.

_____ 14. Market structure involving only one seller of a product for which there are no close substitutes.

_____ 15. Schedule of the amounts of a firm's product that consumers will purchase at different prices during a specified time period.

_____ 16. Major research study that discovered a strong positive relationship between a firm's market share and its return on investment.

_____ 17. State law requiring sellers to maintain minimum prices for comparable merchandise.

_____ 18. Market structure involving a heterogeneous product and product differentiation among competing suppliers, allowing the marketer some control over price.

_____ 19. Measure of the responsiveness of purchasers and suppliers to a change in price.

_____ 20. Market structure characterized by homogeneous products for which there are so many buyers and sellers that none has a significant influence on price.

Part 8 Pricing Strategy

Name_____ Instructor_____

Section_____ Date_____

Self-Quiz

You should use these objectives to test your understanding of the chapter material. You can check your answers with those provided at the end of the chapter.

While these questions cover most of the chapter topics, they are not intended to be the same as the test questions your instructor may use in an examination. A good understanding of all aspects of the course material is essential to good performance on any examination.

True/False

Write "T" for True and "F" for False for each of the following statements.

____ 1. The Robinson-Patman Act often permits firms to set prices on domestically produced goods well above world market levels.

____ 2. The price of an item is what it can be exchanged for in the market place, not necessarily involving money.

____ 3. The basic argument behind fair-trade laws was that a product's image, which is determined in its price, is a property right of the manufacturer who should have the right to protect it.

____ 4. The Robinson-Patman Act is sometimes called the "Anti-P & G Act," because it was designed to curb pricing abuses by large consumer-goods manufacturers like Procter & Gamble.

____ 5. The Robinson-Patman Act absolutely prohibits price discrimination in sales to wholesalers, retailers, and other producers; cost differentials, however, may constitute a defense for price differences.

____ 6. Unfair-trade laws are federal laws requiring sellers to maintain mandated minimum prices for comparable merchandise.

____ 7. The Miller-Tydings Resale Price Maintenance Act of 1937 exempted interstate fair-trade contracts from compliance with antitrust requirements.

____ 8. Price influences a firm's profits as well as its employment of the factors of production because the prices it asks and resulting purchases by its customers determine how much revenue it will receive.

____ 9. Classical economic theory presumes that firms will behave rationally and that this will result in an effort to maximize gains and minimize losses.

Harcourt, Inc.

Contemporary Marketing

_____10. Target-return pricing objectives satisfy the desire to maximize sales in the belief that increased sales are more important than immediate high profits.

_____11. Many firms set a minimum acceptable sales level as their objective and then seek to maximize profits subject to the sales constraint.

_____12. If the price of a product increases 10 percent and sales of the product decrease 8 percent, that product can be said to have elastic demand with respect to price (price elasticity of demand.)

_____13. The demand for a product for which there are a number of close substitutes will tend to be elastic.

_____14. In marginal analysis, profit maximization is achieved when the addition to total revenue caused by selling an additional unit equals the increase in total cost caused by offering that unit.

_____15. Value pricing typically works best for goods and services that are relatively high-priced.

_____16. Economic theory postulates that businesses strive to maximize sales; the truth is that many of them seek to maximize profits, perceived to be a more realizable goal.

_____17. PIMS data reveals that firms with a 40 percent or greater market share earn an average of 32 percent on investment, while those with a less than 10 percent share earn an average of only 13 percent.

_____18. The PIMS study revealed that two of the most important factors influencing a firm's profitability were its markup percentages and geographic location.

_____19. The net result of a "meeting competition" pricing objective is a de-emphasis of price and a stronger focus on nonprice competition.

_____20. Segmentation strategies designed to secure small shares of large markets rather than those seeking to gain large shares of small markets might be the better choice if PIMS data is correct.

_____21. The advertisement of the Bentley Azure that states: "Bentley. You don't park it. You position it" placed in very upscale magazines indicates that its maker is seeking to achieve a prestige pricing objective for this product of the Rolls-Royce Company.

_____22. Since not-for-profit organizations, by definition, do not cite profitability as a goal, they never seek to maximize profits.

_____23. Pure competition is a market structure with large numbers of buyers and sellers of heterogeneous products in which product differentiation exists, allowing the marketer some control over prices.

_____24. The price set for a product in the marketplace must generate sufficient revenue to cover the costs of producing and marketing it.

____25. The price elasticity of demand is the percentage change in the price of a product or service divided by the percentage change in the quantity of the product or service which is demanded.

Multiple Choice

Circle the letter of the word or phrase that best completes the sentence or best answers the question.

26. The federal law passed in 1936 that was inspired by price competition from developing grocery store chains and prohibits price discrimination in sales to wholesalers, retailers, and other producers is
    a. the Clayton Act.
    b. the Miller-Tydings Act.
    c. the McGuire-Keogh Act.
    d. the Consumer Goods Pricing Act.
    e. the Robinson-Patman Act.

27. A defense may be made against a charge of violating the price discrimination provisions of the Robinson-Patman Act if it can be shown that
    a. another firm violated the Act in the same fashion and wasn't caught.
    b. nobody in the firm is competent enough to understand the meaning of the law.
    c. competitors engage in similar behavior on a regular basis.
    d. the firm's price discounts were set to meet competitors' prices and cost differences justify the variations.
    e. the company has been doing this sort of thing for years.

28. A firm using value pricing for a product might promote that product using a slogan such as:
    a. "Great performance at a reasonable price."
    b. "Be the envy of your friends and the talk of your neighborhood."
    c. "Among the most expensive wines in the world."
    d. "The highest quality available – if you have to ask how much it costs, you can't afford it."
    e. "The resort hotel of incomparable service."

29. Which of the following is a target-return pricing objective?
    a. attempting to maintain a 7 percent net profit as a percent of sales
    b. matching the prices of the established industry price leader
    c. establishing relatively high prices to maintain an image of quality and exclusiveness
    d. seeking to capture and retain a specific market share percentage
    e. attempting to assure specific total unit sales in the current year

30. Marginal analysis is the approach used to determine the price to set when a firm's pricing objective is
    a. maximizing sales volume.
    b. maximum profit.
    c. meeting competition.
    d. creating prestige.
    e. market leadership.

31. The net result of the pricing objective of meeting competition is
    a. emphasis of the price element of the marketing mix at the expense of nonprice elements.
    b. a more complex analytical process that must be used when prices are set.

c. maximization of profits at the expense of image creation and prestige.
d. creating an image of quality and exclusiveness to the detriment of revenue.
e. de-emphasis of the price element of the marketing mix and more focus on nonprice competition.

32. Which of the following would be more likely to be a pricing objective of a not-for-profit organization than of a for-profit one?
    a. meeting competitors' prices
    b. achieving a target return on investment
    c. generating a specific dollar sales volume
    d. discouraging consumption of a product
    e. maximizing overall unit sales volume

33. The producer of which of the following products most likely follows a prestige pricing policy?
    a. Sacher Chocolate, "By Appointment to the Imperial Household of Austria-Hungary."
    b. Timex watches, "Stylish, Inexpensive Timepieces Everyone Loves."
    c. Schaefer beer, "The Beer to Have When You're Having More than One."
    d. Ken-l Ration for dogs, "Rover Will Love It."
    e. Coca-Cola, "The Pause That Refreshes."

34. One of the most significant studies of pricing strategies and objectives of the last twenty years was the PIMS project. For what does the acronym PIMS stand?
    a. Project to Investigate Marketing Scientifically
    b. Purdue Institute of Marketing Studies
    c. Profit Impact of Marketing Strategies
    d. Produits Interieur de Marché Solar
    e. Palomar Investigation of Marketplace Situations

35. When a nonprofit organization attempts to get prices on certain products raised by attaching taxes, tolls, or even fines to their use, it is probably driven by the objective of
    a. cost recovery pricing.
    b. market suppression.
    c. profit maximization.
    d. seeking a target return on investment.
    e. providing market incentives.

36. Retail prices that customers have come to expect as a result of tradition or social habit are called
    a. residual prices.
    b. standard prices.
    c. day-to-day prices.
    d. unusual in today's market.
    e. customary prices.

37. A schedule of the amounts of a product or service that producers will offer for sale at different prices during a specified time period is
    a. a demand schedule.
    b. competition in the marketplace.
    c. a description of market structure
    d. a supply schedule.
    e. an equilibrium schedule.

38. A market structure characterized by relatively few sellers, each of which may affect the market, though none of them can control it, is called
    a. pure competition.
    b. monopolistic competition.
    c. an oligopoly.
    d. a monopoly.
    e. perfect competition.

39. The market structure that is typical of most retailing and features large numbers of buyers and sellers of heterogeneous and differentiated products is
    a. pure competition.
    b. modified competition.
    c. perfect competition.
    d. oligopolistic competition.
    e. monopolistic competition.

40. The average total cost of producing a product may be computed by
    a. computing the change in total cost resulting from producing an additional unit of output and dividing by total output.
    b. determining the amounts of costs that change with level of production and dividing by gross revenue.
    c. dividing the sum of total variable and fixed costs by the number of units produced.
    d. dividing revenue by number of units sold and subtracting variable cost.
    e. determining the change in total revenue resulting from selling one more unit of output.

41. Monopoly exists when
    a. there exists only one seller of a product for which there are no close substitutes.
    b. sellers in the market are few but large and product is undifferentiated.
    c. there are few buyers in a market, and sellers have to scramble to keep them supplied.
    d. there are numerous buyers and sellers in the market but communication among them is imperfect.
    e. buyers refuse to purchase what sellers have to offer.

42. Costs which remain stable regardless of the level of production achieved are called
    a. variable costs.
    b. fixed costs.
    c. average total costs.
    d. marginal costs.
    e. average revenue.

43. In the traditional economic model based on analysis of revenue and cost curves, profit maximization occurs when
    a. average total cost equals average revenue.
    b. marginal cost equals average revenue.
    c. average revenue equals average total cost.
    d. marginal cost equals marginal revenue.
    e. average total cost equals marginal cost.

44. The most popular method of price determination used today is
    a. marginal analysis pricing.
    b. cost-plus pricing.

Harcourt, Inc.

c. full-cost pricing.
d. incremental-cost pricing.
e. breakeven pricing.

45. When most of a firm's costs are fixed over a wide range of outputs and the primary determinant of profitability is revenue, it is appropriate to use
   a. full-cost pricing.
   b. incremental-cost pricing.
   c. yield management to set prices.
   d. cost-plus pricing.
   e. the MPMC model as the price setter.

46. Modified breakeven analysis differs from traditional breakeven analysis in that
   a. breakeven occurs when total revenue equals marginal revenue, instead of when average revenue equals total cost.
   b. no consideration is given to the required profit when making the analysis of costs and revenues.
   c. calculations are made using computer programs as the mechanism, rather than manually.
   d. breakeven no longer occurs when total profit equals total variable cost, but rather when total variable cost equals marginal revenue.
   e. consideration is given to evaluation of consumer demand as well as analysis of prices and costs.

47. Basic breakeven analysis
   a. is useless as a pricing tool because it is based on assumptions which are always untrue.
   b. identifies when a company's costs will equal its revenues at some price for the product, assuming that costs can be assumed to be divisible into fixed and variable parts.
   c. has become less sophisticated in recent years because there has been a tendency to abandon it in favor of more useful tools.
   d. is an effective way of recognizing marketplace variables and preparing for them beforehand.
   e. is not described by any of the above choices.

48. In the global market, producers of commodities – products such as bananas and sugar cane – may find this pricing objective more important than do producers of value-oriented products. The objective is
   a. profitability.
   b. market share.
   c. meeting competition.
   d. price stability.
   e. prestige image.

49. The continued development of on-line marketing is expected to further smooth out the friction of time, which should result in
   a. prices shifting up and down in response to supply and demand fluctuations.
   b. greater price stability because everyone will know what market conditions are like.
   c. larger profit margins for retailers as they increase prices.
   d. higher prices for the consumer because he/she is vulnerable to supply manipulation.
   e. chaos and the ultimate collapse of the economy as we know it – like the Y2K bug caused.

50. The Melvin Manufacturing Company makes iron castings for the plumbing industry. They are planning to introduce a new high-style manhole cover assembly targeted at upscale neighborhoods and are wondering how many units they'll have to sell to break even on the deal. Fixed costs to tool

up to make this assembly have been $150,000. Variable costs for each unit produced will be $20. At a price of $50 per assembly, how many units must be sold to break even?
a. 2,500
b. 4,000
c. 5,000
d. 8,000
e. 7,500

Contemporary Marketing

Name_____ Instructor_____

Section_____ Date_____

Applying Marketing Concepts

OilSlick Refining Company processes and sells specialty machinery lubricants under the SlideRite label. Endor Sandovich, director of marketing for the company, was planning a speech to be delivered before the student marketing club at nearby Panthermal University. Endor knew the students would want to know about his company's marketing mix in general, and he also knew that pricing was sure to be an exceptionally hot issue because of a big price-fixing case in another industry that had been heavily covered by the press lately. It would be difficult to explain OilSlick's pricing policies because the firm did not aggressively use price to generate sales. As one of three firms dealing in this rather unique class of lubricants in a five-state area, ORC was satisfied with its third of the market and really didn't want to rock the boat unnecessarily. Prices were set at the beginning of the selling year based on the result of contract negotiations with the suppliers of the raw base-stock from which the lubricants were made. Those prices were then maintained until the next year, subject only to special promotional activities.

In general, prices were set by first estimating supply and demand for ORC's products. Next, the cost of buying and processing the base-stock was computed. Costs that could not be assigned to a particular item were not included in the calculations. Once costs were determined, an amount sufficient to cover selling expenses and provide a reasonable profit was added to determine list price. Since the other two firms in the area used the same method of determining price, initial prices were usually quite close, and were often identical. Differences that existed in the early part of the season "ironed themselves out" by midyear.

Write "T" for True and "F" for False for each of the following statements.

_____ 1. OilSlick Refining Company's pricing objective would be classified as profit maximization.

_____ 2. The company would benefit from using modified breakeven analysis.

_____ 3. OilSlick Refining Company is constrained by customary prices and thus cannot change prices from year to year.

_____ 4. ORC's prices do not take into account demand for their products.

_____ 5. If Mr. Sandovich were to apply modified breakeven analysis to his problem, he would have to use a method that assumes that variable cost would be a constant amount per unit.

Circle the letter of the word or phrase that best completes the sentence or best answers the question.

6. OilSlick Refining Company's pricing objective is
    a. profit maximization.
    b. to maximize sales.
    c. a target rate of return on investment.
    d. meeting competition.
    e. to secure market share.

Harcourt, Inc.

7. Mr. Sandovich's talk is really about setting prices in a
   a. purely competitive market.
   b. oligopolistic market.
   c. monopolistically competitive market.
   d. monopsonistic market.
   e. market characterized by highly differentiated products.

8. The pricing mechanism that the company uses is
   a. the cost-plus approach.
   b. based on breakeven analysis.
   c. basically a modified breakeven process.
   d. based on analysis of demand elasticity.
   e. probably aimed at arriving at a customary price.

9. Mr. Sandovich's method of determining costs for pricing purposes was to apply
   a. full costing.
   b. breakeven analysis.
   c. markup on selling price.
   d. differential costing.
   e. incremental costing.

10. If we had been told that the SlideRite brand was strongly preferred over competing brands in two of the five states where it was sold, we could have concluded that, in those states, SlideRite's market was probably
    a. purely competitive.
    b. monopolistically competitive.
    c. oligopolistic.
    d. poligopolistic.
    e. monopolistic.

Marcelin Plauché is in an enviable position. A graduate of the Ecole Polytechnique du Paris (civil engineering), Technische Hochschüle der Baukunst von München (architecture), and the Parsons School of Design (interior design), he is in such demand as both designer and contractor of office buildings that he can literally name his own price. There are even reports of people hiring "hit" men to eliminate others who sought to use his services. Mr. Plauché realizes that popularity like his won't last forever and has stated in public that his fees are going to be high enough so that when things taper off he, his wife, and their twelve children will be able to live comfortably for many, many years.

The cost of a Plauché-built structure is now about $400 per square foot. The average office building in the area costs around $50 per square foot. Though apoplectic with envy, other contractors continue to build and successfully sell conventional structures at average prices because, even though they would love to be able to, not many firms can afford a building that costs $400 per square foot.

11. Mr. Plauché is well aware that his work possesses an image of quality and exclusiveness that appeals to status-conscious firms, and is pricing according to
    a. a volume objective.
    b. a target return objective.
    c. a prestige objective.
    d. an objective of meeting competition.
    e. an objective of maximizing sales.

12. The structure of the supply side of the building market in Mr. Plauché's part of the country right now is probably
    a. purely competitive.
    b. oligopolistic.
    c. a monopoly.
    d. monopolistically competitive.
    e. monogamous.

13. If we assume that the actual cost of construction of a Plauché-built structure is no greater than that of a home built by a "lesser" contractor and we take seriously his comments about "living comfortably for many, many years," we might conclude that his pricing objective has a component of
    a. securing market share.
    b. profit maximization.
    c. meeting competition.
    d. target return on investment.
    e. serving a selected mareket segment.

14. If Mr. Plauché collects money from his clients by submitting to them the invoices from his subcontractors and suppliers to which he adds (rather large) sums for his own costs and efforts, then the pricing method he is using is
    a. breakeven pricing.
    b. incremental cost pricing.
    c. modified breakeven pricing.
    d. customary pricing.
    e. cost-plus pricing.

Part 8 Pricing Strategy

Name_____ Instructor_____

Section_____ Date_____

Surfing the Net

Keeping in mind that addresses change and what's on the Web now may have changed by the time you read this, let's take a look at some of the places on the Net that reflect aspects of price determination. We are not endorsing or recommending any of these sources, merely making note of the information and services that people have elected to offer through the Internet.

Finding good Web sites to exemplify price determination was not easy. Typically, people's sites give you the results of their pricing decisions, not the logic behind them. On the other hand, where there's a will, there is often a way.

Looking for price determination at its most direct? Check out one or more of the auctions we've discovered. At an auction, the price is determined by direct interaction of supply and demand. If you've never been to an auction, you really should go to one – but leave your money at home. Auctions can be addictive. Some online auctions and their specialties include **http://www.oldandsold.com** that features all sorts of antiques, **http://www.firstauction.com** that specializes in electronic and electrical equipment and appliances, **http://www.philatelists.com** for the stamp collectors, and finally, for the wine connoisseurs among you, there's **http://www.zachys.com** for auctions of wines of various sorts.

Another example of direct interaction setting prices is in the stock market. A good entry to that market is the CNN Financial Network's financial markets service at **http://cnnfn.com.** This site has links to a number of other stock and bond market-oriented sites. Alternatively, you might try Corporate Financial Online at **http://www.cfonews.com** for more detailed analysis of recent activity in the market and other links to important sites.

Finally, you might give some thought to what you're worth – at work, that is – at the JobNet Web site. This site compiles listings of available jobs from a number of sources, with trends in employment and employment statistics built in. Try it at **http://www.westga.edu/~coop/localhome.html**

Sites verified January 22, 2000.

Harcourt, Inc.

Chapter 19

Managing the Pricing Function

Chapter Outline

Use the following as a guide in taking notes.

I. Chapter Overview – Creating and administering the pricing structure

II. Pricing Strategies

    A. Skimming pricing strategy

    B. Penetration pricing strategy

        1. Everyday Low Pricing

    C. Competitive pricing strategy

III. Price Quotations

    A. Reductions from list price

        1. Cash discounts

        2. Trade discounts

        3. Quantity discounts

        4. Allowances

        5. Rebates

    B. Geographic considerations

IV. Pricing Policies

    A. Psychological pricing

    B. Price flexibility

    C. Product-line pricing

    D. Promotional pricing

        1. Leader pricing and loss leaders

    E. Price-quality relationships

Harcourt, Inc.

V. Competitive Bidding and Negotiated Prices

    A. Negotiating prices online

VI. The Transfer Pricing Dilemma

VII. Global Considerations and Online Pricing

    A. Traditional global pricing policies

    B. Characteristics of online pricing

VIII. Strategic Implications

Name_____   Instructor_____

Section_____   Date_____

Key Concepts

The purpose of this section is to allow you to determine if you can match key concepts with their definitions. It is essential that you know the definitions of the concepts prior to applying the concepts in later exercises in this chapter.

From the list of lettered terms, select the one that best fits each of the numbered statements below. Write the letter of that choice in the space provided.

Key Terms

a. skimming price strategy
b. penetration pricing strategy
c. everyday low pricing   (ELP)
d. competitive pricing strategy
e. list price
f. market price
g. cash discount
h. trade discount
i. quantity discount
j. trade-in
k. promotional allowance
l. rebate
m. FOB plant
n. freight absorption
o. uniform-delivered price
p. zone pricing
q. basing-point system
r. pricing policy
s. psychological pricing
t. odd pricing
u. unit pricing
v. price flexibility
w. product-line pricing
x. promotional pricing
y. loss leader
z. transfer price
aa. profit center
ab. cannibalization
ac. bundle pricing

_____ 1. Pricing policy based on the belief that certain prices or price ranges make a good more appealing than others to buyers.

_____ 2. Price reduction offered to a consumer, industrial user, or marketing intermediary in return for prompt payment of a bill.

_____ 3. Pricing strategy involving the use of a relatively low entry price as compared with competitive offerings; designed to help secure initial market acceptance.

_____ 4. Pricing policy based on the belief that prices ending with odd numbers just under round numbers are more appealing – for instance, $9.99 rather than $10.00.

_____ 5. Pricing policy permitting variable prices for goods and services.

_____ 6. System that handles transportation costs by allowing the buyer to deduct shipping expenses from the cost of the goods.

_____ 7. Any part of an organization to which revenue and controllable costs can be assigned.

Contemporary Marketing

_____ 8. Pricing policy that states prices in terms of recognized units of measurement or standard numerical counts.

_____ 9. Offering two or more complementary products and selling them for a single price.

_____ 10. Cost assessed when a product is moved between profit centers within a single firm.

_____ 11. Price that a consumer or marketing intermediary actually pays for a product after subtracting any discounts, allowances, or rebates from the list price.

_____ 12. Price reduction granted for a large-volume purchase.

_____ 13. Practice of marketing different lines of merchandise at a limited number of prices.

_____ 14. Pricing strategy designed to de-emphasize price as a competitive variable by pricing a product at the general level of comparable offerings.

_____ 15. Price quotation that does not include shipping charges; also called FOB origin.

_____ 16. Pricing strategy of continuously offering low prices rather then relying on short-term price cutting tactics such as cents-off coupons, rebates, and special sales.

_____ 17. Refund of a portion of a product's purchase price, usually granted by its manufacturer.

_____ 18. Securing additional sales through lower prices that take sales away from the marketer's other products.

_____ 19. System that handles transportation costs by dividing the market into geographic regions and setting a different price in each region.

_____ 20. Price-setting system that handles transportation costs by quoting all buyers the same price, including transportation expenses.

_____ 21. Payment to a channel member or buyer for performing marketing functions; also known as a functional discount.

_____ 22. Established price normally quoted to potential buyers.

_____ 23. Pricing system common in some industries during the early twentieth century that incorporated transportation costs by quoting factory prices plus freight charges from the basing point city nearest the buyer.

_____ 24. Funds provided by a manufacturer to pay for advertising or sales promotion by other channel members in an attempt to integrate promotional strategy within the channel.

_____ 25. General guidelines based on pricing objectives and intended for use in specific pricing decisions.

_____ 26. Product offered to consumers at less than cost to attract them to a store in the hope that they will also buy other merchandise at regular prices.

_____ 27. Pricing strategy involving the use of a high price relative to competitive offerings.

_____ 28. Credit allowance given for a used product when a new product, usually of the same kind, is purchased.

_____ 29. Pricing policy in which a lower than normal price is used as a temporary ingredient in a firm's marketing strategy.

Contemporary Marketing

Name_____ Instructor_____

Section_____ Date_____

Self-Quiz

You should use these objective questions to test your understanding of the chapter material. You can check your answers with those provided at the end of the chapter.

While these questions cover most of the chapter topics, they are not intended to be the same as the test questions your instructor may use in an examination. A good understanding of all aspects of the course material is essential to good performance on any examination.

True/False

Write "T" for True and "F" for False for each of the following statements.

_____ 1. For a new product that represents a significant innovation, a skimming price conveys an image of distinction.

_____ 2. Many firms begin a penetration pricing strategy with the intention of maintaining that price for a substantial length of time, so that success of the strategy cannot be measured in terms of trial purchases.

_____ 3. During the late growth and early maturity stages of the product life cycle, a product's price is typically increased to compensate for the pressure of competition and the desire to expand its market.

_____ 4. One advantage of a skimming strategy is that it permits the marketer to control demand in the introductory stages of the product life cycle and adjust productive capacity to meet demand.

_____ 5. One of the forms of everyday low pricing involves manufacturers that seek to set stable wholesale prices that undercut those offered by competitors, which often rise and fall due to trade promotion deals.

_____ 6. Penetration pricing works best when a good or service experiences highly inelastic demand.

_____ 7. Retailers universally oppose everyday low pricing strategies because of their use of "high-low" strategies that depend on frequent specials and promotions.

_____ 8. Improvements in existing products are seldom sufficient to allow firms to introduce a skimming strategy where none existed before.

_____ 9. Unless demand is price-elastic, overall price cuts will mean less revenue for all firms in an industry; moreover, low prices may generate an image of questionable quality.

_____ 10. When marketers price their products at the general levels of competitive offerings, they largely negate the price variable as an element of their marketing strategy.

Harcourt, Inc.

_____ 11. Marketers typically avoid combinations of cash, trade, and volume discounts, tending to use one or the other of them exclusively.

_____ 12. Trade discounts are justified on the grounds that large orders reduce selling expenses and may shift a portion of the product's marketing costs to the buyer.

_____ 13. If a trade discount were quoted as "35 percent, 10 percent off list price" for wholesalers, this would mean that wholesalers would pay the manufacturer of the good the list price less the 35 percent that they were to discount the list price to retailers, less another 10 percent of the discounted price to compensate them for their costs, profits, and services.

_____ 14. A vendor who offers a rebate of 4 percent to customers who make annual purchases of at least $30,000 with that vendor is offering a noncumulative quantity discount.

_____ 15. The major categories of allowances are price adjustments and trade-outs.

_____ 16. When "FOB origin" pricing is used, the buyer pays only the cost of loading the merchandise aboard the carrier selected by the seller.

_____ 17. "Uniform-delivered pricing" is sometimes also known as *postage-stamp pricing*, and might be considered to be the exact opposite of FOB origin pricing.

_____ 18. The often-used term "FOB" is really an abbreviation for "Freight Outbound Burden."

_____ 19. Both zone and uniform-delivered pricing have the drawback that some customers will be paying phantom freight.

_____ 20. Originally, odd pricing was used as a cash-control device within the firm, forcing clerks to make change

_____ 21. Unit pricing – pricing goods in terms of some recognized unit of measure or by standard numerical count – has significantly improved the shopping habits of low-income consumers by allowing them to make more meaningful price comparisons.

_____ 22. One-price policies characterize situations in which personal selling is employed, whereas variable pricing is used where mass selling marketing programs are typical.

_____ 23. Product-line pricing allows the shopper to pick a price range and then devote his or her attention to the other features of the product such as color, style, or material.

_____ 24. Loss-leader pricing is prohibited in those states with unfair-trade laws.

_____ 25. Many situations involving government and organizational procurement are characterized by competitive bidding, particularly in cases of nonrecurring purchases like a weapons system for the Department of Defense.

Contemporary Marketing

Multiple Choice

Circle the letter of the word or phrase that best completes the sentence or best answers the question.

26. Williams-Sonoma's Dualit toaster, its most popular catalog item for 1999, was sold using a
    a. skimming pricing strategy.
    b. penetration pricing strategy.
    c. competitive pricing strategy.
    d. "market-minus" price strategy.
    e. functional strategy.

27. Which of the following is one of the advantages of a penetration pricing strategy?
    a. It allows the firm to quickly recover its research and development costs.
    b. It is effective in segmenting the overall market on a price basis.
    c. It may allow a new product to reach the mass market quickly and capture a large share of it prior to entry by competitors.
    d. It permits the marketer to control demand in the introductory stages of the product's life cycle and to adjust productive capacity to meet demand.
    e. It largely negates the price variable in the marketing strategy.

28. When a skimming strategy is used, the product's price is typically reduced during the late growth and early maturity stages of the product life cycle because
    a. volume of production is sufficiently high to allow reductions in the per-unit cost of the product.
    b. competition has been effectively stifled and the product can now be allowed to sell at its "natural" price.
    c. the profits earned during the introductory and early growth stages of the cycle may be plowed into new productive technology, making lower prices possible.
    d. Successive price declines expand the firm's market and meet challenges posed by new competitors.
    e. the product's proprietors have achieved their target objective and can now afford to take less "off the top" for contribution to profit and overhead.

29. Though the one chief disadvantage of a skimming pricing policy is its tendency to attract competition, it may still be used effectively for a relatively long period if
    a. patent rights or some other unique proprietary ability – like a trade secret – can keep out competition.
    b. research and development costs are quite small and can be recovered very early in the product life cycle.
    c. production facilities are able to satisfy all potential demand which may develop.
    d. financial pressure can be placed on potential competitors which will prevent them from entering the market.
    e. inventories of goods are kept larger than any demand for the product which may develop.

30. When a penetration pricing strategy is used,
    a. prices are set at a level well above the prices of existing competing products.
    b. the price of the product is adjusted as necessary to keep it competitive with similar products in the market.
    c. the product is usually already in the decline stage of its life cycle and price manipulation is a normal feature of this stage.
    d. it is necessary that there be no pre-existing competition; otherwise, the strategy won't work.

e. products or services are priced noticeably lower than competing offerings in industries with many competing brands.

31. A penetration pricing policy is likely to be most successful when
    a. relatively few consumers are price-sensitive.
    b. some consumers are price-sensitive.
    c. some suppliers are price-sensitive.
    d. large numbers of consumers are highly price-sensitive.
    e. large numbers of suppliers are highly price-sensitive.

32. In industries with relatively homogeneous products,
    a. competitors must match each other's price reductions to maintain market share and competitive position.
    b. skimming pricing is often used as a differentiating tool among producers of what are essentially commodities.
    c. penetration pricing may provide the consumer advantage necessary for success.
    d. pricing based solely on costs is almost mandatory.
    e. market-plus pricing offers the advantage of high short-term return with little down-side risk.

33. Using a competitive pricing strategy
    a. creates the situation of segmenting the overall market on a price basis.
    b. conveys an image of distinction and appeal to buyers who are less sensitive to price.
    c. shifts the marketing emphasis to nonprice competition in product, distribution, and promotional areas.
    d. is useful to introduce new products in industries where there are large numbers of competing brands.
    e. discourages competition, since the attractive financial returns associated with skimming are not usually present.

34. Which of the following most closely represents the list price of a product?
    a. The amount of money you and your next door neighbor's son both agree is fair to pay him to cut your lawn.
    b. The amount of money you ask for when you decide to sell your 1994 Mitsubishi Montero.
    c. The manufacturer's suggested retail price (MSRP) on a new GE television set.
    d. The advertised price of a home offered "for sale by owner" in a classified newspaper advertisement.
    e. The price you paid for your new set of tires after all discounts and allowances were subtracted from the original price.

35. Reductions in price offered for prompt payment of bills – usually specifying the exact time period involved – are known as
    a. trade discounts.
    b. cash discounts.
    c. quantity discounts.
    d. cutback discounts.
    e. "off price" discounts.

36. If the payment terms on an invoice are shown as 4/10, net 60, then
    a. the full amount must be paid within ten days and legal action will be taken after 60.
    b. the full amount is due in 60 days but if you pay the invoice in ten days you can deduct 4 percent from the total.

c. 4 percent of the invoice must be paid in ten days, and the rest in 60 days.
d. 10 percent of the amount due must be paid in four days, with the rest due at the end of 60 days.
e. four-tenths of the amount billed is due in 60 days.

37. Payments to channel members for performing marketing functions are known as
    a. cash or seasonal discounts.
    b. seasonal or cumulative discounts.
    c. incremental or decremental discounts.
    d. trade or functional discounts.
    e. noncumulative quantity discounts.

38. If a trade discount stated as "50 percent, 15 percent off list" was offered to a wholesaler by a manufacturer, then the wholesaler would pay which of the following prices for a good whose usual retail price to the consumer was $100?
    a. $32.50
    b. $35.00
    c. $37.50
    d. $41.00
    e. $42.50

39. A discount that depends only on the number of units or dollar value of product bought in a single transaction is a
    a. noncumulative quantity discount.
    b. cumulative quantity discount.
    c. promotional quality discount.
    d. cash or standard discount.
    e. market position status discount.

40. Allowances are similar to discounts in that they
    a. provide that larger customers pay less per unit for the things they buy.
    b. are based on the operating expenses of each level in the channel of distribution.
    c. specify deductions from the list price of a product.
    d. alter the financing rates normally quoted to potential buyers.
    e. are used uniformly across the consumer and industrial segments of the market.

41. Trade-ins accepted by the vendors of consumer durables such as automobiles are
    a. trade discounts.
    b. rebates.
    c. market pricing.
    d. allowances.
    e. variable pricing.

42. A means of handling transportation expenses in which only the seller pays the shipping charges is
    a. FOB plant pricing.
    b. uniform delivered pricing.
    c. zone pricing.
    d. all-for-one pricing.
    e. freight absorption.

43. When a lower-than-normal price is used as a temporary ingredient in a firm's selling strategy,

a. it is called predatory pricing.
   b. "market-up" pricing may result.
   c. pass-through pricing is the policy.
   d. "market-down" conditions may result.
   e. it is called promotional pricing.

44. Pittsburgh-plus pricing was
   a. a variety of zone pricing once used in the Chicago meat packing industry.
   b. the basing-point system of quoting prices in the steel industry in the United States.
   c. widely used by manufacturers of parts for automobiles during the 1960s and 1970s.
   d. a type of FOB origin freight allowed pricing typical in the fresh produce (fruits, vegetables, and like goods) industry in the western United States.
   e. a method of determining how much it would cost to ship anything to Pittsburgh.

45. When a retailer prices products in terms of some standard numerical count (by the dozen or the hundred or the gross), that retailer is using
   a. unit pricing.
   b. promotional pricing.
   c. odd pricing.
   d. psychological pricing.
   e. average-cost pricing.

46. The use of a variable price policy by a seller
   a. facilitates mass marketing programs where the customer does not expect to haggle over the price.
   b. creates the possibility of haggling between buyer and seller over the price of every item in the store.
   c. can often be recognized by the preponderance of prices ending in 5, 8, or 9.
   d. is quite common in large-scale department store retailing, where variable pricing is the rule.
   e. may result in retaliatory pricing by competitors.

47. When a retail firm prices goods slightly above cost to avoid violating minimum-markup regulations and to earn some return on promotional sales, it is using
   a. bait and pull pricing.
   b. bull and bear pricing.
   c. leader pricing.
   d. product-line pricing.
   e. multiple-unit pricing.

48. The concept of price limits basically says that
   a. people consciously limit their spending to goods that do not affect their consumption patterns.
   b. a firm may encounter legal opposition if the prices of its products exceed certain limits.
   c. the relationship between price and sales volume is limited to values greater than two.
   d. consumers have limits within which their product-quality perceptions vary directly with price.
   e. individuals expect to be able to limit spending to necessities and a few luxuries, even in bad times.

49. In the governmental and industrial markets, when there is only one supplier of a good or service or where extensive research and development work is called for by a contract,
   a. competitive bidding may nonetheless be required by law.
   b. negotiation is likely to be the basis on which the contract is awarded.
   c. an escalator clause is typically included in the contract to protect the buyer from price increases.
   d. transfer pricing may be used to reduce the process of contracting to a comprehensible level.

e. specifications must be especially carefully written so that breach or abrogation of the contract will be easy to prove in court.

50. FOB origin-freight allowed pricing is also known as
    a. postage-stamp pricing.
    b. pricing to the market.
    c. zone pricing.
    d. basing point pricing.
    e. freight absorption.

Name_____   Instructor_____

Section_____   Date_____

Applying Marketing Concepts

Adastra High Definition Television Corporation manufactures a line of HDTV sets that are distributed throughout the United States. Sold primarily through specialty outlets, Adastra products are recognized as leaders in their field. Sales volume and profits have increased dramatically over the last five years. Adastra sells through its own sales force, but in those parts of the country where sales volume isn't large enough to justify maintaining a company sales representative, it uses electronics wholesalers.

Adastra is a respected name in its industry. Retailers often feature the company's line in their advertising. The company encourages this and gives dealers who advertise their relationship price reductions on Adastra products to help them pay their advertising costs. They also have a somewhat unusual approach to pricing for an electronics manufacturer. Prices on Adastra products are the same, including transportation, to any dealer anywhere in the country.

The company's product line includes three ranges of HDTV set. The "Stellar" units have a 15 by 25-inch picture tube and sells in the $525 to $700 range, depending on special features. The "Galactic" models are somewhat larger with 21 by 35-inch pictures. These units sell for $950 to $1200. The top of the line "Universality" models feature a very nice 27 by 45 inch picture and sell for $1800 to $2200. Adastra publishes manufacturer's suggested retail prices (MSRP's) whose dollar amounts always end in a 98 (like $1098) and encourages dealers to stick with that ending even if they discount the product off the MSRP. It is management's belief that the 98 ending helps sales.

Write "T" for True and "F" for False for each of the following statements.

____ 1. Adastra's pricing policies encourage retailers to sell their products as loss leaders.

____ 2. Since Adastra quotes the same price to all buyers of its products it is using a unit pricing policy.

____ 3. The company is encouraging its retailers to use psychological pricing.

____ 4. If Adastra were to institute a trade-in program, it would be suggesting that retailers sell the company's products at less than list price.

____ 5. By pricing its products in different ranges, the company is attempting to establish definite price/quality relationships in the consumer's mind.

Circle the letter of the word or phrase that best completes the sentence or best answers the question.

6. The discount that Adastra gives wholesalers who sell to retailers is called a
    a. cash discount.
    b. trade discount.
    c. quantity discount.
    d. promotional discount.
    e. rebate.

7. What kind of allowance does Adastra currently grant its distributors?
   a. a rebate
   b. a trade-in
   c. a promotional allowance
   d. an allowance for returned goods
   e. a sales representative's field allowance

8. Adastra's geographic pricing policy is
   a. FOB plant.
   b. FOB plant freight allowed.
   c. zone pricing.
   d. basing point pricing.
   e. uniform delivered pricing.

9. The company's general pricing policy is one of
   a. product line pricing.
   b. unit pricing.
   c. skimming pricing.
   d. penetration pricing.
   e. price fixing.

10. The firm encourages its retailers to engage in
    a. skimming pricing.
    b. penetration pricing.
    c. unit pricing.
    d. odd pricing.
    e. unusual pricing.

Dan Hammer Motor Company is a multi-brand new car dealership in Brawley, Wisconsin. The company sells two American, one German, two Japanese, and one Korean make. Advertising strongly suggests that potential new-car buyers "Watch Dan Hammer down new-car prices," but specific prices are never advertised and each retail customer bargains with the company for his or her own purchase price on a car.

The company is also on the state's "bid list," so it periodically receives requests to bid on providing automobiles for the highway patrol, wildlife and fisheries department, and other state agencies. These bid requests are carefully read, and if what is needed is described clearly enough, the company may enter a bid. Occasionally, the fleet manager will have to call the state capitol in Madison to find out exactly what is meant by certain wording in the request sent out by the state agency.

All cars sold by the Hammer dealership are delivered to the buyer in Brawley. If the buyer doesn't want to take delivery in Brawley, the company can make arrangements to have the car delivered to them by another dealer from his stock for the additional amount of money it would cost to ship the car from Brawley to that dealership.

When asked about his pricing policies, Mr. Hammer said, "One thing we know is that we never want to be the cheapest dealer around nor do we want to be the highest priced. People don't like you to be either one of those things. We just want to sell cars at a reasonable price that people think represents good value for the money."

_____ 11. Though all consumer prices are subject to negotiation at Hammer's, the evidence provided suggests that their pricing strategy is a competitive one.

_____ 12. When a supplier such as Hammer's enters a bid on a state request for bids, they are really opening the process of negotiation to supply those vehicles.

13. Dan Hammer Motor Company's basic pricing policy appears to be a
    a. fixed-price policy.
    b. variable price policy.
    c. list price policy.
    d. product line policy.
    e. zone pricing policy.

14. When the fleet sale manager calls Madison to get additional information on bid requests, he is probably trying to clarify the bid request's product
    a. specifications.
    b. end-use.
    c. price limits.
    d. function.
    e. user name.

15. The geographical pricing policy the company uses for delivery of cars distant from Brawley is
    a. zone delivered pricing.
    b. freight absorption pricing.
    c. postage-stamp pricing.
    d. basing point pricing.
    e. FOB Brawley.

16. Mr. Hammer's comments about not wanting to be too cheap nor too expensive suggest that he is aware of
    a. how fickle the consumer can really be.
    b. the concept of price limits.
    c. the uses of odd pricing.
    d. the essence of the automobile-buying experience.
    e. how difficult it is to make money.

Contemporary Marketing

Name_____   Instructor_____

Section_____   Date_____

Surfing the Net

Keeping in mind that addresses change and what's on the Web now may have changed by the time you read this, let's take a look at some of the places on the Net that reflect aspects of managing the pricing function. We are not recommending any of these sources, merely making note of the information and services that people have elected to offer through the Internet.

Prices aren't always under anybody's control, and the stock market is an interesting example of how a completely open market works. The following is a very interesting Web site in this connection, which, though rather lengthy to access, lets you look at graphs of the ups and downs of prices of a number of stock issues. Try **http://www.stockmaster.com** and take a look.

To compare prices of Internet service in various places, there are a number of sites you might care to explore. Lade's of Cape Coral, Florida, is an Internet service provider in that area that can be reached at **http://www.boblade.com,** while in Worcester, Massachusetts, Flashnet can be accessed at **http://www.2400ad.com/worcester.html.** In the west, the local Internet service provider for Lawtoin, Oklahoma, can be reached at **http://www.lawtonok.net,** while if you're interested in getting hooked up in Sydney or Melbourne (Australia), you should contact **http://www.spin.net.au** In Hamilton, Ontario, Canada, try **http://www.netinc.ca** to access the local ISP, and finally, in the UK, an outfit called Spartiate can be reached at **http://www.spartiate.co.uk.**

Some sites with information about pricing of telephone communication services include **http://www.cellone.com** for Cellular One, while **http://www.pacbell.com** belongs to Pacific Bell Telephone Company, and Sprint may be found at **http://www.sprintlink.net.**

Ever wonder why insurance costs what it does? Take a look at the Web site of the American Risk and Insurance Association at **http://www.aria.org.** There you'll find an explanation of risk theory, the risk management profession, and other neat stuff about this organization.

A most interesting site is found at the BizWeb locus. Billed as "perfect for comparison shoppers," the site has an all-inclusive catalog of products – finance, food, publishing, flowers, clothing. Select a category and you're presented with a list of firms offering the product you've chosen. Then you can move to each one's home page and see who's offering the best deal. The address is **http://www.bizweb.com.**

Sites verified January 12, 2000.

Name_____ Instructor_____

Section_____ Date_____

Cases for Part 8

1. Madame Gremillon's Creole Seasoning Mix

In east central Louisiana south of the Red River and west of the Atchafalaya lies Avoyelles Parish.[1] The people there are Creoles (not Cajuns)[2] who have preserved their French language and customs with little change for the last 250 years. But like their Cajun cousins to the southwest, they are creative and have adapted much of their cuisine to use native ingredients.

Odile Moreau Gremillon is an exception to the comment that "all Creoles can cook and the only people who can cook better than Creole men are Creole women" in only one respect: She can cook *better* than most Creoles, and has a bunch of prizes won at Parish and State Fairs to prove it. For years, friends and local retailers have been urging Odile to sell her famous Creole Seasoning Mix commercially. Today she borrowed $35,000 from the Bank of Moreauville to produce and market her product. As a consequence, she will be facing competition from products already on the market in the local area. Madame Gremillon's Seasoning Mix can best be described as a combination of herbs, spices, and thickeners which, when added to the liquid of stews, soups, and other slow-cooked foods, gives them a delightful bouquet and flavor and adds to them a robust texture which would otherwise be lacking.

Question

What should Madame Gremillon's pricing objective be? Defend your position.

---

[1] Louisiana has no counties. As in France, its civil subdivisions are called Parishes. Admittedly, it can get a bit confusing because many of the civil Parishes bear the same names Church Parishes might, like St. John the Baptist, St. James, and St. Landry, to name but a few.

[2] Creoles emigrated from France to Louisiana directly. Most Creole families arrived before 1760, while the Cajuns (a corruption of the French *Acadien*, were forcibly ejected from what is now Nova Scotia somewhat later in the century. The Creoles (which term is itself a corruption of the Spanish Criollo, meaning a person of European stock born in the New World) landed in New Orleans and moved northward to settle in eastern Louisiana, while the Cajuns settled the southwestern part. There are vast differences in the two cultures, as there are vast differences in their cuisines. Where Cajun food tends to be spicy – heavy with red and black pepper flavor – Creole food relies more on seasoning – onion, garlic, bell pepper, celery, salt, and browned flour – to define itself.

Contemporary Marketing

2. *National Seat and Pew Company*

Sandahl Engstrom, director of market development for National Seat and Pew Company, has been asked by Walt Thornnastor, the company president, to estimate demand after the firm implements a price level change.

National markets theater seats and church pews all over the United States. Their products are used in churches, public buildings, and motion picture and performance theaters all over the United States. There are other manufacturers of similar products that can be used if National's seats are unsatisfactory. National's costs for labor and material have risen to the point where some upward price adjustment must be made. Mr. Thornnastor has considered a 10 percent price increase, but before announcing the change, he wants to know if sales will decline dramatically.

Question

Can Mr. Engstrom provide a reliable estimate of the demand change to Mr. Thornnastor? How should he go about estimating demand?

3. *Sir Henri de Jacques, Kinght Errant (A Tale of Tenth-Century France)*

Sir Henri de Jacques, a journeyman knight and freelance tourniste de joust from Rouen, has developed a revolutionary new style of armor that he thinks will revolutionize the manly art of the Tourney, that periodic test of valor and the manly arts of war in which every right-thinking tenth-century Frank of noble lineage deems is his right and obligation to engage.

His armor has a unique shape that allows it to hold the saddle even when struck directly by the lance of a competitor, but is still light enough and well enough articulated so that its wearer is sufficiently nimble to participate in a bit of friendly murder and mayhem afoot. It is also approximately twice as resistant to cuts, piercing, and blows with blunt instruments as average armor.

De Jacques estimates that he can build his "Rouen Rider" for around 3000 pence (or the equivalent). This includes both fixed and variable costs. Since Sir Henri expects to sell his suits of armor to the better class of tournistes, their material and workmanship must be of the best quality, and the expected lifetime of each suit (assuming it is not lost in battle, hopelessly rusted, or crushed beyond all possibility of repair) will be at least ten years.

The characteristic shape and startling strength of Sir Henri's armor is determined by a special forging process which he himself developed and is done in secret. He fully expects it will be at least fifteen years before anyone else can figure out how he manages to create this result.

Question

Should Sir Henri adopt a skimming or a penetration pricing policy? Why?

4. Intense Lighting, Inc.

Ted Mallon, president of Intense Lighting, feels that his firm has a problem. Distributors are treating the Intense line of outdoor lighting very casually, and don't seem to be making a very active effort to promote its sale. Jan Stockwell, Mr. Mallon's new executive assistant, has suggested a course of action she thinks will go a long way toward solving the problem. Ms. Stockwell believes that Mallon should raise its retail price, thereby increasing the amount of discount per item received by both retailers and wholesalers.

Gene Nolan, sales manager for Intense Lighting, is displeased with Jan's proposal. He favors the use of promotional allowances given for specific purposes. Mr. Nolan would use cooperative advertising and PMs.[1]

Questions

a. Discuss the advantages and disadvantages of each proposal.

---

[1] PMs, or "Push Monies" are payments made directly to sales clerks and wholesaler salespeople. They are usually figured as a certain percent of sales. They are sometimes called "spiffs."

b. If you were the director of marketing for Intense Lighting, which of the two alternatives would you choose? Why?

5. Donald M. Landsdowne, Attorney at Law

Donald M. Landsdowne is an attorney practicing in the state of South Dakota. Mr. Landsdowne specializes in personal injury cases in which he typically represents the plaintiff and is compensated for his services by receiving a percentage of whatever judgment his client receives from the court or he can negotiate with the defendant. Mr. Landsdowne is a very conscientious and thorough practitioner, and his services are considered to be among the best. He has traditionally charged 40 percent of any awards he was able to get for his clients as his fee.

In recent years, there has been an influx of attorneys into the legal profession, and sheer numbers have made the industry very competitive. Mr. Landsdowne has just learned that a number of his fellow attorneys have reduced their fees on personal injury cases to 35 percent, and some are even accepting 30 percent of the award. He is concerned about what to do. He knows that his reputation is well established in this field of legal endeavor, and even with the increase in competition he hasn't noticed any diminution of his caseload. He is concerned because he feels that if he reduces his fees he will be working for less than he is worth, and most of his cases come to him by referral (from people he has successfully represented in the past), anyway.

Question

What should Mr. Landsdowne do?

Creating a Marketing Plan

The information contained in this episode will help you complete Parts III.A. and III.B. of your marketing plan for Telabri Industries. You may wish to review the material in Part Five of the text to refresh your memory before attempting to complete Part III.A.

Episode Seven: How Much Is Too Much? (And How Little Is Not Enough?)

"OK," said Terry, "let me get this straight. We're going to offer 'minimum turnaround' Web site maintenance service aimed primarily at business users here in the New Essex area. We're going to be open 24 hours a day, and we'll serve anyone who is willing to pay our prices. We're going to offer Web site development as well, and that ties in explicitly with the maintenance situation. In other words, we don't care whether we start as the Web site developer or in a maintenance role. A customer is, after all, a customer. I see. That makes me happy. What about you, Brian?"

"I'm fine, too, Ter," Brian said, "I can see where I'm going to be spending a lot of time doing preventive maintenance for people whose sites attract the attention of hackers. You know, I'll bet we're one of the few service firms in town with people who know how to create the right diagnostics to stop those little devils before they can do any damage and then track them down. It should be fun!"

"Right, fellas," Laura spoke up, "but you know we've got to get down to brass tacks on price sooner or later. You guys have fun just going out there and playing around with all those Web sites, but if we don't make some money around here, it's not going to be long before we won't be able to pay the rent. Come look at these figures I've put together. They outline some price information I got my hands on." And so saying, she handed to Brian and Terry a copy of the information contained in Table P7-1.

"Very interesting," muttered Terry, reading the charts he had been handed, "we've really got a wide range of prices here, don't we. It looks like the most common local price for site development is either $180 or $150 per page when you work it out."

"Yes," replied Brian, "but there are five firms charging only $150. I wonder if they know something we don't know – or maybe it's that we know something they don't – (laughing) like how to create good Web sites!"

"Well," smiled Laura, "I've run some figures and if they are right, we can make money according to our expectations at any rate equal to or greater than $150 per page. That price would put us in a very competitive position as far as the other places that offer these kinds of services are concerned."

"Yes, that's true," answered Terry, "but it's still the next-to-the-bottom price for the market. I think we're better than that. I think we should ask at least $160 per page for our services, and there should be a three-page minimum."

"I'll buy the three-page minimum," spoke up Brian, "but the average I see in these figures is $183.00 and change per page. Why don't we want to charge something like that?"

"Let's put that decision off for now," commented Laura, "if we offer maintenance contracts, you know, we're going to have to price them as well. How do you propose we do that?"

Harcourt, Inc.

Table P7-1: New Essex Area Repair Price Data
(From a Survey of 21 Firms)

Charge Per Page	Number	Percent Reporting
$300	2	9.5%
$220	2	9.5%
$200	2	9.5%
$180	5	23.8%
$160	4	19.0%
$150	5	23.8%
$120	1	4.7%

Mean per page charge: $183.33
Median per page charge: $180.00
Modal per page charge: $150.00/180.00

Table P7-2: Typical Development Time for
A New Web site and Renovation Times

Page Type	Initial Time	Time for Renovation	Average Pages Per Site
Home Page	20 Hrs.	2.25 Hrs.	1
Graphics Page	30 Hrs.	2.75 Hrs.	3
Catalog Page	5 Hrs.	0.50 Hrs.	20
Reply Page (Interactive)	10 Hrs.	1.00 Hrs.	2

"I've got that one solved for you, Laura," responded Terry. "An article I read last night gave some actuarial figures and some prices for maintenance contracts and it said that maintenance contracts that sell cost approximately as much yearly as a site renovation."

"You mean a renovation that involves every page on the site?" asked Brian.

"Yes," answered Terry, "and it looks like that sort of thing costs about 10 percent, on average, of what a new site would cost. I think our maintenance contracts should be priced at around 10 percent of the cost of a new site to the client."

Laura entered the conversation at this point to announce, "Good thinking, Ter; I've seen that article and I think you're right. Let's work on that sort of price for maintenance contracts. Now let's get back to the per page price for our Web development service. What price do you think we should set? Let's vote on it."

Guidelines:

a. Outline the company's product/service strategy in your planning notebook. Refer back to the information provided in the earlier parts of this exercise for items that may expand on what you learned in this part. Recognize how this strategy developed to serve the needs of the market and of our entrepreneurial trio.

b. What sort of price structure do you favor for Telabri Industries? Should their page rate be $150, $160, $180 or some other amount? This time, the decision is yours to make, but you should be able to justify it if called upon to do so.

Contemporary Marketing

Creating a Marketing Plan

The material provided in this episode should allow you to complete section III.E. of your marketing plan.

Episode Eight: So When Do We Start To Get Rich?

The three partners, having incorporated their business, have themselves each bought 20,000 shares of the authorized 80,000 shares of Subchapter S common stock for one dollar apiece. They were able to borrow $90,000 from family and friends and have also secured a $90,000 bank loan, both at a rate of 9.5 percent, the whole to be repaid over five years in monthly installments of $3781.80.

Pro Forma Income Statements for the first three years of operation have been prepared and are included in Table P8-1.

Table P8-1: Pro Forma Income Statements for Years 1, 2, and 3
Telabri Industries, Inc.

Year	One	Two	Three
Revenue	$291,460	$346,752	$408,294
Allowances	8,000	9,600	11,448
Net Sales	283,640	337,152	396,846
Internal Services	48,210	49,350	49,840
Employee Wages+	90,000	105,000	120,000
Gross Margin	145,430	182,802	227,004
Operating Expenses	209,718	130,298	126,740
Marketing Expense*	28,718	60,062	64,778
Operating Income(Loss)	(93,006)	(7,558)	35,486

*Includes Sales Commissions, Sales Staff Salaries, and Advertising.
+Compensation to three hired employees not members of the corporation.

The threesome, Terry, Brian, and Laura, will have collected separate commissions and salaries not included in "employee wages" as compensation during the first three years. Those amounts are summarized in Table P8-2.

Harcourt, Inc.

Part 8 Pricing Strategy

Table P8-2: Amounts Paid Incorporators, First Three Years
Telabri Industries, Inc.

Year	One	Two	Three
Administrative Salaries	$60,000	60,000	60,000
Service Salaries	38,400	38,400	38,400
Sales Commissions	13,490	24,494	29,210
Sales Salaries	22,300	22,800	22,800
Total Amounts	$134,590	145,694	150,410

The amounts above were paid share and share alike to each of the three corporate members. They are, of course, due any dividends that they may elect to pay themselves from profits earned in years three and subsequent years.

Guidelines:

Use this information to prepare Part III.E. of your marketing plan. Note that, since this is a startup business, projections have been made pro forma for a period of three years. Impact of the trio's efforts will be evidenced by the degree to which the projections and reality are similar.

Question:

Will it all have been worth it? Considering the future of the company, will the three partners have gotten out of it what they expected to, in your opinion? Remember that the psychic reward of entrepreneurship has some value as well.

Harcourt, Inc.

Chapter 1 Solutions

Key Concepts

1. t	8. d	15. c	22. f
2. h	9. k	16. r	23. ab
3. q	10. p	17. u	24. y
4. e	11. o	18. z	25. j
5. m	12. s	19. b	26. l
6. x	13. g	20. a	27. n
7. v	14. aa	21. w	28. i

Self-Quiz

1. T	11. T	21. T	31. b	41. d
2. F	12. F	22. F	32. b	42. e
3. T	13. T	23. F	33. a	43. c
4. F	14. F	24. F	34. b	44. e
5. F	15. T	25. T	35. c	45. d
6. T	16. F	26. b	36. a	46. e
7. T	17. F	27. d	37. e	47. c
8. F	18. T	28. c	38. a	48. a
9. T	19. T	29. a	39. d	49. e
10. T	20. T	30. c	40. d	50. b

Applying Marketing Concepts

1. T	6. a	11. b
2. T	7. a	12. b
3. F	8. e	13. a
4. F	9. e	14. c
5. F	10. c	

Contemporary Marketing

Chapter 2 Solutions

Key Concepts

1. e	6. j	11. m
2. l	7. d	12. h
3. n	8. i	13. a
4. g	9. c	14. k
5. b	10. f	

Self-Quiz

1. F	11. T	21. F	31. e	41. c
2. T	12. F	22. T	32. b	42. d
3. T	13. T	23. F	33. c	43. b
4. T	14. F	24. F	34. d	44. a
5. F	15. F	25. T	35. c	45. c
6. T	16. T	26. c	36. e	46. b
7. F	17. F	27. b	37. a	47. e
8. F	18. F	28. d	38. e	48. a
9. F	19. T	29. d	39. b	49. d
10. T	20. T	30. a	40. e	50. a

Applying Marketing Concepts

1. F	6. e	11. b
2. F	7. a	12. d
3. T	8. e	13. a
4. F	9. c	14. b
5. T	10. b	

Harcourt, Inc.

Chapter 3 Solutions

Key Concepts

1. g	6. l	11. v	16. i	21. d
2. t	7. r	12. a	17. o	22. q
3. k	8. b	13. f	18. x	23. m
4. c	9. p	14. s	19. u	24. e
5. h	10. w	15. j	20. n	25. y

Self-Quiz

1. F	11. T	21. F	31. c	41. d
2. T	12. F	22. F	32. e	42. e
3. T	13. F	23. T	33. d	43. b
4. F	14. F	24. F	34. b	44. b
5. T	15. T	25. T	35. c	45. a
6. F	16. T	26. d	36. a	46. d
7. T	17. F	27. a	37. c	47. b
8. F	18. F	28. e	38. a	48. c
9. F	19. T	29. b	39. e	49. d
10. T	20. T	30. c	40. a	50. e

Applying Marketing Concepts

1. c	6. d	11. T
2. d	7. a	12. F
3. a	8. c	13. F
4. c	9. T	14. F
5. b	10. F	

Contemporary Marketing

Chapter 4 Solutions

Key Concepts

1. x
2. g
3. m
4. j
5. f
6. h
7. c
8. s
9. t
10. u
11. b
12. r
13. l
14. q
15. e
16. w
17. d
18. k
19. o
20. p
21. v
22. i
23. n
24. a

Self-Quiz

1. T
2. F
3. F
4. T
5. T
6. T
7. F
8. F
9. T
10. F
11. T
12. T
13. F
14. F
15. T
16. F
17. T
18. T
19. F
20. T
21. F
22. F
23. T
24. F
25. T
26. a
27. c
28. e
29. d
30. c
31. b
32. d
33. c
34. e
35. b
36. e
37. a
38. e
39. a
40. a
41. d
42. c
43. e
44. d
45. b
46. a
47. b
48. c
49. d
50. b

Applying Marketing Concepts

1. c
2. d
3. a
4. b
5. d
6. a
7. c
8. b
9. a
10. b
11. a
12. d
13. c

Chapter 5 Solutions

Key Concepts

1. b   7. k   13. m
2. d   8. c   14. n
3. g   9. a   15. o
4. f   10. j
5. h   11. i
6. e   12. l

Self-Quiz

1. F   11. F   21. T   31. c   41. c
2. T   12. F   22. F   32. b   42. c
3. F   13. T   23. T   33. d   43. d
4. T   14. T   24. T   34. b   44. a
5. T   15. F   25. T   35. d   45. a
6. T   16. F   26. e   36. a   46. b
7. F   17. T   27. a   37. e   47. e
8. F   18. F   28. b   38. b   48. d
9. T   19. F   29. a   39. c   49. e
10. F   20. T   30. d   40. d   50. b

Applying Marketing Concepts

1. b   6. b
2. c   7. d
3. e   8. c
4. a   9. a
5. a   10. b

Contemporary Marketing

Chapter 6 Solutions

Key Concepts

1. r	7. h	13. k	19. d
2. e	8. p	14. f	20. q
3. b	9. j	15. i	21. t
4. g	10. o	16. u	
5. c	11. a	17. l	
6. m	12. s	18. n	

Self-Quiz

1. F	11. F	21. F	31. c	41. a
2. F	12. F	22. F	32. b	42. c
3. T	13. T	23. T	33. b	43. d
4. T	14. T	24. T	34. a	44. e
5. F	15. T	25. F	35. a	45. d
6. T	16. F	26. c	36. b	46. a
7. F	17. F	27. b	37. c	47. d
8. T	18. T	28. c	38. c	48. d
9. F	19. F	29. e	39. b	49. b
10. T	20. T	30. b	40. e	50. e

Applying Marketing Concepts

1. a	5. b	9. b
2. b	6. a	10. c
3. a	7. c	11. b
4. c	8. b	12. d

Chapter 7 Solutions

Key Concepts

1. g	6. w	11. e	16. v	21. r
2. q	7. n	12. i	17. k	22. u
3. p	8. l	13. t	18. m	23. o
4. s	9. a	14. b	19. h	
5. c	10. j	15. d	20. f	

Self-Quiz

1. T	11. T	21. T	31. e	41. e
2. T	12. F	22. F	32. b	42. c
3. F	13. F	23. T	33. d	43. e
4. T	14. T	24. F	34. a	44. c
5. F	15. T	25. F	35. e	45. b
6. F	16. F	26. b	36. a	46. a
7. T	17. F	27. c	37. b	47. d
8. T	18. F	28. d	38. d	48. d
9. F	19. T	29. c	39. c	49. e
10. F	20. T	30. a	40. a	50. b

Applying Marketing Concepts

1. T	6. b	11. F	16. d
2. T	7. c	12. T	17. a
3. F	8. b	13. F	
4. F	9. c	14. b	
5. F	10. a	15. c	

Contemporary Marketing

Chapter 8 Solutions

Key Concepts

1. x	5. q	9. r	13. k	17. t	21. c	25. z
2. d	6. m	10. g	14. ab	18. i	22. o	26. aa
3. b	7. f	11. v	15. u	19. l	23. j	27. w
4. a	8. s	12. y	16. e	20. n	24. p	28. h

Self-Quiz

1. T	11. T	21. T	31. c	41. e
2. F	12. F	22. F	32. b	42. b
3. T	13. T	23. T	33. a	43. d
4. T	14. F	24. T	34. d	44. c
5. F	15. F	25. F	35. c	45. a
6. F	16. F	26. b	36. e	46. b
7. F	17. T	27. a	37. d	47. c
8. T	18. T	28. c	38. d	48. b
9. F	19. F	29. e	39. e	49. d
10. T	20. F	30. a	40. d	50. e

Applying Marketing Concepts

1. F	5. c	9. d
2. T	6. c	10. c
3. F	7. e	
4. b	8. c	

Chapter 9 Solutions

Key Concepts

1. v	6. o	11. p	16. h	21. e
2. a	7. m	12. l	17. k	22. n
3. f	8. r	13. t	18. s	23. j
4. g	9. w	14. c	19. x	24. q
5. i	10. b	15. d	20. u	

Self-Quiz

1. T	11. F	21. F	31. b	41. d
2. T	12. T	22. T	32. a	42. b
3. T	13. F	23. F	33. a	43. b
4. F	14. F	24. F	34. c	44. d
5. F	15. T	25. T	35. e	45. e
6. F	16. T	26. e	36. d	46. c
7. F	17. F	27. c	37. a	47. b
8. T	18. T	28. c	38. d	48. a
9. T	19. T	29. d	39. c	49. a
10. T	20. F	30. b	40. e	50. d

Applying Marketing Concepts

1. T	8. F
2. b	9. T
3. d	10. d
4. a	11. c
5. F	12. b
6. T	13. a
7. F	14. a

Contemporary Marketing

Chapter 10 Solutions

Key Concepts

1. y	5. o	9. f	13. j	17. g	21. u	25. t
2. m	6. r	10. l	14. b	18. c	22. p	26. d
3. v	7. x	11. i	15. q	19. z	23. n	
4. w	8. k	12. e	16. h	20. s	24. a	

Self Quiz

1. T	11. T	21. T	31. d	41. b
2. F	12. T	22. T	32. d	42. c
3. F	13. T	23. F	33. e	43. e
4. F	14. F	24. F	34. e	44. c
5. T	15. F	25. T	35. a	45. a
6. F	16. T	26. b	36. b	46. e
7. T	17. T	27. d	37. e	47. d
8. T	18. F	28. a	38. b	48. e
9. F	19. F	29. c	39. b	49. a
10. F	20. F	30. c	40. a	50. c

Applying Marketing Concepts

1. T	6. b
2. F	7. c
3. b	8. c
4. e	9. a
5. a	10. c

Chapter 11 Solutions

Key Concepts

1. b	6. i	11. h	16. d	21. u
2. f	7. n	12. s	17. c	22. v
3. m	8. j	13. l	18. o	23. w
4. g	9. t	14. a	19. p	
5. k	10. e	15. q	20. r	

Self-Quiz

1. F	11. T	21. T	31. c	41. c
2. T	12. T	22. T	32. a	42. a
3. T	13. F	23. F	33. b	43. b
4. F	14. F	24. T	34. c	44. a
5. T	15. F	25. F	35. a	45. e
6. F	16. T	26. b	36. b	46. e
7. F	17. F	27. c	37. e	47. c
8. T	18. F	28. d	38. d	48. d
9. T	19. T	29. d	39. e	49. a
10. F	20. F	30. e	40. d	50. b

Applying Marketing Concepts

1. d	5. b	9. e	13. b
2. d	6. a	10. a	14. a
3. c	7. a	11. c	
4. b	8. b	12. a	

Chapter 12 Solutions

Key Concepts

1. ag	7. x	13. p	19. h	25. aa	31. ag
2. i	8. j	14. r	20. k	26. ab	32. b
3. z	9. ah	15. e	21. l	27. d	33. q
4. af	10. af	16. w	22. n	28. g	34. f
5. ae	11. t	17. c	23. o	29. ac	35. v
6. y	12. u	18. s	24. ad	30. a	36. m

Self-Quiz

1. T	11. F	21. T	31. e	41. d
2. T	12. F	22. T	32. c	42. c
3. F	13. T	23. F	33. a	43. b
4. T	14. F	24. F	34. e	44. d
5. F	15. F	25. F	35. a	45. d
6. T	16. T	26. a	36. a	46. b
7. T	17. F	27. b	37. c	47. d
8. F	18. T	28. e	38. c	48. e
9. F	19. F	29. d	39. b	49. a
10. T	20. F	30. c	40. e	50. b

Applying Marketing Concepts

1. b	6. c	11. e
2. e	7. b	12. d
3. c	8. a	13. a
4. c	9. d	14. b
5. a	10. b	15. a

Chapter 13 Solutions

Key Concepts

1. ag	9. ac	17. i	25. l	33. b
2. d	10. y	18. o	26. w	34. aa
3. g	11. u	19. h	27. v	35. j
4. e	12. r	20. z	28. n	36. q
5. ai	13. t	21. k	29. aj	37. ak
6. s	14. f	22. ah	30. m	
7. a	15. c	23. af	31. ae	
8. ab	16. p	24. x	32. ad	

Self-Quiz

1. T	16. F	31. e	46. a
2. F	17. T	32. b	47. d
3. F	18. F	33. c	48. b
4. F	19. F	34. a	49. e
5. T	20. T	35. a	50. a
6. T	21. F	36. e	
7. T	22. T	37. b	
8. F	23. T	38. c	
9. T	24. F	39. d	
10. F	25. F	40. e	
11. T	26. a	41. d	
12. F	27. a	42. c	
13. T	28. b	43. d	
14. T	29. d	44. b	
15. F	30. c	45. d	

Applying Marketing Concepts

1. b	6. T	11. b
2. c	7. T	12. c
3. d	8. T	13. a
4. a	9. F	14. c
5. e	10. T	15. a

Chapter 14 Solutions

Key Concepts

1. r	11. ar	21. d	31. ai	41. aa
2. p	12. u	22. f	32. e	42. t
3. o	13. as	23. ag	33. s	43. l
4. g	14. c	24. aj	34. ac	44. ad
5. am	15. ao	25. a	35. k	45. v
6. ae	16. ah	26. y	36. b	46. q
7. n	17. af	27. i	37. w	47. au
8. h	18. aq	28. al	38. m	
9. ak	19. ab	29. at	39. j	
10. an	20. z	30. x	40. ap	

Self-Quiz

1. T	11. T	21. T	31. a	41. b	51. a
2. F	12. T	22. F	32. a	42. c	52. d
3. T	13. F	23. T	33. b	43. d	53. a
4. F	14. F	24. F	34. d	44. a	54. e
5. F	15. T	25. T	35. e	45. d	55. c
6. T	16. T	26. F	36. b	46. d	56. c
7. F	17. F	27. T	37. e	47. c	57. e
8. T	18. T	28. T	38. e	48. b	58. c
9. F	19. F	29. F	39. b	49. a	59. b
10. F	20. T	30. F	40. c	50. e	60. d

Applying Marketing Concepts

1. F	6. d	11. b	16. a
2. T	7. d	12. b	17. d
3. F	8. a	13. a	18. d
4. T	9. c	14. T	
5. T	10. b	15. c	

Chapter 15 Solutions

Key Concepts

1. h	6. k	11. o	16. t	21. c
2. f	7. p	12. n	17. r	
3. g	8. s	13. m	18. a	
4. b	9. e	14. d	19. j	
5. i	10. l	15. u	20. q	

Self-Quiz

1. T	11. F	21. T	31. c	41. d
2. F	12. T	22. F	32. d	42. c
3. F	13. F	23. T	33. d	43. c
4. F	14. F	24. T	34. b	44. b
5. T	15. T	25. T	35. e	45. e
6. T	16. F	26. e	36. a	46. a
7. F	17. F	27. b	37. b	47. d
8. F	18. T	28. a	38. c	48. e
9. T	19. T	29. c	39. a	49. e
10. T	20. F	30. a	40. d	50. a

Applying Marketing Concepts

1. a	6. b
2. c	7. d
3. a	8. c
4. d	9. a
5. e	10. c

Contemporary Marketing

Chapter 16 Solutions

Key Concepts

1. n	6. m	11. u	16. aa	21. a	26. d
2. p	7. q	12. w	17. k	22. i	27. v
3. t	8. z	13. f	18. x	23. o	28. e
4. y	9. r	14. b	19. l	24. j	
5. s	10. g	15. h	20. c	25. ab	

Self-Quiz

1. T	11. T	21. T	31. e	41. c
2. F	12. F	22. F	32. d	42. d
3. F	13. T	23. T	33. e	43. b
4. T	14. F	24. T	34. b	44. b
5. F	15. T	25. T	35. c	45. e
6. T	16. F	26. b	36. d	46. a
7. F	17. T	27. a	37. a	47. a
8. T	18. F	28. c	38. d	48. c
9. F	19. T	29. c	39. e	49. d
10. F	20. F	30. b	40. e	50. d

Applying Marketing Concepts

1. e	5. d	9. e
2. b	6. c	10. a
3. a	7. b	11. a
4. c	8. b	

Harcourt, Inc.

Chapter 17 Solutions

Key Concepts

1. o	6. x	11. s	16. aa	21. j	26. c
2. d	7. h	12. y	17. w	22. q	27. z
3. v	8. n	13. a	18. k	23. g	
4. m	9. l	14. e	19. r	24. u	
5. b	10. t	15. f	20. p	25. i	

Self-Quiz

1. F	11. T	21. T	31. a	41. a	
2. T	12. F	22. F	32. b	42. e	
3. F	13. T	23. T	33. b	43. c	
4. T	14. T	24. F	34. e	44. a	
5. F	15. F	25. F	35. d	45. d	
6. F	16. T	26. d	36. b	46. c	
7. T	17. T	27. b	37. e	47. a	
8. T	18. F	28. b	38. c	48. c	
9. F	19. F	29. e	39. e	49. c	
10. T	20. F	30. a	40. d	50. d	

Applying Marketing Concepts

1. c	6. b	11. d
2. d	7. a	12. c
3. a	8. d	13. d
4. b	9. a	
5. c	10. b	

Chapter 18 Solutions

Key Concepts

1. e	7. n	13. k	19. p
2. h	8. f	14. o	20. l
3. s	9. t	15. j	
4. i	10. a	16. g	
5. r	11. d	17. c	
6. b	12. q	18. m	

Self-Quiz

1. F	11. F	21. T	31. e	41. a
2. T	12. F	22. F	32. d	42. b
3. T	13. T	23. F	33. a	43. d
4. F	14. T	24. T	34. c	44. b
5. T	15. F	25. F	35. b	45. c
6. F	16. F	26. e	36. e	46. e
7. T	17. T	27. d	37. d	47. b
8. T	18. F	28. a	38. c	48. d
9. T	19. T	29. a	39. e	49. a
10. F	20. F	30. b	40. c	50. c

Applying Marketing Concepts

1. F	6. d	11. c
2. T	7. b	12. d
3. F	8. a	13. b
4. T	9. e	14. e
5. T	10. b	

Harcourt, Inc.

Chapter 19 Solutions

Key Concepts

1. s	7. aa	13. w	19. p	25. r
2. g	8. u	14. d	20. o	26. y
3. b	9. ac	15. m	21. h	27. a
4. t	10. z	16. c	22. e	28. j
5. v	11. f	17. l	23. q	29. x
6. n	12. i	18. ab	24. k	

Self-Quiz

1. T	11. F	21. F	31. d	41. d
2. F	12. F	22. F	32. a	42. e
3. F	13. T	23. T	33. c	43. e
4. T	14. F	24. T	34. c	44. b
5. T	15. F	25. T	35. b	45. a
6. F	16. F	26. a	36. b	46. b
7. F	17. T	27. c	37. d	47. c
8. F	18. F	28. d	38. e	48. d
9. T	19. T	29. a	39. a	49. b
10. T	20. T	30. e	40. c	50. e

Applying Marketing Concepts

1. F	6. b	11. T	16. b
2. F	7. c	12. F	
3. T	8. e	13. b	
4. F	9. a	14. a	
5. F	10. d	15. d	

Contemporary Marketing

Solutions for Cases to Part 1

1. The Laser Videodisc

a. RCA apparently introduced SelectaVision because it had spent so much time and money developing it. There is no mention of marketing research to assess the characteristics of demand (or lack of it) for the product. Moreover, the lack of the ability to record constituted a major disadvantage when the product was compared with its competition, the VCR. One suspects that RCA also failed to conceive of a rental market for prerecorded tapes (or discs, for that matter), and thought its lower priced product would attract people who might otherwise buy VCRs.

b. The primary factors affecting the market for SelectaVision were competitive, economic, and technological. It was introduced into a market in which an alternative technology had already established itself and over which it did not possess an overwhelming superiority. In addition, considering the types of technology involved, it did not offer a substantial economic advantage in price or cost of materials (given the presence of a rental market which made the cost per viewing using either the disc or tape medium roughly equal).

c. The arrival of the compact disc (CD) as a medium for reproducing sound and storing computer data (CD-ROM) created a window of opportunity for the laserdisc medium. RCA apparently detected a new, more favorable perception of disc-read laser technology on the part of the using public. RCA believed higher video quality would be preferred to the capacity to record program material and that the quality known to be present in the audio CD will be seen to carry over into the video version. The reintroduced product carved for itself a small but comfortable niche in the academic audio-visual market for several years and was still available in 1997, though it seems to have begun to fade soon thereafter. RCA's perception of the competitive, technological, and economic parameters of the market was somewhat better this time than it was the last time they introduced the product.

d. A number of considerations contribute to the relative success of the DVD product. First, the home computer has achieved the status of a serious entertainment alternative. Until recently, there wasn't enough memory capacity available or a video card with the capacity to refresh the screen fast enough to show a movie without a "herky-jerky" look to it on the average system. Now, only the least sophisticated units lack the ability to do all of these. A second reason for the better showing probably has to do with the physical size of the DVD disc – it's only 4.75 inches in diameter, instead of 12, and is much easier to handle, store, and use – in other words, it's a CD with pictures. Last, the DVD disc can be duplicated on a home CD burner should one ever want to do so (though it could be illegal). Finally, the quality of reproduction is better than that of tape, and if one buys a dedicated DVD player, it's quite a lot smaller than a VCR and about the same price.

2. "Cacao Merivigliao"

a. The various entrepreneurs in this scenario are reacting to having a previously unrecognized market dropped in their laps. What the people want has been found out for them, and they are seeking to satisfy the demand for it. In more formal terms, a pocket of unfulfilled demand has been discovered, and people are seeking the opportunity to fulfill it.

b. RAI created the product (as a satire), and may fear that none of the commercial claimants will be able to produce a product that will live up to the claims which have been made for it, in which case RAI could stand to be in somewhat deep legal trouble later for having made the claims in the first place. Secondly, the awarding of the trademark to someone else would foreclose on RAI's ability to produce further "Cacao Merivigliac" satires. Finally, RAI created the concept, and product or no product, undoubtedly feels that it has the right to any benefits which may accrue from production or distribution, should that ever happen (which RAI supposedly seeks to prevent). Both Buitoni and Vignola seek to commercialize the product that RAI has created. Their attempts to trademark the name are certainly opportunistic to the highest degree, but if they are operating in the knowledge that RAI has no intention of commercializing the product, they merely seek to reap the benefit of what could be considered to be the biggest free advertising program in Italy's history.

Mr. Blanga is the most difficult to understand of all the participants in this little scenario. He seems to have no vested interest in this matter, one way or another – which could make him the most suspect person in the lot. Moreover, his involvement in this situation seems peripheral to that of anyone else, seemingly seeking to deny others the use of something to which he seems to have no rightful claim at all.

In short, the ethical constructs of all of the participants in this little drama are suspect. RAI could be considered to be unethical for seeking to deny the use of the name to Buitoni or Vignola; after all, they can't, by Italian law, register it or put it to any use. Buitoni and Vignola are certainly attempting to make a profit from someone else's creation, and Blanga seems bent on acting as though he had at least the same claim to this creation as RAI, which he does not. Ethics are relative to the culture and the society under consideration, and Italy is certainly not the United States, but RAI seems the least unethical of the four involved parties, followed by the two candy companies because they might perceive themselves to have a right to produce a product RAI, by definition, has no intention of producing, followed by Mr. Blanga, who shouldn't be involved in this situation at all.

c. If a change in Italian trademark law were to be recommended, it would be a change to allow anyone who could show first use for whatever purpose to register a trademark regardless of whether or not it were ever to be used on a product, perhaps even with a stipulation in the law that the intent was to protect such marks from unauthorized use by a noninnovator. The law would have to be carefully structured so that innovators could reap the benefits of their innovations without fear of ripoff or could choose not to reap such benefits if they so desired.

d. The motives of RAI, Buitoni, and Vignola are pellucidly clear. RAI wishes to protect its intellectual rights and the latter two wish to develop the brand for commercial reasons. Mr. Blanga, as was stated before, has no reason to be involved in this situation, except that it has often happened that someone sought to register a trademark when it was known that another person desired it. There are, in fact, people who make it a practice to register foreign trademarks in their own country and then offer to sell them to the foreign firms when they enter the local market – forcing them to buy what, by rights, they already own. One might suspect Mr. Blanga of falling into this class.

3. Hargrove Manufacturing Company

If Alicia really wants to do business with the PTT, she has no choice but to "go with the flow" of life in Femerlange. The culture there is typical of the northern rim of the Mediterranean, only somewhat slower. You should understand that the phones *do* work, it's just that the people of the city (and perhaps the country, as well) only want them to work ten hours a day. The public transportation and the taxicabs may be quite good, they just aren't in service at all hours of the day and night. In short, Ms. Truestone has just experienced the beginnings of culture shock, and is just going to have to live

Contemporary Marketing

with it or figure out some other way to get the job done. She really has only two choices: (1) settle in and get to know the Femerlangeans and let them get to know her; or (2) go home. One thing is absolutely for sure: the people of Femerlange are not going to change their way of doing things just to please her.

To better understand some of the subtleties of the cultural differences one is likely to encounter, the work of social anthropologist Edward T. Hall is highly recommended. His three books, *The Silent Language* (New York: Doubleday, 1959); *The Hidden Dimension* (New York: Doubleday, 1966); and *Beyond Culture* (Anchor/Doubleday, 1976), are required reading for persons seeking to adapt in the cultural sphere.

4. The Lifeline Foundation

a. When retail sales are up during periods of recovery or prosperity, Lifeline's receipts of merchandise from businesses will decline because their sales are brisk and inventory leftovers and business failures are fewer. Merchandise received from the general public, on the other hand, will increase in volume because their purchases of products from retailers will require the disposal of the goods they replaced. On the other hand, when times become more difficult, as during periods of recession or depression, receipts from the general public decline and those from businesses increase as they dispose of excess inventories or, in some cases, fail. Contributions dry up from both sources when the economy remains stable for a significant period of time.

b. The Lifeline Foundation, by recognizing these phenomena, can shift its solicitation efforts in recognition of which of the two sources are more likely to be productive at a given point in time. Essentially, all charities are susceptible to the condition of the economy. Lifeline is luckier than some in that it has a source of donations available during both up and downswings of the economic activity level. Its worst times for donations are during periods of stability. At such times, solicitations in both markets may need to be intensified if the thrift shops are to be able to function.

Solutions to Cases for Part 2

1. Where'd They All Go?

a. The most likely explanation for the absence of many of the retailers who were on the Internet three years ago is that they were not prepared for what they had gotten into, didn't maintain their sites properly or successfully carve out a niche for themselves in the cybermarket place, and then withdrew from that arena. The registration of over 25,000 new Internet marketers a month has a corollary – that there must be a certain number of existing Internet registrants who drop from the Net. Let's examine the implications of this realization. Small retailers, of necessity, do business in fairly narrowly circumscribed geographical surroundings and are set up to do so. The Internet looks very attractive to them because of the low cost of entry – preparation of a basic Web site, registration of a domain name, and site placement with an ISP can cost less than a thousand dollars. Listing with the major search engines costs an additional few hundred dollars, and you're ready to go. But when you start getting orders from far distant places and you realize you have to recover shipping and insurance costs to ship goods to those places, and the question of returns – or even of having products on hand to fill orders – comes up, the physical and financial capacities of the firm may become severely strained. Many simply find that the scope of Internet involvement is beyond them and drop out.

b. The relocation of many sites from non-World Wide Web locations to www sites is a natural function of the development of the World Wide Web over the last five to seven years. The Web simply didn't exist when many of the governmental and organizational sites were originally written so they approached the Internet in other ways: through direct hypertext transfer protocols and their own non-Web portals, some of which we still see (the http://sitename.gov calls that still pop up from time to time); as directories on someone else's domain (many early organizational sites were carried in the domains of educational institutions as sitename.something.uiuc.edu, a subdomain, or as directories within a site). The development of the Web created the opportunity to register a very simple domain name under the www "banner," and that is what a large number of sites have done.

c. Registration of domains is first come, first served. There is apparently no explicit recognition of trademarks or copyrighted names on the Web. One can advance a legal explanation for this that states essentially that copyrights and trademarks cannot be assumed to be legally protected everywhere, so that registration of a domain name which happens to be the registered trademark of someone else is fine because the entire world is the venue where that name will appear. The described phenomenon is not as uncommon as one might think. I have seen a number of situations where, while looking for the site of a major company, I have typed in what I thought was the most likely domain name for the company only to find it belonged to someone else – usually another firm not in the same industry, and in several instances the firm was foreign and domiciled far, far away.

Thus, the implications of such a situation are simple: it can and does happen, and if it happens to you, too bad. You might try and buy the name from its present holder, who has no obligation to sell; or you can develop a new name and publicize it to avoid confusion. It is probably a very bad idea to try and pressure the existing holder to give the domain name up, because they can retaliate by doing exactly as this domain holder has done.

2. Was It the Warranty or the Way It Was Honored?

a. Let's begin with the terms of the warranty offered by this manufacturer. Warranties are cost centers for most firms. They evaluate what it will cost them to honor a warranty over its period

offer a warranty that reflects their expectation of what they can afford. It is also a promise to the customer. This car's warranty is almost embarrassingly generous. It exceeds the typical warranty by a large margin. This can mean one of two things, or both: it can mean that the manufacturer expects that this vehicle will give very little trouble (which indeed proved to be the case) or it can mean that the manufacturer wants the customer to own the vehicle for a long time. Either of these indicate a real desire to build a relationship with that customer. The replacement of the radio – though it was technically out of warranty – is also indicative of that attitude. And frankly, the fact that the car WAS so good – well-made and long-lasting, could be read to mean that internal marketing has caused the people who make it to take pride in doing it right and want to make a good product. The magazine, rallies, and other events didn't hurt, either. This firm apparently makes promises it intends to keep.

b. The full tank of gas, immaculate condition of the car on delivery, pride of the mechanic in being able to deliver a good car to its proud new owner all indicate a spirit of trying to be empathetic with the customer and put themselves in his or her shoes. The concern of the salesman for the needs of the customer (note that the car had on it the accessories Tom Beaufort wanted, not those the manufacturer or dealer made the most money selling) was a clue to what might happen next. Dealing with the dealer was pleasant, their prices were fair on both the product and its service, and the work was well done. All of these are evidence of the attempt (in collaboration with the manufacturer) to create the kind of atmosphere that will bring the customer back to the dealership for service work and purchase of more cars.

c. Tom had obviously developed a bond with the people at his (he said it, too) dealership. He thought well of them just as he thought well of the car. He didn't say he was going to shop dealerships – even for that make of car – to buy his new one. He was pleased with how he had been treated during the course of his five-year relationship with these people, and trusted them to treat him fairly in the future.

(This case parallels the author's experience in dealing with a specific dealership for a particular make of automobile in recent history. He might mention here that the same make can be bought at two other dealerships in his immediate area, and during his first buying expedition for this type of vehicle five years ago, he visited both of them and very quickly departed when the pressure was turned on. Thus, the manufacturer's desire to be a relationship marketer has to be advanced by the dealer through the same kind of treatment of customers, or it has little hope of success.)

3. Cyberbeta.com

a. Though cyberbeta.com's e-commerce activities are somewhat more subtle than those of sites such as autotrader.com, for example, where one can purchase, finance, and insure an automobile over the Net, it is still an e-commerce site. It meets all the requirements of the definition. It targets consumers, the people who like jokes and cartoons and the other things it features, collects information from them for its database, engages in transactions with them – largely non-monetary ones, it is true, but transactions nonetheless, and does all this electronically. Another way of putting it would be to say that the site has customers who interact with it – actually two classes of customers – the individuals who come to the site to read the jokes and look at the cartoons, and the advertisers who put their messages in the banners and on the other links spotted about the site's homepage.

b. Yes, cyberbeta.com is an e-marketing site in two respects. It is a business-to-business site offering advertising space to other online marketers to advertise their goods and services, and it is a consumer site offering entertainment to those seeking it in humor. The product is the entertainment derived from the content of the site, "talking" to kindred spirits in the chat room, even participating by sending in jokes, cartoons, and news items. The cost is having to read the ads and the expense in time and effort of submitting material (should one wish to do so.) The site is promoted by its search engine listings, its own appearance, and its contests with their prizes. Thus, though not a blatant "buy-me" type of Internet competitor, this site is definitely engaged in e-marketing.

c. Cyberbeta.com is quite relationship-oriented. There is economic motivation to become involved with the site. One can win prizes by submitting material for inclusion on the site in the form of coffee mugs, writing instruments, and T-shirts. Bigger prizes are possible if one's name is drawn in the weekly drawing. Social bonding and interaction is available in the chat room. There are even rules about what can and can't be done, and they are enforced. Many people find this a very desirable feature. Finally, one can actually be recognized for loyalty and persistence through the citizenship program. One can't help but wonder when the first domain picnic is going to be!

Contemporary Marketing

Solutions for Creating a Marketing Plan

Episode Two

a. The firm's nature is becoming fairly clear in episode two. It is to be a firm specializing in Web site development and maintenance. It will be located in the as yet unnamed home town of the three people who have decided to start it, and they have about $240,000 available to them to get underway. Thus, their geographical scope and their financial resources are limited.

The company is to be a corporation, appropriately licensed and conforming to the constraints of the various environments impinging on it. It has no sales and profits history as yet, just cash on hand and considerable expertise in computer and business-related technology and practice.

b. The data provided are designed to lead our heroes to choose to create a firm that will develop and maintain Web sites with particular appeal to the business user. While there are some 118,925 <u>households</u> in the area which own computers, only 5 percent of those (5,946 households) have a permanent Web presence, and it is dubious if they use non-household members to write their sites or perform active maintenance on them. Under other conditions, it might be desirable to do extensive research into the household market for Web site development, but with the limited resources on hand, the business market for Telabri's services seems far more accessible and the potential much greater.

The 25,895 business firms in the area offer a market with a use level of 35 percent at present, and it is likely that a substantial number of the remainder will need sites soon in the future. It appears as well that the smaller firms have lagged the larger ones in making their presence known on the Net. One reason for this may have been their fear of having to do Web maintenance, exactly the kind of thing Telabri is prepared to do. Moreover, the predicted rate of growth for the maintenance segment of the Web site market is estimated at 33 percent, over twice the rate of growth of other Web-related products and services.

Harcourt, Inc.

Solutions for Cases to Part 3

1. The O'Leary Glass Company

a. The cause of falling sales can't be explicitly determined solely from the type of data given in this case, though some definition of the area in which the problem has developed may be undertaken. Both Central and Southern sales force areas have shown declining sales performance. Only the Northern Area managed to improve its performance this period over last, though cost of sales went up, reflecting the change in sales mix this period. On the other hand, marketing expenses in the North did not decline as a proportion of sales as was the case in the other two areas, leading one to wonder what might have happened in that regard. As a result, the Northern sales force actually contributed less to the bottom line than did either Central or Southern groups.

If one seeks something to look at more closely, sales in the Central and Southern areas seem to be appropriate for closer scrutiny, as does the level of marketing expenses in the North. It is possible that they are scrimping too much in the Southern and Central areas and not enough in the North. In any event, sales have declined for some reason. That reason may be hinted at in these reports, but it may be beyond the control of the field sales force.

b. Other information needed include:
   - Industry sales trend figures;
   - Information on actions by competitors;
   - General economic information;
   - Specific economic conditions in the sales force areas;
   - Sales and cost quotas used by the sales forces as guidelines;
   - Overall cost of sales figures for each product.

2. The Four Wise Men

a. The four samples represent a limited view of only a part of the population. They are biased samples because they were not taken across the whole sampling space. They certainly aren't representative of the population called "this elephant."

b. Each wise man took a nonprobabilistic sample of the convenience type. Each simply acquired data from whatever part of the population he happened to encounter first. Suffice it to say, none of the samples represented the whole population.

c. A redesign of the sample such that the wise men would gather data from all parts of the elephant is certainly in order. The best way to assure that this will be the case is by taking a simple random sample of points scattered all over the body of the elephant. The wise men should, in addition, pool their knowledge. The idea of going off to the king to report individually had the effect of reducing the sample acquired by each to one-fourth its potential size. In the analytical phase, data should be culled of incongruities and if there is persistent conflict between one description and another, a resampling undertaken.

Contemporary Marketing

3. U.S. Grain Exports to Europe: The Data Looks Good But How About the Interpretation?

a. The whole concept of managerial span of control is based on the premise that decisions are made at every level of an organization. This implies that a certain amount of informational filtering takes place as data finds its way up through the chain of command. A problem that is perceived to be within the scope of one's authority to solve is not made known to one's superiors, but is instead solved at one's own level. The problem, of course, is that middle managers may unilaterally decide to act like upper-level managers, and entry-level personnel act like middle managers. In many cases, such actions place people beyond the scope of their experience and competence, and bad decisions result.

b. Had the U.S. officials in Europe made reinspections of the questioned grain shipments or had them made by qualified grain inspectors familiar with U.S. standards instead of turning a deaf ear to the complaints of their European counterparts, it is likely that much of this situation could have been avoided.

c. As was already discussed, field-level filtering of information flows is a necessary part of organizational behavior. Real problems arise when too much information is filtered out or if filtration is selective, removing from the information stream bits of data that might make some particular person or office appear in a negative light. One way of assuring that information is passed along in something resembling its original configuration is by rotation of individuals through the organization so that entrenchment of the communication channel cannot take place. It is, of course, costly to move people about like this, so it is not often done domestically and is even less often done in the international sphere, thus increasing the level of danger that the system will come to serve the vested interests of those who function within it rather than those who pay its bills. For a superb illustration of exactly how this can work, view the PBS television series "Yes, Minister!" or its sequel, "Yes, Prime Minister!" if either is on the air in your area. They chronicle the interaction between Jim Hacker, a fictional British politician who serves in a ministerial capacity in Her Majesty's cabinet, and the British Civil Service, each member of which knows that the government's sole reason for existence is to preserve their bureaucratic positions. (If not being broadcast, these shows may be available on videotape locally.)

A second, more important issue in this case, involves the nature of the role of the U.S. government in commercial transactions. When a transaction occurs between one private individual and another, to what extent does the U.S. government have a role in maintaining levels of quality? The government assigned the grain its grade in the first place. The embassy seems to take the view that complaints must be made officially by the foreign government to be transmitted forward officially to the U.S. government, and the complaints made by the Europeans were unofficial in nature. It is true that importers often complain, just as the embassy official told the inquiring professor about quality when, in fact, they're complaining about what they see to have been a bad deal they've made. The embassy is in no position to make a determination about the validity of simple complaints, but in the interest of U.S. credibility, those complaints should certainly be forwarded for review.

It might be mentioned in closing that inspection of grain shipments for export is now done entirely differently and much more securely than as is described in this case, though the time frame of actual occurrences and the natures of the participants is somewhat different than the case reports.

4. Kaufsaale AG: München Neuhauser-Strasse, Nürnberg, Augsburg, Weihanstephan

Each of the four stores Herr Speigelmann is examining fits one of the stereotypes in the Boston Consulting Group Matrix. The Munich flagship store is a star, growing more rapidly even than the rapidly growing market in which it is situated. The Nuremberg store is a question mark. It is located in a growing market but is faced with competition from at least two other firms. It is, however, a new entrant into the Nuremberg market, so the jury is out on it. These two stores should probably receive a disproportionate share of resources, but they should both be carefully watched to make sure that the conditions under which they are now operating do not get out of hand.

The Augsburg store is a dog. It is a weak performer in a weakening market. Albrecht's may have already driven the last nail into its commercial coffin. This store should be considered for closure. The Weihanstephan store is a cash cow, and given its venerable age, may remain one for another century or two. This store should receive light cultivation but no major commitment of development resources.

As a closing comment, let me point out that the time frame for these sorts of situations is a bit different in Europe than is the case in the United States. It would be somewhat unusual for a store to have been open for over 600 years there, but not outrageously so. There are a substantial number of business firms in Europe that have been active for several hundred years, and quite a few of them are retailers. The store chain on which this case was modeled does, in fact, trace its heritage back to the Hanseatic League and there are, on the gables of a number of its older stores, likenesses in bronze of the thirteenth and fourteenth century trading vessels that were the mainstay of that organization.

5. City Center Cultural Complex

A concentrated marketing strategy seems to be in order for the City Center Cultural Complex because (1) its resources are limited, (2) the competition is using concentrated strategies, (3) consumers perceive differences among products, and (4) it is likely that this class of product is in the maturity phase of the product life cycle. The complex can't afford to be all things to all people. The competition has staked its claims to specific segments of the market, and the City Center needs to find for itself a similar niche to fill or there is a high likelihood that it will fall by the wayside.

Ms. Van Dortmund should study the marketplace, examining the strategies used by each of her competitors and the tastes of the residents of Springfield before deciding precisely where to target her operation. Obviously, modern and traditional values are well-served. The question now is which segments remain for her to consider as possibilities for her facility.

Solutions for Creating a Marketing Plan

Episode Three

Telabri's analysis of competitive conditions in New Essex involves analysis of three aspects of that environment. First, the firm must consider direct competition from firms specializing in Internet-related service. Of these, there are 21 who are potentially active competitors of Telabri Industries. A second source of possible competition are the firms who engage primarily in the sale of computers, but who also do Internet-related work (or say they do). Of these there are 102 who <u>might</u> be active competitors, but a very interesting statistic in this regard is the fact that only 29 firms indicated that they did this sort of work for any but their "regular customers." Telabri will be organized to serve any customer, so the level of competition with these firms will not be as direct or as intense as with the other firms whose main business is Internet-related services. From a marketing planning point of view, the Internet-related service firms appear to be first-line competitors with the computer sales operations constituting a second line of far less serious importance.

The third aspect of the analysis is provided by the subjective comments offered by Laura and Terry. It appears as though the potential competition is not very effective in defining its mission nor in communicating that mission within its own organization or to the using public. A firm whose employee contact with the community via the telephone doesn't even know whether it offers a particular service – much less 8 of them out of 60 – indicates that there is a lack of clarity in the firms' statements of their missions and their orientation to the marketplace. One might even say that their consciousness of the process of segmentation is limited, and it is quite likely that one would be right. It is certainly true that firms which deal with high-tech equipment tend to be started and operated by people who are themselves technologists, not marketers, and often suffer from a lack of skills in human interaction as a result. There is obviously weakness among the competition, and they certainly are not very aggressive, as the two display ads from among 21 *Yellow Pages* listings would tend to indicate.

Lacking information on market share, further analysis of the intensity of local competition cannot be undertaken, but it is quite unlikely that such information would be available in a local market situation.

Solutions to Cases for Part 4

1. Bledsoe Creative (A Derwenter Company)

a. To decide on a target market segment, a sequential process must be followed. First, the dollar return for each unit sold into each of the possible segments must be calculated, as in Exhibit PS4-1:

Exhibit PS4-1: Expected Return Per Unit

Income	Number of Children in Family				
	One	2 or 3	4 or 5	6 or 7	More than 7
Low	$19.00	$19.50	$11.80	$20.60	$19.50
Medium	20.60	19.50	12.90	21.15	17.08
High	20.05	19.50	11.25	21.70	16.75

Next, these expected returns must be multiplied by the total competitor sales for each segment. The resulting total profit potential for each segment is shown in Exhibit PS4-2:

Exhibit PS4-2: Total Profit Potential ($ Millions)

Income	Number of Children in Family				
	One	2 or 3	4 or 5	6 or 7	More than 7
Low	$190.0	$351	$236	$206	$ 39
Medium	288.4	234	206.4	296.1	170.8
High	120.3	117	202.5	260.4	100.5

The highest profit potentials lie in the medium income, 6 or 7 child and medium income, one child segments. These profit potentials, however, do not reflect the preference rankings given the product by these segments. The decision rule is that a higher ranking overwhelms a greater profit potential. Comparing potentials in rank order, the undesirable segments are those that have lower potential than another segment of similar rank. Since all the low income segments ranked MathQuick fifth, the most desirable low income segment would be the 2 or 3 child home; the preferred middle-income segment would be the 4 or 5 child home; and the most desirable high income segment is the one-child home. Using this decision rule, the firm would choose the high income, one child segment. This segment, however, offers a return of only $120.3 million compared to the $206.4 million offered by the middle income, 4 or 5 child segment. It is quite possible that the potential of an additional $86.1 million in return could overcome the rank difference of 1 and 2 offered by these two segments.

b. It would help to know what ranks were assigned to each of the competitive products in the various segments. In addition, market shares currently held by existing competitors would be of use in evaluating the relative meaning of the ranks assigned to the products.

It was assumed in the analysis that total sales in each segment would behave in the same way based upon aggregate data and consumer rankings. That may not, in fact, be the case. In addition, past history doesn't always predict future performance. It certainly wouldn't hurt to have some information on environmental conditions that might affect the acceptance of WarChem. Legislation may be pending or it could be that another competitor is lurking in the wings.

d. The most difficult (and expensive) data to gather is probably the consumer preference data shown in Table P3-1. Sampling reliability calls for the use of at least 30 people in each of the fifteen segments, or a minimum of 450 people.

The rest of the data is probably available in secondary sources such as annual reports, newspapers, and financial review publications. Costs of production and distribution are the easiest information to generate, since they come from internal sources, but could be in error for a new product.

2. Southway Homes, Inc.

Some characteristics which are probably of importance in segment selection for Southway are geographic location, population demographics, psychographics of potential buyers, and the benefits these people expect to derive from living in a rural setting. Where people presently live will certainly affect their probability of preferring Southway's new development, as will location of the development with respect to the place of employment of the prospective homebuyer. Demographics of importance to this analysis include income distribution data, family information, and family size characteristics in the area. Newlyweds certainly want a different type of home than do people with a crop of kids in tow.

Behavioral variables affecting the design of the subdivision include attitudes, motivational makeup, benefits desired by potential buyers, and the influence of group pressures. The newspaper clippings lead one to believe that a prime motive for moving to similar subdivisions is the desire for larger living quarters at a price lower than that asked for an urban accommodation of comparable size and similar features.

3. John Huddleston, Househusband

a. The last thirty years have seen vast, though gradual, changes in American culture and society. Recent data indicate that 70 percent of all adult women are now employed outside the home, and that many of them, like Susan Huddleston, have been successful in jobs that have traditionally been considered male preserves. These changes in the pattern of female employment have had their repercussions in the home. It would not surprise this writer to learn that Mrs. Huddleston's income exceeded that of her husband by some significant amount. Certainly, accommodations of both physical and psychological kinds must be made in acknowledgment of this fact. John is certainly A breadwinner for his family, but he is not THE breadwinner in the family. Many men and women have not been as able to adapt to this realization as John and Susan seem to have been, and this accounts, perhaps, for the 50 percent divorce rate that this country currently faces. Some men, on the other hand, relish the opportunity to spend more time with their wives and children, and with both partners in a marriage gainfully employed, the possibility certainly exists for more family interaction.

b. Mr. Huddleston is involved in tasks in the marketplace which his father, in all likelihood, would never have performed. He buys groceries, does laundry, cleans house, and cooks meals. The likelihood is that he has developed consumer preferences for products in all the lines related to these activities. It is also not at all unlikely that John shops for other products at the request of his wife and children that his dad never even heard of, let alone bought. Marketers must be aware that laundry detergents, peanut butter, pot roast, and a host of similar products are no longer bought exclusively by women, and modify their marketing mixes accordingly. (It might be mentioned here that firms like Procter & Gamble, Unilever, and Colgate are well aware of these changing patterns, and have not only changed the design of their products to accommodate male preferences, but have even changed the formats of their "daytime dramas" [soap operas] in recognition of increasing male watchership.)

c. In years past, segmentation of "family" goods could be done on a "mine, yours, ours, and theirs" basis. Some things were men's things, others were women's, and yet others were children's. The dividing line between autonomic, syncratic, and independent decision making was fairly clear-cut and distinct. Such is not the case today. The amount of buying behavior which is almost organizational in character with influencers, deciders, buyers, gatekeepers, and users participating in the family purchasing decision is on the increase, as is the buying of atypical goods by both men and women. The segmentation process has been affected by these changing and amplified roles so that constant analysis of who is buying which sorts of goods under what sets of circumstances is necessary if successful segmentation decisions are to be made.

Solutions for Creating a Marketing Plan

Episode Four

a. The partners are getting their figures from the data given in this episode as well as information from previous episodes. Their estimate of an Internet-related services market PCs of $78,000,000 in the local area was based on the $15 billion estimate for the national market multiplied by New Essex' proportion of that population, some 0.52 percent (slightly more than one-half of one percent). The $1,131,000 projection for 1 percent of the market five years hence was arrived at by compounding $780,000 (currently 1 percent of the market) at 14 percent for five years, the current year being uncompounded. This is a very lowball or conservative estimate of market potential, as using the projected rate of growth for Web site maintenance would generate a volume prediction in excess of $2,000,000 for the fifth year hence. Laura's comment about doing $375,000 this year and growing at a rate of 30 to 35 percent to achieve the $1,131,000 volume derives from one source: her assumption of $375,000 in volume this year and $1,131,000 in five years.

b. It appears that our heroes have decided that their objectives are to be 1 percent of the market in five years and a rate of profitability of 10 percent on sales at the end of that time. They recognize that, in the meantime, they are likely to lose money for a few years to come, but they are prepared to do so in order for their firm ultimately to succeed. Their business philosophy seems to be very marketing-oriented, with a twenty-four hour a day operation envisioned. They want their customers to be happy with their service and hope to build customer loyalty, which will ultimately result in the writing of a lot of maintenance contracts. Later information may call for revision of the objectives and policies set at this point in the plan.

Solutions to Cases for Part 5

1. Ontario Chemicals and Coatings, Ltd.

This company is obviously a "product-oriented" firm. Stuck (Pun!) with a by-product which happened to be uniquely sticky, the firm tried to dispose of it by adapting it to a use for which it was not suited. This firm would probably define a product as "something we can sell to customers."

A firm should, in fact, be marketing oriented. Instead of merely trying to get rid of a by-product, they should examine it from a marketing point of view – a view toward satisfying needs. Such a view would have led to the pretesting of this product before its introduction and apparent failure, and the failure could have been avoided.

2. Tres Bien Toys

The Tres Bien line are specialty consumer goods. They are well made, safe, and fun – a quality product. They are sold through toy stores at relatively high prices, and customers who have once purchased these toys continue to buy them. They fall into the specialty goods category because of this unique hold they seem to have on their buyers.

3. Herscholdt-Newman Products Company

There are four alternative strategies which can be used to approach the problem of new product development: (1) a new-product committee, (2) a new product department, (3) product management, and (4) venture teams.

The problems experienced by H-N are typical of those experienced by firms which haven't recognized the need for establishing specific methods for locating the responsibility for new product development. New product development plays such a vital role in keeping an organization alive that it is hard to overemphasize the need to establish a formal set of procedures for evaluating new products and for locating the responsibility for this function in an enterprise.

4. Center Point Tool Company

a. A structural failure rate of 110 items out of a production run of 100,000 is rather high by today's standards. Though representing less than 1/10 of one percent of output, such a rate of failure is unacceptable, especially where the possibility of serious injury might exist. One well-known brand of portable work benches, in one guise or another, has been in production for at least 25 years and enjoy a well-deserved reputation as a sturdy, simple tool which will last for a very long time. This is a classic case of a totally no-win situation, regardless of whether the manufacturer is concerned for ethical reasons or not. A lawsuit brought by the seriously injured owner of a product like this, if it can demonstrated that the manufacturer knew of the possibility of such injury, can destroy a firm's reputation, not to mention generating costs of litigation, bad press, and notoriety far in excess of the cost of a product recall of this type. It is obvious that this action had to be taken.

One might question whether Center Point acted quickly enough, and in fact it seems that they might have, because they modified the mold in which these frames were cast in April of 1996, but we don't know <u>all</u> the facts in the case and can't really draw that conclusion.

Harcourt, Inc.

b. It does not appear that CPSC pressure had very much to do with the recall. The phrasing of the notices infers that manufacturers have been rather cooperative with the CPSC in recalling potentially dangerous products. Moreover, it was mentioned that Center Point had received the 110 complaints, not the CPSC, which might well lead one to believe that Center Point was the instigator of the action, not CPSC. CPSC does, in fact, provide an excellent avenue for manufacturers who discover a potentially dangerous defect in a product to get the word to consumers and dealers quickly, efficiently, and cheaply. The CPSC's *SAFETY ALERTS* receive wide distribution to the types of retail outlets where the products with safety problems are sold, to medical clinics, and to the press..

5. Corporate Health Services

The characteristic of service most likely to work in Dr. Reilly's favor is also one that may make the move risky: the inseparability of the service and the service-provider. If, indeed, the people whom he has examined over the last seven years think of him as the service-provider and speak for their companies, he may do quite well. If, on the other hand, they think of CHS as the service-provider, he may find himself with no business at all. This characteristic of services is related to their intangibility. It is possible that Dr. Reilly may benefit or suffer, as well, from the difficulties with service standardization. If he can approach the companies with something they see as better for their purposes, or give them the same thing at a lower price, he may do well. But he's going to have to work very hard to demonstrate that he is, in fact, capable of doing exactly what he has been doing these last seven years. Then, he was CHS; now, he's Dr. Ovid Reilly. There could be a perceived difference between the two.

6. Seagull Computer Corporation

a. Seagull Computer Corporation is certainly selling a combination of goods and services, so it is not at one extreme or other of the continuum. On the other hand, it looks like Sam Seagull's devotion to customer satisfaction positions the company more significantly toward the service end of the continuum than its competitors. A clone is, after all, a clone, but a clone with a high level of customer commitment is another thing entirely. One would suspect from the mention of word-of-mouth and from the rapid growth of company sales that the service provided by Seagull is of a much higher order than is typical in the mail-order microcomputer industry. In short, what we have here is a company which has used a commitment to service to change an otherwise undistinguished product -- almost a commodity -- into one with quite a good reputation and some differentiation..

b. Microcomputers sold by mail are still, more often than not, sold to business/commercial/industrial users. Seagull's use of publications like *Computer Shopper* and *PC Source* is consistent with the idea that it is seeking a market that sees the microcomputer as a tool, rather than as an entertainment product or a toy. Not all industrial or commercial users of computers are large corporations with large numbers of micros in service. Many are small, maybe even one-person operations that need computer support of their operations, but even more importantly need support for their computers. The evidence suggests that Seagull's segment of the market is professional individuals and small businesses with one or perhaps a few micros that are used as tools by people whose interest is in having them available when needed, as needed, with a minimum of hassle.

Solution to Creating a Marketing Plan

There is no episode of Creating a Marketing Plan for this Part.

Solutions for Cases to Part Six

1. Tachikawa Lettuce Farms, LLC

Wholesale middlemen exist because they perform services for their producer and their retailer customers. Mr. Tachikawa, Sr., should give a great deal of consideration to the services Greengrocer Wholesale Brokerage performs for him before implementing his son's suggestion. At this moment, it is doubtful the Mr. Tachikawa knows who the firms are that have traditionally bought his lettuce and cabbage. It is also doubtful that they are aware of him, even if he does package his product in Tachikawa Lettuce Farms boxes for shipment to market. The implication is that the wholesale intermediary has been functioning in the capacity of a marketing department for Tachikawa Lettuce Farms. As a result, the Farms have no sales personnel, no immediate contact with their ultimate customers, and no means of assuring, at least for the immediate future, a market for their output. I would therefore advise Mr. Tachikawa to table – not discard, but table – young Roy's suggestion. Meanwhile, Roy, Jr., should be assigned to gather information about the nature of the overall channel structure in fresh head vegetables and to learn how these vegetables are sold into that market by producers that do not use wholesale intermediaries. He should be sent to learn more about the availability of those special transportation services he was talking about. They may or may not be appropriate for products like this. (In fact, they are, but there are many details that would have to be ironed out before they could be effectively used.)

In short, it may, at some time in the foreseeable future, be possible to implement young Roy's suggestion, but for the moment Tachikawa Lettuce Farms is certainly not in a position to dismiss Greengrocer Wholesale and go out on their own.

2. Airpark Industries, Inc.

a. The idea of selling travel trailers through a used car dealership should be considered in the context of the following variables, among others, before a response is made to Mr. Mingus' offer:

In terms of consumer perceptions:
Is a used car lot an appropriate place, from the viewpoint of consumers, to shop for a travel trailer? Is the image of used car lots and salespeople consistent with the image of new travel trailers?

In terms of product characteristics:
Can a used car dealership provide the necessary level of service and maintenance required for this type of trailer? Will Mingus' personnel be able to properly describe the features of the Airpark line? Again, is the image of the used car lot consistent with the image of the Airpark line?

In terms of distribution:
How would the outlets that currently carry the Airpark line feel about the addition of the new distribution channel? What should the functional (trade) discount for a used car dealer be?

From the producer's point of view:
Does Airpark really need a new channel? How much money is there to finance such a channel?

These questions begin the discussion of the desirability of Airpark selecting marketing intermediaries, particularly the one that has surfaced. Airpark needs to develop a set of specific criteria to apply in the selection of new channels and their members.

b. The steps used in selecting a new channel of distribution are described in this section. The first step is to analyze the market, product, producer, and competitive factors. The second step is to determine the level of intensity of distribution desired.

c. No, I don't think the Mingus offer should be accepted. A used car lot is not a very appropriate place to look for a new travel trailer. Used car dealers don't have the necessary image, nor do they possess the right kind of repair expertise for a product like this. Their personnel aren't knowledgeable about trailers and would have to be trained to do the job correctly. To top it all off, I imagine it would be rather difficult to find a used car lot sufficiently large to do a good job of display and demonstration of an array of travel trailers.

3. Mimi's Mart

a. Voluntary chains provide retailers with several benefits. First, the chain's buying power allows the independent to get product cheaper than would be the case if the independent had to make every purchase from a marketing intermediary. In addition, the voluntary chain can usually provide a private label that the independent can call its own, giving customers the same price line choices as at the major chains. The private label provides some name recognition among customers who have shopped other members of the voluntary chain. Most voluntary chains also provide management information that the independent would have to buy elsewhere for more money. And finally, the wholesaler can provide to Mimi information on product movement and prices that she does not now get.

b. The voluntary chain looks like a good competitive move on Mimi's part. Before going with Mr. Alidont, however, she should shop around to see if there might be an alternative voluntary or perhaps a retailer's cooperative that she could join that would offer better benefits or prices on goods and services of similar quality. Mimi must respond to the challenge posed by Market Giant or she will become uncompetitive, and in the compete-or-die world of modern business, surely perish.

4. Sandoval

Sandoval should move into the new shopping center. If they do not, they will be leaving the suburbs solely to the local department store. The discount department store is not the problem Sandoval seems to think it is. Many shopping centers feature a discounter and a full-service store as their anchor outlets. Generally, people do not shop for the same goods at the two sorts of stores (and some people do not shop one or the other sort, period!). They do not want to go downtown and slug it out with the other store presently located there. Central business districts are risky places in which to locate a department store nowadays. In general, they have experienced economic decline, but some have begun to become resurgent and offer real opportunity. There is insufficient information in the case to suggest that the time is ripe for Seguin City to move back downtown. The only real risk is that the new shopping center will bomb and Sandoval will not succeed in this market.

5. Milkmaid Manufacturing Company

a. Milkmaid can choose from a number of transportation alternatives, including:
- Contract carriers
- Company owned carriers
- Leased carriers
- A new common carrier

Contemporary Marketing

The intermittent nature of Milkmaid's shipping schedule – it is obvious they don't ship milking machines on anything like a regular schedule – tends to rule out the purchase of their own truck or the lease of one for an entire year. The best bet for this company is probably a change of common carrier or the use of a contract carrier on an as-needed basis. The contract carrier, because of the closer relationship between this form of carrier and its user, offers the better choice in this case.

b. A change to contract carriers solve the obvious problem of being forced to maintain four regional warehouses for assembly purposes. Better service, able to make longer hauls with less risk of damage, may make it possible to assemble complete milker units at the factory and ship them direct to dealers. There isn't enough information in the case to make a final decision, but it is reasonable to expect that the idea of reducing the number of assembly facilities will occur to the serious student who reads this case.

6. Wilson Textbook Company

a. One can but wonder how centrally located Ridiculous Falls, Ohio, is to Wilson's market. Even if it is reasonably central, a single facility hardly seems enough to serve the needs of all the country's colleges and universities. Subsidiary distribution centers in, say, northern California, Texas, South Carolina, and Connecticut would spread the load across the entire population of students and make delivery time to any given school shorter.

b. Late orders are not always the professor's fault. Sure, some of us put off book ordering until the last minute, but some schools engage in the "last minute shuffle," changing the courses professors teach up until the last week or so before classes are to meet. Wilson has absolutely no control over this sort of behavior, but might experiment with some of the following ideas:

- Increase sales practitioners' bonuses for accurate estimates of demand.
- Reward sales practitioners who get bookstore orders early.
- Reward bookstores for early ordering.
- Place a surcharge on late orders.
- Increase book prices for late orders.
- Use telemarketing to call bookstores and request early orders.
- Set up a 1-800 number for late orders.
- Ship late orders Federal Express – at the purchaser's expense.

Wilson should assign someone the task of establishing a better procedure for receiving and shipping orders. A combination of the answers to question (a) and one or more of the other suggestions mentioned in this answer would help the company minimize late orders. There will always, however, be emergency orders.

Solutions for Creating a Marketing Plan

Episode Five

Telabri Industries, as a service organization, occupies a somewhat unusual position in the distribution channel. They are providers of a business service, so their channel of distribution will be direct. As participants in the business-to-business market, their initial sales efforts will probably include a lot more personal selling than advertising. At any rate, Telabri will be participating in a marketing channel in which they will be acting as a direct provider of services.

The youngsters have already acquired most of the physical distribution facilities they are going to need: two automobiles in which to make sales and emergency calls and a combination shop/warehouse/office. They are probably also going to need some manual materials handling equipment, like a carry cart and perhaps a hand truck for some of the heavier and bulkier equipment which they will be moving to use in performing their service functions.

Their location was chosen to make them physically convenient to the greatest number of businesses. Obviously, they took some care in the choice. They are certainly aware of the need for a secure location, a particular consideration for firms which produce intellectual property that can be of great damage if it falls into the wrong hands.

Their major physical distribution characteristics, in my estimation, should be accessibility, speed of service, and a high level of accuracy filling each customer's order. Mistakes, though inevitable, are very undesirable for a firm in this position. They should also offer flexibility of scheduling – at their customers' convenience – though this feature is perhaps redundant to mention in this context. It is important to remember that their operating philosophy is "minimum waiting time" for their customers. Moreover, I think it is significant that one of the things they were looking for was a building that wasn't a "dump." While physical beauty is not a necessary attribute of a facility devoted to this sort of activity, it sure doesn't hurt to produce an attractive appearance when customers come to see what kind of work you're doing for them. I can think of several instances when business service firms have lost their credibility with me when I discovered their office was "less than attractive," especially when the condition could have been avoided. More will be said on this under promotion.

Contemporary Marketing

Solutions to Cases for Part 7

1. Servicios Tecnicos y Comercial pro Empresas Pequeños de Cataluña, S.A.

There is not sufficient information in the case to absolutely sure, but it is likely that STECEPCA is suffering from the influx of competition into its industry. STECEPCA needs a new promotional approach to combat this competition. In most countries, firms like these are prohibited by law from advertising much more than what is known as "tombstone" information about their financial offerings – just the facts and only the facts, without projection. STECEPCA must find a new way to promote itself. Their newspaper advertising probably should be continued. To discontinue it would remove them from the day-to-day awareness or potential of it by their most likely market segment. There are, however, alternative approaches that can be tried.

One alternative promotional approach that STECEPCA can probably use to good effect is direct mailings to selected, well-known firms not now among their clients. A brochure featuring the qualifications of STECEPCA's personnel and the services they can provide and featuring a return card or coupon that can be used to request specific information has proven effective for a number of firms in this field. Of course, this assumes that STECEPCA can acquire the names of the firms' decision-makers and direct their mailings to these people. Another device that has been quite effective in this regard is the offering of free investment seminars (by invitation) to decision-makers who are pre-qualified by mailings or particulars they provide on requests for additional product information.

Ultimately, the goal of the basic advertising and sales promotional activities done by this firm is to put qualified investors in contact with sales practitioners who can serve their needs and generate revenues for the firm through sales commissions. Creative prospecting and qualifying are necessary to bring these prospective investors in touch with sales professionals who can fulfill their needs.

2. O. Lee O'Leahy, Inc.

If sales have leveled off, the percentage-of-sales method of allocating promotional dollars will yield a constant dollar promotional budget. The implied objective of the firm is to increase its sales continually. The firm should analyze the market potential and the current nature of the competition to see if such an objective is realistic. If it is (in terms of market potential), then several alternative allocation methods are available.

The most useful budget allocation method is probably the task-objective method. Setting a sales objective and then budgeting to reach that objective is the most logical way to approach a problem of this sort.

3. Large Major Appliance Corporation

The sales force assigned to selling the development packages would undoubtedly have to be quite creative to tie developers to a total need contract for all their appliances. The lead time from contact to sale, however, will undoubtedly be of some considerable duration, so that a plan which features a basic salary every month plus a commission or bonus when a sale is made seems most appropriate.

Harcourt, Inc.

4. Industrial Drive Belt Company

This case should lead you to think about the product life cycle and its influence on the promotional program of the firm. This product is moving (rather rapidly) from the introduction stage into the growth stage. It is now time to shift the emphasis of the promotional program from informative advertising to persuasive product advertising. The appearance of competitors in the market has changed the game plan for Industrial. Until now, Industrial has properly attempted to tell potential users about the existence and advantages of its product, since it was the only game in town. Now, users must be convinced of the advantages of the Industrial product over the products of other makers. The specific goal served by such advertising would be to build customer preference for Industrial over other brands.

Solutions for Creating a Marketing Plan

Episode Six

In this episode, Brian, Terry, and Laura reveal a rather complex but fairly well thought-out promotional plan. They will be using Yellow Pages advertising and newspaper advertising, sales promotional stickers and business cards, personal selling, and even public relations to develop a positive image for their firm. It might be very interesting to attempt to explicitly differentiate among the various forms of promotion that the entrepreneurs plan to use. Are the stickers, for example, advertising or are they sales promotion? My view would be that they are a variety of point-of-purchase advertising, a sales promotion tool. When does personal selling end and sales promotion begin in those instances when one of the selling partners hands a prospect a promotional brochure? A discussion of "supportive literature" could be very beneficial at this point. And let us not forget the importance of the business card. Many of these are saved and filed on the chance that the person who gave it to the recipient will someday be needed in a professional capacity. For the small businessman they are almost literally worth their weight in gold. I am also a big fan of *Yellow Pages* advertising, but not necessarily in the form of major display ads. Certainly a listing is absolutely necessary, and you get that when you subscribe to commercial phone service, but a small, well-written copy box to highlight the business and set it off (differentiation) can be both promotionally and cost-effective.

A very fruitful discussion hinges on the idea of keeping the building clean, neat, and presentable, if only because so many service firms don't bother to do this. If neatness and attractiveness count in a retail environment, why is it that they seem not to at wholesale or for service firms? The answer, of course, is that they do. All other things being equal, a neat, tidy operation has the advantage over one that is kept in a less attractive state. Indeed, the neatness may be reflected in the firm's fire and liability insurance premiums because a neat area is usually a safe area. Some businesses are inherently dirtier than others are – auto repair shops, for example, create more than their share of oily, greasy dirt just because they are what they are. But even these kinds of places can be kept neater than they usually are with a little extra effort that pays big dividends in customer satisfaction.

Students should feel free to suggest alternative means of promotion which Telabri Industries could use. They should, however, be warned, should they suggest using radio or TV ads, that experience has taught us that using these media for this kind of service is generally ineffective for two reasons: (1) the ad is generally lost in the clutter of other advertising unless the service is needed right now, and (2) such advertising tends to create generic demand for the service, seldom specific demand for the services of a specific firm.

Solutions to Cases for Part 8

1. Madame Gremillon's Creole Seasoning Mix

Madame Gremillon can choose from four different pricing objectives: profitability, volume, meeting competition, and prestige. Let us examine Odile's situation before deciding on a preferred strategy. At the moment, the company is a cottage industry. There are no employees and total capital is $35,000. The product is a unique, "home-style" one that may well have an appeal only within a small radius of Mme. Gremillon's home. The potential competition, on the other hand, consists of people like McCormick and Spice Island as well as regionals like the Zatarain, McIlhenny, and Chachere firms. No small potatoes, these. Odile has an advantage in the marketplace among people who like a certain flavor and texture to their food. She does not have any cost advantage over the competition. We must wonder what her motives for going into business are. Does she wish to make a great deal of money, or is she in it for a greater scope of recognition for her culinary skills? The selection of strategy depends on the interpretation of Mme. Gremillon's motives. The inference that many of you will make is that Mme. Gremillon's personal reputation will let her charge a prestige price. This is a logical inference, because her resource base doesn't really allow her to look at the other strategies too closely. We know that she does have an excellent local reputation, and there certainly is no obvious reason why she shouldn't play on it in the early going with her new company.

2. National Seat and Pew Company

Past experience can probably tell Sandahl whether demand will decline precipitately if the price is raised. It is unlikely, however, that he will be able to tell by exactly how much it will decline. Predicting demand responses to price changes is not an exact science. The person changing the price does not really know if conditions are the same now as they were when the last price change was implemented. Inflation, changes in user tastes, and competitor reactions will all come into play in determining what will happen in the marketplace. If it is absolutely necessary to get more information than is on hand, a price expectation or demand evaluation study could be conducted among known purchasers of church and theater-type seating products. It might even be feasible to change prices in a limited geographical area – a sort of test market – to see how seating buyers react to them.

3. Sir Henri de Jacques, Knight Errant

Sir Henri would probably be better off entering the market with a penetration pricing policy. There are several reasons why this choice would be effective. First, his new armor does not immediately tell the potential user why he should buy it. Until one has ridden several tourneys in one of these suits one probably would not be fully aware or appreciate its seat-keeping capabilities. Sir Henri's armor will probably ride and act differently in the saddle than your standard suit of armor, and that will take some getting used to on the part of the rather conservative tournistes. Even though the armor will be well-built and capable of lasting ten years, the rate of losses to enemies, to rust, and even to wear and tear – particularly tear – should create a substantial replacement market once the product has gotten a "foot in the door" and becomes well-known throughout the Holy Roman Empire. All of these factors argue for a penetration price to induce potential buyers to give the product a try. The cost, by the way, is really rather modest. At an approximation based current rates of exchange, it works out to be something less than $500 US, and while price levels in tenth-century France were lower than is the case today, I expect that it's still a small enough amount so that even pricing at penetration levels, Sir Henri certainly should be able to generate enough sales to buy himself a rather nice estate in relatively few years.

4. Intense Lighting, Inc.

a. This case really revolves around attempting to motivate marketing intermediaries by paying them more. Two approaches to this increase in payment are taken. The first suggests the raising of prices to increase the amount of trade or functional discount allowed the intermediaries. This approach has the advantage of not increasing the company's out-of-pocket expenses. The price increase at retail allows the intermediary to keep a greater dollar amount for every unit of product sold. It has two significant disadvantages, however: first, there is the risk that it will not motivate the distributor since the trade discount is considered to be his normal due for performing his distributional functions; secondly, that sales may decrease because of the higher price and the distributor receive the same or less money. It is not a sound business practice to attempt to get something for nothing, and this plan seems to be trying to do just that.

The second plan provides promotional allowances for specific services provided, such as advertising and sales efforts by clerks. It would be necessary to monitor the performance of these specific services, a process which would cost some money. Thus, this approach creates two new costs, the cost of the services themselves and the cost of monitoring their performance. This approach tends to increase costs without impacting price, thus lowering profit margins for Intense Lighting. On the other hand, it does allow Intense Lighting to control the additional services offered by its distributors. It also provides a monetary incentive for helping Intense Lighting's market.

b. Gene Nolan's suggestion seems to have the greater merit for the reasons stated in (a).

5. Donald M. Landsdowne, Attorney at Law

It would appear that the prices of legal services are adjusting themselves to competitive conditions in the marketplace. The influx of new practitioners has, in effect, created an oversupply condition in which a new price schedule is appearing that reflects the relative desperation of the attorneys in the area. In the practice of law as in the selling of hardware, competitive conditions can be competitive, oligopolistic, monopolistic, or monopolistically competitive. One might suspect that Mr. Landsdowne, by virtue of his long experience and good track record, has developed for himself a monopolistically competitive position in the marketplace. He gets most of his cases on referral, which means he has a number of satisfied clients out there who recommend him to their friends when the need arises. When he is successful in a litigation or negotiation, his name appears in the newspaper, reminding people of who he is and what he does. In a situation like this, there doesn't seem to be any reason why Mr. Landsdowne should change his prices. I would recommend no change in his policies at present, but I would advise him to monitor carefully further developments in the marketplace so as to detect any additional information that might change this verdict.

Solutions for Creating a Marketing Plan

Episode Seven

a. It should be well enough established by now that Telabri Industries intends to provide twenty-four hour a day, seven day a week Web site maintenance service directed primarily at the business market that further elucidation would be unnecessary, but one can never be sure. This is, however, the first time the term "minimum turnaround" has been used to describe the firm's mission, and that may be significant in allowing students to differentiate between the personal Web sites and business Web sites. Personal Web site owners do not usually view them as money-making tools that cost money when they are out of service, and hence will tolerate a certain amount of lost access time and "out-of-dateness" on their sites. If a business site goes down or becomes outdated, people cannot get their work done, orders can't be placed, and the company loses money. There is a substantial situational difference here that can be explored at length if it is desired to do so.

b. The partners have any number of prices available to them. We know that $150 per page is their bottom-line minimum price below which they cannot go and achieve their stated objectives of volume and profitability. The data also show that there is quite a lot of clustering at the price levels of $150, $160, and $180. As a new firm entering a fairly competitive market, it is probably unwise to try and adopt a skimming policy even though the quality of their product is ultimately going to be higher than that of the competition's. Their potential customers don't know that, and right now probably wouldn't care, anyway. A penetration pricing strategy would be the best choice in this case. My personal leanings are toward $160 per page with a three-page minimum. This places them almost 15 percent below the average price in the market and twenty dollars below the median price, and still offers profit potential better than they have indicated they need in order to be satisfied. The three-page minimum is reasonable because it is almost impossible to do anything meaningful on a single page. Their pricing of maintenance contracts will be in line with industry practice, and though it may be low when compared with the average of site renovations, being based on their per-page price, must be discounted by the fact that the money is received up front and the work is done later.

It is always well to remember that prices are not etched in stone. If Telabri's quality service develops for them a satisfactory volume of business, price can be adjusted upward or downward to satisfy the goals of the entrepreneurs. We might judge, from some of their discussions, that they really aren't in it just for the money, anyway, and that the desire for profit is the desire to put bread on the table as needed, but also to have a good time while doing it.

Solutions for Creating a Marketing Plan

Episode Eight

Completing this section of the marketing plan completes the entire plan. The crucial question arising out of the projections of sales, costs, and revenues given in this section is meant to be "Will it be worth it?" On first blush, the income figures for these three fairly well educated people may seem a little low: An average of $50,000 per year after three years of hard work – if it all works out!

On the other hand, some would say they have been very generous with themselves. They have drawn three classes of salaries plus commissions while this firm was struggling to get off the ground. What would things have looked like if some of those monies had been left in the business? Let's give Brian, Terry, and Laura just their administrative and sales salaries and plow the rest into the business. Well, the first year's loss of $93,006 would have been reduced to $56,710, the second year's loss of $7,558 would have been a profit of $39,736, and the third year's profit would have been $87,496. Of course, it's their money to do with as they will, and they've weathered the worst of it and are now making a profit even after paying themselves reasonably well.

One can't help but wonder, on the other hand, what happened to the $375,000 in the first year, growing at a rate of 30+ percent per year? Obviously, the original projection of 1 percent of a market of grand scope was a bit overly optimistic — but the business has become profitable, nonetheless.

But there is more to it than may appear just in the raw figures. There is the equity or sellout value in the company once it gets to be a going concern. There is the stream of profits that will just be starting to accrue at the end of that third year. There is the possibility of turning some of the day-to-day operations of the company over to hired employees and taking a little (or a lot) of time off. And, of course, there is the idea of working for yourself, rather than for someone else, which may itself be the motivation to start any small business. Some more dedicated students may attempt to project the income of this firm out for a longer period. If they do, advise them to pick a relatively conservative rate of growth, as was done in the model (20 percent per year). They may assume that gross margin will stabilize at about 80 percent of net sales, and total expenses at about 70 percent of net sales, quite possibly declining slightly as fixed costs become a somewhat smaller percentage of the total.

At the end of five years, if projections are fulfilled, this firm should be grossing in excess of $415,000 and earning a net yearly profit of something in the neighborhood of $50,000 or more, after all expenses and salaries are paid. The question of the worth of that kind of return remains up in the air, and can only be answered in terms of the worth to the three entrepreneurs of being entrepreneurs. Somehow, I think they'll be happy with it.